Yoga, Meditation, and Mysticism

Also available from Bloomsbury Academic

Meditation and Culture: The Interplay of Practice and Context, edited by Halvor Eifring

Meditation in Judaism, Christianity and Islam: Cultural Histories, edited by Halvor Eifring

Pluralism: The Future of Religion, Kenneth Rose

YOGA, MEDITATION, AND MYSTICISM

Contemplative Universals and Meditative Landmarks

Kenneth Rose

BLOOMSBURY ACADEMIC
LONDON • NEW YORK • OXFORD • NEW DELHI • SYDNEY

BLOOMSBURY ACADEMIC
Bloomsbury Publishing Plc
50 Bedford Square, London, WC1B 3DP, UK

BLOOMSBURY, BLOOMSBURY ACADEMIC and the Diana logo are
trademarks of Bloomsbury Publishing Plc

First published 2016
Paperback edition first published 2018

Cover design: Dani Leigh
Cover image © Alfonse Pagano and Dan Barr/Stocktrek Images (gettyimages.co.uk)

A catalogue record for this book is available from the British Library.

Library of Congress Cataloging-in-Publication Data
Rose, Kenneth, 1951- author.
Yoga, meditation, and mysticism: contemplative universals and meditative
landmarks / Kenneth Rose.
New York: Bloomsbury, 2016. | Includes bibliographical references and index.
LCCN 2016016456 (print) | LCCN 2016026079 (ebook) |
ISBN 9781472571687 (hardback) | ISBN 9781472571694 (epdf) |
ISBN 9781472571700 (epub)
LCSH: Meditation. | Contemplation.
LCC BL627 .R66 2016 (print) | LCC BL627 (ebook) | DDC 204/.35–dc23
LC record available at https://lccn.loc.gov/2016016456

ISBN: HB: 978-1-4725-7168-7
PB: 978-1-350-06526-0
ePDF: 978-1-4725-7169-4
eBook: 978-1-4725-7170-0

Typeset by Deanta Global Publishing Services, Chennai, India

To find out more about our authors and books visit
www.bloomsbury.com and sign up for our newsletters.

Dedicated to the memory of
Patrick Rose
and
Elisabeth Boost

Contents

Table of Figures

Acknowledgments

I would like to acknowledge the editorial readers of the proposal for this book, Louis Komjathy and Jessica Frazier. Their cogent and well-aimed comments warned me away from some of the shoals into which a comparative project of this kind can run aground. Many thanks are due to my editor at Bloomsbury, Lalle Pursglove, who gave strong support to this project from beginning to end. I would also like to acknowledge her editorial assistants, Anna MacDiarmid and Lucy Carroll, who handled my various inquiries and other practical matters with friendly efficiency. I would also like to acknowledge the careful copy-editing of Grishma Fredric, account manager at Deanta Global in Chennai, India. I am grateful as well to the faculty senate of Christopher Newport University, Provost David Doughty, Dean Lori Underwood, and Department Chair Kip Redick for the awarding of faculty-development grants, sabbatical leaves, and course reductions over the years, which have allowed me time to research and write this book. I am grateful as well to Tara Dixon, office manager of the Department of Philosophy and Religious Studies at CNU. Playing a central role in our department, Tara keeps it running smoothly so that we can focus on teaching, study, and guiding our students.

I would like to thank Professor Perry Schmidt-Leukel and his wife, Doris, for their hospitality during my visit with my wife Beate to the delightful city of Münster in January 2015. Long will the pleasant images of the elegant and carefully restored streets of Münster, and its fleets of bicyclists stay in my memory. My thanks also go to the students in Professor Schmidt-Leukel's intercultural theology seminar at the University of Münster, with whom I tested some of the ideas that are expressed in this book. They brought a great deal of insight to our discussion, and their responses to my questions and their critical comments were illuminating and stimulating.

Once again, I am thankful and indebted to Jesse Spencer, interlibrary loan librarian at CNU, for unfailingly and efficiently unearthing all of my many and often obscure interlibrary loan requests. Thanks are due also to Mary Sellen, CNU university librarian, for her unswerving support for the robust and highly effective ILL services at CNU's Trible Library.

Among my many family members, I would like to thank my brother Robert Rose for his ongoing support and inspiration. His yogic spirit grows brighter with the challenges and opportunities that life sends his way. Almost to be counted as family is my oldest of friends, Graham Schweig, now a colleague at CNU and formerly a fellow graduate student at Harvard. May we continue, as in the past, to share the fruits of our common and divergent quests for wisdom and yogic balance.

In the ancient Roman city of Trier, which has become my second *Heimat* over the years, I want to note my gratitude for the warm hospitality of the extended Boost and Raltschitsch families. To many friends in Trier, and especially to Sabine Holzer and Klaus Schneider, Monika and Michael Lutz, and Viktor and Inge Schöndorf, I extend thanks for initiating me into the many pleasures of the civilized and urbane life of contemporary Europe. And, above all, I am grateful for the unflagging support of my wife, Beate Boost Rose, whose interest in and enthusiasm for this project helped it to grow and reach completion in the middle of all of our other activities and adventures. May our common passion for yoga and meditative awakening deepen and expand into the unending future.

I dedicate this book to Patrick Rose, author, actor, singer, songwriter, and beloved youngest brother. He was taken from us at far too early an age, yet his happy spirit and untroubled joy in life remain as his example and legacy to all who knew him. I also dedicate this book to Elisabeth Boost, my wife's beloved aunt, who was taken from us not long ago after a long life filled with care for family, delight in the daily pleasures and activities of life, and a deep, contemplatively enriched spirituality. Her warm smile of well-wishing remains a shining image in the memory of each one of us who knew her as the Tante.

Note on Transliteration, Spelling, and Translations

I have generally preferred to use Sanskrit terms untranslated, since this allows for easier study across numerous translations and for working with the original sources. I have often provided a translation, sometimes enclosed in parentheses before the Sanskrit term, or the reverse, depending on the needs of the context. When a translation of a term is given, it is either my own, unless otherwise noted, or it is a common translation not in need of citation.

I have not italicized words that are common in English, such as *karma*, *mantra*, *yoga*, and *yogi*, except when referred to, nor have I used the Sanskrit dictionary form, or the stem form, of these familiar words, which seems overly pedantic to me. I have also decided to use *yogi* (but have retained the Pāli *jhāyin*, which is not widely used in English) rather than *yoginī*, *yogī*, or *yogin* for simplicity's sake and because *yogi* can be made to stand for both genders, given that it is also the neuter singular of *yogin*. I have given other substantives in their dictionary or the stem form, as is common current academic practice, rather than in a declined form, except where relevant. I have given English plural and possessive endings to Sanskrit words when needed in context rather than the Sanskrit plural and possessive endings, which will aid the reader with no knowledge of Sanskrit without posing any difficulty for the Sanskritist. Also, to avoid pedantry, I have not italicized these English plural endings of plural Sanskrit words.

I have used the standard transliterations for the Romanization of Sanskrit and Pāli words, except when citing names and commonly used English words and when quoting a source that does not use transliterations or uses only partial transliterations. In the sections of this book concerned with Buddhism, I have generally favored Pāli instead of spellings, since most of my sources are concerned with the Pāli Canon and commentarial literature in Pāli. I have occasionally used Sanskrit spellings for clarity or comparative purposes.

Traditionally, words in a Sanskrit line were not divided, and there is a variety of methods of separating words when they are transliterated in the Roman script. The system that I have adopted is to separate words in sentences that are not parts of compounds unless this would obscure *sandhi*. To make for easier reading, I have generally used hyphens to separate the elements of longer compounds (*dharmamegha*, but *dharmamegha-samādhi*).

I generally use the common form of Anglicized names unless a variant is used in quotations or when citing a reference that uses a more Sanskritized version of a name. Thus, it can be *Swami Vivekananda* or *Swāmi Vivekānanda* depending upon context.

With respect to the names of varieties and schools of yoga, I follow the usage given in quotations, but in my own exposition, I have favored open compounds and properly transliterated forms.

In book titles such as the *Yoga Sūtra*, I have used open and unhyphenated forms for clarity of appearance and because many of these titles are well known without hyphens (and they are, of course, not hyphenated in the original).

I use the full title of the *Visuddhimagga* or the *Yoga Sūtra* when commenting on these texts in order to avoid defacing the appearance of the printed page and distracting the reader with constant abbreviations. I abbreviate the names of these texts, which are much quoted in these pages, when referring in exegesis to specific passages in these books. Thus, *Vsm* will stand for the *Visuddhimagga*, along with the relevant section number, followed by *Ñ* when quoting or referring to the Bhikkhu Ñāṇamoli translation. *Ñ* will be dropped when referring to or quoting the Pāli text. Similarly, *YS* will stand for the *Yoga Sūtra*, and *Bryant* will be used when quoting of referring to the Edwin F. Bryant translation, which will be dropped when referring to or quoting the Sanskrit text.

Except when referring to the front matter and back matter in Leonora L. Yorke Smith's English translation of Auguste François Poulain's *Des grâces d'oraison*, I will use the following system when quoting Smith's English translation of Poulain's manual: Poulain 14.1, E178. The second part of the citation refers to the page number in the Smith translation, while the first part of the citation refers to the relevant chapter and paragraph in the French and English editions, which, with the minor additions noted below, are identical. When referring to the text without quoting it in either French of English, I will drop the second part of the citation: Poulain 14.1. When quoting the French edition, I will add the page number of the eleventh French edition after a capital *F*: Poulain 14.1, F186. When quoting both, I will blend these approaches: Poulain: 14.1, E178, F186.

Poulain divided the thirty-one chapters of *Des grâces d'oraison* into seven parts, but because he did not begin the numbering of chapters anew in each part, it will be easier to orient ourselves in both the French and English editions of the book by using only the chapter and paragraph number of the cited location. This will save the reader (and author!) the labor of having to look up for each reference the number of the relevant part of the book, which, unlike the chapter numbers, do not appear at the top of the left page. I have generally ignored the finer levels of numbering used in the chapters as well as in the extracts, since they do not affect the numbering of paragraphs within each chapter. When Poulain added a paragraph in later editions, instead of renumbering the paragraphs in the chapter, he helpfully repeated the previously used paragraph number and indicated the new paragraphs with the Latin *bis* after the number ("twice" or "again") or *ter.* (for *tertius*, "third") in order to avoid disturbing the numbering of paragraphs from one edition to the next. Footnotes are numbered in the French original, beginning anew on each page, while in the English edition, they are indicated with various sigla such as *, †, etc. I thus reference the notes in this way: Poulain 29.4n*/1, E533, F565, where * refers to the note in the English edition and the number 1 to the same note in the French edition. This is followed by the relevant page number in each edition.

Prologue

Every author wants to be read, which poses a special challenge for the academic author, whose monographs will almost never show up on any list of bestsellers. In hope of increasing readership, this book's main title has been simplified to *Yoga, Meditation, and Mysticism*, but it would be more precise—and more in line with an academic monograph—to call it, *Saṃyama, Samatha, and Mystical Theology*, a title that purchases topical precision at the cost of wider appeal. As we will see in the course of this book, these three technical terms name carefully defined segments of larger bodies of spiritual practice, which are analyzed in the yoga system of the Hindu commentator Patañjali, the meditative system (*bhāvanā*) of the Buddhist commentator Buddhaghosa, and the mystical theology of Augustin-François Poulain, who was one of the last major Catholic manualists of mystical theology.

In the pages to come, the wider bodies of spiritual knowledge within which these manuals are situated will not be ignored, but my interest here will be the isolation and comparison of what I see as three distinctive sets of "meditative landmarks," which are described in each of these distinctive manuals. My intention is to demonstrate that the yogic and mystical itinerary described in these classic manuals is actually a common itinerary (which I call "the common yogic-mystical itinerary") that is constituted by what I see as shared "contemplative universals" that have been laid down like a rail in our brains, which are genetically coded for transcendence. It is my contention—one that, as we will see in the coming pages, is not uncontroversial—that certain unmistakable commonalties in contemplative spirituality, or mysticism, point to a common spiritual heritage, which is rooted in the structure of the brain, in the genetic code, and in the deep structure of the mind.

This linking of spirituality to scientific concerns does not, however, necessitate materialist conclusions about consciousness, for the appeal to scientific accounts of the contents of consciousness does not require the sacrifice of the findings of the comparative philosopher of mysticism. If, starting from an idealist view of consciousness, one sees the world of experience as a product of shared features of consciousness, then the so-called "hard problem"[1] of explaining consciousness from a materialistic starting point is made much easier by seeing both the brain and the mind as arising in tandem from a base of immaterial intelligence and beatitude, or the sacred, which is the beginning and end of physical and mental life.

This book is unashamedly comparative. As I will argue in Chapter 1, comparing traditions in search of significant patterns is a legitimate concern of religious studies. Inquiry into what religious traditions share is as important in my view as what makes each singular, or what sets them apart. Nevertheless, the central disciplinary focus on studies of singular religious traditions over the last thirty years has emphasized the skills of the historian and the linguist at the expense of the philosopher and the comparativist. Since more academics who read these lines may favor the former skill set over the latter, an unconscious bias against generalizing studies may hinder appreciation of the comparativist ambition of this book. The specialist in the traditions discussed in these pages will undoubtedly note that I am not a specialist in the three religious traditions that I am exploring in these pages, and that I am dependent upon the work of primary scholars in these fields, whose accounts of these traditions provide a rich source of data for generalizing studies. Thus, it needs to be emphasized that my purpose here is not to deepen understanding of this or that epoch and its cultural expressions, but, instead, to illumine particular aspects of the character of the spiritual life wherever it occurs. To take, for example, one area of concern in the following pages, I will note some of the difficulties of interpretation that attend the rise of globalized contemporary yoga. But I will not stop there, since my focus in this book is on the yoga of the *Yoga Sūtra* and not on the various ways in which its variant of yoga has been used, and perhaps misused, in the centuries since its composition. While of great interest as historical and cultural phenomena, these recent controversies are more relevant to the history of yoga and the history of the reception of yoga traditions outside of India than they are to the outlining of a comparative philosophy of spirituality, which is the central concern of this book. As a philosopher of religions, my concern in these pages is not with producing a monograph about the irreducibly diverse historical and cultural dimensions of these three traditions. My concern is rather with addressing philosophical questions about the unity and the legitimacy of human spiritual experience. My concern is thus not philological, text-critical, historical, or cultural—typical and important concerns of Indologists, Buddhologists, and historians of Christianity. It is, rather, a concern with the sorts of systematic and constructive questions that are legitimately raised by philosophers, theologians, and methodological theorists.

Introduction

A New Day for Perennialism?

An odd light flashed in Huston Smith's eyes as he verbally dueled with Steven Katz. The room was filled with religion scholars gathered for what was billed as a showdown between the dominant forces of constructivism, led by Katz, and the all-but-vanquished perennialist camp, whose last great defender, Smith, stood that afternoon in the gap. The time was late 1990, and the venue was the Annual Conference of the American Academy of Religion, held that year in New Orleans. Perhaps because I am a congenital perennialist—I am more a Platonist than an Aristotelian, more an Augustinian than a Thomist, more an Advaita Vedāntist than a Mādhyamika Buddhist—I was pulling for Smith.

But it was clear, to me at least, that the audience of mysticism scholars had already long been won over by Katz, and that the day of perennialism appeared to have faded forever from the scene. Yet, the light in Smith's eyes was perhaps less the recognition of defeat than a visionary glance into a future when perennialism—or at least the enduring essentialist kernel of perennialism that religion and spirituality in their countless, diverse forms express a common core—would once again throw a light of insight into the discourses of religious studies, comparative theology, theology and philosophy of religions, and the comparative philosophy of mysticism and spirituality.

So now, as I begin writing these pages, I sense that we are living in the dawn of that day toward which Smith looked wistfully on that long-lost afternoon. And in these pages, I would like to add my own contribution to the recovery of mystical essentialism with the comparative study of mystical consciousness that I will undertake in these pages.[1]

Religious Pluralism and the Search for Contemplative Universals

A reader of my last book, *Pluralism: The Future of Religion* (Bloomsbury, 2013), might assume that I also belong with Katz among the constructivists, since the central concern of that book is the defense of what I call "apophatic pluralism." In opposition to older pluralisms (or what I call "Type 1 Pluralism"[2]), which see the diverse religious languages of humanity's many religious traditions as expressions of generic teachings such as theism, nondualism, "the divine," "the Real," "the Absolute," love, truth, compassion, wisdom, and so on, I propose in *Pluralism* a new version of pluralism, which I call "apophatic pluralism" (or what I also call "Type 2 Pluralism"). Apophatic pluralism dispenses with the inclusivistic and quasi-exclusivistic generic and substantializing categories of older pluralisms in favor of the nonsubstantialistic and metalinguistic claim that the infinite character of the sacred, or the fullness of being, ensures the ceaseless proliferation of ever new religious discourses, with the inevitable result that no particular body of religious doctrine, shaped as it is by the contingent languages, cultures, and practices of particular contexts, will ever be accepted universally as final and normative for all of humanity. Consequently, I argue in *Pluralism* that apophatic pluralism, as opposed to any variety of religious particularism, whether expressed in stronger exclusivist forms or in weaker inclusivist forms, is the only ethical and durable basis for the religious, theological, scientific, philosophical, and mystical study of religion.

This apophatic pluralistic approach appears, at least at first glance, to imply a thoroughgoing constructivism, one that leaves no logical space for religious essentialism, which, among the perennialists at least, undertook a quest to formulate generic, universalizing doctrines—or what I call "superdoctrines"—that are supposedly common to all religions. What, after all, does Kṛṣṇa have to do with the Lord God or with Awonawilona? The diverse sacred histories centering on each of these divinities can easily run their courses without essential reference to the others, and attempts to make comparative sense of them through such religious abstractions, or superdoctrines, as "the Absolute" or "the Real" will not be as compelling to people living in and practicing these religious traditions as such richly realized divinities as Jesus or Śiva.

Indeed, abstractions such as these can be seen as alternative and perhaps even competing doctrines by adherents of the bodies of doctrine associated with specific religious traditions, and for a religious pluralist to insist on their general applicability would be to fall into the very trap of inclusivism and exclusivism[3] from which pluralism, as envisioned by John Hick in his later writings, was meant to rescue the academic and theological study of human religiosity. Constructivism seems, therefore, to be the appropriate approach to religious differences at the level of diverse bodies of distinctive religious doctrine, which remain resistant to essentialist reduction to generic doctrines for those who are committed to reading them in a literalistic and historicist manner.

Despite this constructivist stance with respect to bodies of religious doctrine more or less taken in a literalistic manner, I think that religious pluralism is consistent with the search for commonalities, or universals, in widely varying religious traditions. I think that one can be both an apophatic pluralist and an essentialist, provided that the helpful emphasis of constructivism on the historical uniqueness of each tradition is upheld.[4] We see no difficulty, after all, in calling both Henry Ford and Ratan Tata "industrialists," for we seem to know what an industrialist is, yet the poverty of such generic religious concepts of perennialism as the One, the Absolute, ultimate reality, and the divine has made many religious-studies scholars wary of formulating and enforcing vague abstractions such as these as the supposed deeper meaning of the quite diverse teachings of these various religious traditions. It is for this reason that I would like to ground a new comparativism upon mystical experience rather than upon the futile search for generic doctrines and concepts that would be acceptable to the diverse groups of people involved in humanity's countless religious movements.

To justify this new comparative approach, I undertake an experiment in comparison in this book by entering into a close study of the three contemplative traditions represented in the *Yoga Sūtra* of Patañjali, the *Visuddhimagga* of Buddhaghosa, and in *Des grâces d'oraison* of the Catholic manualist Augustin-François Poulain. These authoritative cartographers of the inner life have charted in their own distinctive ways a typical and virtually invariant pattern in the development of consciousness as it moves yogically and contemplatively from immersion in mundane consciousness to the flowering of transcendent, beatific insight.[5] As we will see in coming chapters, this pattern unfolds through the cultivation of the deepening states of concentration in the practice of *samatha-bhāvanā* ("calmness meditation") in the *Visuddhimagga*, of *saṃyama* ("focal triad," "restraint") in the *Yoga Sūtra*, and of *recueillement* ("recollection") in *Des grâces d'oraison*. The result of this comparative experiment is that I have isolated what appear to be virtually identical sets of mystical experiences that are induced by the deepening of concentration in each of these traditions. Ensconced as they are in these distinctive and doctrinally irreconcilable religious systems, the progression of concentrative states nevertheless unfolds identically in each tradition as a process of simplification or unification of consciousness.

For example, at the key moment in each contemplative system when the practice of deepening concentration attains fixed absorption, the yogi, the *jhāyin* ("calmness meditator"), and the mystical theologian experience a sudden sense of locking in or steadily focusing on the meditation object accompanied by an unmistakable sense of passing through a portal into a subtle realm of yogic and contemplative experience that is unmediated by the senses. This is but one in a set of five invariant universal human capacities that I call "contemplative universals," which I have named "convergence," "coalescence," "simplification," "quiescence," and "beatitude." (I am not making the claim that these contemplative universals, as distinctively named by me, are part of any religious tradition. They are, instead, justified abstractions denoted with Latinized English words that I deploy to make sense of the experiential identity of the diverse sets of what I call "meditative landmarks"[6] that express the contemplative universals in the irreducibly diverse doctrinal and cultural contexts of each of the three traditions under study in these pages.)

As I hope to show in the following pages, these contemplative universals display the underlying order of the spiritual life wherever it occurs.[7] Without in any way discounting the value of the local and contextual studies that have occupied academic religious studies in the last thirty years, this discovery of a religion-neutral spiritual itinerary constituted by a repeatable and invariant progression of experiential states justifies, in my view, a return to nomothetic—or universalizing and essentializing—explanatory approaches to the study of religion and mysticism, an approach, although long neglected in academic religious studies, that has the advantage of being more in line than merely atomizing, idiographic,[8] or tradition-specific, interpretive studies, with the essentialistic findings of the emerging fields of evolutionary cognitive science of religion (ECSR) and contemplative neuroscience. Viewed from the standpoint of these fields, it is clear that each of these three traditions teaches techniques of moving from spiritual alienation to spiritual completion that run along rails that have been laid down in our brains and minds by the universal requirements of spiritual awakening, which, because we are embodied beings, are also mirrored in our neurobiology. We will explore this still mostly uncharted terrain in the following pages, since it promises to serve as a staging ground for a new and common effort between the various humanistic and scientific disciplines and the practice traditions that research and cultivate yoga, meditation, and mysticism.

Such a move can serve to rehabilitate religious essentialism, but now on the basis of contemplative universals rather than upon doctrinal or symbolic universals, as in the perennialisms of Huston Smith and Mircea Eliade.[9] The failure of a perennialism that is grounded on elusive common doctrines and symbols to find a universally plausible common ground does not mean the search for a genuine comparative methodology and a workable religious essentialism must come to an end. The recognition of the limitations of perennialism should not be seen as a categorical indictment of mystical essentialism itself, but rather as an awareness, gained through the constructivist captivity of the philosophy of mysticism, that the quest for a widely plausible essentialism in the study of mysticism will always take its rise from the shifting languages and multiple conceptualities of humanity's many religious and philosophical quests. Once we see perennialism as merely one now passé though formerly insightful expression of religious essentialism, we can take up the search for a more adequate—at least for now—religious essentialism, one based on contemplative experience instead of religious doctrine and symbolism. This, then, is not a misinformed repudiation of Katzian contextualism and an uncritical embrace of Smithian perennialism, but the recognition that just as abstractions without particulars are barren, so particulars unillumined by general ideas and principles are mute.

Toward a Postconstructivist and Essentialistic Comparativism

While some readers may be tempted to dismiss my quest for contemplative universals as a whimsical quest based on overhasty generalizations and fictive constructs, I think that it draws significant support from three fronts. On one front, there is movement among religion scholars away from noncomparative, tradition-specific studies toward the revival of comparative studies ranging over more than just one tradition. Evidence for this new comparativism is the book forthcoming from Bloomsbury, *Comparison Revisited: Comparative Methods in Religious Studies and Theology*, edited by Perry Schmidt-Leukel and Andreas Nehring, which brings together an international group of leading historians of religion, philosophers of religion, and comparative theologians in search of new approaches to the comparative study of religion. My own contribution to that book, "The Singular and the Shared: Making Amends with Eliade after the Dismissal of the Sacred," seeks to renew the comparative approach of Mircea Eliade by shifting the focus of comparative studies from doctrines and symbols to mystical and yogic experience, as expressed in the three traditions under study in this book and as illumined by contemporary scientific approaches to contemplative experience. As noted above, I attempt to extend my vision of this new comparativism in religious studies in the first chapter of this book by abstracting a set of five contemplative universals from the distinctive sets of meditative landmarks discoverable in the three distinctive mystical traditions under study in this book, a move that is characteristic of a nomothetic, or generalizing and essentializing, approach to the study of global contemplative experience, which is only partially illumined in noncomparative approaches in religious studies that idiographically focus in a piecemeal manner on local traditions in isolation from other similar traditions.

This comparative move is paralleled, on a second front, by a new boldness in moving beyond constructivism toward essentialism by mysticism scholars. I will take up this new discussion in chapter two, where I will also offer an appreciative reevaluation of W. T. Stace's long-neglected and frequently disparaged philosophical study of mysticism. For almost forty years, the Anglophone philosophy of mysticism has been dominated by a constructivistic focus on the contextual differences distinguishing the world's mystical traditions rather than upon what unites them as mystical traditions, which was the essentialist concern of the now discredited perennialism. Enduringly important as the constructivist move was in its time, it lost sight of what, in this book, I call *the mystical*. For if a mystical experience is made mystical only by the local contexts in which mysticism arises, as implied by constructivism, then we will need to ask ourselves, as essentialists do, what makes these unique and local experiences mystical? Unless it is mere habit and convention to call them mystical, we will have to point to an essence, to a universal or common set of features, that gives this term its meaning in each of the various contexts in which it is deployed. Otherwise *mystical* becomes a term chosen more for its historical, celebratory, or emotive value than for its conceptual explanatory force, and a philosophy of mysticism that stands on so unstable a foundation as this will inevitably come undone. As we will see, however, a good case for appealing to the mystical among the mysticisms can be made on the basis of the comparative study of the meditative landmarks and contemplative universals that are the core of this study.

On the third front, my move toward contemplative universals is strongly supported by recent advances in neurobiology, genetics, ECSR, and contemplative neuroscience,[10] which, taken together, uncover patterns rooted in our common neuroanatomy, biochemistry, genetics, and cognitive capacities, thus indicating that the path of spiritual awakening and spiritual advancement is essentially the same for Buddhists, Christians, Daoists, Jews, Hindus, religious independents (SBNRs), and so forth, even though the doctrinal expressions of this universal spirituality vary in different cultural and religious backgrounds, just as Mandarin Chinese differs from German and Arabic. I will explore some of the findings of these sciences in Chapter 3, where I call this turning away from language and culture to contemplative neuroscience and evolutionary and cognitive-science approaches to religion "the neurobiological turn." Because I am a religious-studies scholar and not a scientist, I can say up front that appealing to these emerging sciences is a real exercise in multidisciplinarity for this religious philosopher!

Following these leads, then, I will chart a new comparativism in religious studies that strays beyond its customary haunts in philology, history, anthropology, and social criticism in search of shared meditative landmarks and contemplative universals, which I will take up in Part 2 of this book in a series of chapters dedicated to uncovering what I see as a common yogic-mystical itinerary, which is exemplified in the yoga of Patañjali, the *bhāvanā* of Buddhaghosa, and the mystical theology of Poulain. Supported by these generalizing and essentializing studies, a pluralistic, apophatic, and comparative religious studies can shift the study of religion and spirituality away from the agnostic, distanciated, and often materialistic non-practitioner bias of contemporary religious studies, as well as from the religious particularisms promoted by inclusivist theologies and the sterility of the constructivist/essentialist debate. This nomothetic, or explanatory, approach is thus concerned with what the religions are about rather than with the religions themselves as objects of study, as is the concern of idiographic, or particularizing, tradition-specific approaches. More than just a curiosity about the material and social conditions that determine this or that religious tradition, the nomothetic approach takes religions seriously as speaking about the nature of reality, just as the sciences and different schools of philosophy do. It is my view that detailed accounts of individual religious traditions isolated from questions about what these traditions find meaningful are incapable of providing a full accounting of religion as a whole, just as a description of an individual computer without reference to the principles of computer science could not provide a full understanding of computers.

It is my hope, then, that the study of the common yogic-mystical itinerary and its five moments will help to articulate what is common to contemplative traditions. By rejecting constructivism and idiographic approaches as the only useful methodological approaches to the study of religion and spirituality, we can begin to enrich the currently impoverished and marginalized field of religious studies by supplementing its countless contextualized, richly realized evocations of specific religions with rigorous study of the shared features of religion and spirituality. In so doing, I would like to depart from a model of religious studies that too often is captive to antireligious or nonreligious ideologies, and thus bereft of its own proper subject matter and activity, and move toward research that establishes the reality and universality of mystical experience and its irrepressible power to ground a philosophy of religions that can secure a foundation for the religious life and, more fundamentally, for a meditatively grounded metaphysics.

Part I

Chapter 1

A New Comparative Religion and the Search for Contemplative Universals

The Naming Explosion and Religious Universals in Religious Studies

After a generation of the dominance of the influential views of figures such as the anthropologist Clifford Geertz and the religionist Jonathan Z. Smith, current theorists in religious studies such as Francesca Cho and Richard King Squier are arguing that the discipline of religious studies is now imbued with "the ethos of particularism in which the increasing data of religions are treated like atomistic and self-sufficient units of knowledge."[1] This focus on what Gregory D. Alles characterizes as "loosely connected or disconnected microstudies"[2] has led to what he calls "a naming explosion,"[3] in which religious studies is now glutted with "an overburdening surfeit of concepts,"[4] which have been invented to name and categorize all of this disconnected data. This, in turn, has led to a weariness with mere data that, wittily observes Alles, is like "a slide-illustrated travelogue that goes on for too long."[5] By sweeping aside their mandate to understand and explain religion in generic and religious terms, as once exemplified by such iconic figures as Mircea Eliade, Joachim Wach, and Joseph Kitagawa, religious-studies scholars over the last thirty years have mostly become what Kenneth Boulding calls "walled-in hermits"[6] who have beat a "retreat into local categories,"[7] in Alles's memorable phrase. Thus, in a religious-studies establishment that took the Geertzian call[8] for thickly described histories of religions and ethnographies fully to heart and which was chastened by J. Z. Smith's condemnation of much of what it does as hothouse productions of their solitary workshops, there is now, as Cho and Squier note, a prevalent "prohibition against comparing" in which the anti-syncretistic "we-are-we and they-are-they manifesto" has become "thoroughly normative."[9]

Having surrendered the legitimate and culturally significant critical and interpretive activity of comparing religious traditions, religious studies has in recent decades intensively busied itself with narrow studies of ever narrower ranges of phenomena, for which it borrowed its explanatory methods from other disciplines, whose own formal objects were far removed from the actual practice of religion and its traditional forms of scholarship and practice. This, in turn, led religious studies into a manufactured crisis in which it went in search of its own *raison d'être*, only to conclude that the study of religion should be folded into some other discipline such as sociology, anthropology, history, critical studies, area studies, and so on,[10] leaving its university departments, faculties, and institutions to become what Timothy Fitzgerald calls "the world religions industry,"[11] which is an institutional convenience that offers courses popular with spiritually questioning and questing undergraduates.

Until at least the death of Mircea Eliade in 1986, mainstream academic religious studies evaded the plight and consequences of the naming explosion in the now overly particularistic and atomized religious-studies establishment by using abstraction in the search for religious universals as one of its central explanatory activities. Without neglecting the many other analytical tools available to it, religious studies also sought general names into which to fit and make sense of the many particular names that arise in the various branches of human religiosity. The intellectual action of generalizing over a range of particulars in order to abstract universal features from them is a familiar process, for without abstraction we would not have mathematics, scientific laws, logic, or elementary reasoning. It does not take many instances of encountering cats or dogs before we have abstracted concepts from the individual animals to help us quickly decide that *this* animal appearing to me right now is either a cat or a dog. In religious studies, comparative religion classically sought to abstract universals from religious particulars that could be used to construct the set of concepts that are unique to religion, thereby distinguishing it as a human enterprise from philosophy, psychology, and other bodies of knowledge and practice. Although this venerable approach to the study of religion has for more than a generation been severely out of favor in the research agendas of mainstream academic scholars of religion, many of the classic comparative categories, with various modifications, remain in play in any introductory religion course when religionists talk about scriptures, deities, salvations, cosmologies, the sacred, the holy, prayer, mysticism, and spirituality.

For example, in his standard introductory text, *Exploring Religion*, Roger Schmidt pursues the "comparative study of the primary forms of religious expression" through such familiar themes as the Holy, the Quest, Sacred Stories, Scripture, Salvation, etc.[12] But the antiessentialist and materialist theorist of religion Russell T. McCutcheon dismisses Schmidt's categories as "ill-defined," and takes him to task for his essentialistic, ahistorical, and phenomenological approach.[13] In his social-constructionist view of religion, McCutcheon wants to replace the understanding of religion as disclosing an autonomous realm of meaning with an understanding of religion as a product of the "social and material interests of the institutionalized observer-interpreter who defines, circumscribes, and creates [the] cognitive category" of religion.[14]

Yet, this now familiar and even clichéd criticism is in turn subject to the charge that it misses the specificity of what religion is fundamentally about by reducing the study of religion to the social and political forces that invariably shape religions. No doubt religions are implicated in culture and history, and thus will vary widely from one social context to the next, yet the cultural and historical study of religions does not exhaust the study of religion as an intellectual activity, as the phenomenology of religion, which has long sought to explicate what is experientially common across these cultural chasms, demonstrates. Thus, the abstractions called upon in introductory religion courses clearly retain a pedagogical usefulness because the religious life of humanity, despite its endless diversity, displays numerous regularities or generalities. Returning to a classical type of philosophical expression, I call these recurrent patterns "religious universals." It is my view that, apart from reference to such universals, religious studies will remain absorbed in mostly descriptive accounts of individual religious traditions that, Eliade lamented, because of "timidity" and prudence[15] borrow nonreligious and antireligious theories from other disciplines such as anthropology, sociology, psychology, cognitive science, biology, and neurobiology.

The epistemological notion of the universal is as ancient as philosophy itself. Forming a logical pair with the notion of a particular, the application of these complementary concepts to the strife between particularizing and generalizing approaches in religious studies can provide a way beyond the current impasse that ends the repetition of sterile comparative categories on one side and the numbing enumeration of the disconnected phenomena of isolated religious traditions on the other. The literature and controversies centering upon the ancient philosophical idea of the universals are vast and I have no intention here of entering into these controversies. Whether universals exist only in the objects that express them or whether they have a separate, abstract existence apart from being exemplified in particulars,[16] whether universals are given in the nature of things or whether they can be constructed by perceivers,[17] or whether universals are eternally fixed or can evolve and be sublated through higher awareness are all important questions that must be addressed in setting out a theory of universals. Since this is not my intention, I can avoid these questions in this context, and simply note that the idea of a universal, whether granted or not by my readers, is anciently established in global philosophy, and, so, it will not be a merely arbitrary decision on my part to think that religion and religious experience express, to a significant degree, religious universals (and, as will see in later pages, contemplative universals).

From the massive flow of scholarly activity centering on the discussion of universals, I want to skim out the notion of what Paul C. Hedengren calls "general words," which, he notes, we use "frequently."[18] This use of general words, or religious universals, is exhibited in the comparative explorations of Eliade, Wach, van der Leeuw, among others, and in the use of the words *religion* and the catalogue of comparative terms that are familiar in the phenomenology of religion and thematic introductions to religions of the world, such as Schmidt's. For apart from reference to something like religious universals, we will find ourselves unable to answer the challenge posed by Hedengren: "How do we explain our ability to use general words?"[19]

The philosopher who rejects universals does not thereby evade the ticklish question of why we use general words and their associated concepts to refer to what at first glance may seem to be divergent sets of phenomena. After all, even a theorist who is opposed to all generalizing trends when thinking about matters religious will likely agree that the word *religion* can be used in teaching situations to refer to Vedic rituals and the teachings of Meister Eckhart, but not, except perhaps metaphorically, to athletic rituals and the technical knowledge of a software coder. One answer to this question from a metaphysical point of view is to note that our ability to use words and concepts in this generalizing manner derives from our intuitive familiarity[20] with universals, which are properties[21] that are shared by the particulars that exemplify them. Monima Chadha, summarizing the *Nyāyasūtras*, sees "universals as the meaning of general terms,"[22] a view that is well represented by medieval Western ontological realists, who take "general terms to signify universals."[23]

As a merely verbal formula, this may seem unremarkable until one realizes that generality is the central feature of a universal, which can be defined as having "the capacity for being wholly present at more than one place at the same time."[24] Or, from the Indian tradition, universals are "wholly present and indefinitely repeatable in many particulars."[25] In the case of two gray objects, for example, "There is," according to Chris Swoyer, "a single, universal entity, the property of being gray, that is possessed or exemplified, by each of the two" objects.[26] It is thus not merely an arbitrary and contingent matter of linguistic usage that a general word such as *religion* (along with other general words for abstract objects or entities such as justice,[27] numbers, and propositions) can denote some degree of identity between the otherwise historically quite distinct streams of biological, social, and cultural phenomena of the distinctive religions of the world.

With the help of the concept of religious universals—but not without them—we are able to judge that religions are religions—and not something else, such as a military establishment, a government, a school, a hospital, a corporation, or some other human institution—by virtue of sharing the property of *religion*. No doubt, as the constructivists have helpfully made clear, particular religions contain much more than the shared property of *religion*, just as a red apple is not identical with a red sunset except with respect to redness. But my concern here is with the shared property of religion, rather than the divergent properties of individual religions, which are the concern of purely descriptive studies. Yet, to avoid what on the surface might seem like a circular definition and argument of merely saying that a religion is a religion insofar as it is a religion (or, more precisely, is an instance of the universal of religion), I will have to say what the property named (in English) by the general word *religion* is, which will not be an easy task in the current theoretical context of academic religious studies, which is shaped by particularism, constructivism, and the Wittgensteinian dodge of surrendering the quest to define the property of religion by taking refuge in the idea that because religions, like family members, share only some but not all traits, there is no common property that defines religion.

What is a Religion?

My immediate response to the nearly categorical Wittgensteinian denial that religions have *any* common features is to ask why we call any of them *religions* in the first place? How can we responsibly and accurately describe specific events, practices, ideas, and cultural roles as religious if we lack a metalanguage, a typology, or set of cross-cultural categories, about religious phenomena that are not merely local and contingent? Lacking this, will we not constantly be led into committing just the sort of embarrassing provincialisms described by Gregory Alles, who points out that it is unduly ethnocentric to refer to the *baḍva* of the Rāṭhvas of Gujarat as a *priest* since the two terms are not identical in meaning?[28]

Falling into unwitting and unwanted provincialisms such as this are undoubtedly a risk in comparative work, but it is inevitable that any globalizing view of life must risk some imprecision in order to avoid becoming mired in a merely local knowledge that rejects both the dangers and rewards that come from generalizing over multiple cultures. For the inevitable—but always partial—parochialism of all categorical or typological terms does not mean that a *baḍva* is less like a priest and more like a hunter. A German is not an Italian, that is clear, but neither is a Canadian an Italian (barring, of course, the imprecision of double or triple citizenship!) Inevitably, words must be chosen to make such distinctions, and so long as it is acknowledged that they are imprecise and subject to change even as they carry general meanings, this practice should not be a bar to comparative work.

We thus find ourselves as scholars of religion making use of some implicit or explicit conception of religion, even when it is against the best intentions of some of us. But, to develop a conception of some class of phenomena necessarily involves reference to generality, which is the province of a universal. For despite the obvious differences between religion *x* and religion *y* as unique social, cultural, and biological complexes, we still know, somehow, to call each of them a religion, and this leads us back to the question of how we know what to study as religion in the first place? Our ability to sort phenomenon *x* and phenomenon *y* into the category religion and not into some other category despite all of their other differences depends upon an invariant and general feature of religion, and this invariance and generality is underscored when the words *religion* or *religious* are used by theorists who are otherwise allergic to thematizing the concept of religion.

This contradictory blending of skepticism about the concept of religion even while retaining it in the study of religion is modeled by Gregory Alles in a thought experiment about a hypothetical group of newly discovered people that he calls the Ajnatasthanis. Alles notes that the fact that the Ajnatasthanis are human beings means that we already know a great deal about them that will not need correcting were we actually to meet one. For instance, we know that Ajnatasthanis are two-legged and, while we cannot predict what language Ajnatasthanis speak, we know that they are capable of using language. But, in contrast to the claim that they are human, the claim that Ajnatasthanis are religious, would allow us, thinks Alles, to infer "very little, if anything at all" about the religion of the Ajnatasthanis.[29] This skepticism follows from his view that the concept of religion is "inference-poor"[30] because it refers neither to substances nor to natural kinds, which means that a concept of religion, unlike, say, the periodic table of the elements or the biological classification of organisms, is not grounded upon regularities to which general words apply and which obtain despite the countless ways in which religious traditions differ from one another.[31] This view allows Alles to propose the skeptical formula that "from the knowledge that instance *x* counts as a religion, there is no way to predict many, if any, features of any other instance *y*."[32] In other words, we can have no prior idea of what the religion of the Ajnatasthanis would be like simply from the claim that they are religious. Of course, this means that we will need to abandon the apparently empty notion of religion as a concept without a referent. The price of this surrender, however, is the loss of our ability to speak about the religion of the Rāṭhvas or, for that matter, any other so-called religion of any other group of people. Given the absolute vacuity of the word *religion*, religious studies would really turn out to be a redundant discipline—even if it lingers on institutionally for some time longer in an academe that has all but surrendered to the dominance of the STEM disciplines.

Because, as it turns out, this negation of the concept of religion even while still making use of the word religion is a self-refuting position to hold, Alles retreats into the less skeptical view that even if "there is no such thing as religion,"[33] the study of religion, at least as long as it is descriptive,[34] "will never cease."[35] But this leads us back to the opening question of this section, which is the question of how are we to pick out religions in the first place? Even when limiting religious studies to a merely descriptive role, the continued use of the word *religion* to refer to particular instances of religion calls for an explanation of why Alles feels justified in using this word to refer to more than one instance of religion? For this practice to make any sense there must be at least one generality—or religious universal—that allows Alles to do this. Without reference to such a generality, it is arbitrary to use the word *religion* to refer to certain activities of the Ajnatasthanis while assuming that these activities are only contingently linked to similar activities of non-Ajnatasthanis. This circumstance must either force us to come up with a provisional definition of religion or to simply backtrack into a refusal to face the fact of the reality of general terms, although this will leave us in the contrary position of continuing to make use of the concept of religion as we do our scholarly activity even while we stoutly deny that we are doing any such thing.

A Thought Experiment

Before making my own attempt to say what it is that makes a phenomenon religious, I would like to offer my own thought experiment as a way of showing why my belief that there is a religious something that makes something a religion is not a mere whim of my own choosing. Anjali studies auto engineering and excels in this field. She becomes a senior engineer for Honda, where she concerns herself mostly with theoretical issues involved in increasing fuel efficiency in automobiles. Oddly, Anjali does not own a car, does not have a driver's license, and has, in fact, never learned to drive. As an ardent urban dweller, actual driving is not essential to Anjali's theoretical work as an auto engineer, while her engineering and mathematical skills are paramount.

Devin owns a canary yellow 1957 Chevy Bel Air convertible. He has spent countless hours restoring this car to its original condition by following original factory specifications and through online discussion groups. His knowledge of this specific car is virtually complete, down to part numbers and the shape of every part. His knowledge extends to the specific suppliers of the parts in the car, as well as to the subsuppliers. Devin also has a complete record of all previous owners of this car, and through painstaking oral interviews, he has reconstructed the driving history of this particular automobile. He has created a blog that captures the social history of this particular automobile, in which he documents how it figured in the transformation of working-class city dwellers into middle-class suburban pioneers in the postwar period in the United States. Oddly, Devin has never driven this car since he has no license and is not really interested in driving. Like Anjali, he lives in a city, and takes mass transit and the occasional taxi. He is uninterested in the general principles of auto engineering, since his interest is in this particular car and its specific details as an artifact of a certain period of time and not in abstractions like driving cars or designing cars in general.

Bernd has owned a series of cars from makers around the globe and he has had varying relations with each of these cars, ranging from annoyance to indifference and, once, an odd feeling of affection for one of his better cars. He is not very much interested in the social history of his latest car, nor does he know much about auto engineering. However, he appreciates the fact that his cars have given him mobility, so he maintains them well, although he will not keep a car much beyond the point where it becomes cheaper to buy a new one than to maintain the old one. Besides, with advances in technology, a new car every five or six years serves to keep him and his family safer and reduces the cost of fuel.

With just a bit of imaginative stretch, we see here analogies for three possible ways of approaching the study of religion: the first approach suggests a conceptualism that is cut off from the material and cultural conditions within which abstract forms of knowledge arise, the second suggests a historicism that dispenses almost completely with the abstract and conceptual forms of knowledge that are necessary to give meaning and form to particulars, and the third approach suggests a middle ground between the two, one which tries to avoid the extremes of both conceptualism or historicism.

The first approach is that taken, at least in theory, by the old perennialism, whose own theological and ideological concerns eventually made its categories appear narrow and parochial. The second approach is that taken by the current historicism and constructivism in religious studies, which sacrifices explanation of the general conditions that make particulars possible in favor of the evocation, and perhaps even the fetishization, of the particular. The third approach is the one that we will take in these pages, and it recognizes that all abstractions, concepts, or universals, necessary as they are for explanation, must arise out of the soil of lived, concrete experience. Inevitably, what once were fresh generalizations will over time reveal that they, too, are implicated in the now vanished context and concerns of the people who formulated them. They will inevitably be cast aside, as the quest for understanding once again comes into vivid contact with concrete, empirical, and historical conditions, thereby setting off another cycle of constructivist revolutions and essentialist counterrevolutions in the never-ending quest to understand and explain the religious heritage of humanity. This dialectical interplay of the idiographic and the nomothetic approaches has a distinctive role to play in gaining a wider understanding of religion in general and in particular. For apart from a general theory of what counts as religion, one that is necessarily based on a definition of religion that refers to at least one shared, or general, feature of religion, the study of particular religions is liable to run aground in infinite and disconnected descriptions or in the futile search for a complete *nonreligious* explanation of religious phenomena, one that explains everything about a religious phenomenon except, crucially, its *religious* aspects.

Defining the Universal Religion

The outcome of this thought experiment, for me at least, is the firm conviction that there must be at least one feature, or to use a more technical term, property, in common between two sets of phenomena called *religion* if we are to feel justified in calling both of them by the name *religion*. This is not a merely logical or metaphysical quibble, since it is clear that we are not using the word *religion* in a purely arbitrary manner when we call Hinduism and Islam, but not Apple or Microsoft, religions. But if there is at least one shared property that justifies the use of the word *religion* in both—and other—instances, then we will have discovered that property of religion that must necessarily be in play when we call any *x* by the general word *religion*. What, then, is that property (or properties) that would allow us to use the word *religion* to categorize Hinduism as a religion and not as a business enterprise and Apple as a business enterprise and not as a religion?

A first response to this question might be that we can indeed study religions as businesses, and that people can also have a religious dedication to a corporation. It is clear that, even if only in a metaphorical sense, Apple is a religion for many of its employees and dedicated users of its products, which means that religions certainly have dimensions that can be summarized in a business-school case study.[36] Yet, unless we know in advance how a business differs from a religion, the metaphor of "religious" dedication to a nonreligious activity will make no sense. We can make the concept of religion so elastic that it includes armies, corporations, sports teams, and educational institutions, as well as intense devotion to a higher or greater cause or institution, but in so doing we will have turned the concept of religion into either a uselessly polyvocal term or into an adjective and a metaphor suggesting intense devotion to something or other. This underscores the point that the essential types of religion and business are sufficiently distinct, despite some superficial overlap, that it is not persuasive to say that they are indistinct from each other, for there does remain an essential difference between a human enterprise devoted to profitability and one devoted to negotiating the deep mysteries of life. In its most intense forms, religions awaken passions and inspire commitments that far transcend those evoked in any other area of life, and this is because religions, uniquely, among human activities, claim a special knowledge about life's deepest mysteries, such as those having to do with origins, destiny, good and evil, suffering, and death, a competence that derives from the unique ability of religions to orient human beings to an immaterial dimension of beatitude and deathlessness. Religions also offer ways of coming to terms with these mysteries in communities dedicated to the practice and propagation of methods of negotiating these deep mysteries. I thus propose the following definition of religion, one which defines a universal that will allow us to sort religions from other kinds of human organizations: *Religion is the human quest to relate to an immaterial dimension of beatitude and deathlessness.*[37] This definition suggests that, whatever else religions may be—and they are vast human complexes creating almost total worlds for their adherents—they are, insofar as they are religions, humanity's most reliable and time-tested methods of encountering a quality of life and experience that appears to escape the bounds of finitude and suffering. Of course, no academic religious-studies scholar must subscribe to this sort of view of religion as an article of faith or conviction. One need not, after all, be religious or spiritual to study religion academically, although this should not become a justification for attempting to strip religion of the religious and spiritual aspects that inevitably attend it like fingers to the hand and light to the sun. It seems evident to me that any view of religion that seeks to understand religion *as religion* will find more success of understanding religion *as religion* by making use of a definition like the one just proposed than one that reduces religion to aspects of human culture, psychology, or biology.

This approach to the study of religion will undoubtedly be viewed as "theological" and naïve by theorists of religion who are committed in advance to removing the religious aspect of religion *as religion* from the study of religion. There is, no doubt, real anxiety in the academic study of religion about being stained by theology, a stance that was justified when religious studies was still a newborn discipline in the protective shade of liberal Protestant theology faculties. But a religious-studies establishment that rejects as inadmissible for consideration the view that religion, whether rightly or wrongly, claims a special competence in dealing with the mysteries and rituals of beatitude and deathlessness is in flight from its own formal object of study after abjectly surrendering to a materialistic and reductionistic scientism. And, of course, this scientism, although currently dominant in the more elite levels of the global scientific and academic establishments, is itself an expression of Western religious conflicts since the Enlightenment (which continue with far less sophistication in the religiously charged polemics of the New Atheists).

Questions about the relation of theology to religious studies are undoubtedly fraught, and they go back to the very origin of religious studies as an independent discipline. But the artificial division of religious studies from theological, religious, and spiritual approaches to humanity's religious heritage, which seemed to be an inalterable wall from the late 1970s until the first decade of the current century, is rapidly dissolving in this emerging postsecular age. With the breaching of this wall, a new religious studies, one that is sensitive not only to the canons of the sciences, but also to the intimations of the illumined consciousness of humanity's sacred traditions, is coming into view. This new, postsecular approach to religious studies will not negate the distinction between secular and religious approaches to the study of religion. Instead, it will point out that this distinction is neither absolute nor final. This surprising postsecular turn in religious studies would have been welcomed by the grand old practitioners of religious phenomenology like Eliade, van der Leeuw, and Otto not only because it presages a renewal of interest in their long abandoned projects, but also because it is a symptom of the irrepressible sacred dimension of life that they insightfully charted.

The Dawn of a New Comparative Religion

This turn to the general and the universal in the comparative study of religion is not merely a whimsical product of this religion scholar's study, but is stimulated both by the recognition of similarities in contemplative experience across religious and cultural boundaries and by the growing body of research that suggests that human consciousness, whether due to genetics or a shared contemplative psychology, is characterized as much by general features of contemplative experience as by local differences between historically and culturally quite distinct religious traditions. We can, for instance, discern the dawn of a new comparative religion in the writings of Jeppe Sinding, who addresses "the present plight—and future possibility—of a general and comparative study of religion as a field of inquiry in the human sciences"[38] through pioneering work on the partial rehabilitation of "universals, essences, and nonreduction."[39] This nonreductive and universalizing view expresses Jensen's aim, shared with other new comparativists, of installing "a theoretically oriented comparative and general perspective in the study of religion."[40] Essential to Jensen's rehabilitative effort is the refurbishing of the reputation of leading earlier phenomenologists of religion such as Joachim Wach,[41] whose project is being resurrected in the new nomothetic-friendly environment of a religious studies that is being challenged and inspired, as we will see later in this book, by the nomothetic findings of the new cognitive, biological, and evolutionary sciences of religion.

Other religious-studies scholars are making similar moves of breaking decisively with the constructivist and particularist bases of contemporary religious-studies scholarship. Bernard McGinn adopts an "essential or synchronic view of Christian mysticism"[42] when he claims that "mysticism also has an essence, nature, or set of fundamental characteristics that, while shaped by time, exhibits considerable consistency over the centuries."[43] Providing a rationale for comparative study of multiple traditions, William E. Paden claims that "there is *no* study of religion without cross-cultural categories, analysis, and perspective,"[44] and that the development of these comparative capacities is "the basic, proper endeavor of religious studies as an academic field of inquiry."[45] This new comparativism, as Paden writes, should "neither ignore resemblances nor simplistically collapse them into superficial sameness."[46] Although Paden knows that this approach will be questioned by "postmodernists," this comparative approach "will," in his view, "be obvious to natural scientists, for whom humans appear as a singular phylogenetic kind, with common genetic programming, social predispositions, and infrastructural cultural behaviors."[47]

More directly engaging the findings of neuroscience and cognitive science is Ann Taves,[48] who raises the call for "a comparative neurophysiology of altered states of consciousness."[49] This innovative comparative project calls upon the divergent but intersecting skill sets of comparative religionists and contemplative neuroscientists as they join together in the project of explaining the special kinds of experiences often thought of as religious, which Taves categorizes as instances of a set of "special things" that people often associate with words such as *religion, religious, mystical, superstitious, magical, spiritual,* and spirituality.[50] These experiences are, phenomenologically seen, "relatively stable across cultures," and, neuroscientifically considered, expressions of "dynamic brain processes" and "intersecting physiological continua."[51] Success in this novel endeavor might lead, in turn, to the development of "a cognitively . . . based typology of experiences often deemed religious."[52] Taves's subtly argued comparative project can provide a strong theoretical bridge between a postconstructivist religious studies on one shore and contemplative neuroscience and ECSR on the other.[53]

Unlike the radical empiricists and constructivists who negate the search for the essence of religion, Daniel Dubuisson frankly acknowledges that there is a commonality between the radically diverse worlds presented by the world's religions (which he would include in the larger category of totalizing worldviews, religious and otherwise[54]). But he does not find the "combinatory principle"[55] of comparative religion in the usual places, such as in some general aspect of human biology or psychology, or in what was traditionally thought of as the soul.[56] He also excludes social functions and structures, theological notions of God, divinity, or transcendence,[57] as well as the concept or category of religion, which he views as an invention of the Christian West and, indeed, in his negative evaluation of this concept, as the West's highest cultural achievement.[58] Instead, Dubuisson sees each religion, or, better, each culture, as constituting a total world that, barring some syncretistic fusions here and there, shapes the whole experience of a culture from its grandest cosmogonic conceptions and practices down to its most intimate behaviors. As he writes, "All worlds are worlds, even though none is identical with any one of its congeners."[59] Dubuisson sees human beings as cosmographers, or formers of worlds that, despite their unassimilable diversity, remain as total environments in which we live out our lives. He thus wants to turn our attention away from merely particularistic studies of religion and from the use of the notion of religion[60] to the study of humanity's inveterate and universal activity of creating "cosmographic formations."[61] This, in his view, is an anthropologically sound approach,[62] which avoids what he sees as the failings of the old comparative religion associated with Eliade,[63] yet which allows for a generalizing study of the sorts of cosmogonic activity that is generally associated not only with religion, but also with any totalizing worldview, religious or otherwise.[64]

In a similarly universalizing move, Stuart Ray Sarbacker performs a comparative experiment by situating the notion of *samādhi* within the comparative context of Buddhist and Hindu yoga systems in India and Tibet,[65] as does Randall Studstill, who attempts to overcome the limitations of constructivism by arguing that the application of specific mystical teachings and practices have common effects despite the contextual differences between the traditions.[66] (This latter, anticonstructivist claim has been boldly affirmed by Jeffrey J. Kripal, who, in a discussion of psychic and paranormal phenomena that can easily be applied to mystical phenomena, rejects the reduction of consciousness to local cultures.[67])

A similar comparative case study to those pursued by Sarbacker and Studstill has been conducted by Gavin Flood, who, while denying that "the inner truth of the Buddha is the same as the Christian's God within," there is, nevertheless, "a parallel process of discernment and practice" in both traditions.[68] Confirming the common practical effects of mystical practices, despite the doctrinal divergences of the various home traditions in which these practices are situated, has also been the concern of by F. Samuel Brainard, who—in a philosophically subtle monograph on the comparative philosophy of mysticism published at the turn of the new millennium—was already charting the lineaments of a postconstructivist philosophy of mysticism.[69]

Building upon some of these approaches and attempting to extend them is my own contribution to this new comparativism. As will be seen in Part 2 of this book (and as foreshadowed in the Introduction), my endeavor to distill a set of five contemplative universals from the diverse meditative landmarks of the three traditions under study in this book is an attempt to devise a set of religious universals that are grounded in contemplative experience, comparatively considered, instead of in the comparative study of doctrine and symbolism, which, with notable exceptions such as Rudolf Otto's project, were the main foci of perennialism and earlier comparative phenomenologies of religion. These contemplative universals operationalize my definition of religion as the human quest to relate to an immaterial dimension of beatitude and deathlessness without endorsing any one religious view of life. That is to say, my proposed contemplative universals can best be understood as a means to the realization of the highest and most spiritual aim of religion, which is the establishment of relations with the immaterial dimension of beatitude and deathlessness, rather than as merely efficient methods for achieving the many laudable mental and physical benefits that, as contemplative neuroscience has shown, attend contemplative practices. These contemplative universals, although a product of this religion scholar's study as formulated here, are, nevertheless, not merely products of this comparativist's imagination (or lack of it).[70] Nor are they merely ethnocentric constructs[71] or suggestive notions based only upon apparent resemblances.[72] They are, on the contrary, grounded in repeatable spiritual experiments, such as the one I will undertake later in this book. On the one side, they subserve the formal object of religion, which is the spirituality of deathlessness and beatitude, and, on the other side, they are faithful to the phenomenology of contemplative states as presented in classic manuals in each of these three traditions. I have, accordingly in my recent work, turned away from the comparative study of doctrine to the comparative study of human spirituality, where, I think, the possibility of discovering contemplative universals as a basis for a pluralistic religious essentialism shows more promise of reward.

As can be seen from this brief survey of the awakening of the new comparativism in the study of religion, there is an emerging postconstructivist consensus that comparative studies, and the nomothetic approach more generally, are an essential, if long absent, method in religious studies. I would go further and suggest that the presence of contemplative universals as inevitable structural elements or processes in the diverse spiritualities of the world demonstrates the ontological rootedness of these universals and their grounding, along with culture, psychology, and biology, in a unified metaphysical view of the world. Shifted metaphysically in this way by taking into account the missing aspect of generality in the study of religion, academic religious studies can take an ontological turn and return to one of its earlier concerns, as reflected in the generalizing and universalizing quests of such pioneering and canonical figures as Joachim Wach, Gerardus van der Leeuw, Joseph Kitagawa, and Mircea Eliade, but with this difference: where they sought to provide a general, philosophical account of the human religious impulse in light of doctrine, symbol, and ritual, my approach here will be to range over the meditative landmarks of the three traditions under study in this book in order to abstract from them the contemplative universals that give a regular and discernible form to these otherwise diverse traditions. I will take the general not only as the distinguishing mark of universals but as the distinguishing mark of religion as it moves disciplined human awareness from dissipated lostness in everydayness to the resumption of the mind's birthright of indigenous awareness of deathlessness and beatitude by way of the global contemplative itinerary to be outlined later in this book.

Chapter 2

Recovering the Mystical in the Reign of Constructivism

A Short History of Mysticism

An unanticipated but welcome outcome of the softening of the old dualist, Cartesian and Newtonian materialism in science and the academy is a new openness in the sciences of consciousness to mysticism and to religious experience more generally. During the last two centuries, a period in which the now fading high secularism of the West was dominant,[1] the topic of mysticism became increasingly important for theologians and students of religion who wanted to save religion from the devastating, reductionistic assaults of rationalism, scientism, and secularism on the one side[2] and religious formalism and petrified orthodoxies on the other. The basic strategy of these thinkers was given its original formulation by the theologian and philosopher Friedrich Schleiermacher, who sought the source of religion in an unmediated intuition of that reality, beyond the limits of the world and of human reason, upon which human existence depends.[3] Numerous critiques of this sort of essentializing strategy—such as those offered by R. C. Zaehner,[4] Steven T. Katz,[5] Robert M. Gimello,[6] Wayne Proudfoot,[7] and Grace M. Jantzen[8]—have weakened its standing in the academic study of religion, although it remains, with numberless variations, the prevalent explanation of religious experience outside of the field, among the adherents of mystical, harmonialist, neo-Asian, and contemplative neuroscientific spiritualities, a persistence that indicates that the appeal to mystical experience is a move that is far older than the relatively recent time of Schleiermacher. Indeed, it suggests the perennial character of appeals to the mystical as an alternative to overly formalized, rigidly institutionalized, heavily inscripturated, or authoritarian religiosity.

Mysticism and related words like *mystical* and *mystic* originate, according to a speculative but commonplace etymology, in the Greek word *myein*, which can mean "to close" the eyes or "to be silent."[9] Drawn from the realm of the Hellenistic mystery religions, this word seems to indicate an initiate into sacred mysteries who has closed the outer senses in order to awaken to an inner world of spiritual meaning. In contrast to this experiential meaning, in the early Christian tradition, and under the influence of Judaism, *mystical* came to refer to anagogical interpretations of scripture in which, for example, the city of Jerusalem stands not for the actual city but for a heavenly city.[10] This is a cataphatic approach to mysticism, which focuses on visionary imagery that is generated by the ritually enhanced repetition of and internalization of doctrinal formulas and scriptural passages. (In the bicameral realm of Christian mysticism, cataphatic approaches can be distinguished from apophatic approaches, which take the forms of cataphatic mysticism as penultimate and preparatory for an unmediated reidentification with being, a resumption of our original nature that includes and transcends cataphatic forms. The cataphatic/apophatic distinction has, as we will see, its counterparts in the Buddhist meditative and Hindu yoga traditions and in recent neuroscientific theorizing about meditative taxonomies where this dyad has been characterized as the distinction between the Affective Domain and the Null Domain.[11])

In a somewhat later period in the nascent Christian tradition, an apophatic countermovement arose of approaching the knowledge of God through unknowing, or the systematic negation of theological and biblical knowledge, an approach that the enigmatic Dionysius the Areopagite first called "mystical theology."[12] In contrast to the cataphatic mysticism of which he was also a master, he accented direct experience of the ineffability of the God beyond God, who transcends standard theological and biblical teachings, an apophatic trend that, despite all orthodox opposition, has continued to find major exponents including Meister Eckhart, John of the Cross, and, most recently, Thomas Merton. Both cataphatic and apophatic mysticism grow out of the ancient monastic practice of contemplative scriptural reading, which has recently been revived in liturgical forms of Christianity under the name *lectio divina*, a style of inscripturated meditation that was given its familiar fourfold form by the Carthusian abbot Guigo II in the twelfth century.[13] By intensifying the anagogical reading of scripture into ecstatic and unitive worship, mystical theology and *lectio divina*, when unhampered by doctrinal and institutional scruples, increasingly rise toward an unmediated encounter with the Trinity and the overdeity beyond the Trinity.[14]

Internal to this inscripturated style of mystical theology is the potential to move in either a more experiential, or mystical, direction, or in a more dogmatic, or theological, direction, as indicated by the varying views of this potential that have been staked out in the eastern churches and the western churches. Reflecting the tradition of western churches, Harvey D. Egan, for example, distinguishes mystical theology from dogmatic theology, and holds that originally mystical theology "referred to mystical experience," although "contemporary usage, on the other hand, equates mystical theology with the doctrines and theories of mystical experience."[15] In sharp contrast, the Orthodox scholar and theologian, Vladimir Lossky declared that " 'mystical theology' denotes no more than a spirituality which expresses a doctrinal attitude."[16] And, more stoutly, he affirms that: "Dogma cannot be understood apart from experience; the fullness of experience cannot be had apart from true doctrine."[17]

Generally the province of contemplative monastics in the centuries between Constantine and the Cluniac Reforms, mystical theology at the turn of the second Christian millennium in the West began to take on the vivid form of an intensely personalistic devotion to Jesus. This style of cataphatic mysticism then spread out from Cistercian monasteries under the influence of Bernard of Clairvaux (1090–1153), with the result that personal religion, which once had been the province of the mystery religions and religious philosophies of the ancient Mediterranean world,[18] and which independently had shaped from ancient times the religions of India, began to spread among the European masses, first among Catholic semimonastics like the Beghards and the Beguines, and later through the revolutionary activities of Protestant reformers who wanted to place a Bible in the pocket of every youth driving a plow and to plant within them the expectation of dramatic personal religious experiences.[19]

As the West began to awaken again to the larger world around it, beginning early in the sixteenth century, its most enduring response was colonialism and the spread of hegemonic secular and religious ideologies. This was accompanied by the secularization of society and the neutering of religion by the liberal, universalistic ideals of the Enlightenment. As a consequence, the heritage of the world's religious traditions, which was now being rapidly translated into European languages and categories, was transformed into material for Western consumption while also being used as a tool to silence colonized populations through the deployment of Orientalist clichés.[20] Thus, the image of mysticism popularized a century ago by such writers as Evelyn Underhill and William James could easily be seen as a kind of generic personal religion for deracinated liberal Eurocentric Protestants in search of private meaning in a cultural landscape dominated by triumphant science and normative secularism. Common in current scholarly evaluations of mysticism are nominalistic and skeptical claims such as these, offered by social-constructionist and anticolonialist theorists who claim that the idea of mysticism is a recent construct of Western Protestant post-Christians in search of an antiauthoritarian warrant for a personal refuge from the demands of religious communities and political struggle.[21]

Clearly, a mysticism such as this, one that had diverged widely from its orthodox and classical origins, could be seen as a pastiche lacking the power to offer resistance to secular academic and scientific elites or to entrenched religious interests, even as it became a key element in a new religious syncretism that blended newly encountered Asian spiritualities with orthodox and esoteric Western religious forms. These compelling and now widely diffused syncretisms promote forms of spirituality in which being spiritual (as in "I'm spiritual, but not religious") has been increasingly divorced from traditional religious forms and institutions. This approach has often been dismissed in a cavalier and trivial manner as an expression of spiritual dilettantes practicing "New Age"[22] or "cafeteria religions."[23] Despite often negative and satirical evaluations, this syncretistic approach to human spiritual experience is now being positively reevaluated as the innovative practice of SBNRs (an acronym for "spiritual but not religious" practitioners), who, as seen by Linda A. Mercadante, are creators of new religious forms that foretell the rise of an experiential and pluralistic religiosity that is disruptive of authoritarian and dogmatic religious institutions.[24]

Given the rise of SBNR religiosity as a massive reality in US society and increasingly in other globalizing societies, it seems to me that the older, essentialist and relatively unskeptical and nonreductionistic views of mysticism, which, as we will soon see, prevailed from at least the days of James and Underhill to

W. T. Stace and Ninian Smart, will be more useful for developing a science-assisted, nomothetic account of mysticism than the more recent anticolonialist and social-constructionist dismissal of a globally shared mystical experience as the province of dilettantes, shallow comparativists, and capricious syncretists. To continue this latter, clichéd discourse about mysticism, which, like the crudities of the "New Atheism," dissolves religion and mysticism in a fog of diffuse and suspicious criticism, runs the risk of perpetuating the dualism and hegemonism of previous Western ideologies and hostile critical stances by negating the emic, or insider, stance of people practicing new forms of religion and mysticism in favor of the overextended etic, or outsider, stances of supposedly critical secular and antireligious observers. Ironically, this apparently neutral and rigidly secular approach to religious studies can itself be seen as perhaps the last wave or, to change the metaphor, the fading echo of Orientalism and Western cultural hegemony.

In the conflict of religious and spiritual worldviews with a deadening and dying radical secularism, which grants no intrinsic significance to a spiritual understanding of life, such trivializing views of religion and mysticism, especially when they are uncritically promoted in the academic field of religious studies, can be seen as ironically serving the cause of a once hegemonic secularism instead of the more substantive work of uncovering the common themes of a pluralistic and personally and culturally transformative spirituality. Thus, under the influence of the global return to religion and spirituality that is now, with ambiguous outcomes, undermining the global regime of the secular, a new comparative mysticism that can point out the similarities in the cataphatic and apophatic accounts of the world's many and diverse mysticisms can also serve to direct the energies of postsecularism[25] in a pluralistic but not unspiritual or antispiritual direction.

Yet, an essentialism of this sort is not likely to prevail in the academic study of mysticism without a long debate over the issue of whether the study of mysticism should focus only on materials derived from the unique cultural settings in which the different mysticisms arose or whether it should seek the common mystical dimension in the various mysticisms created over the millennia by humanity.[26]

Mysticism: One or Many?

These last reflections lead us to the central issue of this chapter, one that has divided the Anglophone philosophy of mysticism into two camps over the last forty years: is it the case that "phenomenologically, mysticism is everywhere the same," as Ninian Smart, echoing James and Huston Smith, asserted.[27] Or is it the case that a mystic's mystical experience is to some degree prefigured and thus diversified by the varying contexts in which mystical experience arises, as Steven T. Katz asserts.[28] Or, more simply, we might ask whether mysticism is one or many.[29]

To ask this question is to enter into the inconclusive debates between essentialists and constructivists (or perennialists and contextualists[30]). Instead of looking for a common reality or experience toward which the teachings of the various mystical schools point, constructivists take these diverse teachings as the respective starting points for the study of mysticism. Thus, constructivists use the term *mysticism* "in a qualified sense," according to Bernard McGinn. Instead of speaking of "mysticism" as such, they speak of "Christian mysticism" or "Buddhist mysticism."[31]

In contrast to this currently dominant scholarly approach is an older scholarly essentialism, which in the form of perennialism, or "the Perennial Philosophy,"[32] remains the dominant and pervasive understanding of mysticism outside the academy. While perennialism can be faulted for neglecting the historical and doctrinal side of mysticism,[33] an essentialist approach to mysticism need not undervalue these aspects of mysticism, even if its legitimate concern will always be with the common meaning of global mystical experience rather than with the contexts in which the world's many mystical languages arise. Just as constructivism sees mysticism in the plural as a product of various historical and doctrinal contexts, so essentialism sees mysticism as—at least in central crucial ways—a singular constitutive factor in the generation of humanity's varied religious and spiritual discourses.

As must already be clear to the reader, I side with the essentialists on this issue (which Bernard McGinn calls an "internecine" debate in recent Anglophone philosophy of mysticism[34]). But in so doing, I neither take up blindly the old perennialist approach nor do I simply try to counterargue the constructivists with arguments to which they are opposed on principle, for, as I have learned in trying in the past to harmonize what in the end are intractably divergent bodies of religious doctrine, this would be a futile move, since we are dealing here with fundamental views of the common data of mysticism that represent interests that are so at odds with each other that there can be no resolution of the issue that will be agreeable to both parties. Yet, if we are to find an exit from the dead end and impasse that has stalled progress in the philosophical study of mysticism, we will have to come to terms with the antiessentialist constructivism that has dominated the Anglophone philosophy of mysticism for the last two generations.

Katz's Constructivist Counterrevolution

Although other scholars played important roles in the rise of mystical constructivism in the late 1970s,[35] the central figure was and remains Steven T. Katz, whose name is virtually synonymous with this highly disruptive school of interpretation.[36] Like Kant awakening philosophy from the dogmatic slumbers of his day or like Barth casting bombs of revelation onto the once serene landscape of liberal theology, Katz almost in one stroke exiled mystical perennialism from the Anglophone philosophy of mysticism. Virtually overnight, the widely accepted view of mysticism as a common core of ideas expressed diversely in the world's religious traditions was replaced, if only for academics, by the axiomatic conviction that the world's various mysticisms are, on the contrary, expressions of the "pre-experiential conditions of the mystic's circumstances."[37]

Instead of looking, as had perennialism, for uniform mystical experiences across mystical traditions, constructivism focused on the world's many bodies of mystical literature, which undoubtedly report ultimate experiences in terms that are not identical to each other. Constructivists rejected the idea of a common mystical experience globally uniting those who speak, on the one hand, of God, and those who speak, on the other, of *nirvāṇa*.[38] This claim threw the study of mysticism into disarray and almost immediately made all attempts to articulate a general definition of mysticism seem outmoded and even wrongheaded.[39]

This was a disruption as disorienting as John Hick's Copernican revolution in theology, which he tried to instigate by placing first God (and later the Real) rather than Christ at the center of "the universe of faiths," a metaphor that Hick adapted from the Copernican revolution in astronomy which placed the sun instead of the earth at the center of the solar system.[40] Other Copernican revolutions in human thought included Kant's placing the categories of reason instead of the objective world at the center of philosophy and Schleiermacher's placing of human experience instead of the Bible or doctrine at the center of Christian theology. But in a counterrevolutionary move precisely opposite these Copernican and classically modernist moves, Katz instituted an anti-Copernican reversal of perspectives by placing mystical doctrine instead of mystical experience at the center of the philosophy or mysticism. This disruptive move was, as suggested above, logically identical to the theological counterrevolution patented by Barth much earlier in the last century when he similarly disrupted the theological world of his liberal teachers by placing Christian doctrine instead of religious experience at the center of theology.

Katz, like Barth, thus took a counterrevolutionary move back toward orthodoxy and religious particularism away from the liberal universalism and wider ecumenism[41] of the philosophy of mysticism that reigned from James and Underhill to Stace and Ninian Smart. Katz's disruptive move can perhaps be seen as a reaction to the antitraditional liberalism and radicalism that came to its greatest flowering in the late 1960s and early 1970s, but began to recede in the face of the return of more traditional values and religious teachings beginning around 1980 in the United States. A similar counterrevolution was also influentially and disruptively undertaken in the theology of religions by Gavin D'Costa, who, for a time at least, almost singlehandedly halted the progress of theological pluralism with his antipluralist claim—directed at his own *Doktorvater*, the pluralist pioneer John Hick—that pluralism is actually a covert form of religious inclusivism, or even exclusivism.[42] In both cases, we see a distinctively antimodernist and antiliberal rejection of the universalizing values of the Enlightenment and of modernity.

Although it contradicted almost the whole body of work in the philosophical (as opposed to the theological) study of mysticism that had been assembled over the preceding century,[43] Katz cast aside as a dead end the grounding axiom of the old philosophy of mysticism that a mystic's immediate experience of *x*, where *x* stands for the ultimate reality aimed at by all mystics, is only secondarily expressed in "the familiar language and symbols" of the mystic's tradition.[44] In an intellectual feat that was the equivalent of a yogic headstand, Katz flipped the field upside down by laying down the then counterintuitive axiom that "The Hindu mystic does not have an experience of *x* which he then describes in the, to him, familiar language and symbols of Hinduism, but rather he has a Hindu experience."[45] Where the older philosophy of mysticism saw the Hindu mystic (or, more precisely, the nondual Vedāntist) as applying the name Brahman to an unmediated experience of an ineffable mystical *x*, Katz innovatively saw the Hindu dogma of Brahman, and its originating contexts as prefiguring and preforming the Hindu mystic's mystical experiences.[46] Or, as I formulate Katz's interpretive approach: *mystical outputs are determined by doctrinal inputs.* Not every constructivist will always fully agree with the constructivist principle so stated,[47] but in this strong form of what I will call "the constructivist axiom," it has entered into the mainstream of religious studies over the last forty years as an assumption that has generally stood as exempt from criticism.

Thus, rather than see mystical experience as a way of overcoming or relativizing religious doctrine, as was often one of the intentions of perennialism, Katz sees mystical experience as a derivative of the doctrines of specific religious traditions. Instead of there being a singular mysticism that is variously expressed in Christian Jewish, Hindu, and Buddhist terms, there is, in Katz's view, an irreducibly *Hindu* mysticism, an irreducibly *Jewish* mysticism, and so forth. Undoubtedly, this neo-Kantian move[48] was useful in turning scholarly study back to the religious contexts within which mysticisms arise, for it was certainly the case that the older philosophy of mysticism had construed mysticism as a singular reality with countless expressions. In a contrary move, however, Katz pluralized the core of mysticism, thus disruptively bending mysticism back upon its diverse expressions and reducing it to a pluralized reflection of those diverse expressions. This was a fruitful victory for the historical and linguistic study of particular mystical traditions, as well as for orthodox and mainstream interpretations of mysticism, and it was the academy's answer to Katz's plaintive "plea for the recognition of differences"[49] in the study of mysticism.

Losing the Mystical in the Mysticisms: The Dead End of Constructivism

As important as this turn to differences was in bringing greater sophistication to the academic understanding of the contexts and content of the globe's many mysticisms, it inevitably led to the dissolution of the concept of mysticism.[50] By pluralizing mysticism in its essence instead of in its expressions, the crucial perennialist view of mysticism as a common human capacity prior to and independent of institutionalized and textualized religions and mysticisms was lost in an endless sea of distinctions.[51] This, in turn, led to a nominalism and skepticism about the concept of mysticism that dissolves it in a haze of overheated, self-enclosed, antimystical theorizing.[52] So, after a generation of the dominance of constructivism, we are left with the question of what mysticism as such—or the mystical[53]—is about.

One possibility is that a unitary or essentialist approach to an understanding of the mystical is simply ruled out by the constructivist stress on differences, and the word *mystical* can, as a consequence, be used at best in the metaphorical and celebratory way of Robert M. Gimello, a founding constructivist along with Katz, who sees, "mystical experience [as] simply the psychosomatic enhancement of religious beliefs and values or of beliefs and values of other kinds which are held 'religiously.' "[54] But this is a dead end, since it unjustifiably retranslates *mysticism* from a cognitive to a merely affective use. While this clever deflection is reminiscent of the now almost risibly naïve mid-twentieth-century obfuscations of analytic and positivist philosophizing with respect to religion and metaphysics, it fails to come to terms with the longstanding and widespread understanding of the meaning of mysticism. Nor does it account for the fact that we know how to distinguish, partially at least, the mystical dimension of religion from other dimensions, such as ritual and liturgy, scripture and founding stories, religious jurisprudence and sumptuary codes, and doctrinal and conceptual analysis.

Although the doctrinal content of a Buddhist mysticism is, for example, "near the other end of the mystical spectrum" from the content of a Jewish mysticism, as Katz observes,[55] yet this differentiation of two clearly distinct forms of mysticism only underscores the issue of meaning since, given the radical doctrinal discontinuities between these and other bodies of mystical doctrine, one may rightly ask why Katz continues to refer to all of them with the word *mysticism*? Is this merely a habit born of old conventions that can now be discarded? Or does it raise in even stronger form, now that the Katzian plea for differences has been fully accommodated, the question of what allows us to refer to radically diverse kinds of religious expression as mysticism. But this, of course, is to ask after the meaning of the term *mystical* (just as we did with the term *religious* in the last chapter). And to ask after meaning is to search for a concept, a general idea, or a universal, which is expressed in a potential infinity of limited realizations. The isolation of what I see as religious universals to account for religious and religious activity was the main focus of the last chapter, and from that follows the quest, to be begun in this chapter, of isolating a set of contemplative universals that can account for the regularities that, despite constructivist skepticism, structure global contemplative experience. These contemplative universals are deeply felt internal states that retain phenomenological identity through the diverse contexts in which contemplative experience is expressed, thus allowing us to unfailingly point out the mystical among the mysticisms and, furthermore, to authorize us in calling certain Jewish phenomena *mystical* and certain Buddhist phenomena *mystical* despite the many differences that distinguish these traditions from one another. It is upon these contemplative universals, rather than upon the compelling but nonuniversal differences between diverse contemplative traditions, that, in my view, a defense of the mystical—and more generally of the religious life of humanity *as religious*—can be mounted over against the perhaps now faltering reductionistic, materialistic view of life.

Against the expected nominalistic criticism that there is no shared feature—and thus no essence or universal—corresponding to the general term *the mystical*, I would point out that, as noted in the last chapter, nominalism is but one of a number of classic epistemological theories, none of which have been or likely will be confirmed to the satisfaction of all philosophers. Whether essences or universals exist in an ideal metaphysical space or are abstracted from existing realities,[56] the practical need for them is felt whenever we make a generalizing statement. Unless I want to invent a new word every time I see an apple, I am justified in naming an individual apple with the general word *apple* (or *Apfel*, etc.). The alternative is an ever-expanding dictionary for each set of singulars such as apple, cats, trees, etc. Thus, I might coin a new word for each instance of an apple—this is a *japer*, that a *liduga*, and that a *pralpram*—a situation that becomes almost immediately unsustainable and which is remedied by noting that the sort of thing to which I am now pointing is an apple.

It seems to be the case, then, that unless the mysticisms are linked to each other in a noncontingent and non-stipulative way by way of a general word like *mysticism* or the *mystical*, we have no justification for being able to use the word *mysticism* as a name for this or that distinctive set of religious phenomena. Without acknowledging the mystical *x* that the various mysticisms intend in and through their respective contexts, we have no right to continue calling them forms of mysticism at all. We may continue to do so out of habit or convenience, but, apart from a common reference point, or a contemplative universal or universals, that justifies the use of the general word *the mystical* or *mysticism* when talking about the mysticisms, we may just as well use other words.[57]

This example alone should make it clear that a constructivist approach to mysticism can never bring us anywhere near to a full understanding of mysticism, what to speak of articulating the essence of mysticism, nor can it illumine the perennial arising of mysticism in utterly diverse religious movements. At most, it merely reintroduces under the name of *mysticism* the diversities of religious expression that are studied in other fields, such as historical theology, the history of religions, the sociology of religion, etc. Such an approach is also consistent with merely materialist or social-constructionist approaches, which discount the notion of a sui generis mystical universal and reduce reference to it to the formal object of their respective interpretive methods, whether that be some aspect of culture, biology, psychology, or the physical world. But for religious studies to once again achieve, as it has in the past, an understanding of the mystical as it was expressed by the mystics in their respective mysticisms, it cannot dispense with the task of defining the essence of the mystical, even if this understanding remains wedded to skeptical, agnostic, or dismissive views about the reality of this element. Nor is this a religious or theological claim, since the question of the meaning of the mystical remains just as much a needed preliminary issue for nonreligious and nontheological approaches to mysticism as for religious and theological approaches. One need not affirm the mystics' truths, after all, in order to understand the mystics. The alternative to this needed intellectual activity of essentializing mysticism is the atomizing of language and thought about mysticism and the mystical to the point where each of us latches onto increasingly smaller islands of mysticism that float unrelated to one another in a field of signifiers shifting aimlessly and chaotically toward nonbeing.

Disconfirming Constructivism: Three Perspectives

Constructivism, at least in the strong form in which it is often presented[58] and which I characterize above as the view that mystical outputs are determined by doctrinal inputs, is in my view manifestly inadequate as a theory capable of accounting for the globally available evidence for mysticism and the mystical on both skeptical and unskeptical approaches. Rather than an empirical approach to the mystical evidence, strong constructivism is more of an *a priori*, ideological, and dogmatic approach to the body of mystical evidence than an actual analysis of what the whole body of this evidence suggests. It is not surprising, then, that constructivism has faced a number of well-aimed criticisms, which when supplemented by my own critical stance as suggested above, amount to a refutation of strong constructivism (weaker forms of constructivism, which amount to nothing more than keeping in mind that the mystical is expressed diversely in varying contexts, are not affected by these critiques and should remain a part of the full complement of methodologies that are brought to bear upon the study of the world's mystical traditions). In the following sections, I want to survey the most influential of these disconfirmations of constructivism.

Disconfirming Constructivism: Reducing Mystical Experience to Doctrine

Sallie B. King formulated one of the earliest and most devastating counterarguments to Katz's program when she noted that his approach "improperly reduces mystical experience to doctrine."[59] With the passage of the decades, this trenchant criticism has been sharpened to the point where it is now a refined and standard criticism of Katzian constructivism, in which, according to Jason N. Blum, "mystical experiences have been misrepresented as over-determined by context and as necessarily compliant with mainstream doctrine."[60] Paul Marshall offers a similar negative judgment on what might be called Katz's "over-determination thesis": "Doctrines are cited as evidence for the influence of doctrines."[61]

A few examples of how Katz attempts, although without success, to reduce mystical experience to doctrine show the force of King's devastating criticism. Among the many mystical passages cited by W. T. Stace in his once-standard philosophical study, *Mysticism and Philosophy*, is a selection from Ruysbroeck that recounts a "union without distinction" that is "above reason and beyond reason" and that passes into "a wayless abyss of fathomless beatitude."[62] For Stace, this is one of the many mystical texts that give evidence for what he calls "introvertive mysticism," which has the "nuclear characteristic" of being "an undifferentiated unity devoid of all multiplicity"[63] (which contrasts with the nuclear characteristic of what he, in contrast, calls "extrovertive mysticism," which is a sensory vision that unifies the multiplicity of objects in the universe[64]). Thus, for Stace, this passage, despite the theistic interpretive elements that are included in the selection (but not quoted here), is "as near to uninterpreted pure experience as can be got."[65]

Katz, however, takes aim at Stace by citing this passage in his paradigm-shattering essay and asserting that the theistic and Christian elements in Ruysbroeck's account are essential to Ruysbroeck's mysticism because a Christian mystic experiences "the mystic reality in terms of Jesus, the Trinity or a personal God."[66] In other words—and here Katz restates the axiom of strong constructivism—"The experience that the mystic . . . has is the experience he seeks as a consequence of the shared beliefs he holds through his metaphysical doctrinal commitments."[67] Contra Stace, who held that these theistic elements, as differentiated empirical content, cannot remain in the introvertive mystical experience, Katz thinks that the contextual prefiguring of mystical experience insures that a Christian mystic like Ruysbroeck will have a Christian mystical experience.

But, as Huston Smith notes,[68] this passage from Ruysbroeck actually contradicts Katz's view, since it articulates what for an orthodox believer might be considered to be a highly suspect dissolution of the persons of the Trinity in "the wayless abyss of fathomless beatitude."[69] This apophatic theme, which undercuts the finality of cataphatic doctrinal claims and images, is a constant theme in Christian mysticism from at least the time of Dionysius the Areopagite through Meister Eckhart[70] and down to Thomas Merton (with even a hint of it discernible in the writings of Paul[71]). Not only that, but examples like this are easily multipliable from virtually every tradition. Stace speaks of thousands of "unanimous" reports from all over the globe for the introvertive mystical experience, which undercuts the strong constructivist claim that mystics get from their mystical outputs only the doctrinal inputs that they bring to them.[72] For instance, one can point out that the Buddha entered the central Buddhist trans-sensory, transconceptual, trans-experiential mystical state conventionally named *nirvāṇa* without having first been a Buddhist and without knowledge of normative, orthodox Buddhist doctrine, which did not yet exist.

Another example of the implausibility of Katz's reduction of mysticism to doctrine is his extremely odd, theory-driven claim that yoga "properly understood" is a reconditioning rather than an unconditioning or deconditioning of consciousness.[73] But the second *sūtra* in the *Yoga Sūtra* is more than completely clear in stating that yoga is the overcoming of the vagaries of mental conditioning (*yogaś citta-vṛtti-nirodhaḥ*), which certainly includes all of the preformed expectations and doctrinal commitments that the beginning yogi brings to the practice of *dhyāna* and the cultivation of *samādhi*.[74]

Still another example of the failure of the claim that doctrine determines the central content of mysticism is provided by Buddhism. That central forms of Buddhist mysticism are oriented toward a transdoctrinal, noncontextual state of pure awareness is made clear by Paul Griffiths, who offers a subtle exploration of various possibilities of pure, unmediated, and nondualist consciousness in Buddhism, particularly in Yogācāra Buddhism and its teaching about "unconstructed awareness," or "preverbal, preconceptual awareness."[75] In this same connection, Robert K. C. Forman notes that Buddhist doctrine or categories are left behind in the fifth *jhāna*, a form of pure awareness untouched by doctrinal inputs.[76] As these examples—which can be multiplied many times—show, the extraordinarily sophisticated phenomenological analyses of ordinary and nonordinary states of mind offered in the various Buddhist traditions, which are, I think, far beyond anything yet achieved in the Western exploration of the mind and its contents, are enough to show that there is a centrally important unconstructed dimension in consciousness. In other words, there is more evidence for the claim that mysticism is ultimately oriented to the overcoming of the dissolution of awareness in empirical multiplicity than in affectively rich and emotionally charged reproductions of doctrine.

And, of course, it would almost be impossible to understand a mystic like Plotinus from a purely constructivist perspective, according to Robert K. C. Forman and Steven Bernhardt,[77] given that the encounter with the One (*to hen*) overcomes all differentiation by definition. "This," according to Bernhardt, "is what Plotinus means when he says that 'we are ever present to Him [*to hen*] as soon as we contain no more difference.'" This view is asserted also in the *Kaṭha Upaniṣad*, which states unequivocally that "from death the death he goes, who sees/here any kind of diversity."[78] There is, of course, no end of such passages in the mystical evidence.

It is clear, then, that what Katz refers to as the "mystical evidence"[79] is replete with instances of formless, nonsensory, but wakeful transpersonal awareness, which eludes being shaped by doctrinal inputs, thereby disconfirming the axiom of strong constructivism, and if this archive of textual sources for global mysticism is allowed to speak without constructivist distortion, then it must be acknowledged that this state has been testified to by what Paul Griffiths eloquently names "the religious virtuosi from all cultures."[80] But this is all that is needed to support the notion of the oneness of mysticism and of the mystical, which was defended by mystical philosophers from James and Underhill to Smart and Smith. On this point, at least, the *philosophia perennis* was on to something central to the definition of mysticism.

Disconfirming Constructivism: or Pure Consciousness Events (PCEs)

This talk of unconstructed, formless awareness and deconditioned consciousness moving beyond its doctrinal moorings leads us inevitably to the influential work of Robert K. C. Forman who, along with his collaborators in various edited volumes, produced a formidable disconfirmation[81] of the strong constructivist axiom by developing a careful, comparative phenomenology of what Forman calls "pure consciousness events," or PCEs. This is a state of purified mystical awareness that is essentially devoid of doctrinal and visionary content.[82] Despite Katz's *a priori* rejection of pure consciousness,[83] Forman sees the PCE as a central feature of many kinds of mysticism and contemplative experience, and he defines the PCE variously as states of "wakeful contentless, consciousness,"[84] a state with "no experienced content for consciousness,"[85] "wakeful objectless consciousness,"[86] and "wakeful though contentless (introvertive) consciousness."[87] And it is just such states of awareness, completely inexplicable from a Katzian perspective, but central to the older mystical philosophies of Stace and James, that Forman sets out to restore to a central place in the Anglophone philosophy of mysticism.

Forman begins his critique of constructivism by referring to the trophotropic/ergotropic continuum constructed by a pioneer of neuroscientific studies of mysticism, Roland Fischer.[88] This cartography maps a range of conscious states from the extreme of *samādhi* on the trophotropic side and the extreme of mystical rapture on the ergotropic side, as well as the rebound from each extreme to the other. After summarizing the divergences between these two extremes as indicated by variations in such factors as metabolism, emotional arousal, mental activity, heart rate, skin temperatures, EEG patterns, and galvanic skin responses,[89] Forman concludes that "The two sets of states are unlikely to have identical psychological characteristics, causes, and etiologies."[90] This allows him to distinguish such phenomena as visions, hallucinations, and auditions, which are ergotropic, from tranquil, nonsensory contemplative experiences, which are trophotropic.

Using a once-standard typology in mysticism studies derived from W. T. Stace's influential *Mysticism and Philosophy*, Forman places the ergotropic phenomena in the category of Stace's "extrovertive mysticism" and the trophotropic phenomena under the category of Stace's "introvertive mysticism," which he defines as a state in which there is no awareness of an external world beyond the self[91] (and which, of course, need make no reference to a self). Forman then excludes as mystical such ergotropic, extrovertive phenomena as visions, hallucinations, and auditions, which he segregates into its own category of "visionary experiences."[92] This allows Forman to make the bold but clarifying move of "reserving the term 'mysticism' only for trophotropic" and introvertive states.[93] In this, he harks back to another major preconstructivist philosopher of mysticism, Ninian Smart, whom he quotes as saying: "*Mysticism* describes a set of experiences or precisely, conscious events, which are not described in terms of sensory experiences of mental images."[94] Quite the opposite of this is introvertive mystical experience, which Stace had earlier defined as excluding multiplicity and distinction.[95] By focusing on the PCE and introvertive mystical experience instead of extrovertive experiences, Forman thus narrows his focus to the trophotropic states of deep contemplative calm associated with *dhyāna* and *samādhi*. In so doing, he orients the philosophy of mysticism back to the distinctive kind of trophotropic mystical experience that engaged the field from James to Smart and Fritz Staals.[96]

R. C. Zaehner noted that this sort of "monistic" or "unitive" mysticism is different from inscripturated, doctrinal forms of theistic mysticism,[97] but rather than using this fact to dissolve the notion of the mystical into multitudes of divergent kinds of religious experience (which is a wider category than mystical experience), which are, in turn, sorted into various proliferating typologies, Forman, contrary to Zaehner, but similarly to Stace and James before him, simply excludes as mystical the ergotropic mysticisms and focuses on the key element in nondual ("monistic" and "unitive") trophotropic mysticisms: the PCE. Forman's PCE is a culture-free zone which, as an apophatic space of formless consciousness, is prior to cataphatic, or visionary, kinds of mystical experience. Indeed, it is ontologically prior to all experiential states because it is the timeless and formless ground in which the ever-changing states of experience occur. In direct contradiction of the constructivist focus on individual features of isolated mystical traditions, Forman has prominently and consistently argued, given the pervasiveness of the PCE in the world's many mystical traditions, that "rather than being the product of a cultural and linguistic learning process, [trophotropic] mysticism seems to result from some sort of *innate* human capacity."[98]

To speak about a so-called innate capacity is to use updated language for what comparative theologians and comparative religionists early in the middle of the last century called a sui generis capacity of human beings for spiritual experience. This autonomous, self-generating, and self-justifying mystical endowment, whose onetime grounding in such various locations as religious emotions, the ground of the soul, or the transcendental structure of the intellect was subjected to withering and reductionistic critiques, has begun to resurface recently, after a long winter of rejection and disregard. This is not due to new breakthroughs in theology or philosophy, which remain mired in the dead ends of constructivism and religious particularism. Instead, impulses for a new essentialism are coming by way of the broad revival and wide diffusion of contemplative practices that were once the preserve mostly of monastics in the three traditions under study in this book as well as from the neuroscientific study of meditative states and the cognitive-scientific recognition that human consciousness—what to speak of mystical consciousness—is not shaped exclusively by language and culture.

Disconfirming Constructivism: Bottom-Up Processing

With the weakening of the constructivist ban on essentialism, academic mystical studies is now positioned to profit from current neuroscientific and cognitive-scientific models that are demonstrating that "bottom-up" processes emerging from the unconscious and the brain decisively shape consciousness alongside the "top-down" processes of language and culture, which have been the focus of constructivist approaches to mysticism. Ann Taves, former president of the American Academy of Religion, has begun to lay the theoretical groundwork for religious studies for just such an approach. Her work in this area, which we might call "postconstructivist," was inspired by the neo-perennialist William G. Barnard, who criticized the constructivism of Wayne Proudfoot for failing to account for the mystical experiences of people who were "not engaged in spiritual disciplines" and "had not been primed by a tradition."[99] This devastating criticism of constructivism led Taves to reject a "thoroughgoing constructivist view" (or what I call "strong constructivism" and Forman "complete constructivism"[100]). But this rejection—and this is Taves's intention in her work in this area—opens the door in academic religious studies to the effects of bottom-up processing on mystical consciousness and religious experience.[101] This means that the brain, the unconscious, and even the immaterial environing dimension of being postulated in various forms in the world's religion are increasingly being recognized as shaping human religious experience independent of and prior to the top-down processing stressed by constructivists and social constructionists. From such a perspective, it might make sense, once again, to speak about a religious and mystical sui generis, but this time not just as a special psychological and spiritual capacity within human consciousness, but also as a physical, electrochemical, and neurobiological reality genetically coded into our brains. Thus, we can see that the sui generis mystical capacity, which is being recovered with the help of contemplative neuroscience and the cognitive science of religion, is also an immaterial spiritual reality that shapes the yogic and contemplative itinerary as it moves from conventional everyday consciousness to the summit of nondual mystical insight. For after the door is opened to nonlinguistic and noncultural factors in human cognition, only a strict materialist dogma will refuse to consider the thesis that immaterial realities express themselves neurobiologically by shaping our religious experiences. Rather than double down on a theoretically insufficient materialist stance, we might take the opportunity offered by the resources of contemplative sciences to build bridges between the humanities and the natural sciences.

Disconfirming Constructivism—The Neuroanatomy of Ineffability

As a key practice in the Buddhist contemplative practice of *vipassanā bhāvanā,* or "insight mediation," mindfulness proceeds in part through the anticonstructivist practice of what Ingrid Jordt characterizes as the separation of "percept from concept."[102] This can be taken as a contemplatively operational definition of *ineffability*, which James classically named as "the handiest of the marks" of the mystical,[103] and which has recently been rehabilitated by Jason N. Blum, who holds that ineffability claims are a cross-cultural feature of mysticism.[104] Blum counters the constructivist rejection of ineffability and its neo-Kantian reduction of consciousness to language[105] by drawing upon a vast amount of neuroanatomical evidence that shows that a much of basic human experience is nonlinguistic, a trait that it shares with—as far as we know—all forms of animal consciousness.[106] In the evolution of consciousness, emotions, which are primarily physiological activities of neurobiological and bodily systems, long predate language and cognition.[107] This is clearly reflected in the neuroanatomy of the brain where neocortical structures are much newer than older, subcortical brain structures such as the limbic system.[108]

Of course, as Blum notes, this is not evidence for the "mystic object" sought by perennialists,[109] nor is it likely that scientific approaches will easily revive perennialism among academic religion scholars.[110] But it does indicate that the mystic of any and all traditions who rhapsodizes the ineffable shares with other mystics "a built-in natural human capacity for nonlinguistic experience."[111] While this can be taken as evidence for a materialist reduction of the contents and referents of consciousness to brain states, it can also be taken as showing that a brain is a necessary but not sufficient condition for embodied religious experience.

Conclusion

No doubt many scholars in the humanities and religious studies will be scandalized by this apparent return to outmoded, universalizing conceptions. Scholars for whom the critical analysis of religious texts and religious language and the exploration of the social contexts within which these texts and languages arise will find this to be an alien approach to the study of religion. Perhaps this is the reason why the most compelling and paradigm-shattering work on meditation is being done far beyond the precincts of religious-studies departments in parts of universities where humanities scholars such as I rarely visited in the past: the laboratories and scanners of contemplative neuroscientists and neurotheologians. There are at least two reasons why meditation lends itself to neurobiological study and is thus the best place to begin a scientific study of religion and spirituality. One is that much of the intellectual and visionary content of religious worldviews, as well as the startling capacity of mystics and saints to renounce and transcend conventional ideas, attitudes, and habits, comes from their mastery of meditation in its many forms. Second, meditation, like mysticism is not religion specific. William James famously and epigrammatically noted that the classical texts of mysticism have "neither birthday nor native land,"[112] a claim that can be extended to meditation. The abstraction of a common yogic-mystical itinerary from the local itineraries of the different mystical traditions that I will undertake in the second part of this book is evidence that there is a core mystical path at the heart of the world's great spiritual traditions that is prior to, independent of, and creative of the local mysticisms and meditative itineraries that have been developed in the world's many spiritual traditions. Although this view will likely be rejected by constructivists and social constructionists, recent neurobiological and evolutionary studies of contemplative experience provide decisive evidence that decides this question in favor of essentialism at the expense of constructivism.[113] And to some of these findings we will now turn.

Chapter 3

Biological Essentialism and the New Sciences of Religion

The God Helmet: Triumph of Reductionism or Dawn of Spiritual Neurobiology?

In an odd twist that could not have been predicted at the onset of the rise of the antiessentialist, constructivist approach to the study of mysticism in the 1970s is the current return of essentialism in religious studies with the strong sanction of science. The long dominance of antiessentialist, constructivist approaches to mysticism is being forcefully challenged by the rise of what I call "biological essentialism." Typical of this new essentialism in religious and spiritual areas once considered off limits to science is the provocative experiment of Michael Persinger, who famously devised a helmet that produces the sense of an invisible presence in up to eighty percent of subjects when their right temporal lobes are stimulated with magnetic fields.[1] "Persinger thinks," writes religion scholar Ross Aden "that this experience is the model for the impression of spirits, ghosts, aliens, and perhaps God."[2] This leads Persinger to conclude, according to Aden, that "in whatever way believers understand their experience . . . it is the result of a brief, focused electrical incident in the brain."[3] No stronger rejection of the constructivist reduction of mystical experiences to culture and dogma than this can be offered, even after allowing for contextual differences, or what Aden calls "cultural factors as well as the setting,"[4] in individual instances of religious experience.

Yet, this forceful repudiation of particularist, inclusivist, empiricist, and constructivist interpretations of religious experience may be a pyrrhic victory for the essentialist, nomothetic, and comparative study of mysticism, since it buys victory over constructivism at the apparent cost of the surrender of the specifically spiritual, or nonmaterialistic, aspect of religious experience.[5] This new biological essentialism appears to undercut the conviction that there is a spiritual, or immaterial, dimension of being by showing that religious experience can be accounted for in terms of brain processes. This is a high price to pay, I would say, although the scientific confirmation of the essentialist approach to the study of mystical consciousness is welcome.

Yet, this argument can immediately be flipped on its head, since the scientific confirmation that the brain is intimately involved in producing religious experience decisively undercuts claims that religious experience is merely a culturally shaped mental projection, or just a product of the imagination, or dismissible as the product of an abnormal or diseased brain. My own solution to the threat of biological essentialism canceling out the mystical essentialism outlined in the last chapter while also negating constructivism is the familiar but still important observation that the mind is not the brain, and that, therefore, the mind is only partially expressed through the brain. Stimulating the brain to produce religious experiences, as in Persinger's God Helmet experiment, only maps out possible locations and processes in the brain that filter the spiritual, or immaterial aspect, of being, as Jeffrey J. Kripal argues.[6] Because a filter merely changes the character of light, as with a stained glass window, rather than generating the light itself, Kripal's filter thesis suggests that religious experiences are something more than only psychological features of physical brain states. In fact, a deeper implication of Persinger's experiment, which at first glance seems to confirm the reduction of the spiritual to the biological, is the view that the brain is a tool evolved by a prior, nonbiological dimension of being to express itself in the physical register of being. Thus, the God Helmet can also be taken as a sign both of the end of the era of reductionism and of the dawn of a spiritual, or contemplative, neuroscience. Instead of explaining away religious experience as merely psychological or as only an illusion produced by the brain, the new neuroscience of religious experience shows that human beings are biologically predisposed to experience an immaterial realm of pure consciousness.[7] It turns out that, just as we have evolved material senses to negotiate a realm of physical objects, so we also have evolved brains that register a subtle, immaterial realm of being.

Yet, a claim such as this, especially in an academic monograph on religious experience, runs afoul of what Victoria Nelson and Kripal see as "the greatest taboo among serious intellectuals,"[8] which is "the heresy of challenging a materialist worldview."[9] In response to the idea that immaterialism is an intellectual heresy to be avoided by the serious and responsible academic and scientist, I would point out that, as the history of the rise and fall of orthodoxies and their corresponding heresies in the history of religions make clear, the word *heresy* has no objective significance, since the term is only a way of discrediting people with whom one disagrees religiously. It is an oft-repeated maxim of mine as a teacher of religious studies that one person's heretic is another person's saint. This is no less true in the history of science than in religion, since there are multiple and contrary views of what counts as science. Thus, the scientific orthodoxy of today, as aggressively defended by figures like Daniel Dennett and Richard Dawkins, is, simultaneously, ever more open to the study of consciousness and meditation, as seen in the work of Herbert Benson, Andrew Newberg, Eugene d'Aquili, Richard Davidson, Jon Kabat-Zinn, and many others. It seems that the study of consciousness and meditation almost inevitably lead to a less materialistic and even nonmaterialistic view of the world. This, in turn, seems to be leading to a softer, less aggressively materialistic variant of science.

The New Sciences of Religion

This current unlinking of science and materialism and the rehabilitation of immaterialism are opening the way for a reawakening of the quest for contemplative universals as pursued in the old "science of religion"[10] (an expression that at the turn of the twentieth century was a synonym for comparative religion).[11] Because the search for generality has marked science from its origins in the major cultural hearths of the world,[12] any genuine science of religion, whether new or old, must be a quest, above all, for the universal features of religiosity and spirituality wherever they appear. A genuine science of religion will not suppress nor be indifferent to the incalculable diversity of the world's many religious and contemplative traditions. It will, on the contrary, delight in this diversity as providing the field in which its provisional generalities, or universals, can be formulated, tested, refined, and abandoned or reformulated. A nomothetic quest for generality in the study of religion, then, is not the abandonment of idiographic studies of individual religious complexes, but forms a complementary and necessary branch of religious studies.

Foundational to this new biological essentialism is the view that "there is a universal human nature," which is grounded in "evolved psychological mechanisms" rather than in "cultural behaviors," as Ilkka Pyysiäinen forthrightly declares.[13] Insight into this universal human nature is emerging not through the sort of cultural studies currently dominant in religious studies, but through genetic, cognitive, evolutionary, neurobiological, and contemplative research. Undoubtedly, this claim will surprise particularist, constructivist, and hyper-empirical religious-studies scholars. Yet, as the following brief sketch will convey, the new sciences of religion have returned to the generalizing concerns of the nineteenth century's science of religion. I offer the following examples, not as a comprehensive overview of these emerging fields, but merely to suggest the potential of the emerging biological essentialism to aid in the development of a reinvigorated humanistic study of religion, one that will stand on the triple foundations of biological research in the areas of, first, the evolutionary cognitive science of religion (ECSR), contemplative neuroscience, and neurotheology, second, disciplined yogic and contemplative experience, and, third, the vast array of philological, philosophical, cultural, exegetical, interpretive, and ethnographic skills available to the traditionally trained religion-studies scholar. To the first of these three foundations, I will now briefly turn, while the second is at the heart of the second part of this book. For a discussion of the third of these foundations, the reader is directed to the many standard methodological texts in the classic areas of academic religious studies.

A New Science of Religion: The Evolutionary Cognitive Science of Religion

In current academic religious studies, the most established of these new sciences of religion is a discipline that was first called the cognitive science of religion (CSR), but has more recently taken to calling itself the evolutionary cognitive science of religion (ECSR).[14] Moving in the opposite direction of constructivism and cultural studies in religious studies, the turn by a small group of religion scholars to evolutionary and cognitive studies was, according to Francesca Cho and Richard King Squier, a "reactivating [of] the paradigm of universal theorizing about religion" through the envisioning of "the putative structures that evolution has imparted to human thought."[15] ECSR commenced, according to Steven Engler and Mark Quentin Gardiner, in 1990 with E. Thomas Lawson and Robert N. McCauley's *Rethinking Religion: Connecting Cognition and Culture*, although an argument can be made that it had its real beginning as early as in 1980 with the work of Stewart Guthrie.[16] Of the numerous suggestions made in Lawson and McCauley's book, their identification of religion as commerce with "culturally postulated superhuman beings" came to be seen as "the defining characteristic of religion in subsequent cognitivist work."[17] As used by Justin L. Barrett, for example, the word *religion* can be defined as designating "a shared system of beliefs and actions concerning superhuman agency."[18] This conception, developed rigorously and most famously by Pascal Boyer,[19] has evolved into a mechanistic, phenomenologically innocent[20] model of human religiosity as traceable to a postulated cognitive capacity for "hyperactive agency detection" and its expression in behavior through "hyperactive agent-detection devices" (or HADD)[21]

At its simplest, this model accounts for religion by positing the overuse or misuse of a cognitive capacity in human beings for detecting agency.[22] That is, we seem to have installed within us an Agency Detection Device (ADD), or, more simply, an agent detector.[23] According to this cognitivist and evolutionary model, we human beings have bettered our chances of survival by quickly assuming that sudden movements or other changes in the environment are signs of an approaching predator. Whether we are right or wrong in attributing agency to what might merely be the trembling of leaves in a breeze is less important than the fact that, by reacting appropriately to a predatory agent that may turn out to be imaginary, we may survive still one more day and thereby have another chance to pass along our genes.

Yet this ordinary, and in itself nonreligious,[24] cognitive capacity within humans can go seriously awry, according to ECSR, when despite increasing empirical knowledge of the actual material character of the world and of natural causation, people continue to attribute large-scale phenomena like the existence of the world and small-scale phenomena like changes in people's fortunes for the better or worse to the activity of superhuman agents such as deities, ghosts, spirits, angels, demons, and the like. As fictional add-ons to other, empirically available agents, such as other human beings and various predators, our built-in agent detectors hyperactively conjure up the various religious agents that appear in human religions. These nonordinary agents are accounted for by ECSR as expressions of hyperactive agent detectors functioning unchecked within people.[25] Despite even extensive scientific education, people's hypersensitive agent detectors keep going off and alarm them to the presence of the putative hidden actors behind the scenes who are believed to be responsible for unexpected events, or miracles, and who create the world and reveal religious rituals and religious teachings.

Ilkka Pyysiäinen, a CSR theorist whose views are less adversarial to the insider's sense of the reality of these agents, holds that religious ideas about supernatural agents can be explained as references to agents whose actions or character are "counter-intuitive" in one or more memorable ways to humanity's shared "folk" or "intuitive" (i.e., scientifically unpurged) psychological, biological, theoretical, and ontological expectations (at least as construed from the outsider standpoint of a convinced naturalist and materialist[26]). These religious representations violate to some degree the boundaries of usually separate ontological domains, such as impersonal natural phenomena and living persons[27] (e.g., "benevolent rocks or weeping statues"[28]). For example, the intuitive folk ontology in which agents always have bodies is violated in the case of deities,[29] who counterintuitively are bodiless, although in other respects deities conform to intuitive expectations about agents, such as having desires and beliefs.[30]

A New Science of Religion: Contemplative Neuroscience

In striking contrast to the days of James and even Stace, we now live in a time of rapidly expanding and breathtakingly creative and daring developments in the neuroscience and neurobiology of meditation, which are being expanded and systematized in the emerging fields of contemplative neuroscience, or affective neuroscience,[31] and neurotheology. A pioneer in the medical and scientific study of meditation is Herbert Benson, whose 1975 bestseller, *The Relaxation Response*, offered one of the first positive biological accounts of the physical correlates of the practice of meditation. This iconic book was the first in a long series of medical bestsellers focusing on the body-mind connection and the formerly mostly unexplored health benefits of meditation, which was just beginning in the middle 1970s to venture toward mainstream respectability. The lasting contribution of Benson's research was his discovery that a simple meditation technique can induce a "physiological state of quietude"[32] that is the opposite of the fight-or-flight response. Benson showed that meditation induces a decreased rate of metabolism, or hypometabolism, thus inducing a restful state. This is accompanied by decreases in heart rate, breathing rate, and previously elevated blood pressure, all of which contribute to decreased risk of hypertension and stroke (the conditions that led Benson to explore meditation as a remedy).[33]

Although Benson's work must be credited with creating a platform for the mainstreaming of serious clinical and experimental research about meditation, the antecedents of contemplative neuroscience can be traced back to a study by Arthur Deikman, whose 1963 article "Experimental Meditation"[34] is taken by Richard Davidson as inaugurating contemplative neuroscience,[35] and to the work of three graduate-student friends, Richard Davidson, Daniel Goleman, and Jon Kabat-Zinn,[36] whose later careers would produce research and clinical programs that can be seen as completing the mainstreaming of meditation begun by Benson. Also significant for the development of contemplative neuroscience is the path-breaking work in the emerging field of neurophenomenology of Francisco J. Varela as extended by Evan Thompson.[37]

Other recent discoveries that lend at least indirect support to contemplative neuroscience is that of the so-called God gene by geneticist Dean Hamer, which is as at least as sensational a concept as Persinger's God Helmet. Despite its popular style and the journalistic breeziness of its title, Dean Hamer's *The God Gene*[38] is a worthy successor to William James's *The Varieties of Religious Experience*, and Hamer makes an important contribution to the scientific study of religious experience by showing that human beings have what he calls, "God genes" or a built-in " 'God module' prewired in the brain."[39] More precisely, Hamer's God gene is the VMAT2 gene, whose variations control serotonin and dopamine in order to produce altered states, which are characteristic of even lower-level meditative states. Because twin studies show that this gene is highly heritable, as measured in the Cloninger Self-Transcendence Scale, human beings seem to be genetically programmed for transcendent, contemplative experiences.

The relationship of meditative experience and genes is not a one-way street from genes to experience, as if causality here were only a bottom-up affair. Richard Davidson, along with researchers at the University of Wisconsin-Madison and the Institute of Biomedical Research of Barcelona, has discovered that meditation "reduced levels of pro-inflammatory genes," thereby increasing recovery from stress. It seems, then, that gene expression can be affected positively through meditative calming of the mind,[40] which, as an instance of top-down causation, indicates that meditative experience has genetic correlates that are independent of the cultural forces of the meditator's environment. Contrary, then, to all merely cultural and idiographic explanations of mysticism, neurobiology points toward a biological core that correlates with the phenomenological core of mysticism. As Hamer cogently and colorfully asserts: "Spirituality has a biological mechanism akin to birdsong, albeit a far more complex and nuanced one."[41]

Neuroscientist Patrick McNamara lends support to the idea that religiosity has a neurobiological and neurochemical basis when, after a discussion of Walter Pahnke's famous research on the mystical effects of LSD in *The Neuroscience of Religious Experience*, he tentatively concludes that "Entheogens produce religious experiences by activating the same brain circuit that normally handles religious experiences."[42] As mapped by McNamara, this circuit links "the orbital and dorsomedial prefrontal cortex, the right dorsolateral prefrontal cortex, the ascending serotoninergic systems, the mesocortical DA [dopaminergic] system, the amygdala/hippocampus, and the right anterior temporal lobes."[43] McNamara sees this circuit as composed of "the most important regions of the brain for studies of religious experience."[44] Given these developments in the neurobiology of religion and spirituality, academic religious studies has the opportunity to take what I call the neurobiological turn instead of continuing on with only textual, culturalist, and nomothetic studies of mysticism.

A New Science of Religion: Neurotheology

An influential and often-cited finding in the neuroscience of meditation[45] comes from the research of Andrew Newberg and his first collaborator, Eugene d'Aquili, and later collaborators (Newberg, not without hesitation, calls this approach "neurotheology,"[46] an expression that would better be replaced, in my view, by the less sectarian expression "contemplative neuroscience"). Using SPECT scans to measure cerebral blood flow of meditators from various traditions, they have provided compelling, if not conclusive,[47] evidence that the cultivation of meditative states produces similar neuroanatomically observable changes in the posterior superior parietal lobe of the brain.[48] Ordinarily, the thalamus continuously transmits auditory and visual information to this lobe, which then generates a sense of the body's orientation in space and its relationship to other objects, or between self and other. But through the application of certain meditative techniques, the neural impulses from the left prefrontal cortex increase, with the result that neural activity in parts of the thalamus also increase, thereby suppressing neural impulses to the posterior superior parietal lobe. Then, in a well-corroborated result, the sense of the boundary between self and other dissolves for the meditator.[49] This process of deafferentation of, or decrease in, neural activity in the posterior superior parietal lobe occasions the rise of a nondual, unitive state of awareness that Newberg and d'Aquili call "absolute unitary being,"[50] or an "enhanced non-cognitive state."[51] This finding is a stunning neurobiological verification of what Stace saw, on the basis only of literary studies—for he himself disclaimed having had mystical experiences[52]—as the introvertive mystical experience of "transsubjectivity" in which a mystic senses that "the boundary walls of the separate self fade away."[53]

It is not hard at this point to conclude, on the basis of this signature neuro-anatomical and neurophysiological process, that the brain has, as Newberg thinks, "universal functions" including religious functions, which could serve as a universal hermeneutic in all religious traditions.[54] While theologians and other religious intellectuals have habitually looked to texts for the data upon which to base their interpretations and systematic reflections, and while they have often drawn upon religious experience for these purposes, it has never previously been part of theological, religious, and metaphysical systematics to draw upon the sciences of the brain and its operations. But, given this secure neuroanatomical finding, these fields now have the opportunity to take the revolutionary step of making a religious and spiritual fact rooted in the anatomy and physiology of the brain an ingredient in their speculations and interpretations. In his own attempt at making good on the theological element of neurotheology, Newberg has suggested this principle (among numerous others): "Every brain structure and function must be considered to be useful in understanding theological and philosophical concepts."[55]

It goes without saying that such neurobiological processes are shared among human beings, thus giving support to universalizing approaches to religious experience after decades of constructivist focusing on the cultural divergences that attend this or that individual mystical experience. As noted by Jensine Andresen and Robert K. C. Forman: "Indeed, perhaps the domain of the religious reflects pan-human correlations at a deeper level than conceptuality—electrical activity in the frontal and temporal lobes of the brain, the stimulation of hormone flows, and the ceasing of random thought generation all may be seen as cross-cultural technologies of spiritual experience."[56]

The Neurobiological Basis of the Spiritual sui generis

It appears that Newberg and d'Aquili have provided the clue that is needed to show that a specific type of yogic and mystical (if not always religious[57]) experience is rooted in the physiology and anatomy of the brain. Thus, whenever a human being experiences the sublime mystical state of nonduality, the neural correlates of the nondual condition as it arises in awareness will include as its signature the deafferentation of neural activity in the posterior superior parietal lobe. Ann Taves correctly sees Newberg's and D'Aquili's claim to have found "the biological root of all religious experience" as exemplifying a sui generis and common-core approach to religious experience rather than the ascriptive approach, which she favors.[58] Although she acknowledges the association between "unusual activity" in the posterior superior parietal lobe and a sense of "the absorption of the self into something larger" discovered by Newberg and d'Aquili, she rejects the idea that this brain state and its experiential correlate are religious in themselves, since, in accordance with her ascriptive theory of religion, they could be deemed nonreligious in other contexts. Yet, rather than negating the value of the central finding of neurotheology as grounding mystical experience, Taves's criticism serves to underscore an essential difference between nondual, apophatic, and introvertive mystical experience and other religious phenomena. Nondual, apophatic, and introvertive mystical experience (or the mystical proper) will, in my view, always bear the neurophysiological signature of the deafferentation of posterior superior parietal lobe, while other religious activity and events, insofar as they are experiential events, may or not have the signature of the mystical and can thus be assimilated to many other human activities, which, in accordance with Taves's ascriptive theory of religion, may or may not in various contexts merit the designation as religious events. That is to say, any *x* may or may not be given the label *religious* on an ascriptive view of religion, but the mystical, whether in contexts deemed religious or not, will always bear the neuroanatomical signature of the deafferentation of the posterior superior parietal lobe.

We are now in a position where, aided both by contemplative neuroscience and neurotheology, I can state the axiom that the mystical is sui generis, while other religious events are sui generis only insofar as they are also mystical. This axiom is confirmed, in my view, by the fact that, as has been known since the days of the Buddha and the *Yoga Sūtra*, the mystical can be expressed in any number of doctrinal contexts (as suggested by the Buddha's metaphysical agnosticism and by the adaptability of *dhyāna* to multiple doctrinal contexts in multiple Indian religious systems). Nondual mysticism—or what has variously been called cessative,[59] apophatic, and introvertive mysticism—can thus be used to justify any variety of theistic, nontheistic, religious, and nonreligious teachings, as when, for example, the subjects of study were Tibetan Buddhist monks or Franciscan nuns.[60] We could ask for no clearer marker of the neuroanatomical and neurophysiological basis for introvertive, nondual, apophatic, noncognitive mystical experience than the felt sense of nonduality that arises through the deafferentation of the posterior superior parietal lobe.

Given this scientific confirmation of the central thesis of Stace's introvertive mysticism, and given the functional identity of the human brain from person to person (barring, of course, individual differences at the cellular level), it seems that the basic claim of strong constructivism has been effectively falsified. The neurobiological turn thus confirms the once widespread view in the comparative study of mysticism from James to Stace and Smart that a transconceptual, nondual mystical state is a perennial feature of religion—or what I call a religious universal—rather than a figment of the speculative imagination. By definition, this religious universal, in contrast to more doctrinally shaped forms of intense religious experience, has no sectarian markings. While there can be a Christian religious mysticism shaped by specifically Christian elements, there cannot be a *Christian* introvertive, nondual, or apophatic mysticism except insofar as it is a Christian who is experiencing this transsubjective, noncognitive state. This goes for all other traditions as well, each of which can claim interpretive ownership of its own variously declined varieties of religious experience, but can lay no special claim upon the nondual mystical-yogic state, which, because it bears the neurobiological signature of the deafferentation of the posterior superior parietal lobe, expresses the deep biological structure of religion and spirituality and provides a scientific basis for the study of the mystical and its attendant practices, itineraries, and outcomes. This discovery, in turn, provides a foundation for a pluralistic and essentialistic comparative science of religion. Thus, the door seems now to swing widely open once again for a new perennialism in the study of yogic consciousness and mysticism.

Conclusion

Despite the sensationalism that is easily aroused by the headline-grabbing discoveries of Persinger, Hamer, and Newberg, their findings seem to have gained ground in the neuroscientific mainstream. This is especially true of neurotheology, whose findings have become the main plank in the search for the neural correlates of religious experience.[61] That these neurobiological processes are shared by human beings lend strong support to nomothetic approaches to religious experience after decades of idiographic approaches focusing on the cultural divergences that attend exclusively to individual mystical traditions.

Discoveries such as these are the foundation of a new, postmaterialist science of religion, one that need not, like currently dominant materialist sciences, remain agnostic about whether or not there is a spiritual and immaterial dimension to life.[62] These findings put overly constructivist and particularist views of religion on notice that, despite the richness of diversity that radiates through humanity's religions, there is an underlying core of mystical experiences that shapes individual spiritual experience wherever it occurs.[63]

But again, as at the beginning of the chapter, one note of caution needs to be raised, for while the help of science is useful in recalling religious studies to its neglected nomothetic concerns, it must not be paid for at the cost of blindly adopting a trivialization of religion that sees religion only through the genetic, cognitive, and neurobiological categories that mark the boundaries of a reductionistic materialism. Independent of the views of science, welcome as they may be, religion has its own realm of competence. Surpassing the powers of virtually all other human endeavors, religion promises access to the immaterial and deathless realm of beatitude. Hindu, Buddhist, Christian, and other varieties of mysticisms differ in countless irreducible ways, yet they also share an identical concern with charting a path for contemplatives from unaware submersion in the realm of the senses to awakening into an immaterial realm of deathlessness and beatitude.

Whether one accepts that such a realm exists or not, it is indisputable that religion in general and mysticism in particular aim toward this realm. There is no doubt that cultural, political, linguistic, and anthropological factors shape religions and spiritualities, as constructivism has usefully pointed out. They are, after all, products of the incessant and immensely creative activity of human societies and personalities. Yet, it should be uncontroversial to assert that the purest aim of religion and mysticism is to acquaint human beings with a realm beyond the reach of the senses and death, which is achieved through overcoming the duality of self and other. This is the basis of religious hope and of mystical practice, and it is because of this message of hope that one may hear a religious or mystical eulogy at a memorial service but never a eulogy based on chemistry or economics.

This new religious essentialism is thus less interested in the biographies of religious founders and histories showing how the contexts of their unique hierophanies shaped their personal mystical experiences than in studies that, for example, show how the altered states and nonordinary[64] insights of meditation, which is the key practice of mysticism, affect people's capacity for compassion,[65] the realization of happiness,[66] and the activation of the altruism necessary for group rather than individual selection in evolution.[67] From perspectives such as these, the specific contextual differences between religions and their contemplative practices appear to be less significant than their empirically testable benefits, which inhere in them as forms of religion and spirituality rather than as unique features of this or that sectarian body of doctrines, practices, and historical and institutional characteristics. For, despite the infinite number of differences that distinguish the world's many religious traditions, the essential practices of religion have displayed a remarkable unity over the millennia, as the old perennialists correctly argued. Setting aside the endless varieties of local expression and local doctrinal controversies, religious practices such as ritual, prayer, and meditation seem remarkably similar everywhere they occur, just as writing and talking involve the same bones and muscles in different human societies, even if their verbal and symbolic content changes dramatically from context to context. Up very close, Hopi *katsina* dances appear quite different from Vaiṣṇava *sankīrtana* parties or Pentecostal dancing in the Spirit, yet, within a larger perspective, each of them can be seen as serving the same purpose of awakening a sense of ecstatic connection to unseen realms and powers in the dancers, an experience that, despite its identity across time and cultures, is diversely thematized in the world's many unique religious traditions.

Thus, a basic conviction guiding this book is that while constructivism served for a time as a needed corrective (but not as a substitute) to the abstractions of the earlier perennialist approach, constructivism itself now stands in need of correction. I propose to do this by returning theoretical attention in religious studies to the question of the general aspect of religions, which is to say that I will sift the unique materials contingently produced by the three traditions under review in this book in order to draw or abstract out the contemplative universals, or deeply felt internal states, which retain phenomenological identity through the diverse contexts in which contemplative experience is expressed. It is upon these contemplative universals, rather than upon the interesting but inessential differences between diverse contemplative traditions, that, in my view, a defense of mysticism—and more generally of the religious life of humanity *as religious*—can be mounted over against the perhaps now faltering reductionistic, materialistic view of life. And to a more detailed comparative study of these universals, we can now turn.

Part II

Introduction to Part Two

Charting the Common Itinerary of the Contemplative Experience

Careful study of the stages and landmarks that inflect the unfolding of mystical experience in the degrees of *samādhi* in the Classical Yoga of Hinduism, the *jhānas* of Theravāda Buddhism, and the degrees of *unio mystica* in Catholic mystical theology has convinced me that contemplative experience is the product of the cultivation of ever deepening states of concentration. Mystical experience, from the fraction of an instant when the mind of the yogic contemplative first experiences awareness apart from the mediation of the senses up until the moment of full enlightenment, can be seen as flowing from the unified states of mind generated through concentration that are familiar to the experienced meditator. Although thematized diversely in each of these traditions, their common practical meditative teaching can be summarized as prescribing a common technique for achieving diversely conceived final soteriological end states: the cultivation of deepening states of mental concentration, which produce salvific insight by kindling profoundly penetrating analyses of experience that becomes contemplatively absorbed in its inquiries.

Given its centrality in yogic and contemplative practice, I will, in the next three chapters, use concentration as a key to unlock the inner orderliness of contemplative experience wherever it occurs, since the intensification of concentrative focus is marked by a sequence of experiential meditative landmarks that, despite irreconcilable contextual differences in the traditions as lived on the ground, is virtually identical in each of the three traditions under study in this volume.

The spiritual life is revealed in each of these three traditions as a developmental journey from an uninformed unspiritual way of life to a perfected spiritual way of life, a journey that is expressed in itineraries, or maps, with highlighted junctions or stages, each with its distinctive landmarks or defining characteristics. Each of the yogic-contemplative traditions under review in this book presents this itinerary in its own unique way (the Buddhist and the Pātañjalian itineraries share many explicit commonalities, being sibling traditions in ancient India, yet identical commonalities arise in the historically unrelated—at least as far as the historical archive can suggest—tradition of Catholic mystical theology). These traditions describe meditative landmarks that in their own ways express the five contemplative universals that I name *convergence*, *coalescence*, *simplification*, *quiescence*, and *beatitude*. The virtual identity of these universals in these three traditions suggests that the deep structure of the spiritual life is tradition neutral rather than tradition specific. This common itinerary, or contemplative roadway, is a rail laid down by the nature of the spiritual life in our minds and in our neuroanatomy, a finding that favors nomothetic and essentialistic approaches to the study of religious experience over constructivist and idiographic approaches.

As a guide to much of what is to come in the coming chapters, I present here a brief summary of these five contemplative universals and the meditative landmarks through which they are expressed. For ease of understanding and to follow the discussion in this part of the book, I have summarized the common yogic-mystical itinerary and its five contemplative universals and the distinctive meditative landmarks through which it is expressed in each of the three traditions under study in this book in the following chart.

As a guide to what is to follow in the following three chapters, I would like to offer here a brief overview of these five contemplative universals, a sketch that will be filled out with particular attention to the diverse sets of meditative landmarks that express them in the three traditions under review in this book.

Convergence

Preceded by preparatory practices of Catholic ascetical theology, Buddhist *sīla*, and the yogic *yamas* and *niyamas*, convergence, as the first station on the common yogic-mystical itinerary, is a key stage in the eight limbs of the Pātañjalian Yoga of Hinduism, in the multiple *jhānas* of *samatha* practice in Theravāda Buddhism, and in the degrees of *unio mystica* in Catholic contemplative prayer. Through remarkably similar practices of concentrating the mind in these three traditions, the yogi, or contemplative, accesses an ensemble of subtle inner states characterized by sublime sentiments of tranquility, immaterial sensation, liberative insight, and unitive awareness. The focusing practices that access these subtle inner states are called *recueillement actif* in French, *dhāraṇā* in Sanskrit and Pāli, and *parikamma-nimitta* ("training sign") and *uggaha-nimitta* ("learning sign") in Pāli (these two signs share between themselves the features of *dhāraṇā* in the *Yoga Sūtra*), and I see them as locally distinctive expressions of the contemplative universal that I call "convergence."

Coalescence

The next step in the common yogic-mystical itinerary is the contemplative universal that I call "coalescence." Coalescence is expressed in Pātañjalian Yoga, Buddhist *bhāvanā*, and Catholic mystical theology in the meditative landmarks of *dhyāna*, *paṭibhāga-nimitta*, and *la ligature des puissances*. Each of these terms names a distinctive experience that a skilled yogic contemplative in these three traditions will likely have experienced: the sudden locking in or fixing of the mind on the meditation object after a period of increasingly focused concentration or recollection. This coalescence of the mind and the meditation object is one of the great "landmarks" in yogic contemplation, and it will not go unnoticed or be soon forgotten by the yogic contemplative who experiences it. This coalescent practice opens inner portals into a timeless and always available sublime realm

Figure 1 The Common Yogic-Mystical Itinerary

Contemplative Universals and Their Common Functions	Meditative Landmarks in Theravāda Buddhism	Meditative Landmarks in Pātañjala Yoga	Meditative Landmarks in Catholic Mystical Theology
convergence: mind focuses on meditation object	**parikamma-nimitta** (training sign) & **uggaha-nimitta** (learning sign)	**dhāraṇā** (concentration)	**recueillement actif** (active recollection) **affective mental prayer** leading to **prayer of simplicity, prayer of simple regard, or prayer of the heart** = active night of the senses
coalescence: mind fixes on or locks in on the meditation object	**paṭibhāga-nimitta** (counterpart sign) = **upacāra-samādhi** (access concentration) & **appanā-samādhi** (absorption concentration)	**dhyāna** (meditation)	**la ligature des puissances** (ligature of the faculties)—beginning of recueillement passif (passive recollection) = passive night of the senses/arid prayer of quiet
simplification: mind simplifies itself factor by factor	**four jhānas** ***generating factors*****:** **vitakka, vicāra, pīti, sukha** (applied, or concentrated, thought, sustained thought, or deep reflection, mystical rapture, contemplative happiness)	**saṃprajñāta-samādhi** (mediated recollectedness) ***generating factors*****:** **vitarka, vicāra, ānanda, asmitā** (concrete-reflection recollectedness, abstract-reflection recollectedness, delightful recollectedness, mere self-awareness recollectedness)	**unio mystica** (mystical union): three preliminary stages: **(sweet) prayer of quiet, full union, ecstatic union** = active night of spirit ***generating factors*****:** **intellect, understanding, will, imagination, memory**
quiescence: mind is stilled	**saññāvedayitanirodha** (cessation of ideation and feeling)	**asaṃprajñāta-samādhi** (unmediated recollectedness) dharmamegha-samādhi (recollectedness in the inner raincloud of beatitude)	**la suspension des puissances** (suspension of the faculties)= passive night of the spirit/ spiritual dereliction
beatitude: mind is transcended	Before physical death: **nibbāna** After physical death: **parinibbāna**	**kaivalya** (extrication): Before physical death: **jīvanmukti** After physical death: **videhamukti**	Before physical death: **transforming union** (last stage of mystical union)After physical death: **visio dei, beatific vision**

of the subtle-body states. This realm is intermediate between the physical world and more sublime states of quiescence and insight (treated in the next sections) that escape the nets of cosmological, physical, biological, psychological, social, intellectual, and religious conditioning.

Simplification

Coalescence is followed in the common yogic-mystical itinerary by the contemplative universal that I call "simplification." Simplification is expressed in Pātañjalian Yoga, Buddhist *bhāvanā*, and Catholic mystical theology in the meditative landmarks of the sequential suppression of the sets of factors that constitute the four *jhānas*, the stages of *saṃprajñāta-samādhi*, and the stages of *unio mystica*. It is a notable feature of advancing concentration in each of the three contemplative traditions that the visionary phenomena and the pleasant psychological and bodily states of the earlier stages of meditative absorption gradually give way to a quiet inner stillness in which the mind becomes clear and a stable mirror of what is ultimately real. Now, the tranquilized mind becomes the site of powerful and effective liberative and salvific insights, which weaken to the point of overcoming the cosmological, physical, biological, psychological, social, intellectual, and religious conditioning of the yogic contemplative.

Quiescence

Simplification is followed in the common yogic-mystical itinerary by the religious landmark that I call "quiescence." Quiescence is expressed in Pātañjalian Yoga, Buddhist *bhāvanā*, and Catholic mystical theology in the meditative landmarks of *asaṃprajñāta-samādhi*, *saññāvedayitanirodha*, and *la suspension des puissances*. Now, the mediation of the mind by cosmological, physical, biological, psychological, social, intellectual, and religious conditions ceases, and the yogic contemplative enters into a state of virtual cessation in which the outward faculties have been stilled while awareness is utterly transfixed from within. There is now no further attraction to or concern with the objects of the external realms of the body and the mind, and the yogic contemplative takes their stand upon the ground of immaterial being itself. This condition of cessation is intermittent, so long as physical life continues, and it is experienced, especially in its initial phases, as a spiritual night of disorientation while the contemplative becomes accustomed to this new condition of absolute inner freedom. Over time, this sense of disorientation is transformed into a steadily calm and blissful mood of unwavering inner recollectedness that allows the yogic contemplative to make a return to effective and compassionate external activity until the end of physical life.

Beatitude

Quiescence is followed in the common yogic-mystical itinerary by the religious landmark that I call "beatitude." Beatitude is expressed in Pātañjalian Yoga,

Buddhist *bhāvanā*, and Catholic mystical theology in the meditative landmarks of *nibbāna*, *jīvanmukti*, and transforming union, which is, variously expressed, the condition of perfected, saintly human existence where the yogic contemplative lives simultaneously in the inner and outer realms while exercising mastery in both spheres. This end state of the common yogic-mystical itinerary represents the perfection of the spiritual life in its embodied, human form, and is a foretaste of the transhuman condition of *parinibbāna*, *videhamukti*, and the beatific vision.

Now, with this summary of the set of contemplative universals that mark the stations of the common yogic-mystical itinerary and that are expressed in the distinctive meditative landmarks of the three traditions of Theravāda Buddhism, Pātañjala Yoga, and Catholic mystical theology in hand, we can begin looking at each of these traditions in turn.

Chapter 4

The Concentrative Itinerary of the Buddhist *Jhānas*

The Jhānas *and Early Buddhism*

At the point nearly of death from practicing harsh asceticism, the future Buddha fell into a reverie of despair at his failure to attain awakening. The former prince happened to recall a day in his youth when he sat "in the cool shade of a rose-apple tree"[1] watching his father at work. As he sat under the spreading shade tree, the young Siddhartha unwittingly became mentally and physically calm, and he fell into a focused and delightful state of mind.

In talks he gave later to his disciples and other hearers, he called this state of mind "the first meditation," or "the first jhāna" (*paṭhamajjhāna*), and he defined it as a state of mind that is "secluded from sensual pleasures, secluded from unwholesome states."[2] This seclusion, he explained, when combined with applied, or concentrated, thought (*vitakka*) and sustained thought, or deep reflection (*vicāra*),[3] generates the positive mental states of mystical rapture (*pīti*) and contemplative happiness (*sukha*). While reflecting upon this delightful state of mind, Siddhartha wondered if he had found the way to enlightenment, a question that was immediately answered by a dawning inner conviction that the way of the *jhānas* is, indeed, the way to enlightenment.[4]

This delightful anecdote flows into the story of how the discovery of this delightful and tranquilizing style of meditation led the emaciated ascetic to eat a bowl of rice and porridge, thus ending his long and deadly fast, but allowing him to trace out a new path to awakening, one that moderated the fasts and mental exertions of the asceticism of his day and opened the way to a style of meditation that reveled in calmness, tranquility, mindfulness, and insight.[5]

With this bold move, Siddhartha approached Buddhahood and forged the new and distinctive concentrative practice that would, at least in its beginnings, be at the heart of his new contemplative movement. Even from the beginning, this gentler and spiritually pleasurable style of meditation was condemned by more rigorous ascetics who equated contemplative progress with painful disciplines. "Happiness should not be reached through happiness, happiness should be reached through hardship" complained a shocked contemporary of the Buddha."[6] The common understanding then was that meditation should be difficult, with deadly fasts, painful breath control, the cessation of work and physical activity, the closing down of the senses and the mind, and an intention to pursue yogic discipline even to the point of death and beyond. Against all of this, current trends in research on meditative practices in early Buddhism contend, the Buddha found a new path, one that stressed meditative reflection, inner tranquility and delight, and a gentle abiding in an illumined and pleasant state of equanimity, mindfulness, and liberative insight.[7]

Despite the emphasis in some contemporary Theravāda Buddhist circles on insight practices (*vipassanā*) as specifically Buddhist and a corresponding dismissal as common to other religions of calming practices (*samatha*),[8] such as the one recounted in the pericope cited above from the *Mahāsaccaka Sutta*, the most original path of Buddhist practice appears to have begun with the first *jhāna* and to have deepened into the fourth *jhāna*, where it merged with various wisdom or insight practices and matured in the eradication of the defilements (*āsava*), which is equivalent with Arahantship.[9] Johannes Bronkhorst claims that the cultivation of the *jhānas* was the earliest form of Buddhism:

> Rather than fasting, straining the mind and stopping the breath, one should perform the Four Dhyānas [*jhānas*]. And rather than aiming at the non-functioning of the senses [like non-Buddhist ascetics], [the Buddhist] should remain equanimous in the face of what they offer.[10]

The scholar of ancient Buddhisms will see that I am following Bronkhorst's lead in taking *jhāna*, or concentration,[11] as foundational to the Buddhist path,[12] and I am not unaware that it is a controversial stance.[13] What persuades me to continue down this path is the insight that the sequence of the first four *jhānas* corresponds snugly with the sequence of stages of *samādhi* in Patañjali's yoga, as well as with the sequence of mystical unions in mystical theology, as we will see in later chapters. I also take some degree of confidence that this focus on the *jhānas* is not misplaced when I remember the words of the Buddha:

> There is no meditative absorption
> For one without insight
> There is no insight
> For one without meditative absorption.
> With both,
> One is close to Nirvana.[14]

At the risk of contradicting some influential strains of current orthodox Theravāda Buddhism, a careful reading of the *suttas* makes clear that the *jhānas* must be seen as playing more than an important but merely auxiliary, or even dispensable, role in the movement of the aspirant toward *nibbāna*, since, as Grzegorz Polak has shown, "the jhānas receive the highest praise" of being equated with *nibbāna* in numerous places in the *suttas*.[15] The oft-repeated claim that while other religious traditions may promote spiritualities based on varying degrees of concentration, Buddhism uniquely teaches an insight practice that leads to a liberation beyond that accessible by even the deepest states of absorption is overly familiar in contemporary

Buddhist literature.[16] But attempts at reconstructing early Buddhism by scholars such as Tillman Vetter,[17] Johannes Bronkhorst,[18] Grzegorz Polak,[19] and Rupert Gethin call into question this prioritizing of insight over concentration. It might be useful to observe the caution expressed by Gethin who writes that "[a] simple bifurcation between 'calm' and 'insight' is . . . probably inappropriate in the context of much of the Nikāya material."[20] It may well be the case that this bifurcation is a recent construction of some schools of Buddhism, especially in those that have recently gained prominence in the West, and cannot therefore be attributed to the historical Buddha and the earliest expressions of Buddhism.[21] And, contrary to the views of contemporary Theravāda Buddhism, ancient Theravāda Buddhism was not as certain about the subordination of concentration to insight, since the *Visuddhimagga*, a compendium of Buddhist meditation practices and an inventory of the stages and elements of an introspective and empirical meditative psychology that was composed in Sri Lanka in the fifth century CE by the Indian Theravāda Buddhist monk Buddhaghosa, expresses the view that the supramundane paths of *nibbāna* cannot be obtained apart from *jhāna* (Vsm XIV, 127[22]).

To begin viewing the *jhānas* as foundational, and not merely incidental, to the Buddhist path to *nibbāna* despite the ambiguous textual evidence[23] is not to reverse course and now claim that *jhāna*, or more broadly, *samādhi* and *samatha*, is the only kind of meditation appropriate to Buddhism. Nor is it to claim that Buddhist—or any other kind of meditation—should dispense with insight practices in favor of concentrative practices. This would also be a deformed position, and one that is out sync with the placement of Right Mindfulness (*sammā-sati*) as the seventh limb in the Noble Eightfold Path. Yet, it remains the case that the ultimate limb in this venerable and universal Buddhist scheme is Right Concentration (*sammā-samādhi*), which can, according to Polak, be "simply defined as the four jhānas."[24]

Rather than seeing concentration and insight as irreducibly distinct contemplative competencies, I see them as fused together into the various degrees of *jhāna* (as well as *dhyāna*, or, more precisely, *samādhi* and *unio mystica*, which I will discuss in later chapters), a view that finds support in recent studies of early Buddhism. Polak argues, for example, that "in the original stratum of the *Suttapiṭaka* insight was somehow seen as an intrinsic quality of the state of jhāna."[25] As I see them, then, concentration and insight are concepts that represent two distinctive but ultimately complementary ways of describing the effects of varying degrees of a concentrated and insightful mind. To put that more simply, if more formulaically: the whole ensemble of Buddhist contemplative practices (*bhāvanā*) presupposes and arises only in a concentrated mind, since the insights that dissolve our conditioning do not occur in a distracted awareness, a point that is reinforced by the need even in insight practices that dispense with the cultivation of the *jhānas* for a lesser degree of momentary, or *khaṇika, samādhi*.

Yet, as Tilmann Vetter has observed, "the path to salvation" in Buddhism "has long been considered as being manifold,"[26] a judgment that is faithful to the luxurious richness of the countless meditative practices recommended by the many branches and schools of Buddhism. Consequently, controversies about the nature of early Buddhist meditation and the role of *jhāna* in Buddhist soteriology must remain inconclusive.[27] What, nevertheless, remains supremely important is the end goal of contemplative practice, however it is achieved: a tranquilized and purified awareness directly perceptive of and in nondual union with whatever is ultimately real.

Jhāna *Maximalists and* Jhāna *Minimalists*

Alongside the fraught question of what role the *jhānas* played in early Buddhism is the question of what constitutes a genuine *jhāna*. While the central factors that make up a *jhāna* are clear enough,[28] clarity is elusive when it comes to the question of determining when a meditator has entered into *jhāna*. Later innovations, such as the notion of *upacāra-samādhi*, or "access concentration," in the *Visuddhimagga* and the *navākārā cittasthiti*, or the "nine mental abidings"[29] in Vajrayāna Buddhism, show that this issue has generated a good deal of contemplative experimentation and model-building over the centuries. But now that *jhāna* is a central topic among convert Buddhists and meditators in the erstwhile West,[30] new disagreements are breaking out among current teachers and scholars over how intense and enduring a focused meditative state must be to count as a real *jhāna* and not as a lesser attainment.

The spread in this controversy is wide. Some *jhāna* teachers claim that meditators can enter the *jhānas* on a ten-day retreat and use them to cultivate insight or walking meditation.[31] Others claim that a real first *jhāna* cuts off sensory and bodily awareness and should last for at least four—or even twenty-four—hours.[32] Leigh Brasington, a well-known American *jhāna* teacher and student of Ayya Khema calls the gentler and more lenient concentrative experiences "Sutta Style Jhanas" and the sterner and more rigorous concentrative experiences "Visuddhimagga Style Jhanas."[33] The confusion over what counts as an actual *jhāna* and what is merely a deeply focused state of awareness is not helped by the circumstance that advocates of the *sutta* approach tend to view the rigorists as demanding too much of contemplatives, while advocates of the *Visuddhimagga* approach tend to view the minimalists as exaggerating their achievements. This can lead to what Ṭhānissaro Bhikkhu (Ajaan Geoff) calls "jhāna wars."[34] Brasington has memorably summed this situation up in what I like to think of as the "Brasington Jhāna Axiom":

> An interesting thing that I have observed that holds for most teachers of Jhana is that they tend to regard all Jhana methods with concentration levels less than their own as "not authentic, not real Jhanas," and they tend to regard all methods with concentration levels stronger than their own as "indulging, not useful."[35]

As a result of this fundamental disagreement, the discussion and practice of the *jhānas* is driven by a doctrinal and practical divide between those who promote the idea that *jhāna* is almost impossible to attain except by professional meditators who can maintain *jhāna* for multiple hours while cut off completely from all sensory and cognitive inputs and those who hold that *jhāna* can be achieved relatively quickly by bringing about a fixed focus on the meditation object even while remaining aware to some degree of the eternal world and that one is in *jhāna*.[36]

I must leave the intricacies of this debate to Buddhologists, since my focus here will be on the first four *jhānas* as matters of contemplative experience and not on historical questions about them (and so I will make use of both *sutta* and *Visuddhimagga jhānas*, with a reference to Abhidhamma *jhānas* as necessary). I do think, however, that a solution to the question of what counts as a *jhāna* might be resolvable by bringing into play the methodological principle that Bronkhorst lays out in *The Two Traditions of Meditation in Ancient India*. He attempts there to sort out apparent contradictions in the Pāli Canon by noting whether a practice that is both approved and rejected in the *suttas* is similar to a non-Buddhist practice. In such a case, he sees the practices as, hypothetically at least, not belonging to the earliest form of Buddhism. He thinks, on the contrary, that it is an intrusion of non-Buddhist ideas and practices into the Buddhist texts.[37]

More positively stated, Bronkhorst thinks that the innovation of the Buddha was to depart from the forceful type of what he styles "main stream meditation"[38] that was prevalent among Jains and yogis and which is also described in various early Upaniṣads.[39] Mainstream meditation sought physical and mental immobility as the way to overcome *karma*[40] (equivalent perhaps to what would be characterized later as *nirbīja-samādhi* in Patañjala yoga and *nirodha-samāpatti*, or "the attainment of cessation" in the *Visuddhimagga* (Vsm 2.3.120 Ñ),[41] which is sometimes equated with *nibbāna*[42]). Although Siddhartha had also followed this path, he turned away from it to follow his own way of gentler meditative practice that uses focused reflection (*vitakka* and *vicāra*) to bring the mind into a series of delightful concentrative states (*pīti* and *sukha*), culminating in a tranquil and equanimous awareness of whatever arises in the field of experience.

This new path, which was the distinctive discovery of the bodhisatta,[43] came to occupy a central place in the Dīgha Nikāya and the Majjhima Nikāya, and it came to be known, according to Polak, as "the Sāmaññaphala Scheme" (*sāmaññaphala* means "the fruits of the contemplative life," and it is the name of a *sutta* that teaches the value of *jhāna* meditation). Polak summarizes this "archaic" Buddhist soteriological doctrine as essentially "the release from taints (*āsava*)" occurring "after the attainment of the four jhānas."[44]

Taking a clue from this contrast between ancient Indian mainstream mediation and the new *jhāna* path of the Buddha, I would characterize *jhāna* maximalists as advocating a return to mainstream meditation and the minimalists as more in line with the earliest teaching of the *suttas* and of the Buddha about *jhāna* meditation. I agree with Ajahn Brahm who claims that the word "jhāna designates Buddhist meditation proper" and that "if it isn't jhāna then it isn't true Buddhist meditation!"[45] To back up this claim, Ajahn Brahm cites the *Gopaka-Moggallāna Sutta*, where Ānanda, the Buddha's personal attendant for many years, tells a questioner that the Buddha praised correct *jhāna*, which begins with withdrawal from sensual pleasures and unwholesome states of mind and ends with equanimity and mindfulness.[46] (Despite this ringing affirmation of the centrality of the *jhānas*,

Ajahn Brahm, as noted in an earlier footnote in this chapter, is a *jhāna* maximalist. His belief that real *jhāna* involves a complete cutting of all sensation and thought, and that it should be long lasting indicates that his view of *jhāna* is more like Bronkhorst's mainstream meditation, against which the Buddha developed his own gentler, more pleasant *jhāna* practice).

To say more now on this topic would be to go back on my promise not to trespass upon the domain of the Buddhologists. But this much needed to be said so that I can now move on to the main burden of this chapter, which is to show that the first four *jhānas* are meditative landmarks expressing contemplative universals.

Jhāna *and* Vipassanā*: Bypassing a Forced Controversy?*

One more preliminary needs to be mentioned, however, before we move on—the relationship of the *jhānas* and *vipassanā*, or the practice of insight meditation. Even if, as indicated above, some scholars of early Buddhism fail to find in the earliest strata of the *Suttapiṭaka* a neat division between the path of the *jhānas* and the path of insight, this dyad does form a canonical element in later, more systematized forms of Buddhism, beginning, at least, with the *Visuddhimagga*. In fact, this canonical dyad enables Buddhologists to reduce the welter of Buddhist meditation practices to either the category of *samatha*, which is virtually a synonym for the practice of the *jhānas*, or to the category of *vipassanā*, which stands for the sequence of sixteen insights leading to *nibbāna* in Theravāda Buddhism.[47] As Robert Gimello has noted: "All elements of Buddhist meditation find their place under one or the other of these two general rubrics."[48] Beginning with the pioneering popularizing work of Daniel Goleman,[49] most, if not all, contemporary popular treatments of the *jhānas* take this dyad in its systematized form for granted, as does Bhante Henepola Gunaratana in his comprehensive works on the *jhānas*.[50]

As noted above, it is only recently that the topic and the practice of the *jhānas* has begun to come into view among practitioners of the influential forms of Theravāda Buddhism that have become prevalent outside of Asia in the last forty years, which have generally stressed *vipassanā*, or insight meditation. Of the leading Theravāda teachers who have become prominent in recent decades, perhaps only Ayya Khema, Bhante Gunaratana, and Ajahn Brahmavaṃso (or Ajahn Brahm) have taken the minority view of accenting the *jhānas*. So pronounced is this tendency to focus on *vipassanā* at the expense of *samatha* in contemporary Theravāda Buddhism that Theravāda Buddhist meditation is commonly thought to be only an insight practice with little, if any formal role for, the deep meditative attainments of the *jhānas*.[51]

Recently, however, a few Buddhologists have begun to argue that some of the distinctive meditative practices of contemporary Theravāda Buddhism appear to be postcolonialist innovations of the last century or so.[52] Besides the notable innovation of involving large numbers of laypeople in meditative practices that long had been reserved for monastics, these practices include insight meditation, or *vipassanā*, either without *jhāna* or with only a minimal degree of concentration (i.e., "momentary concentration," or *khaṇika-samādhi*), "pure" or "dry" insight meditation, the downplaying of *jhāna*, or adopting a maximalist view of *jhāna*.

This claim will not likely sit well with the many people around the world who practice in the numerous contemporary Thai and Burmese schools of meditation. My own view is that this claim does seem somewhat excessive, since, as even these critics acknowledge, there is a solid textual basis for many of these practices. Besides indications in the *Suttapiṭaka*, this basis includes the *Abhidhamma* and the *Visuddhimagga*,[53] which seem to have served as the inspiration for figures such as Ledi Sayadaw and perhaps Ajaan Mun as they tried to revive what were in their time the moribund meditation practices of Theravāda Buddhism.[54] In support of this view is the fact that a traditional commentary on the *Visuddhimagga*, written well before the nineteenth century, refers to these practices when it remind meditators "whose vehicle is insight" that "no insight comes about without momentary concentration."[55]

It is nevertheless the case that nineteenth and twentieth-century versions of *bhāvanā* among Theravāda Buddhists do seem to have departed from the balanced view of the *Visuddhimagga*, the *Abhidhamma*, and the *Suttapiṭaka*, which gave a central place to the *jhānas* in the Buddhist contemplative life.[56] So, the current revival of interest in the *jhānas* by both scholars and practitioners, along with the new historical revisionism that calls dominant expressions of Theravāda contemplative theory into question, are welcome.

Rather than seeing these revivals as innovations having no essential connection to the practices of "original Buddhism" (a notion that can also be seen as a scholarly construct),[57] I see them as creative expressions of the contemplative impulse that has animated Buddhism from the beginning. They are authentic renewals of Buddhist meditation rather than just modern fabrications. Instead of thinking now, merely on the basis of current—and always revisable—historical research, that whole generations of recent Theravāda teachers and scholars have been wrong, we can see them as illumined revivers, in the face of colonialism and Westernization, of ancient practices, and that we, who follow after them, can further this process of revival and renewal by making more space in meditative practice and theory for the delightful and liberative states of mind, in all of their diversity, that are named by the words *jhāna*, *dhyāna*, *samatha*, *śamatha*, and *samādhi*.[58]

Besides, even if we could isolate the original meditation practice or practices of the Buddha, this would not invalidate the creativity of contemporary Buddhist meditation masters as they have deftly adapted the two timeless principles of contemplative practice, concentration and insight, to emerging situations unforeseen by the Buddha. Isolating the form of original Buddhist meditation is of value as a historical undertaking, so long as it does not lead to attempts to silence "false" later Buddhisms in the name of a "true" original Buddhism. More importantly, perhaps, the merely historical activity of reconstructing "original" Buddhist *bhāvanā* will likely be of limited relevance to people engaged in serious contemplative practice, since a practicing contemplative can benefit from all of the varieties of contemplative and yogic practices that have been described in ancient and modern Buddhist texts (as well as in yogic and mystical theological texts, as we shall see).

Although my focus here is on the *jhānas*, this emphasis does not imply the rejection of the *vipassanā* side of this dyad, nor does it imply a subordination of *vipassanā* to *samatha*. Since I see *jhāna* as the comprehensive, integral practice taught by Buddha when he pointed to the feet of trees and to empty huts and gave a clear direction to his disciples: "*jhāyatha*" (meditate),[59] I think that *samatha* leads to full awakening through the eradication of the cankers (*āsava*) and the kindling of liberative insight. There is no need to follow a "dry insight"[60] path, especially since, according to Polak, the notion of *vipassanā* has nowhere near the prominence in the Nikāyas as *jhāna* does.[61] Of course, one can follow any path that one likes, but there is no longer any need to go on rejecting the *jhānas* as if they were a false or lesser way to full and final awakening. This was certainly not the view of Buddhaghosa, who sees the *arahant* as one "who has reached the destruction of cankers by augmenting insight that had . . . jhana as its proximate cause" (Vsm 3.62 Ñ).

My own approach to the relationship between *samatha*, or the *jhānas*, and *vipassanā*, or insight practices, then, will be synoptic and integral, taking the Buddhist tradition as a whole—and, indeed, the contemplative heritage of humanity as a whole. So, I will not shy away from blending canonical, commentarial, and contemporary views of scholars and practitioners of the *jhānas* in these pages, although my own focus will be on recovering the *jhānas* for contemplative practice. For systematic and controversial historical, philological, and doctrinal evaluations of these various practices, I will defer, once again, to the global company of Buddhologists.

The Easy Path and the Hard Path

As I now begin to reconstruct the path of the *jhānas*, my approach will assume a minimalist approach to *jhāna*. Thus, I will take the *sutta jhānas* as normative and the *Visuddhimagga jhānas* as representing a movement back in the direction of the kinds of painful asceticism and meditation that the Buddha rejected when he decided that contemplative delight is not to be feared. This is not to say that I will dispense with the *Visuddhimagga*, for, as will be seen in the coming pages, I draw heavily on the *Visuddhimagga* because it is invaluable for its systematic analysis of the *jhānas*, even if this can be overdone to the point of losing the simplicity, ease, and delight of the *jhānic* path described in the *Suttapiṭaka*. This means that, following Polak and Bronkhorst, I will be assuming that the type of *jhāna* often vilified or downplayed by later Theravāda and other Buddhist scholars and teachers, at least until very recently, is very likely a type of maximalist *jhāna* that is opposite to the minimalist *jhāna* of the *Suttapiṭaka*. Since I am not an academically certified scholar of these texts, I cannot provide a philological solution to the problem of what counts as genuine early Buddhist *jhāna*, but I can make clear my own preference in this area and, standing upon the ground cleared by such scholars as Bronkhorst and Polak, I can move ahead in my comparative and systematic study of the *jhānas* as expressions of the underlying structure of human spirituality, which is the main topic of this book.

The practice of minimalist *jhāna* is what I call "the easy path," which following the innovative scholarship of Johannes Bronkhorst, I contrast with what I call "the hard path."[62] The hard path is the way of a renunciation so fierce and an asceticism so severe that many people today are inclined to reject it as life-denying. Under this heading, we can place practices such as extreme fasting, neglect of the body, a steadfast turning away from all sensory experience, and a stern rejection of spiritual consolation, whether it comes in the form of visions of gracious deities or in the form of an upsurge from within of delightful mental states. Rare as expressions of the most austere forms of the hard path now are, its mood lingers on in any kind of spiritual direction or practice that takes suffering, difficulty, pain, endurance, and trials as preferable to their opposites (or what is somewhat quaintly labeled "encratism" in older Catholic writings when discussing the practices of ascetical rigorists). Indeed, followers of the hard path are just the sort of rigorists or maximalists who see danger in spiritual experiences and consolations, and who will be alarmed by the sorts of spiritual experiences that arise in the *jhānas*.

The easy path is, on the contrary, a gentler way that finds material for contemplation—or reflective musing—in every direction. Scriptures, sacred teachings, stories about and images of teachers and divinities, the phenomena of nature and the play of thought—all provide a doorway into the stillness at the root of the mind. This pathway dispenses with all of the heroic—and sometimes sadistic and masochistic—tools of the hard path mentioned above. It reduces asceticism to two mental movements. Its negative move is to practice turning attention away from unwholesome thoughts, situations, and external, sense-mediated pleasures. Its positive move is to turn attention inward by using some subject of reflection to bring the mind to increasing stillness. The interplay of the two movements of this gentle, mental asceticism generates a series of tranquilizing and delightful mental states, which gradually subside into profound tranquility. This inner ground of stillness and silence is the transparent mental plain into which the liberative light of whatever is ultimate dawns and slowly and gently releases the mind from all that is nonultimate.

As discussed in the first pages of this chapter, it was just such an easy path that the young prince Siddhartha first discovered while sitting in the cool shade of a tree watching his father plow a field.[63] The memory of this childhood experience offered him a clue about the way forward in the bitter moments of failure at the end of his quest to attain awakening through the hard path. The memory awakened in him the hope that the experience of *jhāna* might be the path to awakening. This memory was followed immediately by the knowledge (*viññāna*) that "this is really the road toward enlightenment" (*eso va magga bodhāya*). As if to answer the immediately arising criticism of followers of the hard path—which would soon include his five fellow ascetics, he declared that that he did not fear the wholesome and nonsensory happiness (*sukha*) of *jhāna*. He thereby pointed out an easier and more effective path than that of harsh asceticism. Not only was this discovery relevant for Siddhartha and, ever after, for Buddhists, but it can also serve as a reminder that the hard way of radical self-abnegation and of cynicism toward inspiring spiritual experiences is not a more effective path than contemplative absorption, which, grounded upon a gentler asceticism of moderate detachment, opens into a clear seeing of what is.

The Contemplative Path of the Visuddhimagga

In outlining my view of the easy path of the Buddha, I will take my general orientation and framework from the *Visuddhimagga*,[64] a manual widely accepted as authoritative throughout the Buddhist world.[65] At first approach, the *Visuddhimagga* presents a formidable and off-putting façade. Buddhaghosa's penchant, shared with many traditional teachers of Buddhism, for erecting ever more convoluted numbered lists of doctrinal and experiential items threatens to blunt the curiosity of the ardent meditator approaching it for guidance. Yet, beneath this scholastic demeanor, there still beats the ecstatic energy of the meditative path followed by the first Buddhists:

> So freed! So freed!
> So thoroughly freed am I —
> . . .
> Having come to the foot of a tree,
> I meditate [*jhāyāmi*], absorbed in the bliss:
> "What bliss!"[66]

As noted above, the *Visuddhimagga* was composed by the renowned Theravāda monk and commentator Bhadantācariya Buddhaghosa in Sri Lanka in the early fifth century.[67] Buddhaghosa was an Indian Buddhist in a time when Theravāda was disappearing from India and was in a long period of decline in Sri Lanka. New currents of Buddhist thought were circulating internationally in Sanskrit, which by the first century CE had become the language of all Buddhist schools in India, while the Pāli of the Buddhism dominant in Sri Lanka and its ancient Sinhalese commentaries seemed to be a fading tradition. Amid the conflict between the Great Monastery (Mahāvihāra), which preserved the Pāli Canon in Sri Lanka, and the Abhayagiri Monastery, which was the point of contact between Sri Lankan Buddhism and new currents in international Sanskritic Buddhism, an awareness of the value of the venerable Sinhalese traditions as a counterweight to the innovations of the new teachings began to emerge. Sensing that the way forward was to revive the study of Pāli and to recast the Sinhalese commentaries into Pāli, the leaders of the Great Monastery entrusted Buddhaghosa, who, according to the *Mahāvaṃsa*, was sent to the island by his Indian teacher, with the task of weaving new commentaries out of the materials uniquely preserved in Sri Lanka. So successful was Buddhaghosa's masterful commentary—which the *Mahāvaṃsa* claims he wrote three times due to the interference of *devas*—that it reestablished the influence of Theravāda Buddhism and of the Pāli Canon in international Buddhism and put Theravāda Buddhism back into an even competition with the mainland Sanskrit-based Buddhist movements.[68]

Although the *Visuddhimagga* is widely revered as a meditation manual,[69] Polak thinks that Buddhaghosa was more of a text scholar than a deep meditator[70] because it is absolutely certain that Buddhaghosa "himself did not realize the lofty states described in his own treatise," since he was said to have been reborn in the Tusita (Sanskrit, Tuṣita) Heaven, which is a few levels below the "Retinue of Brahman" (*brahma-pārisajja*), the subtle heavenly that is reserved for those who attain the first *jhāna*.[71] Polak thus thinks that the *Visuddhimagga* is more of a "theoretical" treatise and "a tribute to the ancient, heroic times in which the Arahants still walked the earth" than a text designed to spark a meditation revolution.[72] Polak concludes that "there are very good reasons to believe that the famous *Visuddhimagga* was never meant to be a manual of meditation, and that no one has ever traversed the path described in this treatise."[73] Yet, as Erik Braun and also Polak show, this did happen much later in Burma and Thailand in the nineteenth and twentieth centuries, where the *Visuddhimagga* served as a model and an inspiration for the recreation of virtually extinct meditation traditions.

Given the inconsistency of these two views, it seems more likely, then, that Bhikkhu Ñāṇamoli is correct when he writes that "the *Visuddhimagga* is probably best regarded as a detailed manual for meditation masters, and as a work of reference."[74] It certainly would not have been necessary for Buddhaghosa to have been a deep meditator to compose this masterful reference work about meditation, since not all meditators have reached the first *jhāna*, whether construed minimally or maximally. And there is a long history of Buddhist meditators dispensing altogether with the *jhānas*, or deep concentrative meditation, and cultivating just enough concentration to awaken insight. And, of course, apart from speculation about the matter in the absence of direct evidence that Buddhaghosa was not a meditator, or *jhāyin*, there is no reason to conclude that he was merely a masterful commentator and text scholar.

The Training Context of the Visuddhimagga

So, whether one wants to begin with *samatha* or with *vipassanā*, the sequence of practices systematically described in the *Visuddhimagga* follows what has become a canonical itinerary in all Buddhist schools: the procession from virtue, or *sīla* (Sanskrit, *śīla*) through concentration, or *samādhi*, to understanding, or *paññā* (Sanskrit, *prajñā*), a structure that also dictates the three main divisions of the *Visuddhimagga* (Vsm 1.8-10 Ñ). Also known in Buddhism as the Three Trainings of Virtue, Concentration, and Wisdom, this triplex path forms the beginning, middle, and end of the doctrine of the *Visuddhimagga* (Vsm 1.10 Ñ), which thereby points out a venerable and practical path to the seeker undertaking the arduous task of untangling the "tangle" (*jaṭā*) of craving (*taṇhā*) (Vsm 1.2 Ñ, Myanmar Romanized Text[75]) on the heroic journey to purification (*visuddhi*).

What we will find in the *Visuddhimagga*, then, is a schematization of an ecstatic path, well-worn in all contemplative traditions, that leads from conventional awareness diffused into and enslaved by the experience of the body and mind to the synthesis of stillness and intuitive seeing that renders the body and mind transparent, along with all of their endless and compelling transformations. This attainment of transparency is the penultimate event in the journey of the yogi, mystic, or contemplative—indeed, in the journey of life itself, for nothing can be said about what remains after seeing through all forms and dropping them than to repeat the names given to that stateless states by the great saints and seers who have avidly pursued it: *nibbāna*, *śūnyatā*, *mokṣa*, *kaivalya*, *visio Dei*, etc.

In the systematic style of a manual, Buddhaghosa elaborates upon a number of important preparatory themes and practices before coming to what is our main concern, the detailing of the path of the *jhānas*. Long, illuminating, and sometimes entertaining sections follow upon one another in the *Visuddhimagga* before we get down to the business of beginning to meditate. One section describes impediments to meditation such as concerns about food and houses, addiction to books and paranormal powers, and worries about travels, teaching, family, and disciples (Vsm 3.29-56 Ñ).

Another section provides a brief manual of personality types that is reminiscent of the sixteen Jung-inspired Myers-Briggs personality types (Vsm 3.74-103 Ñ). Novice meditators are divided into three classes, each of which has a developed and an undeveloped type. Then follows a catalog of well-observed and sometimes amusing traits that can help the spiritual teacher determine whether a novice meditator belongs to the greedy/faithful category, the hateful/intellectual category, or the deluded/speculative category.

The *Visuddhimagga* next outlines a compendium of forty classic meditation objects (*kammaṭṭhāna*). Expressive perhaps of a mood of contemplative enthusiasm, the title of this chapter dramatically calls the aspirant to seize (*gahaṇa*) one of these meditation objects, which include various kinds of *kasiṇas*, or colored disks, themes for recollection, such as the Buddha, the Dhamma, virtues, and deities, and various sublime states of mind, such as the four divine abidings of loving-kindness, compassion, gladness, and equanimity (Vsm 3.104-122 Ñ). Then, as the chapter concludes, Buddhaghosa helpfully indicates, for the benefit of spiritual directors who use the *Visuddhimagga* as a manual, the personality types that are best suited for the various meditation objects (Vsm 3.121-122 Ñ). As one reads this chapter, one cannot help but hear in the background the voice of the Buddha giving expert guidance to disciples as they set out to meditate at the feet of trees and in empty huts.

Next, Buddhaghosa paints a picture that could flow as vividly today as when it was written from his own experience as one who apparently knew all too well the faults of the cenobitic monastic life (Vsm 4.1-18 Ñ). This is a canny and wry delineation of the eighteen faults of monasteries, such as the petty disturbances and distractions of living in crowded, famous, or new monasteries, the perils of having too many students, or living too close to borders, seaports, palaces, cities, or land rich in forageable leaves, shrubs and fruits, and the random assortment of people that they attract. All of these various disturbances must necessarily be avoided by one who wants to cultivate the *jhānas*.

Yet, these passages offer more than mere diversions or minor preliminaries to the central meditative instructions offered in the *Visuddhimagga*, for these passages also serve as evidence that this is no merely scholastic manual, but is, on the contrary, the vibrant record of what at one point was a vibrant culture of meditation. Reflection upon the themes and ascetical practices (*dhutaṅga*) discussed in these opening chapters of the *Visuddhimagga* grants a foretaste of the purification that is *nibbāna* itself (Vsm 1.5 Ñ) and inspires the contemplative reader to begin or to deepen the practice of virtue.

Approaching the Jhānas *by Focusing on the Meditation Object*

After this instructive series of digressions, Buddhaghosa finally announces that "the time has come for the detailed exposition of all meditation subjects" (Vsm 4.21 Ñ), which signals a lengthy exposition of how the *jhānas* can be cultivated through developing one's skill in working with a meditation object. As if to summarize the journey that is now about to commence, Buddhaghosa offers the meditator a startlingly simple and straightforward set of instructions that can lead one all the way to Arahantship, or the condition of one who is fully awakened in this life. In brief, these instructions are as follows:

Having put aside the lesser impediments (which were mentioned above), the meditator should eat the food gathered on an alms round and take a bit of rest (Vsm 4.21 Ñ). (This is meant perhaps to remove agitation and idleness, which are the twin banes of meditative focus in Buddhism [Vsm 4.72 Ñ]). Then, sitting at ease somewhere quiet, the meditator should bring the mind to focused attention upon a meditation object such as the earth *kasiṇa* in order to "apprehend the sign," or the *nimitta* (Vsm 4.21 Ñ), which is a progressively refined mental stillness that emerges from intense focus upon one's chosen object of meditation. Anchoring one's mind to the "treasure" of the fully developed sign (*paṭibhāga-nimitta*), one "enters upon and dwells in the first jhana" (Vsm 4.22 Ñ). Now, with proper training and practice (or because of *jhāna*-practice in previous lives), the meditator can move toward the fourth (or fifth) *jhāna*,[76] where, like the Buddha, one can develop insight on the basis of the *jhāna* and attain to the fourth degree of *saintliness*, which is the condition of the Arahant (Vsm 4.23 Ñ).

Thus, in one graceful arc of deepening concentration, Buddhaghosa describes how one can move directly from the unenlightened state to the deepest degree of awakening. It is no exaggeration to see this short section as the heart of the *Visuddhimagga*, with everything else as preparation, commentary, and aftermath. What we find here is a classical expression of the easy way, one that goes directly back to the *jhāna* formula so often repeated in the *Suttapiṭaka*, and which succinctly outlines the Buddha's path to enlightenment.

This description of how to go about developing a *nimitta* as a means of accessing the *jhānas* is a model, based on the experience of thousands of Buddhist meditators over many centuries of practice and theorizing, which charts a typical progression of increasingly focused meditative states. The actual experience of developing a *nimitta* in order to enter the *jhānas* will, of course, differ from the model for each meditator. One major divergence between the model and individual experience is that only some meditators seem to have an innate ability to generate a *nimitta* almost effortlessly and seemingly spontaneously, while for many others this is a contemplative competency that must be laboriously developed.

As if in response to questions about this divergence of capabilities for raising a *nimitta* and attaining the *jhānas*, Buddhaghosa notes that, due to practice in a previous life, the *nimitta*, or meditative focus, may arise spontaneously during moments when the mind becomes focused, even accidentally. This was the experience of the Elder Mallaka, notes Buddhaghosa, who experienced the spontaneous arising of a *nimitta* while looking intently at a plowed field (Vsm 4.23 Ñ), an experience similar to what happened to young prince Siddhartha while he watched his father plowing a field.

But for novice meditators without any previous skill with developing the *jhānas*, the path to awakening is longer, since they need to develop the *nimitta* as a tool for entering the first *jhāna*. Buddhaghosa thus lays out a detailed recipe for beginning meditation for novice meditators on how to construct a completely physical and external meditation object (*kammaṭṭhāna*), which is the base for the sign (*nimitta*) that is to be abstracted mentally from the meditation object.

He begins with the first and the most concrete of all of the forty objects, the earth *kasiṇa* (*pathavī-kasiṇa*), which is a physical circle the size of a large plate and made from clay that is "the colour of the dawn," which apparently was available in a local river in Sri Lanka (Vsm 4.22, 24, 4n5 Ñ). (Actually constructing such a physical disk and sitting in front of it is not necessary for those who can already generate mentally this *kasiṇa*).

Having bathed and sat down in front of the earth *kasiṇa* on a low chair in a clean and quite place, the meditator should prepare mentally for *jhāna* practice by reflecting on the pitfalls of sense desires, developing a desire for renunciation, and arousing a sense of happiness by contemplating the virtues of the Buddha, the Dhamma, and the Sangha. This opening period of recollection should close with eagerness to obtain a taste of *jhānic* bliss along with a sense of awe that one is now taking off down the path of renunciation followed by all enlightened beings (Vsm 4.27 Ñ).

For both the novice meditator and the one in whom the *nimitta* arises spontaneously, the *jhānic* journey to *nibbāna* begins with the mental and physical gestures of separating oneself from "sense desires" and "unprofitable things" (Vsm 4.79 Ñ), as prescribed in the classic *jhāna* formula quoted numerous times throughout the Pāli Canon (and quoted in full in the section following the next section). Sense desires, or "lust" (*kāma*), is the first of the five hindrances that prevent the arising of *jhāna* in the *jhāna* formula, while the "unprofitable things" (*akusala-dhamma*) in this formula include the four remaining hindrances of ill will, stiffness and torpor, agitation and worry, and uncertainty (Vsm 4.82, 93, 104). If one is on retreat or living in a disciplined monastic setting oriented to meditation, as in the case of the Elder Mallaka, these gestures should be a natural consequence of the separation from ordinary activities and distractions. As this seclusion, or separation from various kinds of unhelpful mental and physical activity and their associated sensual longings, dissipates through separating, or continual turning away, from them, one finds that one has more time and energy for focusing, or reflecting on the meditation object.

Now that the meditator is ready to commence actual *jhāna* meditation (which, however, will not be successful without observing, in spirit if not in full conformity with the letter, the preceding conditions), Buddhaghosa instructs the trainee to "open his eyes moderately, apprehend the sign, and so proceed to develop it" (Vsm 4.27 Ñ).

Developing the Sign

Buddhaghosa divides the progress of concentration (*samādhi*)[77] into three phases, each characterized by an increasingly more stable focus upon the meditation object. Novice mediators take up the "preliminary work" (*parikamma*) (Vsm 3.62, Ñ), as outlined above, of focusing on the meditation object assigned by the teacher. They develop concentration by returning their attention to this object, which some later commentators name the "starting sign" (*parikamma-nimitta*),[78] whenever concentration wavers. They are instructed to do this "a hundred times, a thousand times, and even more than that until the learning sign arises" (Vsm 4.29 Ñ). The indication that the learning sign (*uggaha-nimitta*) has arisen is that the meditator is able to retain a mental image of the meditation object even with the eyes open, with the result that the meditator is no longer dependent upon the external object (Vsm 4.30 Ñ). As the meditator continues to concentrate on the learning sign, there comes a moment when negative emotions subside and the "counterpart sign" (*paṭibhāga-nimitta*) suddenly arises (Vsm 4.31 Ñ). This is a purely mental object without shape or color that is generated through the power of concentration alone and that is free of the three characteristics of *dukkha*, *anicca*, and *anattā*.

The moment when the counterpart sign arises marks the entrance into *upacāra-samādhi*, or "access concentration," which is described in remarkably experiential terms in a celebrated passage in the *Visuddhimagga*:

> But the counterpart sign appears as if breaking out from the learning sign and a hundred times, a thousand times more purified, like a looking-glass disk drawn from its case, like a mother-of pearl dish well washed, like the moon's disk coming out from behind a cloud, like cranes against a thunder cloud. (Vsm 4.31 Ñ)

So important is this rare meditative attainment that the *Visuddhimagga* warns the meditator to "[g]uard the [counterpart] sign as if it were the embryo of a Wheel-turning Monarch (World-ruler)" (Vsm 4.34, 8.22 Ñ). This significant meditative landmark stands at the passageway between access concentration and absorption concentration (*appanā-samādhi*), which unfolds into deeper states of *samādhi*, or the *jhānas* (Sanskrit *dhyāna*). If possible, the meditator should extend, or deepen one's focus, on the counterpart sign in the same meditation session and move from access concentration to absorption concentration (Vsm 4.34 Ñ). For, as indicated by the name of this degree of *samādhi* (*upacāra-samādhi*, or "access concentration"), this is merely the threshold of the *jhānas*. Although all of the factors of the first *jhāna*—applied thought, sustained thought, rapture, and happiness—are present in this initial stage of recollection,[79] they are still weak and unstable, like a baby when it takes its first steps (Vsm 4.33 Ñ). More training in concentrative techniques is needed in order to deepen access concentration (also sometimes called "neighborhood concentration)" (Vsm 4.74 Ñ) into absorption concentration.

Buddhaghosa now offers a pair of helpful interludes full of tips on how the meditator can guard the counterpart sign from dissipation through idle chatter, uncomfortable food, residences, and postures (Vsm 4.35 Ñ), which are concerns that might seem unduly soft to stern ascetics on the hard path. Next, he drills down more deeply into the causes and conditions that facilitate the rising of the counterpart sign, as an aid to new meditators who fail adequately to guard the sign by losing it in dissipation and distraction. The skills that he recommends include inner and outer cleanliness, striking a balance between energy and idleness when meditating, equanimity, mindfulness, avoiding unconcentrated people, and spending time with people who cultivate concentration (Vsm 4.42-66 Ñ).

The Meditative Sequence of the Jhānas

Returning again to the topic of extending the counterpart sign in order to move from access concentration to absorption concentration, Buddhaghosa now approaches the heart of this book of the *Visuddhimagga*, which unfolds in a sequential manner the *jhāna* series. He quotes in full the standard description of the first *jhāna*, which is part of a larger pericope, or "jhāna formula,"[80] in which the Buddha, throughout the Pāli Canon, unfolds the characteristics of the *jhānas*[81]:

> Quite secluded from sense desires, secluded from unprofitable things he enters upon and dwells in the first jhana, which is accompanied by applied and sustained thought with happiness and bliss born of seclusion. (Vsm 4.79[82])

While the amount of commentary on this formula is virtually endless, the meaning of this part of the *jhāna* formula seems straightforward enough. As one allows one's initially diffused and scattered thoughts (*vitakka*) about the meditation object to unify and become less differentiated (*vicāra*)—a process that we will see retraced in later chapters on other traditions—one begins to sense an experience that is utterly novel and unprecedented for the novice contemplative who arrives at this station in the spiritual life: a sense of intense inner pleasure that is not the result of physical contacts or the savoring of past or potential sensory pleasures. So intense is this nonsensory pleasure that it can feel like an inner storm of pleasure. One may feel as if one could explode with delight or take wing from one's body into a heavenly light. This rapture (*pīti*) is sometimes taken by the novice meditator as a sign of enlightenment and it can become the basis of new revelations, prophecies (since *vitakka* and *vicāra* are varieties of conceptual activity, which is still present at this stage), and new religious movements.

Because of its intensity, rapture (*pīti*) reaches a peak of a sweetly painful intensity, and then subsides, to be replaced by the gentler warmth and light of happiness (*sukha*). This is a quiet sense of inner delight (and, as we will see, it can be taken as a key mark of the Hindu's *sāttvic* state of the quieting of the *kleśas*, or "deadening impulses," or the Catholic's state of grace, or sanctifying grace[83]). During the period of time dedicated to meditation, *pīti* may arise again and again, only to taper off again into *sukha*, which will often remain after the meditation session and suffuse the contemplative's awareness for hours and even days afterwards.

The contemplative who has become familiar with the unfolding and stabilization of these four meditative landmarks, has, as the *Visuddhimagga* says, "attained the first jhana" (Vsm 4.79 Ñ). Aspirants who have anchored their minds on the meditation object and entered the first *jhāna* will undoubtedly think, according to a commentary on the *Visuddhimagga*, "Surely in this way I shall be freed from ageing and death."[84]

Despite this inward assurance, the way stretches on ahead through seven (or eight[85]) more *jhānas*, although it is generally thought that the fourth *jhāna* is the place where, as with the Buddha,[86] the meditator cultivates the insights that lead to full awakening. This is a long journey, and it is intricately detailed by Buddhaghosa. What most concerns us here, however, are the first four *jhānas*, since the last four *jhānas* can be seen as extensions of the fourth *jhāna* rather than as *jhānas* in their own right because liberative insights occur in the fourth *jhāna*, given the impossibility of any sort of cognition in the four "immaterial states" (*āruppa-niddesa*). So, the question naturally arises of how one moves from the first to the fourth *jhāna*.

Now that we are familiar with the four *jhāna* factors (*jhānāṅga*) that generate the first *jhāna*, this is easily answered.[87] The meditator moves from a lower to a higher *jhāna* by surmounting the grosser, or physically and mentally more complex, factors of the preceding *jhāna*(s) (Vsm IV.139). (It goes without saying, of course, that, separation from the five hindrances, which are the initial conditions for access to the first *jhāna*, remains firmly in place for all of the higher *jhānas*.) That is, one moves from the first to the second *jhāna* by suppressing applied thought (*vitakka*) and sustained thought (*vicāra*) in favor of rapture (*pīti*), happiness (*sukha*), and "oneness of mind."[88] One then moves from the second to the third *jhāna* by suppressing rapture in favor of happiness and "equanimity" (*upekkhā*), which now replaces oneness of mind.[89] Finally, one moves from the third to the fourth *jhāna* by suppressing happiness in favor of the "purity" or the "perfection" (*pārisuddhi*) of equanimity and "mindfulness" (*sati*).[90] What remains in the fourth *jhāna* is a state of mindful equanimity free of the painful and pleasurable physical and mental forms of experience. Mindful equanimity now becomes the pervading mental characteristic of the *yogi* absorbed in the fourth *jhāna*, and this becomes the jumping-off point for deeper absorptions and liberative insights (which are outside the scope of this book).

While this might seem overly formulaic, it does correspond with meditative and contemplative experience across the globe, in which deepening concentration is marked by a simplification of consciousness and a diminution of felt physical and psychological factors. In the next section, I will relate these meditative landmarks, as described in the *Visuddhimagga*, to the contemplative universals that of the common yogic-mystical itinerary. These landmarks are evidence for the relatively invariant neurobiological, mental, and subtle-body process of spiritual development that is the foundation of a comparative philosophy of spirituality, which is the main concern of this book.

Theravāda Meditative Landmarks and the Common Contemplative Itinerary

In the first chapters of this book, I discussed the developmental logic of the common mystical itinerary that forms the backbone of my argument for contemplative universals. Below are two columns from the full chart given in an earlier chapter showing what I take as contemplative universals on the left and their Buddhist expressions as meditative landmarks on the right:

Figure 2 From The Common Yogic-Mystical Itinerary

Contemplative Universals and Their Common Functions	**Meditative Landmarks in Theravāda Buddhism**
convergence: mind focuses on meditation object	**parikamma-nimitta** (training sign) and **uggaha-nimitta** (learning sign)
coalescence: mind fixes on or locks in on the meditation object	**paṭibhāga-nimitta** (counterpart sign) = **upacāra-samādhi** (access concentration) and **appanā-samādhi** (absorption concentration)
simplification: mind simplifies itself factor by factor	**four jhānas** ***generating factors***: **vitakka, vicāra, pīti, sukha** (applied, or concentrated, thought, sustained thought, or deep reflection, mystical rapture, contemplative happiness)
quiescence: mind is stilled	**saññāvedayitanirodha** (cessation of ideation and feeling)
beatitude: mind is transcended	Before physical death: **nibbāna** After physical death: **parinibbāna**

As noted in an earlier chapter, I am charting in this book the progression of increasingly refined states of mental focus that are common to mystical traditions, despite their doctrinal divergence from each other. I see this common yogic and mystical itinerary as made up of at least five invariant contemplative universals that are expressed through the locally distinctive meditative landmarks of each of the three traditions under study in this book. Foundational to my approach here and to my understanding of religion and spirituality in general is the conviction that persistent patterns across contemplative traditions are evidence of an identical underlying process that unfolds itself diversely in the world mystical traditions, a view that, as argued in an earlier chapter, seems to be supported, at least from a physical standpoint, by recent developments in the new sciences of religion.

Yogic, contemplative, and mystical experience accesses through heightened concentration of what I have named the common yogic-mystical itinerary and which is an ensemble of inner states familiar to spiritual adepts. These states are suffused with sublime sensations of subtle realms and spiritual intelligences and are radiant with intuitive insights about deathlessness, beatitude, and the unity of life and being. (Skeptics about the reality of such rather common mystical and religious phenomena may make a metaphysical case for their nonexistence or lack of veracity, although it seems impossible to negate the fact that such experiences are universal features of deeper contemplative states.) I have given the names of convergence, coalescence, simplification, quiescence, and beatitude to these five contemplative universals. I now want to go through them in turn to see how each universal lines up with the five meditative landmarks in Theravāda Buddhism that express them.

Convergence: Focusing on the Meditation Object

A universal feature of contemplative systems is training the mind to become focused or concentrated. A concentrated mind is a portal into the subtle realms of the common yogic-mystical itinerary, along with their luminous and liberative insights. But no entrance can be made into this itinerary without a still, calm, and focused mind. So, the beginning stage in meditation is convergence, which, as I am using the word here, might be defined as training the mind (*citta*, or, more fluidly translatable as "thought," which befits Buddhism[91]) to develop skill in focusing on the selected object of meditation. The contemplative universal of convergence is expressed as the meditative landmarks of acquired recollection (*recueillement actif*) in mystical theology and as concentration (*dhāraṇā*) in *patañjala yoga*, which will be discussed in later chapters. In Theravāda Buddhism, the universal of convergence is divided up into the two tasks of generating the training sign (*parikamma-nimitta*) and the learning sign (*uggaha-nimitta*).

The Training Sign (parikamma-nimitta)

The beginning instruction for meditation proper in every contemplative tradition is to bring the attention to bear upon the meditation object and to return it there as often as the mind wavers. This is the first task of coalescence, and it corresponds to the "preliminary work" (*parikamma*) of the *Visuddhimagga* (Vsm 3.62, Ñ) or what the later tradition calls "the training sign" (*parikamma-nimitta*). Far less important than what the meditator focuses upon—for the forty meditation subjects suggested by the *Visuddhimagga* (Vsm 3.104) in no way exhaust the catalog of possible objects of meditation, as is obvious through the study of other meditational systems—is the meditator's succeeding through repeated applications of attention in the preparatory work of overcoming the distractions that divert attention, such as the countless images, memories, hopes, fears, desires, aversions, and everything else that the untrained and unfocused mind continually, like an always-on television, sends the meditator's way.

Not only at the beginning of one's meditative training but even in later stages, the disciplining of the wanderings of a recalcitrant mind is always the first meditative task. It is a common experience, however, that stilling the mind is a difficult task, harder even than taming the wind. Indeed, so challenging is this task that many people give up, and not only after half-hearted attempts at meditation. Some people may conclude that meditation is not for them, given their overactive minds. But a helpful principle to keep in mind at this point, and one that seems firmly grounded in the ascetical theory of the *Visuddhimagga*, is that if the mind will not settle down despite one's best efforts, one should probe to see if any of the five hindrances have become overactive in the meditator's life. It is more likely the case that sense desires, ill will, stiffness and torpor, agitation and worry, and uncertainty about the value of the spiritual life have so irradiated one's mind that it cannot be quieted apart from mindful attempts to uproot these foes of the *jhānas*.

The Learning Sign (uggaha-nimitta)

Although beginning meditation at this stage can sometimes seem dry, fruitless, and frustrating as the meditator struggles with the vagaries of the restless and resistant mind, there is one sure sign that the meditator is making progress. This is when one notices that a trace of the meditation object flickers with almost a life of its own in one's mind, although the meditator must still bring the will to bear in keeping this delicate mental reflection of the meditation object from dissolving into the usual flow of mental distractions.

For this distinctive sign of contemplative progress, the *Visuddhimagga* offers the technical name of "the learning sign" (*uggaha-nimitta*). Its central characteristic is that the meditator can, with the eyes closed, call up and hold in the mind a reflection or trace of the meditation object (Vsm 4.30 Ñ), whether it be an earth *kasiṇa*, a *kasiṇa* of another color, decaying bodies, the Buddha, the body and its parts, the breath, deities, death, or sublime mental states and ethical attitudes toward others.

The *Visuddhimagga* gives a somewhat ambiguous formula for extracting the learning sign from the grosser meditation object (a step unnecessary for those with meditation skills from a previous life, the *Visuddhimagga* frequently points out, who will find that just the sight or thought of the various things used as meditation objects is enough to catapult the meditator into a fully developed counterpart sign [Vsm 4.23, etc.]). Instead of focusing on perceptible aspects of the object, the meditator should, while keeping the object clearly in view, simply repeat any one of its common names, thus bringing attention to the concept that governs the object rather than the object itself. Taking the earth *kasiṇa* as an example, one focuses on the concept of earth as a mental datum instead of the aroma and hardness of the earth (Vsm 4.29, 5.4, etc. Ñ[92]). On the other hand, in its actual description of various learning signs, the *Visuddhimagga* refers to less abstract and somewhat concrete perceptual elements, such as motion for the water *kasiṇa* (Vsm

5.4 Ñ) or a "swirl of hot steam" for the air *kasiṇa* (Vsm 5.11 Ñ), and even defects, such as bubbles of froth in the water *kasiṇa* (Vsm 5.4 Ñ.).

In either case, what we see here is a first step of abstraction that is meant to move from physical qualities through mental qualities toward subtle realities that are neither physical realities nor concepts based on physical realities. Standing midway between the gross realms of physical and mental manifestation and the subtle doorway to the *jhānas* opened by the counterpart sign, the partially independent abstraction of the learning sign marks a clear step away from dependence on the senses and mental images in the development of concentration.

Besides the examples given above, the *Visuddhimagga* refers to a diverse group of learning signs: for the water *kasiṇa*, it has "the appearance of motion"; for the light *kasiṇa*, it is like a "circle thrown on the wall or on the ground"; for mindfulness of the body, it is the perception of animal and human bodily parts as independent of a connection to individual beings; for mindfulness of breathing, it is "a light touch [in the mind] like cotton or silk-cotton or a draught"; and for the repulsiveness of nutriment, it is a sense of the repulsiveness of everything that goes into the gathering, eating, and excreting of food (Vsm 5.4, 5.22, 5.140, 8.214, 11.25 Ñ).

When any of these learning signs (and many others besides) become noticeable in meditation, it signals that the meditator has made real progress in meditation, and the meditator can be assured that by continuing to develop the learning sign concentration will deepen until the moment when awareness becomes unified, which is the terrain of the next contemplative universal of coalescence.

Coalescence: Fixing on or Locking the Mind in on the Meditation Object

The contemplative universal of coalescence is expressed as the meditative landmarks of the "ligature of the faculties" (*la ligature des facultés*) in mystical theology and meditation (*dhyāna*) in *patañjala yoga*, both of which will be discussed in later chapters. As we will see, the various ways in which these three traditions describe how the mind, or more precisely, attention, suddenly locks in or focuses sharply on the meditation object are strikingly similar. So striking is this event, that the skilled contemplative and yogi will not have been able to miss it. Indeed, it is usually taken as one of the great landmarks on the contemplative itinerary, since it marks the point at which the mind begins to experience a purely subtle realm, one that is not dependent upon physical processes. In Theravāda Buddhism, the contemplative universal of coalescence is divided into the two meditative landmarks of generating the counterpart sign (*paṭibhāga-nimitta*), which is equivalent to access, or initial, concentration (*upacāra-samādhi*), and entering into absorption, or full, concentration (*appanā-samādhi*), which commences with the first *jhāna*.

The Counterpart Sign (paṭibhāga-nimitta)

As indicated in the chart above, the counterpart sign is equivalent in the *Visuddhimagga* to *upacāra-samādhi* (access concentration), since the arising of this sign marks the formal beginning of *samādhi*, or concentration, although it is still weak and incomplete. The *Visuddhimagga* describes how the purified, purely mental phenomenon of the counterpart sign arises from the partially sense-based imagery of the learning sign. In place of the intentionally constructed mental image of the starting sign, an object generated purely through perception (*saññā*), there now arises what is felt as a subtle mind-born object that exists from its own side apart from the will of the meditator.

Some examples of counterpart signs, all of which display the transition from sensible to purely mental objects, include some that, although already mentioned above, deserve to be mentioned again. Buddhaghosa dramatically exclaims that the counterpart sign "appears as if breaking out from the learning sign, and a hundred times, a thousand times, more purified" (Vsm 4.31 Ñ). Although this subtle, meditation-born object is beyond all material, sense-based forms, it is, for the sake of communication, likened, as in the case of the earth *kasiṇa*, to the brightness of a mirror pulled out from its dark case, to a sparklingly clean mother-of-pearl dish, to the circle of the moon suddenly appearing from behind a cloud, and to white cranes appearing against the background of a dark thundercloud (Vsm 4.31 Ñ).

Other examples include: for the water *kasiṇa*, a crystal hand fan suspended in the air or a mirror made of crystal; for the fire *kasiṇa*, a piece of red cloth suspended in the sky, a gold hand fan, or a gold column; for the air *kasiṇa*, motionlessness and quiet; for the light *kasiṇa*, "a compact bright cluster of lights"; for the limited-space *kasiṇa*, a circle in the sky; for mindfulness of breathing, a star, clusters of gems or pearls, like the roughness of the cotton-like fibers of the red silk-cotton tree of Asia, "a wreath of flowers," "a puff of smoke"; and for the four divine abidings of loving-kindness, compassion, gladness, and equanimity, the mental breaking down of the barriers between oneself, friends, enemies, and people who are neither (Vsm 5.4, 5.8, 5.11, 5.23, 5.26, 8.215,[93] 9.43, 9.81. 9.87, 9.89 Ñ).

Despite these references to sensible images, the counterpart sign has, in fact, neither color nor shape, since it is not a gross material object knowable by the senses (Vsm 4.31 Ñ). As the *Visuddhimagga* says, the counterpart sign "is born only of perception [*saññā*] in one who has obtained concentration, being a mere mode of appearance" (Vsm 4.31 Ñ). Unlike the learning sign, which, as seen above, retains sensible elements, the counterpart sign, born as it is of the imaginative and conceptualizing capability of the mind, leaps free of sensible traces and partakes of the subtle realms of immaterial consciousness (*rūpabhūmi*), or "the fine material plane of existence."[94] This is a momentous threshold, for it heralds a "change-of lineage" (*gotrabhū*) (Vsm 4.74 Ñ), when the meditator leaves the ranks of those whose experience so far has been limited only to the realm of the senses and desire (*kāmāvacara*) (Vsm 4.74 Ñ).[95]

The suddenness and purity of this sign's sudden arising, even if momentary and flickering, graces the meditator with a sense of awe irradiated with the mystical insight that one has cracked open the mental door (*manodvāra*) to the path to the deathless. As the sensory aspects of the learning sign are left behind, the meditator feels as if the counterpart sign has burst out from the learning sign. Yet, its factors are not stable in one's mind at this point, as they will become in absorption concentration. Buddhaghosa likens the mind at this point to a child who keeps falling down on the ground when it is placed on its feet. In the same way, the mind falters between staying focused on the counterpart sign and falling back into the ordinary flow of consciousness (*bhavaṅga*) (Vsm 4.33 Ñ). And yet, as we will see, just as the child soon learns to stay standing unaided, so the door to the subtle realms will soon open widely for the meditator who continues along this way toward absorption concentration.

Absorption concentration (appanā-samādhi)

As remarkable as the experience of encountering the counterpart sign may be, it remains a preliminary stage to the actual experience of the *jhānas*. The meditator has certainly gained a glimpse into the subtle realms (*rūpabhūmi*), but still stands only on the threshold, or in the neighborhood, of the first *jhāna* (Vsm 4.74). This distinction is not arbitrary, for it is based upon a precise *Abhidhammic* analysis of what actually occurs in the transition between access concentration and absorption concentration. In the view of the *Abhidhamma*, our mind in its ordinary sense- and desire-based operations is absorbed in what it calls "the life-continuum," or the *bhavaṅga* (Vsm 4.33, 4n13 Ñ) This is not the flow of thoughts, which the Abhidhamma calls *cittavīthi*, or the "cognitive process,"[96] but the bare background of awareness in which the flow of mental activity arises. In waking experience, the flow of thoughts continuously plays out against the background of the life-continuum, but in deep sleep or in moments of reverie or perhaps of mental exhaustion, the *cittavīthi* stops for a while, leaving just the *bhavaṅga*, which subsists from the moment of birth to the moment of death.[97] In waking consciousness, the life-continuum is constantly suppressed by sensations streaming into the senses. The *Abhidhamma* precisely divides each of these interruptions of the life-continuum into seventeen discrete moments. Most important for our purposes here is the notion of *javana*, a technical term that Bhikkhu Bodhi suggests should be left untranslated.[98] In general terms, *javana* is the active phase of the cognitive process (*cittavīthi*), or those moments of direct experience of what enters the doors of the senses and the mind.[99] More concretely, *javanas* are the moments when, according to Bhikkhu Bodhi, the mind "'runs swiftly' over the object in the act of apprehending it."[100] These constitute, as Shaila Catherine writes, "the more notable and vivid component of experience."[101]

While this may seem dry and scholastic, it actually provides an illuminating analysis of how the meditator's "jhāna-eye" (Vsm 10.11, 35 Ñ) opens to the subtle realm of the *jhānas*. Not only that, it indicates how to facilitate transitioning from access to absorption concentration. A common mistake when the counterpart sign arises is to become so excited or agitated by its appearance that one suffocates or suppresses the sign. Another is to greedily grasp the sign with the mind and to become inflated with grand ideas about world liberation or other messianic and overblown ambitions. Invariably, the sign disappears because of these reactions, which can be ascribed to the first of the two kinds of failings with respect to meditative focus: agitation or laxity (Vsm 4.72 Ñ). After too many experiences of losing hold of the counterpart sign due to agitation, the meditator may slip into the other failing of laxity and stop developing the learning sign to the degree of intensity needed to generate the counterpart sign. The cure for this failing may well be the same as the cure for excitation, which is to merely stay with the direct experience of the *javana* instead of getting caught up in the various reactions, whether excited or lax, to the *javana*. Indeed, when the meditator begins to realize that excitation and laxity are failings that are correctable by the meditator and not the inevitable outcome of the rising of the counterpart sign, the meditator may be inclined to once again take up the balanced and skillful effort of generating the counterpart sign from the learning sign.

Helpful at this point is Buddhaghosa's account of how the first *jhāna*, or absorption concentration, actually arises. Focusing on the learning sign, one generates the counterpart sign by steady intensification of concentration. Eventually the subtle object of the counterpart sign emerges from the learning sign, and, with a confidence born of practice in balancing excitation and laxity, the meditator senses that now "absorption will succeed" (*appanā ijjhissati*, Vsm 4.74[102]). In place of the usual feed of information streaming into the mind from the senses, suddenly a purely mental door (*manodvāra*) opens into a previously unsuspected immaterial realm of existence, and this is directly followed[103] by a moment of direct nonconceptual experience (a "sublime" *javana*) of the subtle realm,[104] which is equivalent to the dawning of the counterpart sign, the suppression of the hindrances, and the first step into *samādhi* (Vsm 4.32-34, 74). Instead of wallowing in the excess of rapture (*pīti*) that attends the first *javana*, the meditator calmly observes it with neither greed nor pride. At this point, one is able to experience a second, third, or sometimes a fourth *javana*, or direct, nonconceptual experience of the subtle realm, until, finally, in the fourth or fifth *javana*,[105] one breaks free of the sense- and desire-based consciousness (*kāmāvacara*) of the life-continuum (*bhavaṅga*) and is gripped by a pure experience of the subtle realm (*rūpāvacara*).

The experience of the suppression of the life-continuum by this sequence of *javanas* gives the meditator information from the immaterial realm that stretches beyond the limits of the senses and is the subtle location of the realms of the various *devas* and other subtle entities who populate the related cosmologies of Hinduism and Indian Buddhism. Through the cultivation of concentration, the meditator has succeeded in directing, or adverting, the mind door (*manodvāra*) to the subtle realm and away from the usual flow of thoughts (*cittavīthi*) (Vsm 4.74-78).

And now, whether one holds it only for "a single conscious moment" (Vsm 4.78 Ñ) or whether "one carries on with a stream of profitable impulsion for a whole night and for a whole day" (Vsm 433 Ñ) one has attained coalescence.[106]

Simplification: The Mind Transcends Itself Factor by Factor

Coalescence is followed by the contemplative universal that I call "simplification." The contemplative universal of simplification is expressed as progress through the meditative landmarks of the ligature and the preliminary degrees of mystical union (*unio mystica*) in mystical theology and of mediated *samādhi* (*samprajñāta-samādhi*) in *patañjala yoga*, both of which will be discussed in later chapters. It is expressed in Theravāda Buddhism as progression through the four *jhānas*, which I have traced above. I call this process "simplification" because a universal feature of mystical spirituality is the reduction over time of more complex religious ideas, teachings, imagery, and spiritual experiences to simpler mystical forms. This is a countermovement to literalistic, legalistic, particularistic, and constructivist forms of religiosity that prize uniqueness, difference, complexity, and interpretive precision. Even when living quietly within such systems, mystics generally tend to have intuited that the objects of religious ardor in their tradition, when considered in their own right, somehow escape and are prior to the diverse external and culturally mediated aspects of the world's many religious cultures.

I am aware that making such a claim will not sit well with constructivists and particularists (see earlier chapters), but I think that the mystical dimension in religion, by definition, seeks a source of religious vitality that is prior to the material and merely mental dimensions of human experience, That is, whether explicitly or not, mysticism possesses a more or less apophatic tendency, while popular religion is almost invariably cataphatic. Another way of framing this is to think of mysticism as a dominant way of practicing abstraction and simplification in matters religious (another is the generalizing practice of comparative religion, both of which were discussed in an earlier chapter). One example of the process of mystical simplification is the tendency for vivid, richly drawn images of deities to fade away as the center of focus in mystical contemplation. While popular devotion will focus upon these richly realized divinities, a minority of practitioners will discover that the stories of the deities slowly transform into allegories that express the journey of consciousness from dispersion in matter to unification in a supreme state of deathless awareness. In some traditions, this is seen as a journey toward wisdom and spiritual maturity, while in others it is an insight that can be acknowledged, if at all, only at great risk.

In the case of the *jhānas*, we saw the process of simplification at work in the progression from the first to the fourth *jhāna*, a process that moves from a relatively coarse and complex first *jhāna* to a sublime, utterly balanced and simple fourth *jhāna*. This progression involves the step-by-step elimination of the constitutive factors of the first *jhāna*. (These factors, which the *Visuddhimagga* calls "the five factors of possession" [Vsm 4.107 Ñ] have been listed above, but they bear repeating: *vitakka*, *vicāra*, *pīti*, and *sukha*.) Progression from the first through the fourth (or the Abhidhammic fifth) *jhāna* occurs as the meditator successively comes to feel that each of the generating factors in turn is coarse and, as a consequence, is eliminated, thus purifying and simplifying this subtle mental state of focused concentration.[107] (As we will see in later chapters, a similar process occurs with the sequence of the *samādhis* or *samāpattis* in the *Yoga-Sūtras* and in the progress through the degrees of union in Catholic mystical theology).

Quiescence: The Stilling of the Mind

This focused stillness of the mind, or quiescence, is, as indicated in chart 1.2, the outcome of the processes of simplification, coalescence, and convergence. As will be seen in the next two chapters, the contemplative universal of quiescence is expressed as the meditative landmarks of unmediated recollectedness (*asaṃprajñāta-samādhi*) in *patañjala yoga* and as the suspension of the faculties (*la suspension des puissances*), or spiritual dereliction and the passive night of the spirit, in Catholic mystical theology. In Theravāda Buddhism, quiescence is expressed as the meditative landmark of the cessation of ideation and feeling (*saññāvedayitanirodha*), and to this we can now briefly turn.

The Cessation of Ideation and Feeling (saññāvedayitanirodha)

We come now to a rarified contemplative state that is penultimate to the contemplative universal of beatitude. It is aptly and precisely called "the cessation of ideation and feeling" (*saññāvedayitanirodha*, or *nirodha-samāpatti*), or, more simply, "cessation" (*nirodha*).[108] This is the condition just prior to the complete, conscious freedom from the physical, mental, and subtle conditioning of *nibbāna*. Not quite *nibbāna*, quiescence, is a state in which the mind, as well as the body, becomes completely still. This freedom from physical, mental, and subtle conditioning, which is a state of being that is not immediately accessible to biologically and mentally conditioned awareness, is an extraordinarily rare and refined meditative attainment, one that it is virtually impossible to speak about, except, perhaps, negatively, or apophatically. As "a temporary suspension" of ideation and feeling, this state contains, as Steven Collins writes, "no discursive awareness of the kind required for analytical understanding."[109]

While it might seem that such a state is, in fact, equivalent to *nibbāna*, Collins points out that this is contradicted by the well-known Buddhist story about the Buddha's entering cessation when he was at the point of entering *parinibbāna* (i.e., "complete nibbāna," the postmortem *nibbāna* from which there is no return[110]). Ānanda thought that the Buddha had reached *parinibbāna*, but Anuruddha pointed out that he had only reached cessation. The Buddha then emerged from cessation, descended back to the first *jhāna*, and then exited into *parinibbāna* from the fourth *jhāna*.[111] That *nirodha* cannot be the final goal of Buddhism flows from its being a merely temporary condition.[112] So it is, I think, acceptable to see cessation as a "foretaste" of *nibbāna*, perhaps even its analogue, but not its equivalent.[113] Indeed, the *Visuddhimagga* concedes that "it tends toward nibbana" (Vsm 23.50 Ñ).

Here, at the culmination of the concentrative practices begun in *parikamma-nimitta*, the yogi has learned through a self-enacted mental process supported by *samatha-bhāvanā* to decrease neural activity in the posterior superior parietal lobe, thereby causing the onset of a nondual, unitive state of awareness that, as we have seen, Newberg and d'Aquili call "absolute unitary being,"[114] or an "enhanced non-cognitive state."[115]

Beatitude: The Transcending of the Mind

The distinction between *nirodha* and *nibbāna* marks a dramatic division in Buddhism between dimensions of being that, on the one side, are implicated with gross and subtle materiality and mentation and, on the other, a liberation that is utterly beyond all of these conditions. Although almost immeasurably remote from ordinary everyday consciousness, cessation remains a mental state,[116] even if a highly attenuated one. It can perhaps be thought of as the very tip of the fingernail of a finger pointing directly at the moon. One sees the moon toward which the finger points while also still seeing the last trace of the fingernail. This is thus a conditioned mental state whose direct object is the unconditioned non-mental state of beatitude. But beatitude—*nibbāna* in this life or postmortem *parinibbāna*—is unproduced and unconditioned by the processes of the biological, mental, and subtle realms. There is thus no causal link between any of these conditions and beatitude, which stands sovereignly supreme and independent of all conditions. Such a condition is, by definition, beyond the scope of neurobiology, and to postulate it is to postulate a dimension of being that breaks the bonds of the scientific worldview as it is now constructed.

Unlike either *nibbāna* or *parinibbāna*,[117] cessation is the result of the intensification of concentration and the simplification of the contents of the focused mind that make up the *jhāna* series (Vsm 11.124 23.20-21 Ñ). As such, cessation cannot be the end station of the Buddhist path. But if *nibbāna* is taken as a form of liberation-in-life of the Buddhist *arahant* that is akin to the condition of the *jīvanmukta* in Hinduism and the saint who has attained transforming union in Catholic Christianity, then the *arahant* and the sanctified sage or saint will still make use of the whole complement of faculties, physical, mental, and subtle, with which a human being is endowed.[118] Enlightenment in this life, or the condition of the *arahant* who has entered *nibbāna*, is a condition that is other than or more than cessation, for cessation involves a shutting down of the physical systems of the body that it is said not to last for more than seven days (Vsm 12.32, 11.124, 23.42 Ñ). And yet, as is clear, enlightened people may continue to live and teach for years after experiencing *nibbāna*.

Since *parinibbāna*, or full liberation after life might be operationally defined as the ending of all formations (*saṅkhāra*), it must, by definition be beyond the reach of cessation, which although a "produced," or conditioned, form (Vsm 23.52 Ñ), allows a glimpse of the unconditioned state in a body, mind, and *karma*-stream that has been brought to cessation but neither to death (Vsm 23.51 Ñ) nor to the final dissolution of full and final enlightenment (*parinibbāna*).

It seems possible to me, then, that the attainment of cessation is an example of the stealing back into the gentler fourfold *jhāna* path of the Buddha of the end goal of Bronkhorst's mainstream meditation, which sought the stopping of all physical and mental processes as a way of stopping karma and, thereby, rebirth. Cessation is the ultimate degree of concentration (Vsm 23.18 Ñ), but concentration on its own is not the end of the Buddhist path, as is shown by the example of the Buddha abandoning cessation for the "blissful abiding" (Vsm 11.124 Ñ) of the fourth *jhāna* as the place of exit into *parinibbāna*. Thus, early Buddhism abandoned painful asceticism and its explicit rejection of physical, mental, and subtle goods in favor of a gentler path that delighted in the goods of the ethical life, sublime powers, and liberative insight in a state of conscious tranquility and ecstasy. This integrated and human path is the gift of the Buddha to humankind, and one that is no less relevant today as it was when the young prince turned Awakened One wandered the roads of old Bharata.

Chapter 5

The Concentrative Itinerary of Yogic *Samādhi*

Classical Yoga, Rāja Yoga, Pātañjala Yoga—or Something Else?

The Sanskrit word *yoga* is at least as familiar now outside of India as the Sanskrit word *karma* (or, more precisely, *karman*). Yet, familiarity does not in any way amount to clear understanding of this word, not only because the popular contexts in which it is deployed have dramatically increased in the last twenty years, but also because scholarly evaluations of what counts as yoga have dramatically shifted in the same period.[1] This would be more troubling than some commentators think, except for the circumstance that the notion of yoga has been polyvocal and subject to diverse and not often easily synthesizable definitions since the earliest times in India. If David Gordon White is correct, then the earliest and most widespread use of the word *yoga* in its various Vedic forms had nothing at all to do with yoga in any of its later meanings, since it referred to the yoking, or "hitching," of a "chariot warrior" to his chariot, or "rig" in battle, which, if death was the result, led the warrior in his ascent to the heavenly reams through the doorway of the sun.[2]

Novel as this view of the origin of yoga is, it would seem to be of little or no relevance to either the meaning of yoga that is central to the later Indian traditions, or to the export versions of yoga that are now prevalent around the globe. Yet—and more relevantly for later forms of yoga—White points out that in these same early Vedic traditions, the word *yoga* "also came to be applied, with increasing frequency, to the practice of Vedic priests who yoked their minds to poetic inspiration."[3] If these quite diverse meanings are discoverable in the Vedic use of the word *yoga*, then it presents a compelling case for the notion that religious ideas often undergo over time in cultures and in individual personal experience a subtilization in which formerly external, physical, and historical teachings transform into inward, mental, and subtle realm teachings.[4]

However, White's thesis is more sweeping than this historical reconstruction suggests, since the central contention of his acclaimed *Sinister Yogis* is that the power to take over the bodies of other beings, and not a meditative yoga grounded in *āsana* and culminating in *samādhi*, is the "sine qua non of a yogi's practice."[5] This is a very strong claim, for despite the apparent countervailing evidence of the *Ṛg-Veda*,[6] the later classical Upaniṣads,[7] the *Carakasaṃhitā*,[8] *Mokṣadharma Parvan* in the *Mahābhārata*,[9] the *Bhagavad Gītā*,[10] the *Yoga Sūtra*,[11] and the teachings of the Pāśupatas,[12] White maintains that yogis "*never* portray their practice as introvertive or introspective—but rather as extrovert, if not predatory."[13] Clearly, this will require a good deal of explaining, which White—whom his disciplinary colleague Andrew J. Nicholson calls "an Indological provocateur"[14] and another colleague, James Mallinson, calls "the most insistent of *pūrvapakṣins*"[15]—proceeds to provide in a chapter fittingly called "*Ceci n'est pas un Yogi.*"

In building his case, White calls into question the prevalent academic practice—the "modern-day sensus communis"[16]—of referring to the yoga of the *Yoga-Sūtras* as *rāja yoga* or classical yoga. He rightly traces the wide contemporary prevalence of these terms to the pervasive influence of Swami Vivekananda,[17] whom he characterizes as "a giant of neo-Vedānta reform"[18] as well as a "dilettante on the subject of yoga."[19] White, following Elizabeth De Michelis, rightly notes that Swami Vivekananda identified *pātañjala yoga* with *rāja yoga*, or with classical yoga,[20] a move that would pervasively shape modern understandings of the *Yoga Sūtra.*[21]

It can be conceded quickly that it is wrong simply to identify the yoga of the *Yoga Sūtra* with *rāja yoga*, given that the Patañjali's yoga is just one of the many varieties of meditative yoga that fall under the term *rāja yoga.*[22] And while it is clear that the expression *classical yoga* is of recent coinage, this admission should not lead to suspicion about the expression *rāja yoga*, which has been used for over a millennium, if only sporadically at first,[23] and with some dizzying transpositions[24] to distinguish between meditative yoga (*rāja yoga*), or more precisely, *samādhi*,[25] and the yoga of *siddhis*, *vibhūtis*, and physical prowess (*haṭha yoga*).[26] The now globally familiar distinction between *rāja yoga* and *haṭha yoga* first "became codified" in the fifteenth century in Svātmārāma's *Haṭhapradīpikā*[27] and was given canonical expression by Vijñānabhikṣu in the sixteenth century, long after its first appearances in the scriptural tradition centuries earlier.[28] It is clearly wrong, then, to refer to it as "a modern accretion," as De Michelis does,[29] and to fault Vivekananda for making use of this distinction. At the very least, it is clear that the expression *rāja yoga* as referring to meditative yoga can be traced back to long before 1893, when Swami Vivekananda first entered upon the international stage. The same can be said for *haṭha yoga*, which was systematized as early as the thirteenth century,[30] although elements of it can be traced in leading Indian religious movements of the first millennium[31] and, some argue, even earlier.[32]

While one can readily agree with White that the yoga traditions more concerned with physical prowess, mastery of subtle realms,[33] and magical powers have been overlooked and deserve more substantial and serious scholarly attention, this should not become the basis for minimizing the fact that something recognizable to us today as the more popular contemporary classical yoga or the much older *rāja yoga* makes its appearance in the Upaniṣads,[34] where a six-step process similar to the *aṣṭāṅga yoga* of Patañjali's *Yoga Sūtra* is clearly called "yoga" (*ṣaḍaṅgā ityucyate yogaḥ*)."[35] Later, the *Bhagavad Gītā* also describes a similar type of meditative yoga, and it paints an evocative picture of the yogi seated in a classic meditative posture while progressively focusing attention within.[36] The picture of yoga in the *Bhagavad Gītā* accords well with the description of yoga given in the *Yoga Sūtra*, even if it cannot and should not be identified exclusively with *pātañjala yoga*. It is thus difficult to see meditation-based, and enlightenment-oriented, yoga as merely a product of the last century or so. South Asianist James Mallinson concurs, and notes, that White "leaves no room for nuance, ignoring everything that argues against his position, in particular the elephant in his room—the huge body of Indic texts written over the last two thousand years which teach a meditation-based yoga."[37] By sharply distinguishing between the words *yogi* and *yoga*,[38] White attempts to cast doubt upon the antiquity of seated, meditative yoga in the Indian traditions and he also suggests that seated meditators were not called *yogis* before the seventeenth century, a claim that seems to fly in the face of the passage in the *Bhagavad Gītā* noted above.

Influential as this line of debunking reasoning has become,[39] it seems too thin of an argument to undercut an ancient tradition. Although White repeatedly calls the current equation of yoga with meditation and with the use of expressions like *rāja yoga* and *classical yoga* abusive,[40] his approach underestimates what even his own survey shows[41] to be a fairly continuous tradition in India over the last two millennia of the kindred *pātañjala yoga* and *rāja yoga* traditions, even allowing for some gaps in the historical record and for the episodic demotions by orthodox Brāhmaṇas and devotional theists of Patañjali's version of a comprehensive meditative, enlightenment-oriented style of yoga topread.[42]

This underestimating of the durability of the meditative and Pātañjalian varieties of yoga is evident in the preface to White's biography of the *Yoga Sūtra*, where he, with great verve, contrasts the view of ancient India that has been emerging over the last forty years among academic Indologists with the views of "most Indians, Indophiles, and renaissance hipsters."[43] While the latter may think that India's ancient traditions are "ageless verities" unchanged over time, academics such as White now think that "much of what is thought to be ancient in India was actually invented—or at best reinvented or recovered from oblivion—during the time of the British raj."[44]

These claims appear, with a kind of unwitting irony, to display an Orientalism,[45] or perhaps a neo-Orientalism,[46] along the lines of the arch Orientalist, Sir John Strachey, a nineteenth-century British colonial administrator in India, who dismissed the idea of "India" as naming a singular nation or culture as an invention of the West. "The first and most important thing to learn about India is that there is not and never was an India"[47] was his opening comment in his classes training future British civil servants for their activities in India. Similar in iconoclastic and skeptical temper are White's overstated views of the *pātañjala yoga* and *rāja yoga* traditions. It appears to me that White's daring—even astonishing claims—stand on the shaky ground of equivocation, since invention is not equivalent to reinvention nor to recovery from oblivion. To credit imperial Orientalists with rediscovering an old practice is an entirely different matter than claiming that it was invented by them. The latter is a more volatile claim than the first, and perhaps this is why White weakens his initially bold claim in later writings with less sweeping claims.[48]

In response to White, it can readily be admitted that a yoga that involves *dhyāna* and *samādhi* and oriented toward spiritual enlightenment is scarcely to be found in the Vedas outside of some references in the later classical Upaniṣads and the passage, noted earlier in this chapter, in the *Ṛg-Veda* (5.81.1).[49] Even this scanty evidence suggests, however, that these practices are, on the basis of scriptural evidence, upwards of two millennia old, if not much older. It is also to be conceded that the yoga of the *Ṛg-Veda*[50] and the Brāhmaṇas,[51] if not exclusively of the classical Upaniṣads and the *Mahābhārata*,[52] celebrated the cult of the heroic chariot warriors, as White argues, yet this does not rule out the possibility that central features of what we currently call *yoga* arose outside or alongside the Vedic traditions, as is clear when White himself notes that the meditative practices of early Buddhism and Jainism use variants of the word *dhyāna* instead of the term *yoga*.[53] This leads one to conclude that Mallinson is correct in suggesting that it is "often unclear whether White is exploring the history of the word *yoga* or of yoga itself."[54] It is this equivocation that allows White to begin his history of yoga with Vedic warriors yoked to their rigs[55] instead of the yogis of the Indus Valley seals.[56] This move effectively disenfranchises the obviously very ancient Indian spiritual practices that were designed "to stop, still or immobilize" various aspects of the body and the mind, which, although inconsistent with his focus on sinister yogis, White offers a "general" definition of yoga.[57]

Rather than choosing one or the other of these uses of the word *yoga* at the expense of the others, it makes more sense, I think, to follow Indian tradition at this point, where the word *yoga* came to be applied to practices as diverse as that of the chariot warriors, power-seeking *tāntrikas*, and meditators. While the first stream has disappeared altogether (or blended into later Hindu views of poetic inspiration as a form of yoga[58]), the latter two streams of yoga, or the *bubhukṣu* tradition, which is more concerned with physical prowess, uncanny powers, and mastery over the living and the dead, and the *mumukṣu* tradition, which is focused on transcendence, the overcoming of suffering, and enlightenment, have long since intertwined with each other, as evidenced in the *Yoga Sūtra* itself.[59] This is also evidenced by the fact that, as Mallinson argues, "the *mumukṣu* tradition of *haṭhayoga*, which is espoused by the Rāmānandīs and the Daśanāmīs has been the predominant variety of yoga practice for at least five hundred years and is the basis of much of the yoga practiced in the West."[60] This would include, of course, the yoga movements founded by Swami Sivananda of Rishikesh and his major disciples.[61] Clearly, the *mumukṣu* tradition of *haṭhayoga* has assumed the mantle of yoga on the global stage in the last centuries, at the expense of the long moribund *yogayukta* chariot-warrior tradition and of White's *bhoga*-seeking "sinister yogis," a situation that White is seeking to remedy.

Alongside the influential criticism of White is another, allied strand of what I like to think of as neo-Orientalist Western academic criticism of contemporary global yoga. This stream has made news for itself in the academy and the global yoga community with its sensational, Twitter-feed ready proclamation that "Modern Postural Yoga" is mostly an invention of Tirumalai Krishnamacarya (1888–1989) and the yogis of the Mysore Palace *yogaśālā* who spread his teachings to the rest of the world. This charge hangs ultimately on the claim that most, if not all, of the *āsanas* taught there were also invented there. This claim was pioneered in its strongest form by N. E. Sjoman, who claims that the *āsanas* taught in the

Mysore Palace tradition "have no textual support" and "no lineage of teachers" prior to the nineteenth century.[62] This judgment is taken as canonical, if somewhat less categorically by Mark Singleton,[63] David Gordon White,[64] Gerald Larson,[65] and Autumn Jacobsen,[66] and it has become the main critical weapon wielded by the current crop of academic opponents of what might be called "transnational Anglophone postural yoga."[67]

It is undoubtedly fascinating to learn about the syncretistic gym and yoga culture of the Mysore Palace *yogaśālā*,[68] which stretches back to the late eighteenth century. No doubt the athleticism and astonishing physical dexterity of the schools of *haṭha yoga* originating in this new tradition owe much to British acrobats and wrestlers and other current trends of the time.[69] But once again this seems to be a blunt scalpel in an attempted academic surgical removal of the legitimacy of the global yoga movement.

Despite the current prevalence of this line of argument, three stubborn bits of information disturb Sjoman's and his followers' argument: first, the yoga of Swami Sivananda. This style of yoga, known as Sivananada Yoga, was first taught in the West by Swami Vishnudevananda and is now, alongside the schools descending from Mysore, a globally widely prevalent variety of yoga. With this one must connect the Integral Yoga of another Sivananada disciple, Swami Satchidananda, whose variant of Sivananda Yoga is less widespread but virtually identical to Sivananda Yoga. Even less well-known is Yoga Vidya, a school of Sivananda Yoga rooted in the tradition of Swami Vishnudevananda that is widely prevalent in Germany and is spreading throughout Western Europe. As even Sjoman acknowledges, Sivananda Yoga has a different and perhaps even older source than the Mysore Palace in Swami Sivananda's Diksitar family, who, Sjoman notes, are "the traditional custodians of the Cidambaram temple."[70] Also, as Sjoman admits, the *āsanas* taught by the disciples of Krishnamacarya are similar to those taught by the disciples of Swami Sivananda, as well as the *āsanas* of other traditions.[71] This, along with Sjoman's concessions that the Mysore Palace yoga tradition does seem make use of "older sources" such as the *Mallapurāṇa* that make "a distinct reference to āsanas" and that Prince Wodeyar's *Śrītattvanidhi* is "an attempt to synthesize an āsana tradition from many sources,"[72] seems to indicate to me that some sort of common *āsana* tradition preceded the Mysore Palace *yogaśālā*.[73]

Second, as often is the case in his book, Sjoman contradicts himself when he claims a "total absence of connection between the traditional sources and modern traditions" while also acknowledging that the *Haṭhapradīpikā* describes fifteen *āsanas*.[74] This view also fails to recognize that, as Autumn Jacobsen has pointed out, there is some overlap between the *āsanas* of the Mysore Palace *yogaśālā* and of the *Haṭhapradīpikā*.[75] A similar sloppiness mars Sjoman's work when he says that the *Yoga Sūtra* mentions no *āsanas*. Besides giving a succinct and famous definition of an otherwise unspecified *āsana* as "steady and easy" (YS 2.46),[76] the text does describe what sounds like a supine *āsana* of resting, like Ananta, or Śeṣa, "the cosmic serpent," "on the waters of infinity."[77] Sjoman, quite inconsistently and in direct contradiction of his claim, traces "the few āsanas referred to in older texts" to *Yoga Sūtra* 2.47, which, he points out, states "the basic principle of yogic movement"[78] in *āsanas* as *prayatna-śaithilyānanta-samāpattibhyām*, which he translates as: "Relaxing or loosening the effort and by meditating on the endless." He then concedes that the word *prayatna* here suggests "a system of *āsanas* which includes more *āsanas* than the sedentary meditation positions found primarily in later texts."[79] Although the extensive catalog of postures that defines contemporary *āsana*-based yoga is not to be found in the *Yoga Sūtra*, it does, as Sjoman points out, teach "a functional perspective on āsanas"[80] rather than specific *āsanas*. Patañjali's functional definitions of *āsana* accents steadiness, comfort, and the relaxing of effort, qualities that can be associated with various postures, whether derived from old indigenous sources, from the gymnastic traditions of recent centuries, or developed in a *yogaśālā* in Mysore, Pune, or San Francisco. Despite the destructive uses to which, Singleton, White, and others want to put Sjoman's analysis, it serves in the end to support the functional connection of contemporary *āsana*-based yoga to the *Yoga Sūtra*. In the face of these confusions in Sjoman's argument—and perhaps even because of them—it does not take much imagination to see, despite inevitable evolutions in style, that the fifteen *āsanas* described in the *Haṭhapradīpikā* are part of the later *āsana* regimens of Mysore and Sivananda Yoga. Moreover, the claim of the *haṭha-yoga* tradition that there are 84,000 *āsanas*,[81] of which only thirty-two or eighty-four have currency among human beings, as well as the mention of thirteen meditative *āsanas* by Vyāsa on his fifth-century commentary of the *Yoga Sūtra*,[82] reflects a tradition of *āsana* in India significantly older than the Mysore Palace *yogaśālā*-cum-gymnasium.

Third, a plausible case can be made that *āsana*-based yoga is evidenced as far back as an Indus Valley civilization seal that appears to depict a *yogi*, surrounded by animals, seated with folded legs in a classic *āsana* (a variant, perhaps, of *bhadrāsana*).[83] While many Indologists, including Edwin F. Bryant,[84] Barbara Stoler Miller,[85] Ramdas Lamb,[86] David Frawley,[87] Christopher Key Chapple,[88] and Jean Varenne[89] appear to have taken this claim for granted,[90] this claim will elicit amusement among other yoga scholars, who are more inclined to see this presumed *yogi* as a buffalo or a bull[91] or to become skeptical about the meaning of the seal and, thus, its links to later *āsana*-based forms of yoga.[92] But, in my view, these new reinterpretations are neither more nor less plausible nor authorized than the older view. Given the current state of the evidence, it is not possible to decide this issue either way. But if this ambiguous artifact cannot be used to ground *āsana* in ancient India, as the old view presumed, neither can it be used to undermine the antiquity of *āsana* in India, as in current opinion. It does, however, seem reckless to suggest, as White does (perhaps ironically) that the figure in the seal is "a proto-yogic impersonator."[93]—This is a cheating and "abusive"[94] move that unjustly aligns the cheating yogi-impersonators that White studies with the figure in the seal, which appears to offer clear evidence of ancient meditative and *āsana*-based yoga traditions in India.

For all of these reasons, I think that we should be careful in too quickly dismissing the antiquity and integrity of meditative, *āsana*-grounded yoga traditions, along with the most serious contemporary styles of yoga, which cultivate both mundane (*bubhukṣu*) and salvational (*mumukṣu*) ends—sometimes at the same time! It is perhaps more a matter of differing emphases and the vagaries of diverse cultural settings than any violation of the core concerns of traditional Indian yoga that today's global yogis blend the *bubhukṣu* interest in toned muscles and stress-reduction with the *mumukṣu* concerns of being a better person and gaining moments of transcendence. If traditional Indian yoga is rigidly reduced to being either the yoga of austere world-renouncers or the yoga of those in search of magical powers and worldly gain, then contemporary globalized yoga can be caricatured as a hodgepodge that carelessly confuses the two aims of traditional Indian yoga. Yet, insofar as contemporary global yoga blends these two aims, it can be seen as continuous in its core identity with traditional Indian yoga.

The animus of many academic scholars of yoga toward the organic continuity of the always innovative and diverse yoga traditions of India and now around the globe is rooted, I think, in essentialized and traditionalistic images of what yoga should and should not be. Quite helpful as a voice of clarification and moderation in the overheated debate about the legitimacy of contemporary global yoga is the distinction that Andrea R. Jain makes between "the Christian yogaphobic position" and "the Hindu origins position," both of which rely "on definitions of yoga as a homogenous, static Hindu system" and which "presume that a narrowly selected list of characteristics is essential to Hinduism and, more specifically, to yoga."[95] As shown by Jain, one of the odder ironies of contemporary global yoga is the agreement of some Christian exclusivists with some Hindu nationalists and reformists in decrying what they see as the distortion of the essence of yoga by contemporary global yoga. I would also extend Jain's incisive analysis to a third group that is party to the negotiations over the meaning of yoga: the many current academic experts on yoga who, in another sharp irony of contemporary global yoga, display just the sort of "Hindu origins," or essentializing and Orientalizing, tendencies that they would normally reject yet seem to fall into when it comes to making sense of the global yoga movement initiated by Swami Vivekananda.

This seems clearly to be the case in the analyses of pioneering contemporary yoga-scholar Elizabeth De Michelis, which do seem to be an instance of what Andrea L. Jain names "the Hindu origins position" (see below), and which can lead to a dismissal of contemporary expressions of yoga as "Orientalist,"[96] "New Age,"[97] "occult,"[98] or "esoteric,"[99] and as not representative of "classical" Hinduism. On this view, Swami Vivekananda, a founder of contemporary global yoga, becomes more of a "New Age" and neo-Vedantic occultist and esotericist than a representative of "traditional" or "classical" Hinduism.[100] By interpreting Swami Vivekananda as serving the "cultic milieu" of his Western followers by blending Hindu teachings with Western occultism, esotericism, alchemy, astrology, magic, Theosophy, mesmerism, and Neoplatonism—all of which were in Swami Vivekananda's time to be found in varying degrees in the currents of alternative spirituality—De Michelis exoticizes and distanciates Swami Vivekananda, especially for people, including many academics, who may be wary of alternative spirituality.[101] (Jeffery Long has begun to push back at the recent tendency to disparage Swami Vivekananda by Western academics.[102]) The tendency of such scholars to make, what I think is, an overly sharp distinction between "classical" or "untouched" forms of Hinduism and "modern" Hinduism (as expressed in a chart by De Michelis[103]) reflects a lack of appreciation for the syncretistic character of all religious movements.[104] Were this same way of thinking to be applied to contemporary "seeker-sensitive" Christianities over against some selected version of "classical" Christianity, the newer forms of global Christianity might also be suspiciously theorized, thickly historicized, and deconstructed as inauthentic blends of the same currents of contemporary spirituality that converge in a strip-mall yoga studio. Nevertheless, few people outside of academia would be likely to see the "classic" but not the "modern" versions of Christianity as truly Christian and the other deserving, at best, the term neo-Christian.

Mark Singleton, in an essentialistic approach that is similar to De Michelis's approach, detects a chasm between what he calls "modern, transnational, Anglophone postural yoga" and the older Indian *haṭha-yoga* tradition.[105] He attempts, nevertheless, to overcome the "rupture"[106] between "classical" forms of yoga and "modern postural yoga" through what he calls a "dialectical homology," which turns more on the homonymy rather than the synonymy of the word *yoga* in its many uses.[107] In his view, the many varieties of yoga share only the name *yoga* instead of a common core of concerns. This move, which mimics the Wittgensteinian family-resemblance theory of religion, seems to be an ad hoc device meant to ward off charges that Singleton and his collaborators drive too deep of a wedge between newer and older forms of yoga.[108] Singleton's lingering essentialism, as encoded in his rhetorically successful yet hypostatized and linguistically provincial notion of "modern, transnational, Anglophone postural yoga," remains inadequately sensitive to the ongoing creative energy of the syncretistic processes that are inherent in all religious movements, new and old. It is this nostalgia for the apparent purity of the idealized types of traditional Indian yoga that drives those contemporary academics inclined toward Jain's "Hindu origins" approach to sharply demarcate traditional India yoga from contemporary global yoga.

In any event, my own reading of Swami Vivekananda's *Rāja-Yoga* reveals no evidence of the sort of "cultic milieu" of esotericism and occultism traced by De Michelis.[109] Indeed, a clear and bracing emphasis upon a scientific approach to *rāja yoga* pervades the book, and Swami Vivekananda forthrightly rejects "anything that is secret and mysterious," along with all "mystery-mongering."[110] His references to spiritualism[111] when discussing *prāṇa* can be seen as an attempt to relate to a spiritual movement that was then as mainstream an interest as postural yoga and mindfulness are today. Mindful of the interest in "occult" or "mystical" interests of his mainstream audiences, he argued that these interests are actually a search for the kind of yoga that can master *prāṇāyāma*.[112] But this kind of "occultism" is no invention of nineteenth-century occultists and esotericists, since Vivekananda's views of the subtle force of *prāṇa* have their first literary witnesses in the ancient teachings of the Upaniṣads.[113] His genius lay in his ability to form a bridgehead between two diverse civilizations on the basis of spiritual realities that had been all but forgotten in Western societies, where "mysticism" and "occultism" are often used as derogatory names for spiritual views that transgress the boundaries of the exclusivistic reductionistic materialism and fetishization of conventional experience—including conventional religiosity—that pervasively shape the mindset of the contemporary scientific and academic establishments.

Swami Vivekananda, who also possessed an excellent Western education along with traditional Hindu learning, found numerous points of contact with his audience, including references to Kant and Mill.[114] And his musings about science and consciousness seem quite modern in tone (even when advances in knowledge of the brain since then are accounted for), and his views would be consonant with those recently expressed by neuroscientist and popular spirituality and atheism writer Sam Harris.[115] As for Swami Vivekananda's approach to the *Yoga Sūtra* in his famous and widely read *Rāja-Yoga*, it blends the old tradition in India of commentaries consisting of what Joseph Alter characterizes as "*ṭīkā* glosses" and "the *vṛtti* style of nonargumentative redaction" with "the well-defined 'tertiary' and synthetic literature" about the *Yoga Sūtra* that came into existence in the late nineteenth century and its precedents in the commentaries of such earlier figures as Vijñānabhikṣu, Nārāyaṇ Tīrtha, and al-Bīrunī.[116] Swami Vivekananda's commentary is more traditional than many other influential English-language commentaries published since 1896, including, for example, I. K. Taimni's, yet it is not at all idiosyncratic, esoteric, or occultic.[117] Not only does Swami Vivekananda refer to the commentarial tradition ("the commentator," i.e., Vyāsa[118]), but he also distinguished between what he calls "the Patanjali Yoga Philosophy"[119] and the teachings of "later yogis"[120] when, for example, he discusses the notions of *prāṇa* and *prāṇāyāma*, which, as he notes, are not yet so developed in the *Yoga Sūtra* as they would be in later yoga traditions.[121] It thus seems to be a libel to assume that the Swami was, as White thinks, a "dilettante" who took his ideas about "classical yoga" from Madame Blavatsky.[122] This makes for a cutting witticism, but it does not seem to be true to Swamiji's commentary.

Mostly, Vivekananda's commentary expounds traditional Hindu philosophy[123] in the facile manner of a master communicator between two civilizations that were only then through him just beginning to communicate as equals. (It seems condescending to assume that traditional ideas such as these must, somehow, be "New Age" borrowings by Vivekananda as he tries to create his own esoteric "*Naturphilosophie*,"[124] as De Michelis suggests.) That he was not at all condescending to his audience or merely pandering to the interest of marginal groups in esotericism and occultism is clear from the fact that he presented new ideas to a mass (not a scholarly) audience when he used such Sanskrit expressions as *prāṇa*,[125] *iḍā*, *piṅgalā*, *suṣumnā*,[126] and *kuṇḍalinī*,[127] which must have been a sensation, challenge, and aspirational summons to his readers long before the publication of Sir John Woodroffe's *The Serpent Power* in 1919.[128] Reading the commentary today—which can easily stand alongside many other nontechnical but faithful interpretations—it is easy for one inclined toward spirituality to find oneself inspired by Swami Vivekananda to take up the practice of concentration and *prāṇāyāma*.[129] If this is so after a gap of more than a century, after so many other figures have come from India to deepen global knowledge of India's yogic traditions by building upon the foundation laid by the swami,[130] then it is easy to understand the wide appeal of his teachings and personality at the end of the nineteenth century. Despite De Michelis's extended ad hominem that represents the swami as servicing his "cultic milieu," he appealed in his day to the upper echelons of polite culture and to the mainstream hunger for a broad and tolerant religious teaching. There was likely no message more electrifying in 1893 than his declaration that it is "a standing libel on human nature" to call human beings sinners.[131] It is no wonder that he became an overnight superstar in the age of the telegraph, the railroad, and newspapers.[132]

I have come away from a reading of Swami Vivekananda's *Rāja-Yoga* with a sense that it remains a sound and sure guide to the practice of inner yoga, which, in his view, is "in the main mental," while allowing that "part of the practice is physical."[133] Despite exaggerations about his suppressing or rejecting *haṭha yoga*,[134] Swami Vivekananda allowed that it can help people to remain healthy and to live long lives, which is essential to attaining the goal of *rāja yoga*.[135] He also recommended some of its minor practices as well, such as drinking cool water through the nose (*neti kriyā*) to avoid headaches.[136] Not only that, but, prior to his first journey to the West, he went through a period of wanting to learn *haṭha yoga* from a well-known *haṭha yogi*, but was dissuaded from this path by three visions from his deceased guru, Sri Ramakrishna.[137] To Singleton's apparently devastating question, "How could Vivekananda see fit to omit treatment of [*āsana* and *haṭha yoga*] in his new synthesis?" there is an easy answer: Swami Vivekananda could do so because he was a *rāja yogi* and a disciple of Sri Ramakrishna.

In my mind, the ultimate extreme of Orientalism is not a Western ashram led by initiated disciples of an Indian teacher who came to the West to share Hinduism with non-Indians. After all, as Jeffery Long, a leading non-Indian Hindu and South Asianist replies to people who question his bona fides as a non-Indian Hindu: "I am not crashing this party. I was invited by Swami Vivekananda."[138] Nor is the specter of Orientalism most prevalent at a strip-mall yoga studio that stresses the health and therapeutic benefits of yoga even while opening classes with the respectful intonation of *praṇava* and offering teacher-training programs that focus on the *Yoga Sūtra* and the *Bhagavad Gītā*. After all, this approach was founded by Indians in India (e.g., Swami Kuvalayananda,[139] Shri Yogendra,[140] Tirumalai Krishnamacarya,[141] and B. K. S Iyengar) and numerous Indian swamis have come in the last century and a quarter from India to teach countless non-Hindus to live by these and many other Hindu scriptures.

The ultimate instance of a demeaning Orientalism, in my mind, is the current cadre of contemporary global-yoga-bashing Western and Westernized academics, invariably trained in the arch-Orientalist and arch-colonialist discipline of Indology, or South Asian studies, and allied modernist disciplines such as anthropology, critical theory, and religious studies, who themselves as often as not are neither adherents nor practitioners of what they study, but who insist on subjecting India's religious heritage to sometimes savage and acerbic scrutiny through the lenses of a countless array of ever-shifting modern and postmodern Western ideological and "critical" perspectives.

As anthropologists (along with theologians and religion scholars) who are rehabilitating the concept of syncretism in the study of living cultures have begun to argue,[142] supposedly pure cultural forms are reifications of what is the always fluid syncretistic context within which all religious traditions are constantly reshaping themselves in relation to emergent threats and opportunities. On this approach, Swami Vivekananda can be viewed as a reformer of the yoga traditions of India, which had in the centuries before his birth become dominated by power-seeking forms of *bubhukṣu* yoga and colonial prejudices against yogis.[143] He was part of an emerging stream of Indian and European reevaluations of yoga that sought to reinstate the then-eclipsed styles of meditative and enlightenment-oriented *mumukṣu* yoga[144] in a context in which yoga had become associated in the Western imagination with the feats of fakirs and the acrobaticism of Indian contortionists.[145] That yoga is now so popular on the global stage is testimony less to modern yoga's "radical innovation and experimentation"[146]—which may trouble the historian but not the student of the living forms of the religious life—than to the recovery of profoundly attractive and easily exportable aspects of the ancient yoga traditions of India that for too long had been upstaged by more dramatic and perhaps even sinister styles of yoga.

Perhaps, then, a better approach to the academic study of yoga is to use the word *yoga* to name its many diverse expressions, including modern innovations, as Christopher Key Chapple does in the closing pages of *Yoga and the Luminous*,[147] which fuses the stances of the Western academic scholar of yoga and the dedicated yoga practitioner. At the beginning of a short but comprehensive survey of the varieties of contemporary, internationalized yoga over the last almost two centuries, Chapple articulates a principle that is not only true to the spirit of yoga but one that might helpfully guide contemporary academic, practitioner, and popular evaluations of yoga: "Yoga, throughout its history, has exhibited both flexibility and adaptability."[148] Rather than seeing the various uses of the word *yoga* as homonyms, as Singleton suggests,[149] we might see, as Jean Varenne suggested in an earlier decade, the names of the many varieties of yoga as adjectives that qualify *rāja yoga*, which is the "total yoga."[150] According to Varenne, "There is only one yoga," which is "treated unanimously in the tradition as the valid reference" of the word *yoga*.[151] This yoga, which in Varenne's view, is "the supreme form of the discipline, the immutable structure into which all the specific methods favored by any particular yoga school must be inserted," is the yoga that has been given classic expression in the *Yoga Sūtra*, the *Bhagavad Gītā*, the Upaniṣads, and, with specialist variations, in the Tantras, *the Haṭhapradīpikā, the Gheraṇḍa Saṃhitā* and other related texts.[152] As support for Varenne's "synthetic view" of yoga,[153] we might consider the measured words of Barbara Stoler Miller, author of one of the best English translations of the *Yoga Sūtra*: "Through the centuries since its composition, [the *Yoga Sūtra*] has been reinterpreted to meet the needs of widely divergent schools of Indian yoga, for which it remains an essential text."[154]

To these traditional schools of yoga, Stephen Phillips, philosopher, South Asianist, and yoga practitioner, would likely add the yoga studios where he has taken classes and his numerous yoga-studio teachers, since for these teachers and the new global institution of the yoga studio, the *Yoga Sūtra* has become a central canonical sacred text.[155] His respect for yoga-studio yoga and his yoga-studio teachers presents a welcome corrective to the more usual snide and clichéd dismissals by many journalists and academics.

In my mind, this approach, which allows free rein to the nonexclusive character of yoga—what Phillips calls the "Yoga umbrella"[156] and what Carol Horton characterizes as "yoga's easy hybridity"[157]—is in accord with the first instruction of yoga, which is *ahiṃsā*, or nonviolence.[158] It is also an expression, with salutary global consequences for almost two centuries now—if we take Thoreau as the first modern Western *yogi*—of the nondual pluralism that is one of the main strands of the Vedic view of life. *Ekaṃ sat viprā bahudhā vadanti* proclaimed an ancient Indian *ṛṣi*, and in the same spirit, we should accept the many ways (*bahudhā*) inspired teachers (*viprāḥ*) express (*vadanti*) yoga as integral expressions of the one reality (*ekaṃ sat)* that sources, environs, and resumes all that was, is, and will be.

This famous expression exemplifies the nonexclusive character of many, if not all, expressions of Hinduism, and it has its counterpart in the *Yoga-Sūtra*, which concludes a section on cultivating mental steadiness by stating that steadiness of mind may be cultivated through "meditation upon anything of one's inclination" (YS 1.39 Bryant). In a lucid response to the general academic tendency of dismissing contemporary global yoga along with its devotion to the *Yoga-Sūtra* and the practice of *āsana*, Edwin F. Bryant applies the broadmindedness of this aphorism to this not-always charitably pursued critique. Rather than seeing the modern focus upon *āsana* as aimless innovation, Bryant views it as a way of promoting the ideals of meditational yoga that "might be best suited" for "many people in the West."[159] In the spirit of Patañjali's methodological tolerance, the modern focus on *āsana* can thus be seen as a "unique contribution" to the history of *pātañjala yoga*, one that increases "the participational possibilities" of this kind of yoga "in a present mainstream context."[160]

Academic opinion may eventually rebalance itself and come to see that Swami Vivekananda, along with most of the other leading transmitters of yoga to West such as Paramahansa Yogananda, Swami Sivananda, Swami Vishnudevananda, Swami Satchidananda, B. K. S. Iyengar, Indira Devi, and Sri Pattabhi Jois, was clearly correct in trying to reposition old traditions of meditational and postural yoga in the West that had become occluded in the preceding centuries in India by the sort of power- and enjoyment-oriented "sinister" yoga celebrated by White.[161] This seems to have been a wise choice, not only because it gave new life to an enlightenment-oriented type of yoga, but also because it succeeded in presenting to the world a wholesome, health-giving, and spiritually elevated yoga, one that has contributed to the overcoming of the disrepute of yoga and *yogis* in village India and among the old Orientalists and early missionaries, whose one-sided view of yoga Swami Vivekananda almost singlehandedly undermined.

And, given the common experience, which Bryant also rightly notes,[162] that the practice of any of the limbs of *pātañjala yoga* tends to lead to steadiness and luminosity of mind, the widespread worry that global yoga will ultimately cheapen or hijack yoga[163] is likely unfounded. It is more likely that the practice of *āsana*, now globally prevalent for the first time in the history of yoga, will serve as the first stage in the global spread of other yogic values such as nonviolence and the cultivation of a bright and simplified awareness suitable to the kind of depth spirituality that for too long has been all but absent in societies dominated by the gaze of reductionistic science and the mentally flattening effects of historicism, exclusivist religious and secular ideologies, frantic production and consumerism, and the hyper-digitization of the lifespace.

Instead, then, of uncritically acceding to the current scholarly trend of debunking the *Yoga-Sūtras* as a legitimate text for use as a practice manual in contemporary global yoga, we might see it as a text that is once again finding an appropriate readership, as it did earlier in its Indian career when its appearance helped solidify yoga as one of the six classical *darśanas*, or philosophies, of Hindu orthodoxy[164] and in its later period of international use a millennium ago when it was commented upon in Arabic and Old Javanese and was read in Kashmir, Central Asia, and Indonesia.[165]

Global yoga is thus recapturing long-neglected aspects of the *pātañjala yoga* traditions, such as its *śramaṇic, mumukṣu*, non-tantric stances and its optional, nonstandard theism. In the current global appropriation of Asian spiritualities, the many schools of Buddhism and Hinduism, along with various expressions of classic Chinese spirituality, syncretistically interact, with the result that many people practicing yoga today are far more comfortable or at least somewhat conversant with Buddhist and nontheistic perspectives. For many such practitioners, *śramaṇic* Buddhist themes and the optional theism of the *Yoga Sūtra* (apart from the prolixity of its theistic commentators[166]) will be readily accepted, perhaps even more than the Hindu *devatās* by many practitioners of global yoga. For many practitioners today, globalized Buddhism and yoga provide a satisfying alternative spirituality to theistic and book-based religions, a role that the *śramaṇic* traditions also played in ancient India.

Moreover, the *Yoga Sūtra* provides a clear and succinct eightfold path from false consciousness to full enlightenment, along with many ancillary practices. The yogic path as iconically laid out in the *Yoga Sūtr*a is metaphysically underdetermined and can be associated with theistic, dualistic, nondual, or scientific metaphysical frameworks, as well as with various Hindu, Buddhist, Jain, and now Christian, Jewish, and Western metaphysical viewpoints. It is this fluidic and dazzling versatility *of pātañjala yoga* and not mere sleight of hand on the part of the founders of global yoga that accounts for the centrality of the *Yoga-Sūtra* to the global yoga movement, a view that is ratified by Ian Whicher, who views the *Yoga Sūtra* as "one of *the* seminal texts on yogic technique" in Indian philosophy and as "one of the most influential spiritual guides in Hinduism," which, because of its influence on contemporary global yoga, is "one of India's finest contributions to modern/postmodern struggle for self-definition, moral integrity, and spiritual renewal."[167]

Now, after this historical detour, we can get down to the business of charting the yogic and contemplative itinerary of the *Yoga Sūtra*.

The Contemplative Path of the Yoga Sūtra

Concentrative Meditation in the Yoga Sūtra *and the* Visuddhimagga

Since the *Visuddhimagga* and the *Yoga Sūtra* are both products of India's ancient yogic spiritual culture, they share numerous features. Most striking—and central to our comparative work in this volume—is the schematic description of the stages of concentrative, or absorptive, meditation that each contemplative manual, with notable differences, describes. What we find in each of these texts, whether in the *samatha-bhāvanā* of the *Visuddhimagga* or in the *saṃyama* of the *Yoga Sūtra*, are influential codifications of the stages of concentrative meditation, or *dhyāna*,[168] which, according to Vedic scholar Jeanine Miller, has been "the crux of yoga" since the Ṛgveda.[169]

My procedure in this chapter will be the same as in the last chapter. There I looked to the *Visuddhimagga* for detailed information about the distinctive stages of the contemplative itinerary of concentrative meditation in Theravāda Buddhism. Here, I will look to the *Yoga Sūtra* for more succinct, but precise, descriptions of its distinctive but related yogic itinerary. To accomplish this, I will first sketch the contemplative arc of the *Yoga Sūtra*, which will show where the stages of *saṃyama* fit in the larger training context of the *Yoga Sūtra*. Then, I will relate these meditative landmarks to the contemplative universals of common yogic-mystical itinerary, which answers to the larger, comparative purpose of this book.

The Training Context of the Yoga Sūtra

Because the traditional Indian genre of the *sūtra* favors conciseness at the expense of narrative, the *Yoga Sūtra* may seem abstract and lacking in narrative drama in comparison to the *Visuddhimagga*. Yet, the drama of the journey that the *Yoga Sūtra* calmly, expertly, and audaciously charts is not obscured by its technical and sometimes remote façade. The ancient and modern appeal of the *Yoga Sūtra*, both in India and far beyond its borders, is testimony to its capacity to inspire and to guide its students in awakening from the hardships of dissipated, frayed, and distracted awareness.[170] To those who have obeyed this call and placed themselves on the way to yoga, or "union," the *Yoga Sūtra* offers precise insights into the cognitive and psychological sources of the disquiet that seeps into even our best moments. For, beyond providing us with a merely technical or academic knowledge of our predicament, the *Yoga Sūtra* offers a wide and extensive collection of coordinated practices for overcoming the distracted mind.[171]

This ensemble of coordinated practices is detailed concisely in the four *pādas*, or chapters, of the *Yoga Sūtra*, each of which focuses on a main theme in a logically conceived structure that, first, analyzes the basic theory of yoga, second, indicates how to apply the theory in practice, third, catalogs the diverse outcomes of the practice, and, fourth, offers a picture of the final outcome of the practice of yoga. Perhaps a more detailed exploration of some of the major themes of each of these chapters will suggest the scope of Patañjali's spiritual ambition and demonstrate his competence to lead the novice yogi to the end of the yogic path.

A Summary of the Four Chapters of the Yoga Sūtra The first chapter, aptly named *samādhi-pāda*, or "Chapter on Recollectedness," expresses the yogic itinerary tersely as a movement that rises from a mind encaged by its habitual mental patterns (*citta-vṛttis*, YS 1.2) to the stillness of a purified, detached, and fully concentrated mind, which abides in the knowledge of immaterial witnessing awareness (*puruṣa-khyāti*, 1.16). The sublime austerity of this arc of mental disengagement from absorption in the gross and subtle elements of nature (*prakṛti*) is broken and graciously humanized by the detailing of numerous practices that can aid the yogi whose commitment to practice may be weak, medium, or strong (YS 1.22) in achieving concentrated stillness of the mind. This ensemble of coordinated practices, like the multiple teachings of the Buddha, begins with ethical training without which no progress in the spiritual life is possible. (Thus, the first chapter of the *Visuddhimagga*, in accordance with Buddhism's "Three Trainings" [*tisikkhā*], is concerned with *sīla*, or "virtue.") Except for the possibility that a spiritually ripe novice might attain *kaivalya* (extrication) merely by hearing the seed teaching of the *Yoga Sūtra* that "yoga is the overcoming of habitual mental patterns" (*yogaś citta-vṛtti-nirodhaḥ*, YS 1.2), the first training suggestion for achieving this overcoming of mental patterns is to cultivate *abhyāsa* (ongoing practice) and *vairāgya* (disinvolvement), or a moderate but uninterrupted asceticism (YS 1.12).[172]

Essential as this foundation is, caring, conscientious, and dispassionate behavior is only the threshold of the spiritual life, and to further develop it Patañjali suggests nine other training techniques[173] in this *pāda* that make the mind supple and sufficiently fit to begin the practice of concentration, meditation, and recollectedness (*dhāraṇā*, *dhyāna*, and *samādhi*, YS 1.32, 39). Each of these nine training methods cultivates the key yogic practice of gathering the mind together into single-pointed focus, which is the portal into the subtler realms of *prakṛti*, or the "primal matrix,"[174] and ultimate reunion with *puruṣa*, or "pristine, nonobjective witnessing awareness." (The first method, the cultivation of *abhyāsa* and *vairāgya*, can be seen as preparation for the nine focusing, concentrative practices recommended in this chapter.) The default methodological pluralism of the *Yoga Sūtra* is on display here (*yathābhimata*, "as one likes," YS 1.39), when it offers a pleasing variety of practices that appeal to people of varying temperaments (YS 1.12, 23, 28, 32-39; 32 and 39 are essentially the same technique).

Already, even without moving on to the coming chapters, Patañjali has described almost the whole yogic itinerary, and has outlined a complete path for the serious (*tīvra*, YS 1.21) student, and even touched upon the subtle teaching about *samādhi* (recollectedness) and the *jhāna*-like *samāpattis* (unifications[175]) at the end of this chapter (YS 1.41-51; this topic is taken up again in *pādas* three and four, and I will unpack it later in this chapter). It is sufficient now merely to say that the practice of the yogic unification of the otherwise distracted mind leads to the uncovering of the natural luminosity of the pristine, nonobjective awareness of the immaterial inner witness (*puruṣa*, YS 1.47), which is accompanied by deep insight into the patterns that unfold in the visible and invisible worlds (YS 1.48). Far beyond the scope at this point of the conceptualities of philosophy, the way forward (YS 1.50) now opens out into the penultimate stage, or degree, of *samādhi* (*nirbīja-samādhi*, or "de-seeded recollectedness," YS 1.51). This is the jumping-off point (YS 1.51) for the now virtually dismantled and packed-up mind (*citta*) into the infinite waters of *kaivalya*, which is the reunion of *puruṣa* with itself after its long sojourn in the nurseries, schools, prisons, hospitals, workhouses, theaters, libraries, temples, pilgrimage sites, and monasteries of *prakṛti*, the primal matrix (YS 2.18, 21, 22, 4.32).

Chapter 2, as the name *sādhana-pāda*, or "Chapter on Practice," suggests, moves from theory, which is the central nerve of the first *pāda*, to the laying out of a practical program of action (*sādhana*) that promotes the progressive concentration and subtilization[176] of the mind. Expressive of its profound pluralism, which it shares with the indigenous religious traditions of India, the *Yoga Sūtra* begins this *pāda* by offering a simplified, preliminary[177] yoga practice (*kriyā yoga*) with just three components: self-tempering (*tapas*), mantra chanting and intensive scriptural study (*svādhyāya*),[178] and submission to Īśvara (*īśvara-praṇidhāna*), the timeless, pure, all-knowing teacher of ancient teachers (YS 2.1, 1.23-27, 1.45). (These three practices are repeated later in this chapter, where they are placed within the context of the five *niyamas*, or "minor vows," which make up the second limb of Patañjali's *aṣṭāṅgayoga*, or "Eight-Part Yoga," [2.32, 43-45]).

Similarly to the first chapter, the second *pāda* of the *Yoga Sūtra* offers much in the way of practical psychological advice about how to pursue a gentle asceticism[179] that begins to make the mind ready for meditation (YS 2.10), *samādhi*, and direct perception of the immaterial witnessing awareness (*puruṣa*, 2.24). Yet, even in this practical chapter, theory is never far from mind, particularly when it can give practice a strong undergirding, as when Patañjali points out that the root of all our difficulties (*kleśa*) is misknowledge (*avidyā*, YS 2.4), which is the mistake of seeing our timeless, incandescent, and well-advantaged self as temporary, unillumined, and thwarted (YS 2.5). Not long after giving this diagnosis, Patañjali once again foreshadows the ultimate aim of yoga, *kaivalya*, and, in a sentence as sharp as the edge of a razor (YS 2.26), he states that the one certain remedy (*upāya*) for our misknowledge is ongoing *viveka*, which names a spiritually crucial process of mental sifting and sorting[180] that I call "clarification" and that calls to mind the process of removing solids from a liquid. *Viveka* is the process through which the yogi removes the matter of *prakṛti* from *puruṣa* by carefully sorting through the transformations of *prakṛti* and sifting *puruṣa* out of the obscuring mental fluctuations of *prakṛti*.

But this is a steep path, and to ask all but the rarest and most ripe of novices who awaken merely by hearing this teaching about *viveka* to follow it is to ask for what is almost impossible. So, having now reminded his hearers of the heights that the yogi seeks, Patañjali is ready to lay out his full yogic program for developing the *viveka* that cuts through misknowledge and penetrates into the trackless expanse of *kaivalya*.

Preeminent among the numerous techniques that Patañjali introduces in the *Yoga Sūtra* is a series of eight progressively ordered practices, or *sādhanas*,[181] that stand out as iconic in traditional and global yoga. As—dare we still say it?—classically articulated in the *Yoga Sūtra*, Patañjali's Eight-Part Yoga (*aṣṭāṅgayoga*) is designed to move the novice yogi from dissipation in *prakṛti* to the integrated fullness of those who have attained full enlightenment even while still living in the body.[182] In a *sūtra*

(YS 2.29) that is almost as well-known in global yoga today as the iconic second *sūtra* of the first *pāda*, Patañjali tersely defines the eight *sādhanas*, or practices, of *pātañjala yoga* as major guidelines (*yama*), minor guidelines (*niyama*),[183] meditative sitting (*āsana*), controlled breathing (*prāṇāyāma*), sense withdrawal (*pratyāhāra*), concentration (*dhāraṇā*), meditation (*dhyāna*), and recollectedness (*samādhi*).

Reflecting the foundational importance of ethical behavior and asceticism in comprehensive yoga training, Patañjali initiates his Eight-Part Yoga with a code of ten ascetical and ethical prescriptions, or the *yamas* and the *niyamas*. The first *sādhana* of Eight-Part Yoga includes the five *yamas*, or major guidelines (YS 2.30-31), which are nonnegotiable and indispensable for the yogi who is fully committed to the attainment of extrication (*kaivalya*) from the primal matrix (*prakṛti*). These guidelines include nonviolence, truthfulness, not taking what is not one's own, celibacy, and greedlessness. These five guidelines for the practice of liberative yoga are of such foundational importance that Patañjali bundles them together into what he calls "the Great Commitment" (*mahāvrata*) and notes that it has global validity independent of personal circumstances. Of less social significance,[184] but crucial to the purification of the consciousness of the individual yogi, are the five minor guidelines (*niyamas*) of the second *sādhana* of Eight-Part Yoga, which include self-purification,[185] serenity, and the three practices of preliminary yoga (*kriyā yoga*) recommended in YS 2.1: self-tempering, mantra chanting and intensive scriptural study, and submission to Īśvara (YS 2.32). Then follow a series of epigrammatic sentences or maxims that encapsulate generations of practical wisdom for leading the gentle, self-composed, and contemplative yogic lifestyle that is consistent with the major and minor guidelines (YS 2.33-45).

In preparation for the inner turn and ascent to our truest self, Patañjali now teaches us to take a still (*sthira*) and relaxed (*sukha*) seat (*āsana*) (YS 2.46) and to explore our breath (YS 2.49-50). Our realizations while engaged in the third (*āsana*) and fourth (*prāṇāyāma*) *sādhanas* of Eight-Part Yoga initiate us into a subtle realm that stretches beyond our physical forms even as it encircles them (YS 2.50-52), These realizations ready us finally for meditation (*dhyāna*, YS 2.53).

Now our karma begins to weaken and the light of own natural goodness, or *sattva*,[186] begins to penetrate our minds, whose stillness correlates precisely with the long and subtle breathing that results from training in *prāṇāyāma* (and the cultivation of which precludes following an elaborate regime of physically complex *āsanas*, thus explaining perhaps their absence from the *Yoga Sūtra*[187]). In this light, we begin to awaken to a luminous and sublime inner world that lies hidden and unsuspected behind the veil of ordinary perception (*prakāśa-āvaraṇa*).[188] Almost of its own accord now, the reports of the senses become of less interest to us, and we find ourselves engaged in the fifth *sādhana* of Eight-Part Yoga, which is evocatively named *pratyāhāra*, or the ingathering of the senses into the mind (YS 2.54). In this *sādhana*, the aspirant draws the mind away from the presentations of the senses, just as bees follow the queen bee in its movements,[189] and focuses instead on the inner world of the mind itself until the senses come fully within the command of the yogi (YS 2.55). Then, in a move that is at first perplexing at this moment of high drama in the contemplative journey, Patañjali suddenly interrupts his outlining of the stages of Eight-Part Yoga by inserting a chapter break instead of finishing his charting of the remaining and conclusive practices of Eight-Part Yoga.

Given the rhetorical plainness of the *Yoga Sūtra*, this is a dramatic move, and it has certainly been staged to make a point, one that is signaled in the name of this third chapter, *vibhūti-pāda*, which can be translated as the "Chapter on Sublime Powers." Although, as Bryant points out,[190] the question of the odd division of chapters at this point has not been addressed by the traditional commentators, my own view (and one also stated by Bryant[191]) is that, on the one hand, this chapter division is meant to highlight the difference between the first five outer practices (*bahiraṅga*) and the last three inner practices (*antaraṅga*) of the eight *sādhanas* of Eight-Part Yoga (YS 3.7.8). On the other hand, this division (also noted by Bryant[192]) suggests that *saṃyama*, or the simultaneous practice of concentration (*dhāraṇā*), meditation (*dhyāna*), and recollectedness (*samādhi*), which are the sixth, seventh, and eight *sādhanas* of Eight-Part Yoga, produces numerous *vibhūtis*[193] (sublime capabilities) and *siddhis* (extraordinary capabilities, YS 3.37). Although the *Yoga Sūtra* catalogs an extraordinary array of these powers (YS 3.16-49), they are subordinate to and perhaps even a danger (YS 3.37, 51) to the attaining of the supreme fruit of the combined practice of these three *sādhanas*, which is to attain extrication (*kaivalya*) from the primal matrix (*prakṛti*, YS 3.55). Patañjali's real concern is the cultivation of the triad of progressively deepening concentrative practices of concentration, meditation, and recollectedness so that the mind can overcome itself through a self-initiated process of self-evaporation, subtilization, or reabsorption into its primordial matrix, or *prakṛti*.

This reference to *kaivalya* signals the denouement of both the *Yoga Sūtra* and of the whole yogic itinerary itself in the fourth and final chapter, which is aptly named *kaivalya-pāda*, or the "Chapter on Extrication." Before coming to its finale, however, the *Yoga Sūtra* takes a technical[194] turn into such matters as karma, the ability of the accomplished yogi to generate multiple bodies, the nature of time, and the objectivity of the extramental world, all of which make this section of the *Yoga Sūtra* seem inconsistent with the otherwise pragmatic approach taken by Patañjali elsewhere in this practice manual. Indeed, one suspects that this is the least read and least understood part of the *Yoga Sūtra*, even among avid yogis.

Yet, even here Patañjali raises issues immediately relevant to the experience of the ardent yogi. While discussing, for example, the workings of karma (action), or the pan-Indic principle of causation, as well as the consequences of one's actions, Patañjali makes the startling claim that, unlike other people's karma, the karma of the yogi is neither white nor black, that is to say, it is neither good nor bad (YS 4.7). At first glance, this may seem like an antinomian (*pratiloma*, or *parāvṛtti*[195]) assertion, granting license to bad behavior by yogic practitioners by drawing an equivalence between good and bad actions. But, given the foundational stress that Patañjali lays upon the moral cultivation of the yoga practitioner, this interpretation can be ruled out. What this *sūtra* seems to be describing is the exalted state of the accomplished yogi who has renounced self-regarding actions of all kinds and who is, as a result, no more on the receiving end than on the giving end of good or bad karma. This, of course, is an attribute of the state of *kaivalya*, which is portrayed in the last *sūtra* of the

Yoga Sūtra as the final delinking of the *puruṣa* from the *guṇas* (the three combining factors of *prakṛti*, or the primal matrix), at which point, the *guṇas* and *puruṣa* go their own ways,[196] since the purpose of *prakṛti* as the temporary reflective mirror of *puruṣa* (2.18, 4.24, 4.32, 4.34, 4.55) has been fulfilled in the perfected yogi's now completed journey away from dispersion in the realm of *prakṛti*, with its mediated forms of consciousness, toward the utterly unencumbered force of awareness (*citi-śakti*, YS 4.34) native to the *puruṣa*, or pristine, nonobjective witnessing awareness, which is our deepest, original, truest, and final identity.[197]

This, in summary, is the momentous journey proposed to the novice yogi by Patañjali in the *Yoga Sūtra*. In the next section, we will focus on the concentrative path through which the mind reabsorbs itself into its source, of the primal matrix (*prakṛti*).

Pātañjalian Meditative Landmarks and the Common Yogic-Mystical Itinerary

Now, after surveying the whole sweep of the yogic path as envisioned by Patañjali, we are better positioned to turn to the main concern of this chapter, which is identifying the meditative landmarks specific to Patañjali's yogic itinerary and linking them to the contemplative universals of the common yogic-mystical itinerary, which is witnessed to by the other contemplative traditions under study here, as well as by contemplative neuroscience. As in the last chapter, I reproduce below two of the columns from the full chart that was given in an earlier chapter, which shows what I see as religious or contemplative universals on the left and their Pātañjalian expressions as meditative landmarks on the right:

Figure 3 From the Common Yogic-Mystical Itinerary

Contemplative Universals and Their Common Functions	**Meditative Landmarks in Pātañjala Yoga**
convergence: mind focuses on the meditation object	**dhāraṇā** (concentration)
coalescence: mind fixes on or locks in on the meditation object	**dhyāna** (meditation)
simplification: mind simplifies itself factor by factor	**saṃprajñāta-samādhi** (mediated recollectedness) ***generating factors***: **vitarka, vicāra, ānanda, asmitā** (concrete-reflection recollectedness, abstract-reflection recollectedness, delightful recollectedness, mere self-awareness recollectedness)
quiescence: mind is stilled	**asaṃprajñāta-samādhi** (unmediated recollectedness) dharmamegha-samādhi (recollectedness in the inner raincloud of beatitude)
beatitude: mind is transcended	**kaivalya** (extrication): Before physical death: **jīvanmukti** After physical death: **videhamukti**

I will concentrate in the coming pages on the last three of the eight *sādhanas* of *pātañjala yoga*: *dhāraṇā*, *dhyāna*, and *samādhi* (the reader may consult the studies referenced in the bibliography for discussion of the remaining *sādhanas*). Taken together, they form a unified group of concentrative practices that the *Yoga Sūtra* calls *saṃyama* (YS 3.4). This term can be translated dryly as "restraint," but it also connotes the drawing of the mind together into the progressively deeper stages of concentration that we will explore in the next section, as well as the act of tying up one's hair in a knot over the head,[198] which is an old practice and sign of the yogi and a reminder of Śiva, the archetypal yogi. As a name for the last three specifically concentrative, inner *sādhanas* of *pātañjala yoga*, *saṃyama* corresponds to the concept of *samādhi* (or *samatha-bhāvanā*) in the *Visuddhimagga*, where the term *samādhi* has a more general use than in the *Yoga Sūtra* as the name of the whole path of concentration and its division into the *jhānas*, as well as a more limited use as part of compounds that name the threshold of concentration (access concentration, or *upacāra-samādhi*) and achieved concentration (recollectedness concentration, or *appanā-samādhi*). *Samādhi* has a narrower application in the *Yoga Sūtra*, where it stands for achieved concentration instead of the practices leading up to it. In the common yogic-mystical itinerary that I see as underlying the higher ranges of the contemplative path wherever it occurs and that is also engraved in the brain, I follow the lead of the *Yoga-Sūtra*, and divide the arc of concentrative intensification into three contemplative universals of *convergence*, *coalescence*, and *simplification*. The sequential and progressively focused and simplified stages of concentration are expressed in *pātañjala yoga* by the meditative landmarks of *dhāraṇā*, *dhyāna*, and (*saṃprajñāta*) *samādhi*. (These are succeeded by the contemplative universal of *quiescence* and its *pātañjalian* landmark, *asaṃprajñāta-samādhi*, and the contemplative universal of *beatitude* and its *pātañjalian* landmark, *kaivalya*, both of which will be discussed in concluding sections of this chapter).

Convergence: Focusing on the Meditation Object

The Sanskrit name of the *pātañjalian* meditative landmark of *dhāraṇā* is generally translated as "concentration." The root of *dhāraṇā* (√*dhṛ*) suggests, among many other meanings, the practice of calling something to mind. As a yogic practice, this involves repeatedly returning wandering attention to a meditation object, of which Vyāsa gives a list of evocative examples.[199] *Dhāraṇā* is the repeated effort of focusing the internally withdrawn (*pratyāhāra*) and purified attention upon the meditation object, yet it lacks, as we will see, the episodic attentional fixity that characterizes *dhyāna* and the extended fixity and mental simplification (*pratiprasava*) that characterize the ascending degrees of (*saṃprajñāta*) *samādhi*. Strictly speaking, *dhāraṇā* is pre-yogic because it is preparatory to the fixity of mind on the meditation object, which is essential to *samādhi* and which first dawns in *dhyāna*, as we will see. This, we might recall, is consistent with Vyāsa's definition of yoga as *samādhi*.[200]

As an expression of the contemplative universal of convergence, the meditative landmark of *dhāraṇā* can be compared with the meditative landmarks of the "training sign" (*parikamma-nimitta*) and the "learning sign" (*uggaha-nimitta*) in Theravāda Buddhism and to active recollection (*recueillement actif*) in Catholic mystical theology, all of which require repeated efforts or returning to the mediation object in order to overcome distraction.

Coalescence: Fixing on or Locking the Mind in on the Meditation Object

The *Yoga-Sūtra* offers a succinct and experientially verifiable description of the meditative landmark of *dhyāna* (concentration) as the "locking in there (in *dhāraṇā*, that is) on the object (of meditation)" (*tatra pratyayaikatānatā dhyānam*, YS 3.2), which arises through the deepening of concentration (*dhāraṇā*). This locking in, or fixing, of the mind (*citta*) on its object is likened by the commentators to the continuous flow of oil or honey from one container to another and is contrasted with the noncontinuous succession of drops of water, which is the characteristic pattern of *dhāraṇā*.[201] Another way of understanding the experiential progression from *dhāraṇā* to *dhyāna* is to point out that *dhāraṇā* requires repeated efforts to bring a wandering mind back to the meditation object, while *dhyāna* is a period of yogic contemplation initiated by a suddenly arising awareness that the mind is adhering to the meditation object with no further effort. This dawning of *dhyāna* may first be experienced as a short burst of intense concentration, lasting less than a second, of suddenly focused and effortless attention to the meditation object. I call these "suddenly arising mystical experiences," and they can also arise during times of intense concentration outside of fixed periods of meditation and with objects other than a formal meditation object, while listening to music, for instance, or while contemplating a scene or object of great beauty or sublimity.

As an expression of the contemplative universal of coalescence, the meditative landmark of *dhyāna* can be compared with the meditative landmarks of the "ligature of the faculties" (*la ligature des puissances*) in Catholic mystical theology, which marks the beginning of infused recollection, and with the rise of *paṭibhāga-nimitta* ("counterpart sign") in the *Visuddhimagga*, which signals the onset of *samādhi* (*upacāra-samādhi*) in the *Visuddhimagga*. (In another point of convergence between *pātañjala yoga* and *samatha-bhāvanā*, the meditative fixity of the mind first experienced in *dhāraṇā* can be seen as the initial moment of yogic *samādhi*). In each case, there is a distinctive experience of the locking in of attention on the meditation object and a spontaneous ability to retain this focus for at least a few moments without further volition. Correlations such as these are evidence, in my view, of the universal spiritual itinerary that appears with instructive regularity in the world's numerous soteriologies and is also incised on our nervous system.

Simplification: The Mind Transcends Itself Factor by Factor

Not only does the concentrative focus of the yogi simplify itself as it coalesces in the first two stages of *saṃyama*, it also further simplifies itself to the vanishing point (YS 1.50-51) in the next contemplative universal of simplification. As we have seen in the case of the *Visuddhimagga* (and in the next chapter on Catholic mystical theology as well), this is a process of moving from dispersion in mundane consciousness to contemplative unification by way of overcoming in a stepwise manner the central factors of the concentrated mind, moving identically in each of these three traditions from the most concrete to most subtle factors. In the *Yoga Sūtra*, this contemplative simplification of concentration occurs, as we will see, in the movement from "particularity" (*viśeṣa*) to "indeterminacy" (*aliṅga*), which can be taken as the essential process of *saṃprajñāta-samādhi* (YS 2.19). Before taking up this process of yogic simplification in detail, however, a few conceptual issues concerning the notion of *samādhi* call for our attention.

Distinguishing Samādhi *from* Samāpatti Apart from its undeviating aim of moving toward extrication (*kaivalya*) as the goal of yoga, training in *samādhi* (recollectedness) can be seen as the central concern of the *Yoga Sūtra*, a view shared by commentators as widely separated as Larson and Vyāsa. "Yoga is *samādhi*" (*yogaḥ samādhiḥ*) proclaims Vyāsa at the beginning of his commentary,[202] while Larson holds that "the overall focus of the entire *Yoga* Sūtra is the proper cultivation of 'concentration' (*samādhi*) in all of its modalities."[203] Yet, despite its centrality and significance, the explanation of *samādhi* in the *Yoga Sūtra* contains some notable and potentially confusing gaps, as in Patañjali's use of the related but distinct terms *samādhi* (recollectedness) and *samāpatti* (unification),[204] which has long vexed the patience of commentators. It should be pointed out at the outset that these terms are not merely synonyms[205] deployed only, as is often the case in English, to avoid repetition. Instead, Patañjali uses these two terms to highlight the distinction between, as Larson notes, concentration itself (*samādhi*) and the object of concentration (*samāpatti*).[206] Similarly, Feuerstein sees *samādhi* as the "formal category" within which *samāpatti* is the actual unfolding of *samādhi* as it occurs.[207] *Samādhi* is thus the more general term, since it names both *samādhis* with *samāpatti* and those without *samāpatti*, *as well* as those that have no mental contents whatsoever, such as *asaṃprajñāta-samādhi* and *dharmamegha-samādhi*. But the clarity of this distinction is dulled by an apparent gap[208] between *Yoga Sūtra* 1.17, with its list of four *saṃprajñāta-samādhis*, and the closing section of the second *pāda*, which seems to fumble in naming two *samāpattis* for *vitarka-samādhi* and *vicāra-samādhi*, but not for *ānanda-samādhi* and *asmitā-samādhi*, a circumstance that led, as we will see below, to the invention of four hypothetical *samāpattis*: *sānanda-samāpatti*, *nirānanda-samāpatti*, *sasmitā-samāpatti*, and *nirsasmitā-samāpatti*. This distinction would be neater if each level of *saṃprajñāta-samādhi* possessed a corresponding *samāpatti*, but they do not, and this is an apparent logical gap that has caused much concern among commentators over the centuries. My own solution is to equate *samāpatti* with the first two stages of *saṃprajñāta-samādhi*, which take concrete as well as subtle meditation objects.[209] In this, they differ from the last two stages of *saṃprajñāta-samādhi*, which move beyond such meditation objects and, instead, are two increasingly subtle types of objectless, transcendental awareness, the first of which abides in spiritual delight *(ānanda-samādhi)* and the second of which has reabsorbed (*pratiprasava*) everything else into mere self-awareness (*asmitā-samādhi*). I have summed up this solution in a *sūtra* of my own devising: only a *samādhi* that takes either a concrete or a subtle meditation object (*ālambana*) is a *samāpatti*.

Identifying the Stages of Samādhi Another source of confusion when approaching the *Yoga Sūtra* is getting clear about the number of distinctive stages or varieties of *samādhi* that appear in the Yoga Sūtra, an issue on which classical and contemporary commentators disagree. As far as I can tell, the number of distinctive *samādhis* named in the *Yoga Sūtra* range from six to ten, with seven as the choice of Bryant[210] and eight as the choice of Larson.[211] Both agree on the four *saṃprajñāta-samādhis* that Patañjali calls (without actually using the word *samādhi*) *vitarka-samādhi, vicāra-samādhi, ānanda-samādhi,* and *asmitā-samādhi* (all of which will remain untranslated for now, YS 1.17). Yet, they and all of the other commentators would accept the Pātañjalian *asaṃprajñāta-samādhi* and *dharmamegha-samādhi* (although Patañjali refers to the former *samādhi* only as "the other," or *anya*) in the *Yoga Sūtra* (1.18), even if they do not include one or the other or both of them in their final counts. Although Larson seems not to include either in his total, and Bryant seems not to include *dharmamegha-samādhi* in his count, they could, barring terminological or exegetical concerns, change their counts to ten and eight, respectively, without in any way affecting their divergent understandings of the *samādhi.*

Yet, this still leaves four *samādhis* unaccounted for in each taxonomy. Two of these can easily be accounted for by pointing out that later in the *Yoga Sūtra* (1.42-44), Patañjali subdivides *vitarka-samādhi* and *vicāra-samādhi* into positive and negative forms (while renaming them as *samāpattis*). Thus, these two *samādhis* multiply into four *samāpattis*: *savitarka-samāpatti, nirvitarka-samāpatti, savicāra-samāpatti,* and *nirvicāra-samāpatti* (oddly, there is no reference to an *ānanda-samāpatti* or an *asmitā-samāpatti* in *sūtras* 1.41-44, 46, a gap that has puzzled and tempted the commentators.[212]). We have now reached the count of seven (or eight) *samādhis* acknowledged by Bryant, which leaves us with the two acknowledged by Larson but not by Bryant.

At this point, before naming these last two *samādhis* (or *samāpattis*), it needs to be said that they do not appear in the *Yoga Sūtra* itself, but have their source, according to Larson and Bryant, in the commentary of Vācaspatimiśra,[213] which Dominik Wujastyk considers to be "the least useful early commentary."[214] These last two *samādhis* (and, in this hypothetical case, *samāpattis*) are generated by again adding prefixes to the canonical *sānanda-samāpatti* and *sasmitā-samāpatti,*[215] which turns these two *samādhis* into four *samāpattis*: *sānanda-samāpatti, nirānanda-samāpatti, sasmitā-samāpatti,* and *nirsasmitā-samāpatti.* But, in agreement with Bryant, Whicher, and Feuerstein,[216] who find no canonical basis and no basis in Vyāsa's commentary for this innovation, I also will set it to the side.

In my attempt, then, to chart the contemplative arc of *samādhi* in the next pages, I will confine myself to the eight distinctive stages of *samādhi* named by Patañjali (and I will set aside the term *samāpatti* in discussing them from this point forward, given its inconsistent application in the *Yoga Sūtra*). These include the six stages of *saṃprajñāta-samādhi*, which is made up of *savitarka-samādhi, nirvitarka-samādhi, savicāra-samādhi, nirvicāra-samādhi, ānanda-samādhi*, and *asmitā-samādhi*, along with the stages of *asaṃprajñāta-samādhi* and *dharmamegha-samādhi* (which, if taken as a synonym for *asaṃprajñāta-samādhi*, would reduce the number of *samādhis* to Bryant's seven. I will have more to say about this *samādhi* a bit later in this chapter).

There are two other sets of *samādhis* that are often brought into play when discussing *samādhi* in the *Yoga Sūtra*: *savikalpa-samādhi* and *nirvikalpa-samādhi*, neither of which seems to appear in the *Yoga Sūtra* (although *vikalpa* does appear in different contexts, YS 1.6, 1.9, 1.42). These terms, which are used widely but in varying senses in Indian philosophy,[217] seem often to be used as synonyms for *sabīja-samādhi* and *nirbīja-samādhi* as well as *saṃprajñāta-samādhi* and *asaṃprajñāta-samādhi*.[218] And, despite what I see as some logical gaps in the *Yoga Sūtra* on this point (YS 1.46, 1.51 3.8),[219] I follow many commentators in taking *sabīja-samādhi* as a synonym for *saṃprajñāta-samādhi* and *nirbīja-samādhi* as a synonym for *asaṃprajñāta-samādhi*.[220] But, since only the four *samāpattis* are characterized as *sabīja-samādhi* (YS 1.46), this seems to distinguish them from *nirbīja-samādhi*, which might then, although inconsistently perhaps,[221] include *ānanda-samādhi* and *asmitā-samādhi*, as well as *asaṃprajñāta-samādhi* and *dharmamegha-samādhi*. Or, some concentrative expressions of *ānanda* and *asmitā* might arise, one by one from *savicāra-samāpatti*.[222] Or, the conceptual discordance here between the *samādhis* and the *samāpattis*, with the resulting ambiguous place of *ānanda-samādhi* and *asmitā-samādhi*, as well as the unresolved issue of whether they are seeded or unseeded forms of *samādhi*, indicates that different conceptual schemes have only been partially synthesized in the *Yoga Sūtra*.

My own strategy here will be to blend the *samprajñāta-samādhis* and the *samāpattis* and to treat them as constituting six stages of *samprajñāta-samādhi* (which seems to be the exegetical solutions taken by commentators such as Vyāsa and Bryant[223]). I will, however, follow Feuerstein[224] and Whicher,[225] in principle, at least, in taking *nirvicāra-samāpatti* as the ultimate stage of *saṃprajñāta-samādhi*, and treat *ānanda-samādhi* and *asmitā-samādhi* as contained within *nirvicāra-samāpatti* (although I will continue to see them as *samādhis* in their own right, given their appearance in YS 1.17, and also as *samāpattis*, given that the more systematic and comprehensive notion of *samāpatti* in the *Visuddhimagga* includes the eight *jhānas* and *nirodha-samāpatti*, or, more technically, *saññāvedayitanirodha*, which has its counterpart in Vācaspatimiśra's eight *samāpattis*[226]). As issues such as this seem irresolvable, and given the practical and experimental focus of the yoga tradition, I will move beyond these issues at this point, leaving further analyses to the specialists.

To simplify matters somewhat when dealing with the apparently somewhat unorganized analysis of *samādhi* in the *Yoga Sūtra*, I offer the following chart, which will serve as my own map in the upcoming narration of the dramatic arc of the yogic journey through *samādhi* as envisioned by Patañjali:

Figure 4 The Eight Types of Samādhi in the Yoga Sūtra

0 saṃprajñāta-samādhi (YS 1.17) = sabīja-samādhi = savikalpa-samādhi
0 vitarka-samādhi
1 savitarka-samāpatti (*sabīja-samādhi*, YS 1.46)
2 nirvitarka-samāpatti (*sabīja-samādhi*, YS 1.46)
0 vicāra-samādhi
3 savicāra-samāpatti (*sabīja-samādhi*, YS 1.46)
4 nirvicāra-samāpatti (*sabīja-samādhi*, YS 1.46)
5 ānanda-samādhi (no equivalent *samāpatti* in the *Yoga Sūtra*)
6 asmitā-samādhi (no equivalent *samāpatti* in the *Yoga Sūtra*)
7 asaṃprajñāta-samādhi (YS 1.18) = nirbīja-samādhi = nirvikalpa-samādhi
8 dharmamegha-samādhi

(Note: *Saṃprajñāta-samādhi* is numbered zero here because, unlike *asaṃprajñāta-samādhi*, it arises in various forms, depending upon its seeding meditation object. Given that *dharmamegha-samādhi* seems to name the *samādhi* in which there is no danger of regress to acting under the impulsion of the *kleśas* ("deadening impulses") and karma,[227] I take it as the perfected form of *asaṃprajñāta-samādhi*, and, thus, as the eighth distinctive *samādhi* in the *Yoga Sūtra*, one that is penultimate to *kaivalya*. Although the actual word *samādhi* is not used in YS 1.17, 18, nor is *asaṃprajñāta* used in 1.18, they are clearly implied by in context.)

Progressing through the Stages of saṃprajñāta-samādhi More significant than its apparently inconsistent taxonomy of the stages of concentration is the notion of *pratiprasava* in the *Yoga Sūtra* (YS 2.10, 4.34), which can be translated as "reabsorption" or "simplification." Charts of the stages of *samādhi* and *samāpatti* will be subject to varying interpretations and disagreement, given that the flow of the mind from dispersion in *prakṛti* to the verge of *kaivalya* can be artificially and variously divided at virtually any point along the way. Instead of continuing to supplement Patañjali's taxonomy, I will focus on the outworking of the fundamental process of *pratiprasava* in *saṃprajñāta-samādhi* and describe how central factors of concentrated awareness, *vitarka*, *vicāra*, *ānanda*, and *asmitā* come into play and dissolve or are simplified in the progression through the stages of *saṃprajñāta-samādhi*, just as they did in the sequence of the *jhānas* discussed in the last chapter.[228]

I see *pratiprasava* as the central nerve in Patañjali's system, which he uses to show how the world of experience can be reabsorbed back into primordial *prakṛti* through yogic *samādhi*. Not only is this a psychological process, but it is also a reversal of the eternal, cosmological process whereby *prakṛti* unfolds itself from a primordial, potential state in a stepwise manner that begins from the heights of *buddhi*, the pure intellect, and ends in the world of the *bhūtas*, or the traditional physical elements of space, air, fire, water, and earth, along with the physical senses (*indriyas*) and bodily actions (YS 2.18). What is often called "the real world" by naïve but often quite convinced realists is thus actually the lowest and last world produced from the womb of the primal matrix (*prakṛti*). So, the task that is set before the yogi—those, that is, who have tired sufficiently of unconscious dispersion in *prakṛti*—is to heed the yogic summons of return that perpetually emanates from *puruṣa*, which hides (*āvaraṇa*, YS 4.31) behind the coverings of the deadening impulses (*kleśas*, YS 2.3-13) and karma (YS 4.30), and to begin mentally to fold the extremities of extended *prakṛti* back into itself step by step. In the most general sense, then, Patañjali's Eight-Part Yoga can be seen as a procedure for reabsorbing these projected bits of differentiated *prakṛti* back into its pristine, stabilized, and potential form (*guṇānāṃ pratiprasavaḥ*, YS 4.34, see also 1.45) at which point *puruṣa* shines clearly in the purified mind ("*sāttvic citta*"[229]) of the perfected yogi (YS 1.47).

This is not only a speculative, philosophical schematization of the structure of the mind, and hence of the cosmos, but is also a clear yogic itinerary that leads the dedicated yogi from dispersal in the cosmic flow to the leaping-off point into pure, ineffable freedom. This process is yogically cultivated by reabsorbing[230] the extruded (*prasava*[231]) elements of *prakṛti* by collapsing them through deepening concentration in the progressively subtler (*sūkṣma*), or less concrete (*sthūla*), stages of *saṃprajñāta-samādhi*. This is accomplished through a sequential deepening of contemplative focus, which begins already, as we have seen, in *dhāraṇā* and ends on the threshold of *asaṃprajñāta-samādhi*. This movement is traced by the initial cultivation and subsequent abandonment of the four characteristics, or factors, of *saṃprajñāta-samādhi*: *vitarka*, *vicāra*, *ānanda*, and *asmitā* (YS 1.17), which can be translated as "concrete-reflection recollectedness," "abstract-reflection recollectedness," "delightful recollectedness," and "mere self-awareness recollectedness."[232] Although each of these generating factors of *saṃprajñāta-samādhi* is subtle in relation to ordinary, dispersed consciousness, each is less subtle than the factor that succeeds it. Abstract as it may appear on paper, I think that this process of reabsorption of the mind (*citta*) into *prakṛti* through the unfolding of *saṃprajñāta-samādhi* is the core of the *pātañjala yoga* practice and is also a radiant expression of the common yogic-mystical itinerary that I am tracing in this book. Indeed, so central is this yoga practice that Swami Satchidananda, founder of Integral Yoga, recommended to his students that "the samprajnata samadhi with its four varieties should be practiced."[233]

As we will see in the detailed mapping of the itinerary of *samādhi* in the next section, each stage of this process of sublimation, reabsorption, or subtilization is linked to one of the four distinctive aspects of the *guṇas*. *Guṇa* (combining factor) is a familiar term in Indian thought, and it usually calls to mind the three qualities of *sattva*, *rajas*, and *tamas* (or goodness, passion, and ignorance), the continual interplay of which constitute the eternal play of *prakṛti*. The *Yoga Sūtra* speaks, however, of four *guṇas*, or more precisely, the four "phases" (*parvan*) of the *guṇas*. Patañjali calls these phases *viśeṣa*, *aviśeṣa*, *liṅga-mātra*, and *aliṅga* (YS 2.19). Each of these phases is related, in turn, to one of three essential aspects of each thought or cognitive act: that which is knowable (*grāhya*), the act of knowing (*grahaṇa*), and the knower (*grahītṛ*) (YS 1.41), which, as *samādhi* deepens, become increasingly fused, leaving only a unified awareness, which is the jumping-off point (YS 1.18, 50) into unmediated recollectedness (*asaṃprajñāta-samādhi*).[234]

This process of reabsorption defines the contemplative arc of the *samādhis* and the *samāpattis*, and I would like to trace this here briefly before getting into more detail about each stage of *pratiprasava* in the discussion to follow, in which I will link the Pātañjalian meditative landmarks of *vitarka*, *vicāra*, *ānanda*, and *asmitā* to my postulated contemplative universals of convergence, coalescence, simplification, quiescence, and beatitude by way of the four phases of the *guṇas*. It may be helpful if I briefly outline the logic of the process of *pratiprasava* before taking up the synthetic work of bringing together the factors of *saṃprajñāta-samādhi*, the phases of the *guṇas*, and the contemplative universals.

Viśeṣa, which can be translated as "particular," refers to reflection upon individual items or objects in the familiar physical world, which is made up of the five senses (*buddhīndriyas*), the five bodily actions (*karmendriyas*), and the mind or *manas*.[235] At this level of reflection upon ordinary experience, the focus is on what is knowable (*grāhya*), or the specific qualities of specific things or objects, in the tripartite division of cognitive acts. In connection with *vitarka-samādhi*, it is developed by focusing on some particular aspect of the world of physical and sensory experience, whether that is a point on the body, a physical object, or some physical religious object or image.

Aviśeṣa can be translated as "general" or "universal," and it refers to the subtle elements (*tanmātras*), such as sound, touch, form, taste, smell,[236] and *asmitā* ("mere self-awareness"),[237] which in Sāṅkhya philosophy is situated between the *tanmātras* and *buddhi* ("contemplative insight"). At this level of reflection,[238] one also focuses on what is knowable (*grāhya*), but in their subtle forms. Now, the objects of sensory and physical experience lose their individuality and are perceived as potential entities inherent within the subtle elements,[239] just as gold contains as potential the many forms into which it can be shaped. Where *viśeṣa* focuses on the unique features of specific individual things and objects, *aviśeṣa* reflects upon properties that are shared by many things and objects.[240] In connection with *vicāra-samādhi*, this is developed by focusing on the generic aspects of things, such as the subtle elements and the I-factor, the essential ideas, concepts, or forms that infuse the world of concrete objects, things, and events, or the common attributes of the sacred personages, divinities, of the world's religions.

Liṅga-mātra can be translated as "indicator," and it refers to *buddhi*, which is the first evolute of *prakṛti* and, as such, it indicates,[241] or perhaps contains in seed form, all of the subsequent twenty-two evolutes of *prakṛti*. At this level of reflection, one becomes aware of the knower (*grahītṛ*) and thus of the cognitive, affective, volitional, deliberative, and discriminative processes sponsored by *buddhi*,[242] along with the supreme function of *buddhi*, which is to clarify the distinction between *prakṛti* and *puruṣa*.[243] In connection with *ānanda-samādhi*, this is developed by learning to clarify ever and again the immutable distinction between these two ultimate realities (*tattvas*) of Sāṃkhya and to revel in the delight that this rarefied level of contemplation brings.[244]

Aliṅga, or the "unindicated," refers to *prakṛti* itself, the penultimate *tattva*, or principle, in Sāṃkhya, which in its pure potential state is prior to all of the indications or divisions that evolve from it, beginning with *buddhi*. At this level of reflection, one becomes aware only of the purity of unmanifest *prakṛti*, which serves as an immaculate mirror for *puruṣa*.[245] This is as close as the mind can come to *kaivalya* without finally relinquishing itself, and it marks the end not only of mental reflection but also of *saṃprajñāta-samādhi*. In connection with *asmitā-samādhi*, this would seem to be a pure, non-intentional awareness with neither shape nor form that immaculately mirrors the ineffable and unsayable reality of *puruṣa* and is the jumping-off point (YS 1.50-51) for extrication (*kaivalya*).

At this point, we are ready to begin our journey through the subtle realms of meditation disclosed by mediated recollectedness (*saṃprajñāta-samādhi*) (summarized in tabular form in Figure 1 above). As a prelude to what is to come, I will briefly note Gerald Larson's suggestions as to what kinds of intellectual activity are associated with each of the six stages of *saṃprajñāta-samādhi*.[246] He sees *savitarka-samādhi* expressed in the concentrated focus of well-trained and competent engineers, athletes, and musicians. *Nirvitarka-samādhi* is the experience of engineers, athletes, or musicians when they become completely absorbed in their activities. *Savicāra-samādhi* is the rarefied awareness of abstract objects contemplated by theorists in the fields of mathematics, physics, and music, while *nirvicāra-samādhi* is a subtler level of complete absorption in which even these abstract objects as well as the contemplator vanish from awareness. *Ānanda-samādhi* is a more rarefied mental state, as Larson acknowledges, and his references here to the sublime aesthetic experiences of artists, mathematicians, and connoisseurs can be supplemented with the descriptions of pure, spiritual delight described by the saints of the world's many religions. *Asmitā-samādhi*, also a rarefied experience, moves beyond the reaches, in my view, of all the special sciences, art, and music to the purely philosophical awareness of the distinction between the knower and what is known and to the dissolution of even this rarefied insight in pure being itself (Larson divides these last two stages, as did Vācaspatimiśra, into positive and negative forms, although these are not to be found in the *Yoga Sūtra*.)

The *Yoga Sūtra* needs only a few *sūtras* to describe the process of *saṃprajñāta-samādhi*, yet these *sūtras* precisely trace the path of mediated recollectedness. In order to trace for ourselves these tightly packed *sūtras*, I will show how *saṃprajñāta-samādhi* unfolds itself in meditation on two different objects (*ālambana*[247]): a rose[248] and a deity of one's choice (*iṣṭa-devatā*, YS 2.44-45). (Meditating upon a personally chosen deity is one of the many meditation objects indicated by Patañjali and other commentators. Indeed, as Bryant and Feuerstein make clear, theistic forms of yoga have long been central in the yoga traditions of India.[249]). In beginning our exploration of the six stages of *saṃprajñāta-samādhi*, which is the real kernel or heart of the *Yoga Sūtra*,[250] we will assume that all of the preceding stages of Eight-Part Yoga have been sufficiently mastered to allow the yogi to move effortlessly into *dhyāna*, which is equivalent to *savitarka-samādhi* and is the portal into *saṃprajñāta-samādhi*. (It might also be noted that this is the beginning of yoga proper, since, as Vyāsa, noted, "yoga is *samādhi*" at the beginning of his commentary.)

Recollectedness with Concrete Reflection (savitarka-samādhi) The stage of *vicāra-samādhi* can be divided into a *sa-* and a *nis-* (or *nir-*) phase: *savicāra-samādhi* and *nirvicāra-samādhi*. In this section, I will take up the first, leaving the second to the next section. *Savitarka-samādhi* is a conceptually mediated stage of *samādhi*, which is suggested in my translation, "concrete-reflection recollectedness" (and which is also suggested by the character of the Buddhist *jhāna* factor of *vitakka*, which was discussed in the last chapter). At this point, *samādhi* is still somewhat diffuse, as in the deepest, mind-stilling reflections that arise in mantra chanting and intensive scriptural study (*svādhyāya* or, in the tradition that we will engage in the next chapter, *lectio divina*), in the savoring of the details in the meditation object, such as a rose, or the characteristics of the *iṣṭa-devatā* (to continue with my examples). It is thus possible in this stage of *samādhi* to note that one has entered into it, that the mind has become relatively still, and that there has been a relaxation of the intentional effort of *dhāraṇā* as the mind enters into and continues to remain focused in *dhyāna*. Given that the mind in this stage of initial *samādhi* is coalescing with the meditation object in its most concrete form (*sthūla*), there will also be a kind of virtual movement in the mind that continuously takes in or notes the potentially infinite aspects of the meditation object (*ālambana*). (If any of these mental notations strays beyond the meditation object, which can happen in this lowest stage of *samādhi*, one must conclude that, at least for those moments, *dhyāna* and, therefore, *savitarka-samādhi* have been broken). As long as they stay connected to the meditation object, these mental notations are not included under the five categories of *vṛttis*, as defined by Patañjali (YS 1.6-7), and so cannot be thought of as ordinary, discursive thinking arising out of karma-generated *saṃskāras* ("predetermining impulses"). They are, instead, corrective insights, or countervailing *saṃskāras* (YS 1.50, 3.9-10),[251] emanating, as I think, from *buddhi* (contemplative insight), which is the first evolute of *prakṛti* and which always, like the moon in relation to the sun, reflects the light of *puruṣa*.[252] These direct the increasingly *sāttvic* mind of the yogi toward the realization of *puruṣa*, which hovers beyond the flux of the mind.[253]

This beginning stage of *samādhi* deals with the *viśeṣa* phase of the *guṇas*, which means that the yogi has cultivated *dhāraṇā* and *dhyāna* by focusing on a singular item in the realm of concrete sensory and mental experience, such as the socially constructed and empirically available image and knowledge of a rose or of a chosen deity (to continue with my examples) and now, in this first of the six stages of *saṃprajñāta-samādhi* (YS 1.42), the unification of the yogi's mind with the highly particularized (*viśeṣa*) object of meditation is coarse (*sthūla*), indistinct (*saṅkīrṇa*), and incomplete. Other than the countervailing *saṃskāras* and memory (*smṛti*, YS 1.43), there are no other thoughts (*citta-vṛttis*) at work here to disturb the unwavering fixation of the mind on the object (in the next degree of *samādhi*, *smṛti* will fade away, to be followed by the fading away of countervailing *saṃskāras* at the end of *saṃprajñāta-samādhi*, YS 1.51-52). Thus, as Patañjali notes, the mental image of the meditation object as it presents itself at this point in the relatively stilled mind[254] of the yogi remains mixed up with (*saṅkīrṇa*) the whole array of names, ideas, opinions, biases, explanations, and evaluations that are part of the conventional view of the object and remain in the yogi's still active memory. Patañjali summarizes these potentially infinite aspects of the meditation object under the three categories of the *śabda, artha*, and *jñāna* of the object, or the customary names applied to the object, the standard meanings of these names, and the conventional scientific or theological knowledge accumulated about the object. Although the yogi is not thinking or reacting negatively or positively to any of this, all of it still conditions the mental image of the meditation object.

Thus, the mental image that the yogi holds of a rose will be shaped by the native and learned languages of the yogi and the words used for "rose" in those languages, the yogi's actual experience or inexperience with roses, the positive or negative associations that the yogi has for roses, and the degree of knowledge the yogi has about botany and horticulture. When it comes to the yogi's personally chosen deity,[254] the fixed mental image that the yogi has of the chosen deity will be shaped by the native and learned languages of the yogi and the words used for supreme divine beings in those languages, the yogi's personal experience, for both good and for ill, with these divine beings, and the level of training of the yogi in the various branches of theology, ritual, religious law, and, when relevant, scriptural studies. At this stage of *samādhi*, the image of the rose and of the chosen deity are embedded within all of these associations.

In the case of the chosen deity, this degree of *samādhi* can also be experienced by religious exclusivists, religious literalists, authoritarian religionists, and narrow sectarians in sessions of deep reflection and contemplation, and the sense of unity that arises in this *samādhi* at such times can seem to confirm the truth or finality of the teachings or claims associated with a specific chosen deity or ideal human teacher. It is for this reason that it must be pointed out that this is only the first and not the last degree of *samādhi*, and that the way forward lies through allowing this *samādhi* to mature into the next stage of *samādhi*, where, as its name implies, the verbal and conceptual aspects associated with the meditation object disappear.

Recollectedness without Concrete Reflection (nirvitarka-samādhi) Gradually, over multiple meditation sessions as *savitarka-samādhi* almost imperceptibly deepens, focus on the object becomes more simplified as the noting of features in the meditation object decreases until there comes another dramatic moment in the yogic itinerary, when, suddenly, the meditation object shines forth on its own in the mind of the yogi. This transition into the second phase of *vitarka-samādhi*, which is called *nirvitarka-samādhi*, or "recollectedness without concrete reflection," occurs just at that moment when the increasing focus on the meditation object succeeds in bringing about the first in multiple stages of what I call "simplification" in the common yogic-mystical itinerary by eliminating the factor of *vitarka* (a movement indicated by the privative *nis*, or *nir*, in this case) from *samādhi* (YS 1.43). This occurs precisely at the moment when memory, or *smṛti*, which was the only *vṛtti* still at work in *savitarka-samādhi* in the otherwise stilled mind of the yogi,[256] is voided of contents, allowing the meditation object to appear just as it is devoid of conditioning by the conceptual, scientific, traditional, and personally shaped associations that the yogi unconsciously brought to the object when entering into the preceding stage of *samādhi*. (This, it might be noted, constitutes a direct negation of Katzian constructivism and particularly of Katz's claim that yoga is a "*re*conditioning of consciousness"[257]). The apparent emptiness of the mind implied by Patañjali at this point betrays the exclusive focus of *samādhi* on that which is knowable (*grāhya*).[258] Later, in *ānanda-samādhi*, the knowable will collapse into the act of knowing (*grahaṇa*), which will in turn collapse into the knower itself (*grahītṛ*) in *asmitā-samādhi*.

The key feature, or meditative landmark, of this stage of *samādhi*, one that would on principle be rejected by constructivists, is direct, unmediated awareness of the meditation object, which now replaces the mediated object of the preceding stage of *samādhi*. The yogi now directly accesses the object through what the commentator Vyāsa calls *para-pratyakṣa*[259] (higher seeing, or supreme intuition), which reveals the object in a pure, sui generis, mode of appearance that is free of the limitations of conventional, naively objective knowledge and opinion. As a meditation object, the rose now shines with a pristine luminosity in the mind of the meditator, revealing a prior reality that is sublimely transcendent and independent of the conventions that are the material from which memory weaves a thick blanket of concealment (*āvaraṇa*) around the self-generating reality of objects. This encounter with the nameless, transcendent entity that appears as this rose in conventional awareness revolutionizes the consciousness of the yogi by conferring initiation into the realm of direct yogic experience of reality and emptying the goods of this world, including wealth and family, of ultimate significance.[260]

In the case of the chosen deity or ideal human teacher, a clear awareness of the difference between traditional verbalization and conceptualization (or doctrine) about the chosen deity or human ideal teacher and the unencumbered mystical presence in the unified mind of the chosen deity or ideal human teacher now becomes evident to the contemplative. In the theological traditions of the West, this realization marks the beginning of apophatic mystical theologies, which is felt by the contemplative as a sharp and growing sense of discordance or inadequacy between the chosen deity or ideal human teacher as expressed in traditional doctrine and ritual and the direct, unmediated awareness of the chosen deity or teacher as experienced in this second stage of *samādhi*. Entrance into this phase of *samādhi* may inspire purifying or reforming movements that seek, on the one side, to get back to the original or authentic teachings and images of the chosen deity or ideal human teacher, and, on the other side, to challenge and critically undercut conventional and traditional religiosity and images altogether.

Since, as Vyāsa notes in his commentary, this level of *samādhi* is the "root" (*bīja*, but here *vīja*) from which inferential reasoning and scriptural revelation arise (*tataḥ śrutānumāṇe prabhavataḥ*),[261] the yogi who attains it has direct personal experience of that which is prior to and inspires scriptures and logical reasoning. No longer dependent upon these subordinate or preliminary methods of gaining sacred knowledge (*pramāṇa*), such a contemplative may continue to make use of them for teaching purposes.[262] Or, indeed, the one who has attained *nirvitarka-samādhi* may begin to compose scriptures or other sacred literary works that have the ring of genuine revelation.

Recollectedness with Subtle Reflection (savicāra-samādhi) Patañjali briskly describes the two phases of *vicāra-samādhi* by tersely noting that they are explained in the same way as the two phases of the last stage of *vitarka-samādhi*, except that now the meditation objects are subtle (*sūkṣma*) instead of concrete (*sthūla*) (YS 1.44). The focus of the two phases of this stage of *samādhi* is on objects that are invisible to the eyes and discerned only with the mind of the yogi.[263] These include such subtle aspects of consciousness as sound, touch, form, taste, and smell (*tanmātras*[264]) and the subtle, generic sense of self (*asmitā*). These subtle realities (*tattvas*) are the subtle, nonphysical sources of the traditional concrete elements (*mahābhūtas*) of the physical world in Indian thought: space, wind, fire, water, earth,[265] and of the social and physical self with its senses and bodily actions, and socialized and karmically shaped sense of self. *Vitarka-samādhi* in its two phases took its meditation object from the latter group of concrete realities (*tattvas*), while *vicāra-samādhi* in its two phases takes its meditation object from the former group of subtle realities (*tattvas*). And, as in *vitarka-samādhi*, *vicāra-samādhi* can be divided into a *sa*- and a *nis*- (or *nir*-) form: *savicāra-samādhi* and *nirvicāra-samādhi*. As with *vitarka-samādhi*, meditation still takes an object in *vicāra-samādhi*, although now the object is subtle, and so this degree of *samādhi* also focuses on the knowable (*grāhya*) in the tripartite division of cognitive activity. In contrast, however, to *vitarka-samādhi*, the objects in *vicāra-samādhi* are universals (*aviśeṣa*). Rather than specific physical objects, these are the general conditions, or dispositions, that allow a particular object to arise. In terms of Western philosophy, these would be the ideas or forms (*ta eidea*) thought by Plato to be the general, formal causes of specific objects. (Under the influence of Aristotle, these formal causes came to be known in the Latin West as universals.[266]) Particularly in the case of Plato and his followers through the millennia, the ideas as formal, or ideal, causes simultaneously immanent in all their realizations, or particularizations, were perceived by an intellect purified of passion and materiality (and not "blear-eyed with wickedness," as Armstrong's translation of Plotinus's *lēmōn kakias* memorably rendered it[267]). Although this mystical Platonism has long been met with varying degrees of skepticism in Western thought and seems to have been abandoned by all but the occasional mathematician, a mystical sensitivity akin to it has long been accepted almost without comment or controversy as a kind of higher seeing, or supreme intuition (*para-pratyakṣa*) in many schools of Indian thought. It is just this ability to detect the formal patterns (*ideas*) or realities (*tattvas*) underlying physical realities that is clarified and purified in this stage of *vicāra-samādhi*, although in the Indian context the formal cause of the differentiated concrete realities is obviously neither Platonic ideas nor Aristotelian universals, but the five subtle realities (*tanmātras*) mentioned above.[268]

In the first, or *savicāra*, phase of *vicāra-samādhi*, the meditator focuses on the subtle sources or causes of a concrete object. Since these subtle causes (*tattvas*) are not perceptible to a mind (*citta*) that is still captivated by or blinded by the concrete expression of these subtle forms as particular physical or socially available objects, the whole preceding practice of Eight-Part Yoga was needed in order to arrive at the movement of simplification (*pratiprasava*) that was enacted in the move from *savitarka-samādhi* to *nirvitarka-samādhi* and that resulted in the sudden appearance in the mind of the meditator of the concrete meditation object as it is in its own sui generis form of self-presentation, which is empty of the personal, social, and biological conditioning that the meditator brought to that first stage of *saṃprajñāta-samādhi*. Thus purified, the yogi now dives more deeply into the object and moves from the concrete level of reality to the subtle dimensions of reality, or the realm of the subtle body (*sūkṣma-śarīra*), which is the vehicle or body that moves between the many higher and lower subtle realms of the traditional Indian cosmology.

As one bores more deeply into the meditation object that now presents itself in *savicāra-samādhi* as devoid of the personal commentary of the yogi, the fact that it is actually an instance or expression of an invisible, subtle, and universal reality and not an absolutely individual and particular entity dawns in the mind. This is a notable meditative landmark, since it marks the entrance or portal into nonsensory perception (*para-pratyakṣa*). One who crosses this threshold, even just once, will never again be able to take the surface,[269] or physical, dimension of the world as ultimate. Indeed, from this point forward, the yogi will know with unshakable certainty that the world revealed by the senses is but a veil concealing (*āvaraṇa*) an immaterial dimension of being where words like "birth," "suffering," "gain," "loss," and "death" lose their force. Although one has now been initiated into the subtle world of invisible but potent universal realities (*tanmātras*), one's attention is still riveted by *this* rose, even if one's focus is not on the concrete rose stripped of its human associations (as in *nirvitarka*), but rather on *this* rose as an instance or expression of the *tanmātras*.[270] Beyond its own concrete appearance, *this* rose participates in a network of subtle, causal principles (*tattvas*) that also make all other roses possible.

Let's now return to our example of the rose as a meditation object. In *nirvitarka-samādhi* the yogi purified the rose of its conventional associations and united with it as it is presented itself from its own side, unencumbered by the local and transitory meanings that the yogi had brought to meditation. Now, in *savicāra-samādhi*, the mind seeks to rest in what all roses hold in common. Whatever it is that makes a rose a rose and not a tulip and makes a rose a plant and not an animal is the subtle object of interest at this point. More than just an abstraction drawn from surveying a large numbers of roses, this is the formal pattern, or archetype, of the rose, which is the design or plan for generating *this* and *that* rose out of the *tanmātras*.[271] The existence of formal patterns such as these is made evident by our continued and persistent use of them in our interactions with the teeming vitality that constitutes the world of experience, although radical empiricists would deny their existence.

The yogi who venerates a chosen deity or ideal human teacher now begins to sense that the many deities and divinized teachers of the world's religions including the yogi's own, are individually and historically distinct but not final or ultimate expressions of a common divine reality that includes all of them while infinitely transcending all of them. In Christian mystical theology, this is the transition from a sense of the ultimacy of the triune God to the more universal notion of the godhead, a teaching frequently expressed, for example, by Meister Eckhart.[272] It was from this level of mystical theological realization that Paul Tillich spoke when he wrote about "the God beyond God,"[273] as did Gordon D. Kaufman when he distinguished between "the real God" and "the available God."[274] Countless Christian mystics have discovered this path, and, as I have argued earlier in this book and in *Pluralism: The Future of Religion*, this level of theological insight inspires pluralistic, apophatic mystical theologies. In Advaita Vedānta, this level of mystical experience corresponds to the recognition that formless (*nirguṇa*) Brahman sublates the varieties of Brahman with form (*saguna*), as expressed in the sacred ultimates of Hinduism and the world's many religious traditions. While the individual deities of the worlds' religions remain available for veneration to devotees who contemplatively arrive at *savicāra-samādhi*, the many faces of the divine are now experienced as disguises or costumes thrown over the transcendental divine ground of being by the conditioned mind (*citta*).

Abstracted from a particularistic attachment to local names and forms, the deeply absorbed *citta* now senses the one word (*śabda-tanmātra*) of revelation, or the disclosure of being, that radiates through all human and divine speech and thought and is the instigator of all poetries, metanarratives, sciences, theologies, metaphysical researches of philosophy, and sacred texts; the one caress of grace (*sparśa-tanmātra*) that is felt through all human and divine care and is the inspirer of all doctrines of grace and deeds of mercy; the one light (*rūpa-tanmātra*) that is the subtle medium of all seeing and especially of the mystical seeing that discerns not only the variegated and dappled forms of the world of experience and its unity, but also mystically sees the one path of return from dispersion in *prakṛti* to its creative and salvific source (*kaivalya*, *mokṣa*, etc.); the one savoring (*rasa-tanmātra*) that helps us distinguish right from wrong, true from false, the beautiful from the graceless, the refined from the coarse, and is the inward monitor that generates the practical and axiological branches of philosophy; the one aroma (*gandha-tanmātra*) that is perfused though the holiness of the saints of all traditions, that is the nutritious food obtained through the rituals, sacraments, and *saṃskāras* of all religions, and that nourishes the journey of the seeker of liberation on the journey beyond finitude (*saṃsāra*).

Recollectedness without Subtle Reflection (nirvicāra-samādhi) In the second, or *nirvicāra*, phase of *vicāra-samādhi*, meditation upon the subtle aspect of the meditation object deepens to the point where even the subtle objects lose their individual forms and are experienced in a simple, unified intuition (*pratibhā*[275]) as if flowing into a radiant sea of pure, immaterial potency. As one passes through this phase of *nirvicāra-samādhi*, a second simplification (*pratiprasava*) occurs as the subtle objects (*tattvas*) dissolve into *ahaṃkāra*, (I-factor), the prior reality in the Sāṃkhya psycho-cosmology which is both their source and their end.[276] The yogi has now arrived at the level of awareness that Uddālaka elaborated with many memorable illustrations in his discussion with his son Śvetaketu in the *Chāndogya Upaniṣad*.[277] In one of his many instructive similes, Uddālaka points out that just as none of the rivers flowing into the sea still imagines that it is this or that river, so the many creatures of this world lose their sense of separateness from being itself (*sat*). This is the realization of Stace's introvertive mysticism,[278] and it is from this outlook that the yogi and the mystic speak about a beatifying dimension of life that eludes final description.

Not only does the apparently objective world, in both its concrete and subtle aspects, flow into the indistinction of nonduality at this stage, so do the subtle senses. Where in *savicāra-samādhi*, the yogi could distinguish the subtle aspect of luminosity[279] (*rūpa-tanmātra*) immanent in the sun from the subtle aspect of the sound of revelation immanent in this or that scriptural utterance, now the yogi experiences all of the *tanmātras* in one subtle synesthetic intuition, just as if all of the subtle senses, which are capacities of our subtle bodies, had become one sense.[280] Here, where the *tanmātras* blend into one, is where the poetic and sacred visions of humanity have their source and end.

Just as the rivers have become one sea, so here the rose disappears as a meditation object and is replaced by the plenitude of radiant being itself. The chosen deity or divine human teacher similarly disappears at this point, which is the portal to Ruysbroeck's "wayless abyss of fathomless beatitude."[281] Although it may seem radical to one whose contemplation has yet to touch this level of *samādhi*, it is here, where the mind of the yogi is absorbed by the universals that underlie all particulars that the world's many deities and divinized teachers disappear as distinct entities in the radiant sea of universal being, just as the rivers passing into the sea can no longer be thought of as rivers. Especially for theistic meditators, however, the final phases of *nirvicāra-samādhi*, which are the last steps of the mind before its cessation in *asaṃprajñāta-samādhi*, may be experienced as a time of great loss, or what, for example, the Catholic mystical theologian John of the Cross vividly called "the Dark Night of the Spirit." (More will be said on this obscure but pivotal phase of the spiritual life in the next chapter.)

Delightful Recollectedness (ānanda-samādhi) Because *nirvicāra-samādhi* corresponds with the fusing of all of the subtle principles and of their absorption into *ahaṃkāra*, which is their transcendental ground, all meditation objects (*grāhya*) have now been annulled (while meditating at least). The focus turns now to the act of cognition itself (*grahaṇa*). This is perhaps the reason that Patañjali does not speak about further *samāpattis*, which, as I argued above, take either a concrete or a subtle meditation object (*ālambana*). More curiously, he does not mention in this context the last two *samādhis*, *ānanda-samādhi* and *asmitā-samādhi*, which have led some commentators to question the unity of the authorship of the authorship of the *Yoga Sūtra*[282] and others to invent *sa-* and *nis-* (*nir-*) phases of the missing *samāpattis*, which would double the four *samāpattis* that Patañjali does discuss to eight. An elegant solution is at hand, however—one that avoids both of these alternatives, and that is simply to see *ānanda-samādhi* and *asmitā-samādhi* as later phases of *nirvicāra-samādhi* (or, to use Patañjali's terminology, *nirvicāra-samāpatti*).[283] These last stages of *saṃprajñāta-samādhi* are, as phases of *nirvicāra-samādhi*, transcendental rather than objective, as in the preceding phases and stages of *samādhi*.[284]

In *ānanda-samādhi*, all objectivity ends and the focus of meditation makes a transcendental shift from the concrete and subtle dimensions of *prakṛti* to the cognitive act itself.[285] "Delightful recollectedness," or *ānanda-samādhi*, is thus, a transcendental state of awareness and contemplating it confers pure bliss (*ānanda*). It banishes the anxiety generated by the vagaries of the differentiated entities of *prakṛti* that make up life in the subtle and concrete realms of the primal matrix, and the yogi enters into a mood of singular regard for the act of meditation itself. Now, the meditator becomes aware of—and perhaps enamored of[286]—a luminous and gentle sense of delight that confers upon the yogi a sense of freedom, deathlessness, and invulnerability. This is subtler and more delightful than any sensation of pleasure that one has experienced in relation to objects of the senses, and the yogi now realizes that she or he has discovered a source of spiritual pleasure that does not depend upon the senses for its generation.[287] The encounter with this unanticipated awareness is, like the entrance into *dhyāna* discussed earlier in this chapter, one of the most majestic landmarks of the contemplative life, one that confirms for the contemplative the supreme value and independent reality of the spiritual life.

At this point, it makes little sense to continue speaking about meditation objects, such as roses, deities, or divinized human beings, since they have all now been absorbed into the delightful *sāttvic* flow of undifferentiated awareness itself. Where before one may have attributed the delight that one took in devotion to one's chosen deity or teacher to that sacred personage, now it becomes clear that the deity or the teacher was only a symbol or sacrament through which the basic goodness of the far more profound, completely transcendent reality of *puruṣa* reveals itself. This bliss itself now becomes one's deity and teacher, since, at this point, one has reabsorbed all of the distinctions used by cognition along with cognition itself into the transcendental ground of the I-factor (*ahaṃkāra*). Thus, any spirituality that is based on such contingent characteristics as personality or personhood, shaped as they are by our biological heritage as human beings, is now transcended and left behind.

Mere Self-Awareness Recollectedness (asmitā-samādhi) As one continues for some time, whether in one or many sessions, in *ānanda-samādhi*, the intensity of this imageless bliss begins to feel hot and intense, leading the yogi to begin detaching from it. There is now a kind of tranquilizing of the fever of delight that one experienced in the preceding stage of *samādhi*, almost as if one were to pour cooling water on the ardor of the singularized and intensified mind. As delight recedes from view, a vista like that of infinite space or a shoreless ocean dominates awareness. This is the dawning of *asmitā-samādhi*, or recollectedness in an absolute, uninflected sense of mere self-awareness—our most basic sense of self without any of the identifying aspects of the body, our social condition, our will, preferences, beliefs, and so on. We now abide with virtually no mental activity in an awareness of our deepest self, and the focus of meditation becomes completely transcendental as it shifts to the knower itself (*grahītṛ*). The *citta*, which become still and purified when it collapsed into *ahaṃkāra* in *nirvicāra-samādhi*, has now attained the level of *buddhi* (*liṅga*), or contemplative insight, itself, and it becomes a mirror[288] for the pristine purity of *puruṣa*, the formless transcendental reality that ever underlies all of the changing states of consciousness.

The transition into "mere self-awareness recollectedness," or *asmitā-samādhi*, marks the third simplification (*pratiprasava*) in the spiritual life, as the sense of delight (*ānanda*), along with the act of cognition itself, dissolves into the knower (*grahītṛ*), who now almost directly contemplates *puruṣa* through *buddhi*, which is the last veil of *prakṛti* (*aliṅga*) cloaking *puruṣa* from view.[289] Now, there is no more talk of chosen deities and teachers or even references to one who could be guided or enlightened by such personages, since the meditator's own awareness, simplified to the point where there is no longer any remaining sense of self or other, becomes the one point of focus. If one may say it, purified and simplified awareness itself now becomes the meditator's chosen deity and teacher.

In this condition of pure *sāttvic* awareness (*vaiśāradya*), the yogi encounters a pure liberating (*tāraka*, YS 3.54[290]) light from the deepest ranges of the mind (*adhyātma-prasāda*) (YS 1.47[291]), which conforms the yogi with a mystical wisdom that harmonizes the yogi with the ancient and eternal cosmic and moral order of the world, or Divine Providence (*ṛtambhara prajñā*, YS 1.48[292]). In following this inner wisdom and guidance, the yogi receives countervailing *saṃskāras* that block karma-generating *saṃskāras* (YS 1.50.) And when even these countervailing *saṃskāras* are blocked (*nirodha*), then the yogi has reached the jumping-off point into *asaṃprajñāta-samādhi* (YS 1.51). Now, having seen all that *prakṛti* has to offer and ceaselessly practicing the extraction of puruṣa from *prakṛti* (*viveka*), the yogi is able to bring the mind and all its fluctuations into episodes of utter stillness (*nirodha*, YS 1.18[293]). Continued practice of *nirodha* will eventually confirm the yogi in *asaṃprajñāta-samādhi* (YS 1.51[294]).

In preparation for this final leave-taking from *saṃprajñāta-samādhi*, the yogi now enters fourth simplification (*pratiprasava*) of the spiritual life. This transition phase away from *saṃprajñāta-samādhi* begins when one senses that even the absolute, uninflected sense of mere self-awareness cultivated in this final phase of *asmitā-samādhi* is, despite its force and authority, nonfinal, that it is, in fact, the last construct of the mind, which still needs to dissolve itself back into *prakṛti* before the pure awareness of *puruṣa* can return to itself and remain in itself, at which point, the whole world of experience slides like a closing accordion into the transcendental self, which itself then disappears without remainder. At this point, the yogi drops any sense of personalized identity and simply abides as the pure awareness[295] of a mind that has absorbed all but its last traces into its source, *prakṛti*. As in the old Indian simile of the mind as the stick that is used to tend a fire, this is the moment when the stick itself is dropped into the fire.[296]

Quiescence: The Stilling of the Mind

Unmediated Recollectedness (asaṃprajñāta-samādhi) Through the repeated practice[297] of *asaṃprajñāta-samādhi*, or "unmediated recollectedness," the yogi begins to dwell continuously in utter mental stillness (*nirodha*), which allows *puruṣa*, the immaterial inner witness that is unmediated by any of the *tattvas* of *prakṛti*, to resume its independent and sovereign status as the pristine, nonobjective witnessing awareness that has always been the only awareness that has radiated through all of the disguises of *prakṛti*.[298] Now, the yogi attains the condition of supreme dispassion (*para-vairāgya*[299]) in which even the attraction of omniscience (YS 4.29) is turned aside. This attainment should not be thought of as a kind of final dissolution of the body and mind, as in death as envisioned by the currently dominant worldview of scientific materialism. Instead, the yogi retains the ability to reactivate the stilled mind in order to engage in service to humanity. This is possible because the condition of *kaivalya*, or extrication, is not a stage of insentience or unconsciousness. On the contrary, it is full awareness, unhindered by the evolved conditions of our physical and subtle bodies and their limited capacities. To resume the stilled mind or to yogically create a new one (*nirmāṇa-citta*) by one who has come to abide as *puruṣa* in *kaivalya* is similar perhaps to the ability of a bilingual or multilingual person to once again converse in a language after a period of disuse.

Recollectedness in the Inner Raincloud of Beatitude (dharmamegha-samādhi) The one who dwells in this state imbibes from within the ambrosial beverage of the most sublime stage of mystical contemplation, which the *Yoga Sūtra*, in a clear reference to the *bodhisattva* ideal of Mahāyāna Buddhism,[300] evocatively names *dharmamegha-samādhi, or* "recollectedness in the inner raincloud of beatitude."[301] Because, as I noted earlier in this chapter, I take *dharmamegha-samādhi* as that phase of *samādhi* in which there is no danger of regress[302] to acting under the impulsion of the *kleśas* (deadening impulses) and karma,[303] I see it as the perfected form of *asaṃprajñāta-samādhi*, and, thus, as the eighth distinctive *samādhi* in the *Yoga Sūtra*, one that is penultimate to *kaivalya*. (Given that the mind has ceased from action in this *samādhi*, as well as in *saṃprajñāta-samādhi*, so that there is no need to engage in such mental activities as *dhyāna*, or focusing consciousness to attain *samādhi*, we can take the continued use of the word *samādhi* here as metaphorical.[304]) Although the notion of the one who is freed while still living (*jīvanmukta*) does not appear in Patañjali's text,[305] it is assumed by Vyāsa,[306] and this does seem to answer the question of what happens to the one who attains extrication (*kaivalya*) while still possessing a living, sensing, and acting bodily form. It seems that such a yogi, utterly freed of necessary engagement with the forms generated through the play of *prakṛti*, can engage it at will, perhaps for humanitarian reasons. Yet even in these situations, this liberated one remains animated from within by a sublime downpour of wisdom, virtue, and blessedness from the transcendent dimension of *puruṣa*. As Swami Vivekananda noted, "Dharma Megha, the cloud of virtue," is a "peculiar knowledge, a particular light" that comes to the yogi. "All of the great prophets of the world whom history has record had this. They had the whole foundation of knowledge within themselves."[307]

This graced state of awakened awareness inspires the poetic imagination to call forth such evocative descriptions of the last moments of *samādhi* as *adhyātma-prasāda*, *ṛtambhara-prajñā*, and *dharmamegha-samādhi*. These resonant expressions should dispel the idea that *pātañjala yoga* is only a matter of willed self-determination, for they suggest that the yogic path, with its stages and fruits, is not a product of the individual will and imagination, but is a gift inspired for our benefit by *puruṣa*. For *puruṣa*, although apparently remote from our usual distracted consciousness, perennially calls us through the "three hardships" (*duḥkhatraya*[308]) caused by our own thoughts and actions, the social and biological world shaping our bodies and minds, and overarching cosmic, karmic, and divine forces to begin making our way back our original identity as *puruṣa* by way of the path of yoga.

Here, at the culmination of the concentrative practices begun in *dhāraṇā*, the yogi has mastered the art of deafferentation of the posterior superior parietal lobe, as described in an earlier chapter of this book. The yogi has learned through a self-enacted mental process supported by Eight-Part Yoga to decrease neural activity in the posterior superior parietal lobe, thereby causing the onset of a nondual, unitive state of awareness that, as we have seen, Newberg and d'Aquili call "absolute unitary being,"[309] or an "enhanced non-cognitive state."[310]

Beatitude: The Transcending of the Mind

As in the section on beatitude in the last chapter, we come now to questions that are just this side of conceptualization, while the answers to these questions, dealing as they do with matters that are, strictly speaking, inexpressible, are almost without meaning, if *kaivalya* (extrication) is, as virtually all commentators understand it,[311] a state, or force, of unencumbered awareness (*citi-śakti*, YS 4.34) that owes nothing to *prakṛti*. If it is, in the strictest sense of the word, transcendent, then it stands completely outside out of this world, having absolutely no commerce with it or anything in it. For the *kevalin* who has returned to *puruṣa*-awareness, the world has ceased, and the dance of *prakṛti*, which was performed for the pleasure and salvation (*bhoga* and *apavarga*, YS 2.18) of *puruṣa*, is now finished, and she has, in the famous trope from the *Sāṃkhyakārikā*, retired from the scene.[312]

But how can we who are not yet *kevalins* imagine such a state? What would that awareness be like? If it can literally be like nothing that we know, how or why would we want it? Can we even begin to desire it, given its complete unlikeness from our most base and our most sublime desires? Perhaps to soften what will seem to some as an unattractive and inhuman soteriology, Ian Whicher has developed the novel view, initiated perhaps by Christopher Key Chapple, that the still-embodied *kevalin* enjoys awareness of *puruṣa* through the medium of a purely *sāttvic* mind, which, however, holds no intrinsic attraction for the *kevalin*. This leads to a reconceiving of *kaivalya* as an attitude of disidentification with and detachment from *prakṛti* rather than as an absolute and final disassociation from *prakṛti*.[313] While such a view is attractive to those who are animated by universal compassion or who remain subtly identified with their *prakṛtic* selves and the world of experience, it does seem to evade the clear teaching of the *Yoga-Sūtra* and Sāṃkhya.[314] Yet, this leaves us with the unavoidable conclusion that entrance into *kaivalya* can only occur with the final extinction of the body and mind at death (*videhamukti*), when the yogi, now freed of *kleśas* (deadening impulses), *saṃskāras* (predetermining impulses), and karma through the practice *of asaṃprajñāta-samādhi* and *dharmamegha-samādhi*, stops existing in the realms of *prakṛti*. So, to soften this uncompromising teaching, the genial and more humanly accessible teaching emerged that the fully perfected but still-embodied yogi is supported from within by an inner wisdom and guidance (*ṛtambhara-prajñā*, YS 1.48), which is inspired by the closeness of the stilled and purified *buddhi* (contemplative insight) to *puruṣa*. Although the doctrine belongs to Sāṃkhya and is not mentioned by Patañjali (as noted above), the yogi who has attained and remains in *dharmamegha-samādhi* is thought to live on as an enlightened sage (*jīvanmukti*) teaching saving knowledge (*upadeśa*) to seekers while awaiting the body to run itself out, just as an unattended potter's wheel slowly stops spinning.[315]

Yet, it seems clear to me that the *Yoga Sūtra*—in contrast to some of its current commentators—proposes a robust view of *kaivalya* as a complete and final break with *prakṛti* (YS 1.2, 2.25-26, 3.50, 4.34[316]). Consistent with this view, Patañjali asserts that "everything is indeed hardship" (*duḥkham eva sarvaṃ vivekinaḥ*, YS 2.15[317]), yet, in a realistic recognition that so elevated an ideal will have limited appeal, he qualifies this famous claim by suggesting that it is evident only "to the wise," or those who continue to sift *puruṣa* from *prakṛti*, even when gifted with the highest rewards of embodied existence or the most sublime spiritual attainments. So long as people are willing to pay the hardship tax that is inevitably levied on the many real pleasures, delights, gratifications, satisfactions, and spiritual attainments that grace our embodied existence, they will want to limit the scope of the claim that hardship (*duḥkha*) is universal. But the yogi who turns away from things that are seen and that are promised in scriptures (YS 1.51), from omniscience and omnipotence (YS 3.49-50[318]), from the distractions suggested by celestial beings, and, finally, from pride in the strength of one's own renunciation (YS 3.51[319]) is ready for the uncompromising truth of the utter transcendence of *puruṣa*. This can require a superhuman aversion to sentimentality and all compromises with our humanity, but it does seem to be the ideal of the purer expressions of India's ancient *śramaṇic* spiritualities, or "main stream meditation"[320] which, as noted in the last chapter, Johannes Bronkhorst contrasts with the Buddha's gentler path of the *jhānas*, and which is a close cousin to the *samprajñāta-samādhi* of the *Yoga Sūtra*.

Yet, the question remains whether so complete a break from the human experience, or more broadly, from *prakṛti*, is a worthwhile soteriological goal. It matters little how one answers this question when one is confronted with the suffering of a child, the weak, and the dependent or whenever one is called upon to act ethically in trying circumstances. The difficulty and the unique meaning of such moments are not altered in the slightest by our views of final liberation, and it would be inhumane to withdraw into nonreactivity and stillness in the face of such challenges. It is therefore difficult to give final allegiance to a soteriology that implies complete indifference to the world that appears to us and that presents us with both hardships and delights. This is not merely a scruple that betrays the Western and Christian upbringing of this writer, for I have been shaped throughout my adulthood as well by various schools of Vedānta, devotional Vaiṣṇavism, tantrism, *haṭha yoga*, and many schools and branches of Buddhism, all of which in varying ways modify the rigor of the old "main stream" *śramaṇic* traditions of India and make room for sanctified appreciation of and concern for the world of experience.

And yet, the attraction of the austere ideal of an utterly transcendent soteriological end-state remains undiminished for me, since it serves as an abiding reminder that the ultimately real will always infinitely exceed the grasp of even the most spiritually developed mind, what to speak of a mind constrained by the limits of a sophisticated primate brain. It reminds us that our highest values will eventually be taken up and exceeded in values now unimaginable to us in the present universe, which is but one in endless arrays of universes splaying out in all directions from the womb of being. Mature philosophies and theologies take this pluralist insight as nonnegotiable, and they remind us in countless ways that the ultimately real cannot be reduced to final and exact formulas and ways of life, although it can be experienced through the limited but useful channels of language and ritual. No school of philosophy or religious movement can be final and universally normative in an infinite universe, yet each mature and integral philosophy and religion, chastened by this insight, can reliably point out and lead us to the supreme awakening.

Before moving on to Catholic mystical theology, this is the appropriate place to suggest that our survey of two distinctive but related mystical traditions has shown clearly that their divergent sets of meditative landmarks are expressive of a set of common meditative universals. It seem safe to say, then, that the disciplines of *saṃyama* in *pātañjala yoga* constitute one local but highly articulate expression of a universal path that seems to spring up in human experience just as soon as human beings turn themselves seriously to the question of ultimate freedom. More persuaded now, after seeing that the meditative landmarks of *pātañjala yoga*, like the meditative landmarks of Theravāda Buddhism, point toward the contemplative universals of the common mystical yogic path, we can now explore the landmarks of Catholic mystical theology to see if they also express the contemplative universals of the common yogic-mystical itinerary.

Chapter 6

The Concentrative Itinerary of Catholic *Unio Mystica*

The Return of a Vanished Classic

This chapter opens a door onto a now infrequently visited wing of the mansion of Catholic spirituality. The names of its leading figures appear to have slipped beyond the recall of current Catholic spiritual writers,[1] although some were towering figures in mainstream Catholicism as late as a half century ago. Few take the time to study today the great flood of manuals of mystical theology that begins with Scaramelli and continues in full force through Verhaege, Saudreau, Poulain, Tanquerey, Lejeune, Devine, Lamballe, Farges, and Garrigou-Lagrange, but which narrows to a small stream with Bouyer and Aumann. One still senses in the early writings of Thomas Merton the monumental presence of the manualists' settled and stable world of spiritual and monastic formation emanating out of the great centers of mysticism and spirituality in traditional Catholic Europe. Yet, one also sees in the increasing religious pluralism and religious hybridity of Merton's later writings and career how traditional mystical theology, with a few exceptions such as Dubay, Groeschel, and Johnston, appears, with the arrival of the fresh winds of change inspired by the Second Vatican Council,[2] virtually to have vanished, perhaps beyond all hope of recovery outside of the small circles of traditionalist Catholics who continue to republish some of the theoretical and eminently practical books of the great manualists of mystical theology.

The central figure in this chapter is Augustin-François Poulain, a French Jesuit who, at the turn of the twentieth century, published *Des grâces d'oraison* (*The Graces of Interior Prayer*), which was one of the last manuals of experiential Catholic mystical theology.[3] Poulain's comprehensive and practical account of mystical theology opened a door to the practice of mysticism that had been closed to most Catholics since the seventeenth century.[4] Despite the clarity and onetime popularity of Poulain's manual, it, along with the other pre-Vatican II manuals, has fallen into disuse in mainstream Catholicism, although it lives on with traditionalist Catholics, investigators and theorists of the mystical life,[5] and the occasional philosopher of religion.[6] This minor classic of modern mystical theology was well received by a pope and by spiritualists and occultists.[7] It ran to at least eleven French editions as late as 1931, with over 25,000 copies in print,[8] and was translated into at least four languages by that time,[9] which justifies the view of some of his contemporary interpreters that Poulain's book helped to popularize the study of mysticism.[10] The 1910 English translation by Leonora L. Yorke Smith was reprinted numerous times over the decades and remains available digitally on Google Books and in print from various reprint publishers.

This is no small accomplishment for a book that was written by a Catholic cleric in a time of rapidly expanding secularism on the arcane topic of mystical theology, a topic which occasioned unease among some clergy of the Catholic Church in his day[11] and which more or less fell out of the syllabus of Catholic theological schools in the wake of the Second Vatican Council. The book remains popular in traditionalist Catholic circles, and still holds appeal for those studying the subtle phenomena of the spiritual life as practiced by master yogi-contemplatives in any contemplative tradition. It has retained its relevance as a chronicle of unusual phenomena associated with Catholic mystics, and has found a worthy successor in Michael Murphy's pluralistic and comparative *The Future of the Body*.[12] And now, with the reawakening of interest among Christians in *lectio divina*, contemplative prayer, and Christian meditation in and outside of the Catholic Church, Poulain's book should find an even wider readership because his manual traces the mystical-theological itinerary of Catholicism with a descriptive freshness and analytical clarity that is relatively free of the theological overloading that is evident in many of the other traditional manuals produced by such mystical theologians as Réginald Garrigou-Lagrange, Paul Lejeune, Adolphe Tanquerey, Émile Lamballe, Arthur Devine, Louis Bouyer, and Jacques Maritain.[13] Its pleasing and crisp style, which an early editor praised as refreshingly "up-to-date" (*très moderne d'allure*)[14] (a trait that also led to the book's being dismissed, at first at least, as insufficiently learned and overly popular[15]) partially accounts for the never completely extinguished interest in it outside of Catholic circles. More significant, however, is Poulain's avowedly descriptive rather than speculative, or theological, approach.[16] His book breathes the air of early-twentieth-century scientific enthusiasm and optimism, a mood that placed its trust in an approach that was more empirical than the theological and biblical approach favored by other contemporary manualists such as Tanquerey and Garrigou-Lagrange.

Poulain's descriptive method—or what one reviewer in his day called "spiritual vivisection"[17]—allowed him in a surprisingly naturalistic manner to uncover the underlying structure of what Daniel Considine, in his preface to the English translation, saw as "a process," displaying "an orderly evolution" expressed in a set of "laws" and "successive stages."[18] Because of Poulain's anatomical[19] and taxonomic interest in the "physiognomy" (*physionomie*) of mystical union (Poulain 5.4, E65, F70), he was able to think of mysticism as a science (Poulain 30.1, E539), a stance that, apparently at least, is at odds with his view of mysticism as a gift of grace.[20] In his own view, however, his "dissection" (Poulain 30.4, E542[21]) of the stages (*étapes*) of mystical theology is in the tradition of the psychologically and mystically astute description and classification of the stages of contemplative prayer crafted by Teresa of Ávila, whom Poulain sees, in a naïve but telling metaphor possible in that vanished time, as having put mystical experience "under the microscope" (Poulain

30.2, E540[22]), or perhaps, to update the metaphor, in an fMRI scanner. This may be due to the fact that, although Poulain was a Jesuit, he was not a theologian, but a professor of mathematics. He was, as a result, chided for superficiality by contemporary theologians.[23] This relative lack of training in theology allowed him, however, to bypass what his theological colleagues undoubtedly saw as a needed foundation in traditional dogmatics and historical theology and to study the mystical graces of mystical theology in an almost naturalistic and empirical manner.

Poulain's comprehensive[24] and innovative manual has fallen into neglect among contemporary academic theologians due, in part at least, to the intense deference to secularism of the mainstream academy and in the divinity schools and seminaries of mainline churches and Catholicism in the middle and later twentieth century. This deference was expressed in the academic dominance of constructivist and supposedly "empirical" approaches to the study of mystical experience and in the now passé secularizing theologies that streamlined or eliminated the traditional content of religion that appeared to be impossible or abnormal from a rigidly secularist perspective. Such approaches, even when, as in current academic religious studies, they are rich in historical and cultural detail, miss, undervalue, or reinterpret in light of alien ideologies the dimension of rich spiritual experience that is shared by mystical traditions. Now, however, in our postsecular period, the sacred has begun to return, accompanied by a renewed respect for traditional storehouses of mystical wisdom such as those under study in this book, Encased as they no doubt are in ideologies of particularism reflecting the epoch of their composition, they remain nevertheless as important spiritual resources, which have an appeal far beyond the traditional boundaries of their originating religious communities. This kind of respect has, as we have seen, been accorded of late to the Buddhist contemplative tradition by the medical, psychological, and neurobiological professions. Attention is now turning to the massive and highly detailed contemplative traditions of Hinduism, as represented by the various yoga traditions. Now, it seems to me, more attention of this kind should be given to the far less studied Catholic mystical-theological tradition, which I will do in this chapter as part of the larger project undertaken in this book of comparing the meditative landmarks of these three traditions in search of the contemplative universals that make up the stations of the common yogic-mystical itinerary. This chapter is thus animated by the hope that the invaluable psychological and mystical insights winnowed from over almost two millennia of contemplative and yogic practice and preserved in classic manuals of classical mystical theology such as Poulain's can be made available today in a pluralist manner for use by researchers and practitioners in the fields of comparative mysticism and contemplative neuroscience.

A religious particularist and mystical constructivist might assume that the cultural differences between these three traditions, and particularly between the Indic traditions and the Catholic tradition, make such a comparative project dubious and likely to fail. The *Visuddhimagga* and the *Yoga Sūtra*, as products of India's ancient yogic spiritual culture, are cognate traditions and share influences that can be subjected to fruitful historical and comparative study. *Des grâces d'oraison* comes, on the contrary, from a cultural context that, in its medieval expressions, shows little to no conscious awareness of the religious traditions of the world beyond Europe and its borders. This situation had improved somewhat when *Des grâces d'oraison* appeared at the turn of the twentieth century, for although much that counted as knowledge of Asian traditions was still based upon the often elementary and woefully inadequate knowledge of these traditions brought back to the West by travelers and missionaries, a new and more authentic—if still far too Eurocentric—awareness of these religious traditions had begun to take shape in the rise of comparative religion, beginning with the influential work of F. Max Müller. This was continued by figures such as Rudolf Otto and Mircea Eliade and was paralleled by the new ethnographic approach of Franz Boas and his students. Despite the lingering Eurocentrism of these newer approaches, they marked a real advance on the misinformation and biases of the old reports. Even more important for promoting a better understanding in the West of Asian traditions was the epochal 1893 Parliament of the World's Religion in Chicago, which brought the first of many representatives of these traditions to the West. As in the case of Swami Vivekananda, which was discussed in the last chapter, they challenged inadequate Western views of their traditions with their own understanding as accomplished indigenous practitioners of these traditions.

Despite these signs of the dawning of a new age of religious pluralism, one finds little influence of the new awareness in Poulain, whose confused and biased views of the yoga traditions of India are typical for his time and social location (Poulain 31.23, E565-566), which was quite removed from the world of Indian spirituality, central aspects of which have now become almost mainstream in numerous societies outside of India in the century since Poulain's book was first published. Despite this parochialism, the book is not marred by expressions of overt exclusivism and triumphalism. Indeed, Poulain's empirical and descriptive approach to mystical theology is in the same mood as the contemporaneous mystical researches of William James, and Poulain's synthesis of the Catholic mystical tradition is relatively free of the excessive inscripturation and theologizing that we see, for example, in Garrigou-Lagrange's massive systematic mystical theology, *Les trois ages de la vie intérieure: prélude de celle du ciel* (The Three Ages of the Interior Life: Prelude of Eternal Life). This makes Poulain's manual useful for providing a body of evidence for comparative mysticism and contemplative neuroscience.[25] Since my concern here is cartographical, typological, and philosophical rather than historical (a diachronic undertaking, which is governed by a different set of concerns and methodologies than the systematic and constructive concerns that animate this synchronic study), these contemplative similarities are sufficient to ground and justify my comparative approach to these three traditions.

Before moving on to charting Poulain's mystical theology, two other preliminary issues need to be addressed, the disappearance of richly felt mystical experiences in current Catholic spiritual theologies and the issue of the role of self-effort and divine grace in the production of the mystical graces of mystical theology.

The Vanishing of Mystical Experience in Contemporary Catholic Spiritual Theologies

Virtually vanished along with Poulain in mainstream Catholicism is the traditional name for the field in which he once labored: *mystical theology*. In place of this ancient technical name for the field,[26] we now have the more approachable "spiritual theology," "spiritual formation," or just "spirituality."[27] At first glance, it may seem that this change of terminology was motivated by professional academic and theological nervousness with the wider, popular use of the word *mystical*, which names a wide array of phenomena ranging from spirit photography and conversations with spirit guides through reality-shifting visualizations, brain-altering mindfulness practices, and the ecstatic experiences in deep meditation of yogis and contemplatives.[28] And while essential themes of mystical theology remain within contemporary spiritual theology and spirituality, the real reason that these newer spiritualities have shied away from the word *mystical* is that they have, for the most part, set aside the robust stress on the felt experience of God's presence and progress through distinctive stages of union with God that was at the center of interest in the old mystical theology since at least the sixteenth century, if not much earlier. The elision of the word *mystical* from these contemporary theologies of spirituality seems consistent with the neglect of the older mystical theologies, which stressed the mystical graces of the various stages of mystical union with God as signs of infused or mystical contemplation.

Even when Poulain wrote his manual, the time of favor for experiential mystical theologies was fast running out, as antimystical forces set in motion centuries before by the challenges of Quietism[29] on one side and Protestantism[30] on the other finally triumphed in mainstream Catholic spirituality, and the "mystical graces"[31] or "mystical consolations," so treasured in the older mystical theology, were ruled to be "extraordinary graces," like prophecy and speaking in tongues, rather than the highest fruit of sanctifying grace for the pilgrim Christian en route to the beatific vision after death.[32] As a consequence, the mystical graces are now often thought by Catholic spiritual theologians to be nonmystical and inessential to the spiritual life, serving only, at best, as purifying experiences for beginners in the spiritual life,[33] as consolations dispensed by God to people with difficult emotional backgrounds,[34] as aids to married people and clergy and religious working in non-contemplative ministries outside of cloistered settings,[35] or as the productions of overly "expectant" and "credulous" contemplatives.[36]

A Comparative Theology or a Comparative Phenomenology?

If I were to write this chapter as a Catholic mystical theologian, it would be untrue to my calling and professional responsibilities to discuss mystical theology and the sequential unfolding of the stages of mystical union without referring to the question of whether these are purely gifts of grace, which can in no way be produced by the contemplative, as taught in traditional Catholic mystical theology (Poulain 1.1, E1), or whether one can generate these states through one's own unaided efforts at developing concentration. Taking up this issue would require making excursions into such issues as whether the mystical graces, or the stages of mystical union, are infused or acquired, whether they are the perfection of sanctifying grace or are additional, or gratuitous, graces (*gratiae gratis datae*), and thus, strictly speaking, unnecessary graces. Answering such questions would necessitate taking up the old question of whether all Catholics are called to mystical contemplation or whether it is reserved for an elite. This might lead then to the more contemporary theology-of-religions issue of whether such graces and the mystical life itself are reserved only for Catholics, or whether they extend to other Christians (which might include or exclude non-Nicene Christians) and to people of different religious traditions, of no religious tradition, and to people who hold purely physicalist views of the mind as an efflux of the brain. Because I approach these topics as a religious-studies scholar and comparative philosopher of religions and not as a theologian, I can put these questions to the side and focus only on the phenomenology of the mystical graces. My purpose in this chapter is the simpler one of detecting similarities in the three traditions under study in this book and suggesting that these commonalities are evidence of the constitutive role that neurobiology and, prior to the biological and physical order, the ontological order of being play in the arising of mystical experience.

The principle that guides me here is one that was stated by perhaps the last major Catholic mystical theologian with a robust sense of the significance of felt mystical experiences, Réginald Garrigou-Lagrange, who held that the stages of mystical union, as influentially named and enumerated by Teresa of Ávila (Poulain 3.5) are "successive stages in a normal development" (*les moments successifs d'une évolution véritablement normale*[37]). This stance is consistent with a contemporary, nontheological view of mystical graces as successive stages of deepening concentration, which are coded in our neurophysiology and engraved upon the ontological character of being, and which unfold naturally, or better, spontaneously, in the experience of the committed contemplative. Whether one thinks in terms of grace or not, these stages of concentration unfold in the Catholic tradition in a sequence that is virtually identical to their unfolding in the schema described in the *Visuddhimagga* and the *Yoga Sūtra*. Surprising as it may appear, the discovery of phenomenological similarities between these traditions is to be expected and is predictable, given that all human beings share the same neurobiology, psychology, and ontology.

Thus, as we will see below, the threshold to the mystical life in Catholic mystical theology came to be known from the time of Bossuet by a somewhat artificial but entirely accurate expression: "the ligature of the faculties" (*la ligature des puissances*, Poulain, 14.2, E178, F186). As defined by Poulain, the most enduringly popular of the last wave of Catholic manualists of mystical theology, the "ligature of the faculties," or "the ligature" for short, arises suddenly as a novel experience after a period of actively cultivated recollection (*recueillement actif*), a practice that can be assimilated to *dhāraṇā* in the *Yoga Sūtra* and the sequence of *parikamma-nimitta* and *uggaha-nimitta* in the *Visuddhimagga*. As Poulain describes it, the ligature is the unmistakable sensation of the recollected inner faculties suddenly being "seized upon, *riveted*, by a higher object" (*elles sont saisies,* fixées, *par un objet plus relevé,* Poulain 14.2, E178, F186). This sense of being seized by a higher object gives rise to the traditional Catholic belief that the ligature and the mystical graces that follow in its wake are passively received states, which are infused directly into the mind of the contemplative by the action of God.

But, from a phenomenological perspective at least, the sense of suddenly being riveted by a higher or subtler object is also a feature of the meditative landmark of *dhyāna* ("meditation") and of the meditative landmark of *paṭibhāga nimitta* (counterpart sign). Yet, the latter two landmarks are, in their respective Indic traditions, seen as resulting from the sustained application of volition and intention by the yogi and the *jhāyin*, while the invocation of the gracious action of infusion by a deity is either not taken, as in the case of the *Visuddhimagga*, or is invoked as an available but not necessary aid and option in the *Yoga Sūtra* (YS 1.23). From the Indic perspective, one may view the sensation that one's faculties have suddenly become unified as flowing either from divine grace or as the natural outcome of disciplined concentration.

The simile of a child suddenly finding the power to stay standing after many tries with parental assistance, even if the stance is wobbly in the beginning (Vsm 3.32 Ñ), clarifies the difference between access concentration (*upacāra-samādhi*) and absorption concentration (*appanā-samādhi*) in the *Visuddhimagga*. But in the context of mystical theology this simile could indicate the interplay of volitional and gracious elements in the establishment of a concentrated, mystical state (and as suggesting an unthematized element of grace in the *Visuddhimagga* when the question of who or what stands the wobbly child on its feet is posed).

Although either approach—or a combination of them—can be fruitful in different contexts, I will focus here on the wobbly but freely standing child as the metaphor for my approach rather than on the child who must be helped to its feet in the first place and steadied along the way until it learns to stand on its own. One may stress the assistive role of the adults, which stands for the assistive, background role of grace in the Catholic and Hindu traditions.[38] Or, given the inward impulse to stand that moves a child to try to walk, a process that is aided but not initiated by adults, one could also take the apparently more volitional approach of the *Visuddhimagga* and see the stages of the contemplative life as arising spontaneously in novice yogis and contemplatives who consistently apply themselves to the art of concentration. (But, even here, the role played by the genetically coded inner impulse to stand and walk can be likened to the role played in Indic traditions by the notion of *dharma*, which exists independently of individual volition).

Although Poulain sees the mystical graces of union as "infused" gifts of grace that cannot be produced, "even momentarily" (*même un instant*) by human effort (Poulain 1.1 E1, F1), this sense of passive reception of a higher or subtler state of being is also an essential characteristic of *dhyāna* and the *jhānas*, where they are seen as natural outcomes of the application of focused intention (and as optionally granted by grace in the *Yoga Sūtra*, 1.23). Thus, instead of seeing passivity as a sign of grace, I will, without in any way becoming dogmatic on this point, simply hew to the phenomenological datum of passivity in each of the three traditions and see these states as effortlessly enduring states that are preceded by ascetical and concentrative effort, a position that is easily discoverable in the *Visuddhimagga* and the *Yoga Sūtra*, and is even, unintentionally no doubt, discoverable in the *Des grâces d'oraison*, where Poulain notes that the infused graces are not purely passively received graces in which the contemplative is completely inactive, but are simultaneously passive and active states, like the relation of the senses to that which they receive, which involves not only reception of the objects of the senses but also a response to them (Poulain 1.14).

From a contemporary neurobiological perspective, Poulain's felt sense of grace in the arising of mystical states can be attributed to bottom-up processing of the basal ganglia while the volitional attempts to master recollection can be attributed to the top-down processing of the left prefrontal cortex (see Goleman, *Focus*, 25–28). A task such as the initial attempts to stabilize intermittent concentration is at first governed top-down by the PFC, but when it becomes habitual in stabilized or fixed concentration, it is governed bottom-up by the basal ganglia. Thus, just like the driving of an experienced driver or the fielding of a ball by a seasoned athlete, stabilized concentration can arise apart from conscious activity by a contemplative and yogic adept. It is easy to imagine that this spontaneously arising concentrative absorption might be a gift of grace, a view taken by Poulain, but not by Buddhaghosa, and as but one among a number of options by Patañjali.

The Contemplative Path of Des grâces d'oraison

Because the body of literature associated with Christian mysticism, especially in its Catholic expressions, is vast, as is the literature of yogic meditation and Buddhist meditation, I have, as in the chapters on yogic meditation and Buddhist meditation, simplified my comparative project by selecting one classic Catholic contemplative manual to serve as the main guide to the mystical itinerary of traditional Christianity. For Theravāda Buddhism, my guide was the *Visuddhimagga* of Buddhaghosa, for meditative yoga, it was the *Yoga Sūtra* of Patañjali, and now for mystical Christianity, it will be Poulain's *Des grâces d'oraison*. Given the de-emphasis (noted above) of mystical experience in contemporary spiritual theologies, there seems to be a tendency to fall prey to a mistake that Poulain was careful to point out and avoid: the reduction of mystical theology to ascetical theology. Poulain thus carefully delineated his area of focus by immediately setting ascetical theology, the traditional preparation for mystical theology, off to the side while announcing that his concern is with mystical theology (Poulain 1.15[39]). The former is concerned with the inculcation of virtue necessary for the Christian life and ordinary, or nonmystical prayer, which arises from human effort, while the latter is concerned with mystical prayer, which, in Poulain's view, is a gift of grace and cannot be produced by human effort (Poulain 1.15). Countless treatises have appeared on both topics, and Poulain resists the tendency in his day to reduce mystical theology to ascetical theology.[40]

The Training Context of the Des grâces d'oraison

My procedure in this chapter will be the same as in the last two chapters. In the first of these, I looked to the *Visuddhimagga* for detailed information about the distinctive stages of the contemplative itinerary of concentrative meditation in Theravāda Buddhism, while in the second, I did the same for the Hindu yoga traditions by looking to the *Yoga Sūtra*. Now, I will look to *Des grâces d'oraison* for its more affective and effusive yet still precise descriptions of the common yogic-mystical itinerary as expressed in the Catholic path of mystical union with God. To accomplish this, I will first sketch the contemplative arc of Catholic mystical theology as developed up until its almost final summation in *Des grâces d'oraison,* thereby indicating where the stages of mystical union fit in the larger training context of the *Des grâces d'oraison*. Then, as in the last two chapters, I will relate these meditative landmarks to the contemplative universals of common yogic-mystical itinerary, which answers to the larger, comparative purpose of this book.

The Degrees and Stages of Prayer in Catholic Mystical Theology

Although the mystical tradition that Poulain charts and describes seems neglected today, it is a tradition rich in detailed and experientially based mystical experience. Especially in its description of the stages (*étapes*) of mystical prayer, *Des grâces d'oraison* can stand on the same level as the *Visuddhimagga* and the *Yoga Sūtra*. Poulain begins his exposition of the degrees (*degrés*) of ordinary prayer and the stages (*étapes*) *in media res* with affective mental prayer (Poulain 2.2) and devotes a mere paragraph to the two lowest degrees of prayer, as befits a manual of mystical theology (traditionally, the degrees of ordinary prayer were assigned to ascetical theology). Although Poulain's topic is mystical prayer, or contemplative prayer, in the strictly technical sense of the four passively received and divinely infused states of mystical union and the passive phases of the two mystical nights (which I will examine in the following pages), he devotes a long chapter to affective mental prayer and the prayer of simple regard as a prelude to his real concern, the stages of mystical prayer. Both to fill in the lacunae in Poulain's manual and as a handy roadmap for what is to follow, I have inserted the adjoining chart, which should give a sense of the underlying logic of the traditional itinerary of Catholic mystical theology as outlined by manualists such as Poulain:

Figure 5 The Degrees and Stages of Prayer in Catholic Mystical Theology[41]

THE DEGREES OF ORDINARY PRAYER
The Purgative Way
(*purgatio*)

- Public prayer (the Divine Office, the Mass)
- Vocal prayer (set prayers, the Rosary) (Poulain's first degree of ordinary prayer)
- Meditative prayer (*meditatio:* "discursive meditation," *lectio divina*: "sacred reading") (Poulain's second degree of ordinary prayer)
- Affective mental prayer (*oratio,* "affective meditation") (Poulain's third degree of ordinary prayer)
- The Prayer of Simplicity (habitual, acquired, or active recollection, active night of the senses, the Prayer of Simple Regard, the Prayer of the Heart, or the Prayer of Active Recollection) (Poulain's fourth degree of ordinary prayer)

THE STAGES OF MYSTICAL, OR CONTEMPLATIVE, PRAYER
The Illuminative Way
(*illuminatio*)

- The Passive Night of the Senses (the Arid Prayer of Quiet)
- The Ligature (beginning of infused recollection)
- The (Sweet) Prayer of Quiet (incomplete union; weak non-transforming union) (Poulain's first stage of mystical union)
- Full, or Simple, Union (semi-ecstatic union; medium non-transforming union) Poulain's second stage of mystical union)
- Ecstatic Union (ecstasy; strong non-transforming union, spiritual betrothal) (all 3 = the active night of the spirit) (Poulain's third stage of mystical union)

The Unitive Way
(*unio*)

- The Passive Night of the Spirit (arid and painful transforming union)
- The Transforming Union (deifying union, spiritual marriage) (Poulain's fourth stage of mystical union)

The most basic principle structuring this chart is the classic distinction in Catholic mystical theology between ordinary, or nonmystical prayer, and mystical, or contemplative prayer. This important distinction is not well-understood outside of traditional Catholic mystical theology (and sometimes not even there as well, Poulain 1.15). Indeed, the tendency in contemporary Catholicism is to see the strict equation of contemplation with the mystical stages of union and the passive night of the senses and the spirit as innovations traceable to Teresa and John of the Cross and to revert to the less ramified view of contemplation that previously prevailed in medieval and ancient Christianity, which saw contemplation—correctly, if simply—as a wordless and imageless abiding in the presence of God beyond all understanding.[42] I will, however, take the more ramified view of Teresa and John for two reasons: first, this is the approach taken by Poulain and the other manualists up, at least, to Garrigou-Lagrange; second, this richer view of the contemplative life provides distinctions that foster comparative engagement with such contemplatively highly ramified and introspectively precise manuals of the Indic traditions as the *Yoga Sūtra* and the *Visuddhimagga* (a precision that is beginning to be measured and mapped by neuroscientists[43]). Rather than adhering to modernist streamlining of experientially based mystical theologies, it seems more valuable to follow the examples of the Indic traditions and to elaborate as many conceptual aids as possible in mapping out the stages of spiritual awakening on the road to enlightenment and beatitude.

To return to the distinction between ordinary and mystical prayer, the former, which is the topic of ascetical theology, is concerned with the cultivation of virtues and avoidance of vices, which are necessary but not a sufficient conditions for the reception of mystical, or contemplative, states, in traditional Catholic spiritual theology. The proper arena of ascetical theology is the ordinary degrees of prayer (Poulain 1.15), which I will briefly review below. Mystical prayer, or contemplation strictly defined, was seen by the manualists as a divine gift, which comes to the contemplative independent of all personal desire and activity (Poulain 1.1, although Poulain at various points hedges on whether the mystic can generate and maintain these states through self-action, Poulain 16.6, 17.2). Poulain followed Teresa in elaborating four stages of contemplative prayer, or mystical union, which I will also briefly review below.

The Three Ways of Catholic Mystical Theology

Before briefly expanding upon the degrees of ordinary prayer and the stages of mystical prayer as summarized by Poulain, it should be noted that the chart in Fig. 5 is an elaboration of the ancient convention in Catholic and Orthodox mystical theology that divides the spiritual life into the *via triplex*, or "the three ways," of purgation, illumination, and union.[44] To these stages of the spiritual life correspond the ranks, respectively, of the beginner, the proficient, and the perfect.[45] The elegant and simple metaphor of the three ways can inspire the imagination with a clear view of the path toward the summit of spiritual fulfillment, although these rankings can wrongfully be taken to imply that there is a smooth movement from one stage to another, an outlook fostered by the precise cartography and scientific aspirations of manuals of mystical theology such as Poulain's. But the path is not smooth and straight, nor is it a special science for monks and nuns, as suggested by this idealized, smoothed-out typology. Actually there is nothing particularly Catholic or even Christian about this inwardly and universally available way of spirituality, since, as we can see from the last two chapters, this threefold way can be homologized to the Three Trainings of *sīla*, *samādhi*, and *paññā* in the *Visuddhimagga* and, implicitly, at least, to the division in the *Yoga Sūtra* between the preparatory phases of *yama* and *niyama*, the further training stages of *āsana*, *prāṇāyāma* and *pratyāhāra*, and the strictly contemplative stages of *dhāraṇā*, *dhyāna*, and *samādhi*. In Catholic mystical theology, the threefold way has been conceptualized as a kind of mystical ladder with three steps:

1. The Purgative Way (*purgatio*): the beginner (*incipientes*)
2. The Illuminative Way (*illuminatio*): the proficient (*proficientes*)
3. The Unitive Way (*unio*): the perfect (*perfectos*)[46]

This ancient threefold way can be fitted neatly into the more modern division between the degrees of ordinary prayer, which includes the practices and experiences of the purgative way, and the stages of mystical, or contemplative, prayer, which includes the practices and experiences of the illuminative way and the unitive way.

The Degrees of Ordinary Prayer

The Purgative Way

As the first great way of the *via triplex*, the purgative way is the way of preparation for mystical, or infused, contemplative prayer and its various stages. The way of ordinary prayer is, strictly speaking, part of the purgative way, since these forms of prayer can dispose one to meditative and even contemplative prayer. Yet, not all who follow the ordinary way of prayer do so with the ardor and discipline—what classical writers such as Garrigou-Lagrange call "generosity" (*générosité*)[47]—which are necessary to enter these higher stages of prayer. Indeed, some may engage in these forms of prayer without any real interest in the deeper stages of the spiritual life. Since the methods of prayer that I will now briefly describe require consistent commitment and willingness to seriously address the contemplative's own ethical failings and challenges, only when the contemplative has begun to advance toward these sorts of prayer, even if only in intention, can the contemplative be said to have entered upon the purgative way.

The various practices associated with this first great phase of the spiritual life call for a thorough cleansing, or purgation, of the mind and heart (the "soul")[48] of those sins, or failings, that were anciently listed by Evagrius Ponticus as gluttony, impurity, avarice (greed), sadness, anger, acedia (restlessness, apathy, boredom, or weariness), vainglory (show or display), and pride.[49] The spiritual practices of the purgative way are called "active" and "acquired" because one must make a personal effort to efface and overcome these failings, thereby acquiring the desired stage of prayer through one's own personal practice. This sort of self-purifying activity is traditionally called "asceticism" in Catholic spiritual theology, a usage that recalls the ancient Greek idea of athletic training, but which acquired a negative image of self-torture in the later Christian era, due to the extreme methods adopted in some ancient and medieval monastics. The formal study of the practices of this great phase of the spiritual life was, as noted above, traditionally named "ascetical theology" in order to distinguish it from "mystical theology," which studies the stages of mystical union that first begin to emerge (at least in my version of this typology) in the opening phases of the illuminative way.

Public Prayer and Vocal Prayer Poulain's first degree of ordinary, nonmystical prayer includes the kind of set, or fixed, and easily recited, whether publically or privately, vocal prayers that can be found in Catholic prayer books, missals, and breviaries, as well as more elaborate forms of vocal prayer, such as the recitation of litanies and the Rosary, the retracing of the Stations of the Cross (*via crucis*), or the making of novenas, all of which can lend themselves to meditative and even to the beginning phases of contemplative prayer. Ordinary prayer also includes the daily performance by Catholic religious and clergy of the Mass, or Eucharistic Liturgy, and the Divine Office, or the Liturgy of the Hours, which is an anciently established program of the reading and chanting of fixed verbal prayers and scriptural passages in the houses of religious orders, churches, and monasteries. Ordinary prayer, performed privately or corporately, can be a rote, and mystically ineffective activity, but, when performed in a deeply reflective manner, it is conducive to meditative and contemplative prayer.[50]

Meditative Prayer This kind of prayer leads naturally, if pursued in more than an occasional and distracted manner, to meditation, or meditative prayer, which is the first stage of mental (as opposed to vocal) prayer and is Poulain's second degree of nonmystical prayer. The Catholic mystical tradition has worked out an elaborate system of mental prayer (*meditatio*), which uses spiritual reflection (or *meditation* in the older and now virtually archaic sense of "reflection"[51]), on religious themes to awaken spiritual sentiments, consolations, and intentions.[52] A characteristic practice of meditative prayer is, at least in its first two stages, *lectio divina* ("sacred reading"), an ancient ritualized style of private devotional reading that follows the four stages of the *scala claustralium* ("the ladder of the cloistered, or the monastics") named by Guigo II (1140–1193), onetime abbot of la Grande Chartreuse in France, in his *Epistola de vita contemplativa*: *lectio* (slow, personal scriptural reading), *meditatio* (discursive, or reflective, meditation), *oratio* (mental prayer), and *contemplatio* (mystical contemplation).[53] This venerable—and now widely practiced—method of meditation begins discursively, that is, as a kind of inner discussion with oneself and God by way of highly detailed reflections, or "meditations" (again, in a now virtually archaic but traditional sense of that word) on the theme of the meditation, which can include scriptural passages and pious imaginings of sacred scenes accompanied by fervent resolutions and acts of faith. Yet, this kind of prayer is considered to be mental, as opposed to vocal prayer, because it goes beyond the mere recitation of set prayers to an inner spiritual drama that is intellectually shaped by elaborate theological and scriptural reflections, affectively caught up in effusive expressions of feelings of love, praise, and hope, and volitionally engaged in the making of resolutions and acts of faith.

Affective Mental Prayer As these mental states become more a matter of deeply felt personal experience than just meditation topics derived from scripture or a meditation manual (as in *lectio*), the overly conceptual, emotional, and vow-making praying of meditative mental prayer begins to quiet down into a simpler and quieter form of mental prayer, which, because it is more affective, less volitional, and only minimally reflective, is called "affective mental prayer" (*oratio,* see Poulain 2.2). In this, Poulain's third degree of ordinary prayer, the stress is on the affective dimensions of inner prayer rather than upon the conceptual and volitional elements that are dominant in meditative mental prayer. Here, the meditator begins to encounter the characteristic process that Poulain calls "simplification" (Poulain 2.3 E8, F9), which replicates in a religiously different context the process of *pratiprasava* described by Patañjali in the *Yoga Sūtra*. As in the two other yogic traditions under review in this book, as prayer becomes more mature and developed, its themes, moods, and intentions undergo a process of unification and subtilization, or simplification. Where before, prayer was almost as intense, varied, and passionate as the untrained mental activity of a non-meditator, now it begins to divest itself of the surface level of the mind as awareness awakens to what it perceives as the outer radiance of the divine presence, which is the singular goal of the meditative mind. Thus, in this degree of nonmystical prayer, the "affections," or emotional and volitional responses, to a meditational theme are now more numerous, notes Poulain, than "the considerations and the arguments" (*les considérations et les raisonnements*, Poulain 2.2, E7, F8). As the meditator now feels less of a need mentally to rehearse theological teachings and to bring the will under control by means of the constant making of resolutions, the heart and mind become unified, or simplified, and only a few occasionally remembered images or thoughts about God or divine truths are sufficient to keep one inwardly recollected. As Thomas Keating explains, in this degree of prayer, one moves "from discursive meditation to affective prayer or aspirations of the will, then to repeating the same aspiration over and over again."[54]

The Prayer of Simplicity As this desire for God or divine truth continues to be simplified through deepening recollection, affective mental prayer moves into a transitional degree of prayer that borders upon and begins to ascend toward truly contemplative, or mystical prayer (Poulain 2.11). This is the "prayer of simplicity," and it is Poulain's fourth degree of ordinary, nonmystical prayer (Poulain 2.3 E10). This degree of prayer has a number of alternative names (Poulain 2.3, 8), such as the prayer of "simple regard," "the prayer of the heart," or the prayer of "active recollection" (which is a "habitual" or "acquired" recollection that is actively cultivated by the meditator). The word *recollection* (*recueillement*), which is a central technical term in Catholic mystical theology, signifies the same process of concentration that brings about the simplification of the contents of the mind that we saw at work in the *saṃyama* of the *Yoga Sūtra* and in the *samatha-bhāvanā* of the *Visuddhimagga*. Recollection is seen, in the tradition of the manualists (if not of Teresa herself), as having two phases: *recueillement actif* ("active recollection") and *recueillement passif* ("passive recollection," Poulain 29.3-5, 533-534, F565). The essential distinction is between an inner, increasingly deeper and steadier focusing on the object of meditation, which is initiated and sustained by the meditator, as in the case of active recollection (Poulain 29.4n*/1, E533, F564), and an inner seizing of the faculties as if by a divine force apart from any activity or volition on the part of the contemplative, as in the case of passive recollection (Poulain

29.4n†/2, E533, F565). In her simile of bees withdrawing into a hive, for example, Teresa describes a type of recollection that is clearly active, or self-cultivated.[55] She also uses, as Poulain notes, the image of the "tortoise or sea-urchin, which retreats into itself" (Poulain 29.3-4, E533-534) to describe active recollection (Poulain 29.4n†/2, E533, F565). I will have more to say about passive recollection later, but for now it is sufficient to note that for Poulain the onset of active recollection occurs in this degree of prayer and that, over time, *recueillement actif* simplifies into *recueillement passif* (whether solely by grace or to some degree, more or less, personal action and volition).

As the prayer of simplicity deepens, the meditator senses a delightful space of inner quietness in which the process of simplification, already noticeable in the transition from meditative to affective mental prayer, reduces the understanding, will, and emotions, to a unity and inactivity in which there is a simple affective regard for God without much reasoning or volition. At this point, the meditator becomes aware of an inner stillness and a facility for resting in quietness, or what Keating calls a state of "resting in God"[56] and Poulain calls "the prayer of loving attention to God" (*l'oraison d'attention amoureuse à Dieu*, Poulain 2.15, E13, F15). Perhaps now, suggests Poulain, the meditator senses in place of conceptualizations about God and divine truth the gentle burning within of "a sacred flame" (*un feu sacré qui brûle tout doucement dans l'âme*, Poulain 2.15, E13, F15). This radiant awareness of God's presence draws the meditator to the very edge of mystical contemplation and the stages of mystical union with God.

The Stages of Mystical, or Contemplative, Prayer

The Illuminative Way

The Passive Night of the Senses (the Arid Prayer of Quiet) But before the meditator can become a contemplative by passing fully from ordinary to mystical prayer, an unexpected pass—and one difficult to negotiate—now comes into view. This is the purgative, or purifying crisis of the passive night of the senses, which was first noted and described by John of the Cross.[57] This trying time in the life of the advancing meditator, which Garrigou-Lagrange saw as a second conversion for the nascent contemplative,[58] is the bridge between affective mental prayer, which is "acquired," or achieved through self-effort, and mystical contemplation, which, according to Catholic teaching, is infused into the inner life of the contemplative. This, as Adolphe Tanquerey, one of the last traditional manualists following in the wake of Poulain, notes, is a "complex state of soul,"[59] and it is difficult to say whether it is itself a first participation in the mystical grace of contemplation or whether it remains within the general realm of meditation. Poulain hesitates to fully place it on the side of contemplation (Poulain 15.1), while Tanquerey resolves the issue by seeing the passive night of the senses as the first taste of the "prayer of quiet," the first Teresian and Poulainian stage of mystical prayer, which arrives for Tanquerey initially under the aspect of an "arid" (*aride*) contemplation brought on by the inner appearance of a "crucifying" (*crucifiante*) light from God, but which later transforms itself into the "sweet" (*suave*) mystical grace that is more generally associated with the prayer of quiet.[60]

Now, and not without a sense surprise at this turn of events, the contemplative begins to suffer under the growing and gnawing sense that God has become absent, or, more precisely, that God is no longer available under what Thomas Merton called the "simple and primitive images"[61] that have so far nourished one's spiritual life. The contemplative now finds, often with dismay, that even the simplest of conventional thoughts or feelings about God are empty of real substance, and it becomes impossible to inspire the heart and mind with them. To continue trying to do so, either out of a narrow dogmatic or sectarian view of what counts as normative knowledge and experience of God or because of a lack of mystical guidance, may instigate a crisis of inner dryness (*la sécheresse*[62]) in which the usual themes of meditation leave the meditator feeling inwardly dry and painfully aware that God—about whom the meditator now, paradoxically, thinks almost constantly (Poulain 15.6)—dwells infinitely beyond the reach of traditional and conventional religious images and concepts. At this unexpected and puzzling turning point in the life of prayer, the meditator arrives at what Poulain names as the "extreme borderland" (*l'extrême frontière*) between ordinary and mystical prayer (Poulain 15.1, E200, F208).

Impeding the transition from meditation and the purgative way to the illuminative way and mystical contemplation is, as Catholic mystical theology makes explicit, an ensemble of subtle failings, unique to serious but still unripe meditators. These failings, which mirror at a higher level some of the failings, or sins, addressed in ascetical theology and the active night of the senses, include "spiritual pride," "spiritual sensuality," and "spiritual sloth,"[63] a string of interconnected subtle spiritual faults that begin with the greed of the neophyte for spiritual experiences, the exaggerated disappointment and even abandonment of the spiritual path by the advanced neophyte when these abate, and the sometimes humorous and sometimes insufferable pride of advanced beginners as expressed in premature claims to mastery, an exaggerated sense of self-importance, a preening sense of being one of the chosen, or the elect, and extreme rigorousness about the perceived failings of others. Even the mere awareness that one is caught up in some or all of these failings is mostly beyond the ability of the neophyte meditator, and, the dawning of this awareness in a more advanced beginner is occasioned by an often distressing sense of spiritual dryness and emptiness. These are sure signs that one has, in the Catholic mystical tradition begun the transition from ordinary to mystical prayer by way of the passive night of the senses (or the arid prayer or quiet, both of which are different ways of naming the first emergence of the ligature), which marks the traditional entrance into the illuminative way, and into what I call "coalescence." Newly born contemplatives will now begin to note how their practice is saturated with these failings. Certainly, no meditator can pass into the next stages, that of real if incipient contemplation, without first having the root of these failings more or less removed from one's mind. (In the traditional conception, passive purification is an action of grace, and it uproots the meditator's defects more effectively than the meditator, using self-power alone, can achieve).

The Ligature Now, before moving on to the sweet prayer of quiet, is the appropriate moment to speak about one of the most distinctive topics in *Des grâces d'oraison*, or what Poulain calls "the ligature of the faculties" (*la ligature des puissances*, Poulain, 14.2, E178, F186) or "the ligature" for short. Poulain describes this as an unmistakable sensation of the actively recollected inner faculties being suddenly "seized upon, *riveted*, by a higher object" (*elles sont saisies*, fixées, *par un objet plus relevé*, Poulain 14.2, E178, F186). To this phenomenological description there can be added Poulain's formal statement of the principle of the ligature: "It impedes to a greater or lesser degree the production of certain interior acts" (*elle gêne plus ou moins le production de certains actes interieurs*, Poulain 7.1, E114, F118). The ligature is thus the bridge between nonmystical and mystical prayer, and it is first felt as aridity and the inability to engage in reflective meditation, which are key signs of the passive night of the senses (Poulain 14.7). For Poulain, the ligature "indicates that the soul is in the condition of a man whose limbs are *bound* more or less tightly by bands, and who can only move therefore with difficulty" (*indique que l'âme se trouve dans l'ëtat d'un homme dont les membres seraient liés plus ou moins fort par des bandelettes, et qui dès lors ne pourrait se mouvoir qu'avec difficulté*, Poulain 14.2, E178, F 186). This distinctive experience of the ligature, according to Poulain, "surprises us during vocal prayer" (Poulain, 14.1, E178), when, as noted above, the faculties "are seized upon, *riveted*, by a higher object" (Poulain 14.2, E178). Speaking of the onset of passive contemplation, which I take as marked by the onset of the ligature, Tanquerey notes that the mind (*l'âme*) is caught up in "a sort of *divine possession*" (*une sorte de* possession divine),[64] while another manualist, Émile Lamballe, speaks of how, just by thinking about God, "God may strike and 'arrest' a loving soul," thus initiating mystical union.[65]

The ligature is, thus, the first mystical grace because it involves a noticeable inhibition, if still very partial, of the mind's tendency to wander back to its own concerns. This sense of being bound by a higher or subtler power, called *God* in this tradition,[66] is the beginning of passive recollection (*recueillement passif*), which grows more powerful as it overcomes the waywardness of the mental faculties. Indeed, all four stages of mystical union, which we will treat sequentially in the following sections, can, in my view, be seen as intensifications of the ligature. This power of inhibiting the mental faculties, which is a central feature of the mystical graces, is first encountered in the arid night of the senses, and it foretells the arising of the higher stages of mystical union.

Poulain, tentatively but suggestively, theorizes that it is "*a priori* probable" that the ligature is to be found in each stage of contemplation from the prayer of quiet to ecstatic union in accordance with "the law of continuity" (*a priori la loi de continuité rend probable cette idée*, Poulain 14.3, E178, F186)—an expectation borne out, in his view, by the experience of Catholic mystics (Poulain 14.3). Stating the venerable principle of traditional Western natural philosophy that nature does not make disconnected leaps, Poulain claims that, just as there are no breaks in the continuity of natural forms so there are no breaks in the stages of prayer (Poulain 2.11). Poulain's naturalism on this point provides a basis for comparative study of the identical meditative phenomena of *dhyāna* ("concentrative stability"), *paṭibhāga-nimitta* ("counterpart sign"), and *recueillement passif* ("passive recollection") as locally unique but phenomenologically identical expressions of the basic human capacity for focusing on or locking in on some selected aspect of conscious experience, a capacity that, as noted in earlier, is being intensively researched by neuroscientists and psychologists.

An Aside on the Ligature: Gift of Grace or Consequence of Concentration? Poulain's view that the ligature is, in accordance with the law of continuity, probably present in the degrees of mystical contemplation up to and including ecstatic union conflicts with his view that the stages of mystical union, and thus, *a fortiori*, the ligature, are gifts of grace, which are beyond the power of human volition to generate (Poulain 1.1). But since, as Poulain admits, the alienation of the senses in ecstatic union, which can be seen as the most mature expression of the ligature, is widely known to be produced by the "concentration of the faculties" (Poulain 31.33 E571), the fraught question for a person in Poulain's historical location with his theological commitments arises of whether the mystical states are products of the ligature, and thus of concentration, or of divine grace alone and having a source other than the ligature and, thus, of concentration. Although Poulain's theology seemed to require him to affirm the latter position, the actual phenomenological identity of the ligature, *dhyāna*, and *paṭibhāga-nimitta* as functions of deepening concentration imply that, apart from theological special pleading, the mystical states can be produced by the contemplative through developing the arts of concentration, as in the yogic traditions of India. For, despite his formal declaration that these states are beyond human power to produce (Poulain 1.1), his postulation of the natural continuity of the sequence of mystical stages with the degrees of ordinary prayer, as when he seems to characterize the prayer of simplicity in such a way as to suggest that it almost imperceptibly slides off into the mystical prayer of quiet (Poulain 2.17), seems to undercut, or at least blur, the strong distinction that he, in strict obedience to his tradition, wants to draw between natural and supernatural forms of prayer (Poulain 1.1).

Elsewhere throughout *Des grâces d'oraison*, one notices occasional slips like this, which suggest that the Catholic contemplative, similarly to the yogi and the *jhāyin*, can make preparations to receive these graces through the cultivation of concentration as well as through ascetical practices (Poulain 9.25, E7.3, 5, 9). Thus, Poulain suggests that a mystical state such as the prayer of quiet still requires effort. Although he quickly tries to circumvent the implication that this stage of prayer is self-generated by claiming that the "substance" (*le fond*) of this stage of prayer is given by God, he nevertheless details the practices needed to sustain this level of mystical absorption: resisting distractions and not succumbing to the weariness (*l'ennui)*, aridity, and fatigue that accompany this weak degree of absorption (Poulain 10.3-7, E138-139, F 143-144). He also allows that contemplatives can dispose themselves for mystical union through virtuous living and active recollection (Poulain 7.9)—which is no more than to agree with the *Yoga Sūtra* and the *Visuddhimagga* on the need for ethical purification and the cultivation of concentration as factors leading up to *dhyāna* and the arising of the counterpart sign (*paṭibhāga-nimitta*), and through the practice of *lectio divina* (or *meditatio scripturaram*[67]), which along with conversations about God can bring on mystical union.

Despite this concession, Poulain immediately tries to weaken the pluralist implication of this acknowledgment by offering the apparently ex post facto claim that the mystical state has, nevertheless, God for its "sole cause" (Poulain 7.9, E116, F121), a claim that is immediately weakened by his concession that mystical union is occasioned by sacred reading or pious conservation because "God takes account [*Dieu tient compte*] of the dispositions in which he finds us" (Poulain 7.9, E116, F121). Other self-cultivated conditions that, in Poulain's view, also tend toward mystic union include striving for ethical improvement (Poulain 12.6), the cultivation of solitude, and "self-abnegation" (*l'abnégation*), or a program of asceticism (Poulain 12.9).

In my view, the strongest evidence in Poulain's manual that the contemplative can generate the ligature comes from Poulain's own presentation of what he calls "natural" and "semi-natural" ecstasies (Poulain 31.13-27 E558-568). Although his understanding of yoga is absurdly uninformed and even offensive, based as it is on the twisted hearsay of travelers in India (Poulain 31.23), he comes close to the central teaching of the *Yoga Sūtra* that yoga is the overcoming of the vagaries of mental conditioning (*yogaś citta-vṛtti-nirodhaḥ*) through concentration and allied practices. Yet, Poulain tries to evade the connection between what he sees as the mystical grace of ecstatic union and what he sees as the natural ecstasy of yogis, philosophers, and other deeply reflective persons by suggesting that, in contrast to the natural ecstasies, the absorption of the inner faculties in the mystical state does not occur because of the concentration of the faculties and, thus, of the ligature, a move that neatly but groundlessly eliminates the concentration of the faculties, especially that which is cultivated by artists, yogis, Buddhists, and philosophers. In a passage sadly muddled by *a priori* and ad hoc reasoning, Poulain dismisses the evident and widely accepted role of concentration in producing the full ligature as the alienation of the senses in ecstatic union (Poulain 31.33) by suggesting that because this alienation is not complete in lower degrees of mystical union, the ligature in the weaker degrees of mystical union is not caused by concentration. The implication of this suggestion is that there is a unique mechanism, which, in distinction from the concentration of the natural ecstasies, produces the mystical concentration—or the ligature—of the mystical graces. Indeed, he claims that "this other cause" (*cette autre cause,* Poulain 31.34, E572) or mechanism "plays the principle part" in bringing about the ligature and the mystical graces (Poulain 31.34, E572). Yet, when it comes to stating what this mysterious *x* is, that which presumably distinguishes mystical from natural ecstasy, he demurs and pleads ignorance, and even hides on this point behind Teresa, who, in a situation more fraught with theological danger than Poulain's, confessed a similar lack of knowledge (Poulain 31.34).

In either case, the key point is implicitly acknowledged, for it seems that, apart from theological considerations, the ligature, like *dhyāna* and *paṭibhāga-nimitta*, is produced by deepening concentration, which is grounded on the prior ascetical and volitional activity of the contemplative. This is the key phenomenological and neuroscientific point, and it grounds my comparative project. There may well be a specific theological element that remains lost in mystery in Poulain's considerations on the cause of the ligature, but, discerning that is beyond the scope of this study.

The (Sweet) Prayer of Quiet (incomplete union; weak non-transforming union) After the long season of aridity, there comes, like the first hint of spring after a bitter winter, the first taste of the mystical graces of the illuminative and unitive ways. Thomas Keating evocatively describes the beginning of the sweet prayer of quiet:

> The first grace that emerges as the night of sense nears its completion is a mysterious awakening, as if a breath of fresh air has entered one's spirit. . . . Now the former dryness seems to have a delicious spiritual savor that attracts us from the center of our being. Spiritual consolation does not come through the external senses; it wells up from a source deep within.[68]

Where the meditator had only an abstract knowledge of God in the degrees of ordinary prayer, the contemplative—now weaned from these laborious stages of prayer—gains "an experiential, intellectual knowledge" of God's presence (*une connaissance intellectuelle expérimentale*, Poulain 5.3, E64-65, F70; 31.46; 31.48). This imageless knowledge is intuitive rather than discursive and leaves aside the products of the imagination, which is dependent for its material upon the senses (Poulain 16.23). It is also often attended by a sense of "ardent delight" (*une délectation très vive*) that is sometimes so strong that contemplatives may feel as if they are being clasped or embraced from within into the unitive state (*l'ètreinte unitive*, Poulain 16.26).

With the transition to the sweet prayer of quiet, we enter fully into the second great phase of the spiritual life, as conceived in classical Catholicism: the illuminative way. This division of the spiritual life, unlike the purgative way, is fully contemplative and mystical, since the mystical graces encountered here are passively infused into the mind of the contemplative by God, according to the tradition. As charted by Poulain in the tradition of Teresa, there are four stages of mystical prayer, although the fourth, transforming union, is seen by Poulain as different in kind from the first three because it is not a mere intensification of the mystical union that begins weakly in the prayer of quiet and ends strongly in ecstatic union, but is a fundamental modification of mystical union (Poulain 3.6). To pay due regard to this distinction, I place the fourth stage of mystical prayer, transforming union, in the unitive way, while leaving the first three stages of mystical prayer in the illuminative way.

Poulain's discussion of the four stages of mystical union, which he derives from Teresa, (Poulain 30.9), assumes the existence of a collection of traditionally analyzed powers of the mind that include the intellect (*l'intellect*), the understanding (*l'entendement*), memory, imagination, and the will (*la volonté*). These mental faculties are informed in his mystical anthropology on one side by the five sensory faculties and on the other side by the realm of immateriality, or pure spirituality, which moves up from the human mind through the angelic ranks to the Trinity and beyond to such virtually ineffable and incommunicable attributes of God as infinity, eternity, and aseity, which can only be approached through the negative way of apophatic mystical theology (Poulain 6.88, 18.25). The intellect is the faculty that, when purged of the passions, can intuitively discern the outer and inner attributes of the divine (Poulain 9.31[69]). Even unpurged, the intellectual function of the mind is capable of intuitively discerning, or seeing without any medium other than itself, mathematical and logical truths, the immaterial dimension of beauty, the imperatives of ethical goodness, and one's own existence as a spiritual being (Poulain 6.1, 6.1*/1, 9.5-6[70]). Lower than the intellect is the understanding, which, informed by the senses, the will, memory, and imagination, and the understanding, is the domain of calculative, reflective, prudential, and other forms of discursive, sequential reasoning, or the ordinary rational operations of everyday life (Poulain 15.3).[71] It is these latter faculties that must be bound by the ligature in order to allow the intellect to regain its natural luminosity, where it begins intuitively to see the divine, which begins as awareness in the prayer of quiet of an immaterial light of something "external [to the individual soul that is] subtle, mysterious [and] immense" (Poulain 16.27, E228). The intellect itself, that divine capacity at the apex of the mind (*apex mentis*, Poulain 9.28 E.133, but not in French ed.), as in the ancient neo-Platonic psychology that informs the Catholic mystical tradition,[72] is not subject to the ligature, which removes impediments to mystical seeing rather than impeding this mystical seeing itself (as implied by Poulain, 16.27).

As we progress through the stages of mystical union, these faculties are sequentially inhibited, bound, or simplified through the action of the ligature, thus allowing a distinction to be made between these first three stages of mystical prayer as the weak, medium, and strong "state of the grace" (Poulain 3.5, E53). The will alone is bound in the first stage of mystical union (or the prayer of quiet), leaving the other faculties free as well as the operations of the senses.[73] Although the will adheres to God, the imagination—and with it—imagery derived from the senses and memory—can still arise in this prayer (Poulain 3.8, E54), as when it represents "the certain sight of God" that it first obtains in this mystical grace as "a luminous space" or "a whitish atmosphere" (Poulain 16.30, E229, F239). (This distinction, grounded in Poulain's own evident experience of the prayer of quiet, is acute and accurate, and it corresponds to the distinction made in the *Yoga Sūtra* between *puruṣa-khyāti* and the purified sattvic state of *citta* in which it is reflected. This comment alone reveals Poulain to have been a masterful mystical phenomenologist).

It should be noted that, mystical though it unmistakably is (Poulain 14.6), the prayer of quiet indicates its incipient or weak status through the distractions that the not fully absorbed or simplified mental faculties still bring into play, along with the remaining and still virtually unimpeded sensory awareness. Another sign is the sense that, although the contemplative has truly begun to possess God, the possession is still transient and meager, which is a continuation of the intense yearning for God that began to be felt in the passive night of the senses (Poulain 16.32). This process of simplification and absorption, which is the tightening of the ligature from its first appearance in the prayer of quiet (arid and sweet) up to its fullest expression as "the suspension of the faculties" (Poulain 14.2-3, E178) in ecstatic union, is here only felt in its most preliminary but still genuinely mystical expression.

Full, or Simple, Union (semi-ecstatic union; medium non-transforming union) First discussed by Teresa (17.3), full union is an intermediary stage of mystical prayer and an intensification of the action of the ligature, resulting in a stronger suspension and unification of the understanding, memory, and the imagination (Poulain 3.8, E54[74]). Poulain refers to this stage as "semi-ecstasy" (*semi-extatique*) because, while the inner faculties are bound as fully together in their adherence to "the divine object" in this stage of prayer as in the next stage of prayer, ecstatic union, the senses remain free in full union to engage with the external world (Poulain 3.8, E54, 17.2, E237). The unitive clasping, or inner embrace, first felt in the prayer of quiet, becomes more pronounced in full union (*l'ètreinte unitive est beaucoup plus forte*), while the effort needed to remain in this stage of mystical prayer is reduced to almost nothing (Poulain 17.2, E237, E6.17). Also, the sense of the divine presence is experienced with much greater certainty than in the prayer of quiet (Poulain 17.2, E237).

Ecstatic Union (ecstasy; strong non-transforming union, spiritual betrothal) In ecstatic union, the "concentration of the faculties upon their object" (Poulain 33.33, E571) increases to the point that the external senses are alienated, or suspended, thus bringing about a total unification or simplification of all of the lower faculties (Poulain 3.8, E54[75]). Stilled and simplified, the mind is now closed off to the outer world and to the lower mental world, oriented as it is to the external world.[76] Open now only to the higher, purely spiritual worlds through its purified intellect, the mind now intuitively apprehends the divine reality in a mood of unbroken absorption. Ecstatic union is thus an intensification to the strongest degree of the mystical, unitive clasping from within of the ligature, which began faintly in the prayer of quiet and strengthened to the middle range in full union. Poulain distinguishes different degrees of ecstasy: "simple ecstasy," which arises slowly, "rapture" (*ravissement*) when it arises with sudden force, and "flight of the spirit," (*vol de l'esprit*) when the mind feels itself being rapidly pulled away (Poulain 18.4, E244, F254). Corresponding to this profound absorption in the divine object and virtually complete suspension of the inner and outer faculties are notable physical effects such as immobility and coldness of the limbs and a virtual cessation of breathing (Poulain 3.2).

Added to this is the most significant feature of this stage of union: the mind begins to see the divine by means of the purified and luminous intellect. These "intellectual visions of the Divinity" (Poulain 18.23, E249) occur in a brilliant obscurity, reminiscent of the mystical theology of Dionysus the Areopagite (Poulain 18.26), in which the brightness of the divine blinds as much as it illumines the creaturely intellect graced by this divine knowledge (Poulain 18.24). This "blinding contemplation" (*contemplation aveuglante*) reveals the three persons of the Trinity, "incommunicable attributes" (*les imparticipables*) such as "infinity, eternity, the creative power, universal knowledge, immutability, aseity," and the virtually nondual[77] identity of these attributes in the divine reality (Poulain 18.25, E250[78]). The sense that we are beyond our natural cognitive limits when we begin to see these radiant and endless attributes inspires a negative, or apophatic, theology, which indirectly approaches these infinitely positive attributes by laying aside human conceptions. As a mere exercise of forming negative ideas about God, negative theology is not itself mystical contemplation, but only a negative manner of conceptualizing the incommunicable attributes of the divine, which can, however, be attained to as positive attributes in God (Poulain 18.26), through infused, or mystical contemplation, which exceeds the range of reason and the negations that it helplessly produces here at the limit of its own powers (Poulain 18.25-26). Now, in this most profound contemplative vision, the mind, moving beyond its own native powers, begins to see to some degree, at least, God's own inner nature (*in seipso*) and to participate in "the light of glory" of the postmortem beatific vision (Poulain 31.28, E568-569[79]), which is the supreme soteriological destination of the Catholic faith.

At this point in retracing of Poulain's itinerary, it should be pointed out that schematizations such as this may become overly rigid, and the drive to follow the logic of an abstract schema may obscure the living spontaneity of the actual mystical journey. Thus, various schematizations of the stages of mystical union have been developed by other manualists, who sometimes prize taxonomic precision over faithfulness to the living tissue of contemplative experience (as also noted amusingly by Poulain, 30.9-12). So, expressive of a different set of conceptual concerns than Poulain's, Garrigou-Lagrange places ecstatic union along with transforming union in the unitive way, leaving the prayer of quiet and full union in the illuminative way.[80] The rationale for this seems to be that the former stages both involve a complete inner unification of the faculties of the mind, differing only in that in ecstatic union the senses are alienated, or inactive, while they resume their natural activity in transforming union. Consistent with this division of the *triplex via*, Garrigou-Lagrange follows John of the Cross in making the passive night of the spirit the portal to the unitive way,[81] as does Poulain (Poulain 15.42).

The Unitive Way

The Passive Night of the Spirit (arid and painful transforming union) The contemplative who has attained to the penultimate stage in mystical prayer of ecstatic prayer may, with some degree of self-satisfaction, assume that the end of the journey has been reached, yet this would be a premature judgment. Indeed, the subtle spiritual pride that still affects the outlook of the contemplative who has attained to the sublime visions and sensations of mystical union in ecstatic union needs to be uprooted before the last grace of mystical prayer can be conferred upon the contemplative. This is the function of the passive night of the spirit, which removes the last vestiges of the narcissistic self-promotion, complacency, and spiritual consumerism that often mar the spirituality of advanced practitioners. This second passive night is, like each of the other stages of mystical prayer, the infused light of God flowing into the mind of the contemplative (Poulain 15.42[82]), although it is now experienced not as light and delight, but as darkness and suffering (Poulain 15.40). Thomas Keating captures the pathos of this unexpected reversal in the spiritual journey of advanced contemplatives: "All felt mystical experiences of God subside and disappear, leaving persons who have been led by the path of exuberant mysticism in a state of intense longing to have them back."[83] Poulain, following John of the Cross, counsels those proficients who find themselves in this unanticipated valley of discontent to accept the aridity and lightlessness of this stage of prayer, and accept with a lightless and arid faith that it is the portal "to a *new* and higher mode of operation" (Poulain 15.42, E217-218). If they remain in this mood of unknowing or dark faith during this trial, they will eventually be purged of that subtle sense of chosenness and proficiency that often mars the mentality of advanced contemplatives. More surprisingly, they may find that, as Keating warns, "our idea of the spiritual journey and the means we should use to pursue it, and our idea of our vocations, the Church, Jesus—even God himself—may be shattered."[84] Spiritual complacency, which relies upon a reputation for spirituality, membership in a special community of faith, or critically purified notions about God, Christ, and the church, will be uprooted at this point and washed away. Abiding in this shattering of spiritual complacency and pride and making the inwardly elicited renunciations, so subtle that they may not be apparent to anyone but the one traveling in this night, is the only way forward at this point on the contemplative journey.[85]

In keeping with the radical evaluation by contemplatives of their motives and attitudes in this night is the recognition that (not unlike Patañjali's view that "everything is indeed hardship to the wise," *duḥkham eva sarvaṃ vivekinaḥ*, YS 2.15) all of the stages of mystical prayer up to this point are, despite their obvious benefits, better understood as expressions of the arid and crucifying passive night of the spirit, since all of these penultimate stages involve varying degrees of darkness and multiple dissatisfactions (a view, incidentally, that Poulain shares with John of the Cross, Poulain 15.40-42). These defects of the penultimate stages of mystical union are felt first as the aridity of the ligature in the passive night of the senses (or the arid prayer of quiet). It is felt again as the progressive suspension in the penultimate stages of full union and ecstatic union of the natural use of the sensible, appetitive, affective, cognitive, and volitional faculties, a situation that can cause perplexity as well as secret pride or spiritual greed in the advancing contemplative (Poulain 15.40-43[86]). Finally, at the conclusion of ecstatic union and as a signal of transition into the final stage of mystical prayer, or transforming union, the infused light of the divine once again turns arid, as in the first night. Although it will not be evident to the contemplative who is enduring the darkness and discomfort of this second dark night, it is actually the prelude to the purely spiritual, nonbiological, and nonpsychological mode of being and awareness that emerges in the next and last stage of the contemplative journey, transforming union, which is a sublime condition devoid of darkness and dissatisfaction.

The Transforming Union (deifying union, spiritual marriage) In transforming union, which is the final stage of mystical, or contemplative, prayer, all of the faculties are, as in ecstatic union, inwardly unified in the divine reality, but with the key difference that the external senses are now free either to remain inwardly absorbed or to attend to their natural objects (Poulain 19.9). In either case, the mind remains inwardly fully absorbed even in the middle of external activities on the divine reality (Poulain 19.5), which is now experienced directly as it is in itself without the mediation of sensory images or intellectual conceptions. Poulain sees transforming union, or what is also known as the spiritual marriage, as a state of deification in which the contemplative "becomes *like unto God*. He is *deified. dii estis*" (Poulain 19.11 E287, italics in source). As Keating describes it, in transforming union, the contemplative lives "without the consoling spiritual experiences of the past, but with the mature awareness of a purified faith and love that is open to the divine energy of grace directly and continuously."[87] Indeed, God now lives consciously within the contemplative to such a degree that the acts of the contemplative become divine acts, and the contemplative's faculties are the "branches" in which the "divine sap" circulates (*nos facultés sont des branches où nous sentons circuler la sève divine*, Poulain 19.13, E288, F299, E9.31 *bis*). This, according to Poulain, is "the essential part of the spiritual marriage," and it is a foretaste, as close as one can come in this present embodied life, to the beatific vision, which will be the possession of the blest in Heaven, where and when the outer and inner operations of the faculties become unified again in the perfected resurrection body (Poulain 19.13). Now, as noted by Teresa and Poulain, contemplatives become their own masters, given the sublimity of the truth that has been seen (Poulain 20.39).

Although the brain is still needed for recording and remembering this ultimate degree of awareness, it is neither a state of the brain nor does it require a brain to instantiate itself. As ultimate reality, pure being, *śūnyatā*, *nibbāna*, *puruṣa*, *brahman*, *ātman*, and so on, it simply *is*, as affirmed by all of the world's traditional ontologies. The contemplative who arrives at this end station of the human spiritual journey is now simultaneously a citizen of two worlds: the physical world, which includes our bodies, brains, and minds, and the spiritual world, which includes not only the angelic and heavenly realms, but, as its final ground, the immaterial and imageless presence in chartless freedom and immaculate beatitude of pure being. So distinctive is this dual capacity for what might be called contemplative multitasking that the mind appears to be divided into two minds: one completely united to God *as* God in continuous mystical union; the other engaged in the various social, mental, and physical activities attendant upon this body in its physical and social locations (Poulain 19.4).

Catholic Mystical-Theological Landmarks and the Common Contemplative Itinerary

Now, after surveying the whole sweep of the contemplative path as envisioned by Poulain, we are better positioned to link the meditative landmarks of Poulain's mystical-theological itinerary to the contemplative universals of the common yogic-mystical itinerary, which is witnessed to by the other contemplative traditions under study here, as well as by contemplative neuroscience. As in the last two chapters, I reproduce below two of the columns from the full chart that was given in an earlier chapter. Here, I list what I see as the five contemplative universals of the common yogic-mystical itinerary on the left and their Poulainian expressions as meditative landmarks to the right:

Figure 6 From The Common Yogic-Mystical Itinerary

Contemplative Universals and Their Common Functions	**Meditative Landmarks in Catholic Mystical Theology**
convergence: mind focuses on the meditation object	**recueillement actif** (active recollection) **affective mental prayer** leading to **prayer of simplicity, prayer of simple regard,** or **prayer of the heart** = active night of the senses
coalescence: mind fixes on or locks in on the meditation object	**la ligature des puissances** (ligature of the faculties)—beginning of recueillement passif (passive recollection) = passive night of the senses/arid prayer of quiet
simplification: mind simplifies itself factor by factor	**unio mystica** (mystical union): three preliminary stages: **(sweet) prayer of quiet, full union, ecstatic union** = active night of spirit ***generating factors:*** **intellect, understanding, will, imagination, memory**
quiescence: mind is stilled	**la suspension des puissances** (suspension of the faculties) = passive night of the spirit/spiritual dereliction (Poulain 14.1.2)
beatitude: mind is transcended	Before physical death: **transforming union** (last stage of mystical union) After physical death: **visio dei, beatific vision**

Convergence: Focusing on the Meditation Object

The serious and committed practitioner who succeeds in transitioning through the first three degrees of ordinary prayer to the fourth degree of ordinary prayer, or affective meditative prayer (as laid out above in figure five), discovers that the relative complexity of the preceding degree of ordinary prayer, or simple meditative prayer, especially when it makes use of laborious imagistic reflections assisted with operatically intense resolutions and emotionally rich religious episodes, now becomes more simplified as an approach is made to the fourth and last degree of ordinary prayer: the prayer of simplicity. This simplification in mental prayer is accompanied by a pruning away from the intellect and the will of most but not all of the disordered affections, known traditionally as "the seven capital sins."[88] This is accomplished through the ascetical practices that are detailed encyclopedically in ascetical theology (which, as noted above, must be carefully distinguished from mystical theology, Poulain 1.15, E12.8n*/1). These practices are preliminary, both practically and conceptually, to the dawning of contemplative experience, which, in the Catholic mystical tradition, is the rare but expected fruit of ascetical theology (*le but final*, Poulain 31.39, E576, F610). As can be seen from the similar foundational role played by *sīla* in the *Visuddhimagga* and by *yama* and *niyama* in the *Yoga Sūtra*, the continuation and deepening of asceticism is a necessary but not sufficient prerequisite for arriving at the contemplative universal of convergence. This thus seems to be a universal feature of contemplative and yogic experience, and it is impossible to imagine that the highest levels of the spiritual life can be attained apart from a significant and ongoing effort of ascetical and ethical self-cleansing. This suggestion is not meant to endorse any historically conditioned system of asceticism and ethics as final or essential to the spiritual life. What in different contexts will count as nonnegotiable ascetical and ethical principles will need to be discerned through comparative research that is fully committed in advance to a pluralistic and apophatic approach, one that is always ready to challenge and revise its always preliminary ascetical and ethical formulations in light of wisdom and charity and insight and compassion.

Because the asceticism of the higher degrees of ordinary Catholic prayer is self-generated rather than initiated by God, it has, since the time of John of the Cross,[89] been seen as the active phase of the night of the senses and it is accompanied in the serious meditator by a significant deepening of the practice of active, or self-generated, recollection, which must be distinguished from the later phase of passive recollection, a mystical grace that Teresa and Poulain think can be initiated only by God (Poulain 29.4n†/1, E533, F565). Teresa describes a type of recollection that is clearly active, or self-cultivated (although she appears not clearly to make the active/passive distinction, as noted above),[90] in her simile of the bees withdrawing into a hive to make honey, an image that is reminiscent of the similar simile of the queen bee in Vyāsa's discussion of the practice of *pratyāhāra*, as defined by Patañjali in the *Yoga Sūtra*[91] (As mentioned earlier, Teresa also uses, as Poulain notes, the image of the "tortoise or sea-urchin, which retreats into itself" [Poulain 29.3-4, E533-534] to describe this kind of recollection).

In each of these traditions, then, concentration is seen as having a number of major phases. In the Catholic mystical tradition, as cataloged by Poulain, there is *recueillement actif*, or "active recollection,"[92] which, as a product of ordinary prayer, is contrasted with its mystical complement and result, *recueillement passif*, or "passive recollection." *Recueillement actif* corresponds to *parikamma-nimitta* (training sign) and *uggaha-nimitta* (learning sign) in the *Visuddhimagga* and to *dhāraṇā* (concentration) in the *Yoga Sūtra*, while *recueillement passif* corresponds to *paṭibhāga-nimitta* (counterpart sign) in the *Visuddhimagga* and to *dhyāna* (meditation) in the *Yoga Sūtra* (Poulain 29.3-5, 533-534, F565). Given the real difference in quality and intensity between these two phases of concentration, the three traditions mark them with conceptually divergent but phenomenologically similar, if not identical, ways. (In the Catholic case, the transition from active récollection to passive recollection marks the transition from the self-generated concentration of the purgative way to the divinely granted recollection of the illuminative way, which is the first of the two mystical paths in the *triplex via* [Poulain 31.45]. Thus, I place the active phase of recollection under the universal of convergence and the passive phase of recollection under the universal of coalescence in my itinerary).

As noted above, there is a real phenomenological justification for this division in that the characteristic sense of sudden locking in or fixing on, even if only momentarily, on the meditation object by the mind can be characterized as a movement from the active willing and intentionality of *recueillement actif*, *dhāraṇā*, and *parikamma-nimitta* and *uggaha-nimitta* to the sense that the mind has suddenly fallen into a deeper and characteristically different degree of concentration, one that is not episodically and fitfully concentrated, but which attains longer periods of union or fixation upon the meditation object, a condition that gives the appearance of being passive in the same way that a skydiver's falling through the sky after throwing oneself out the door of a plane is a passive action that befalls the skydiver. And yet, without the preparatory activity that preceded jumping through the plane's door, the passive experience of falling would not occur. Similarly, as noted in the chapter on the *Yoga Sūtra*, *dhāraṇā* can be seen as pre-yogic, if yoga is, as defined by Vyāsa, *samādhi*,[93] which first dawns in *dhyāna*, just as the practice of returning attention again and again to *uggaha-nimitta* (learning sign) is pre-*jhānic*. Since the emergence of the counterpart sign (*paṭibhāga-nimitta*) from the *uggaha-nimitta* in the *Visuddhimagga* is an event that marks the entrance into *upacāra-samādhi* (access concentration), which, though still weak and incomplete, is the formal beginning of *samādhi*.

I will have more to say about the corresponding and later phases of concentration in the next section, but the main point to take away from this brief discussion of convergence in these three traditions is that without mastery of the initial phase of concentration, aided by the interiorization and simplification of the various meditation objects and a consistently applied ethical asceticism, there can be no movement away from the surface life of the senses and the sense-oriented mind (or what Garrigou-Lagrange refers to as the imagination occupied with unhelpful sensory—or sensible—imagery and the "sensible memory," which recalls these unhelpful images[94]) into the inner realm of the unified and awakened intellect and purified will.[95]

Coalescence: Fixing on or Locking the Mind in on the Meditation Object

A glance at the common yogic-mystical itinerary shows that the *Yoga Sūtra* requires only one concept to express the contemplative universal of coalescence, while the *Visuddhimagga* calls on two concepts to express it: *paṭibhāga-nimitta* (counterpart sign), which announces the dawn of *samādhi* as *upacāra-samādhi* (access concentration), and its completion as *appanā-samādhi* (absorption concentration).

In *Des grâces d'oraison*, this universal is expressed through an ensemble of concepts that include *la ligature des puissances* (the ligature of the faculties), which marks the beginning of *recueillement passif* (passive recollection) and its dawning in the, at first surprising and enigmatic, experience of the passive night of the senses (also called the arid prayer of quiet). What all three sets of meditative landmarks share are phenomenologically precise descriptions of the virtually identical manner in which the mind, or attention, after a long training in the preliminary concentration-development practices of convergence, suddenly locks in, or focuses sharply, on the meditation object. In commentaries on the *Yoga Sūtra*,[96] convergence is likened to the continuous flow of oil or honey from one container to another, while in the *Visuddhimagga*, convergence is likened to the moon emerging from behind a covering of clouds or to white birds shooting suddenly past a dark raincloud (Vsm 4.31 Ñ). And mystical theology likens it to being bound suddenly with cloth strips or tape (*bandelettes*, Poulain 14.2, E178, F 186).

The ligature, which is first felt as the arid prayer of quiet, or the passive night of the senses, and which slowly matures, under ideal circumstances, into the sweet prayer of quiet, full union, ecstatic union, and transforming union, is, I would argue, the chief mark, of the mystical in Catholic mystical theology. It is phenomenologically and psychologically—and, I would hypothesize, neurobiologically—identical to *dhyāna* and *paṭibhāga-nimitta* both in its opening phase and also in its full expression in all the stages of mystical contemplation to the unfolding of *saṃyama* in the *Yoga Sūtra*, which begins with *dhāraṇā* and matures through *dhyāna*, *saṃprajñāta-samādhi* (*asaṃprajñāta-samādhi* is, of course, beyond the process of simplification and belongs therefore to the contemplative universal of quiescence) and also the unfolding of the first four *jhāna*s in the *Visuddhimagga*, which begins with the commencement of *upacāra-samādhi* in *paṭibhāga-nimitta* and matures into *appanā-samādhi*.

As noted previously, this is so striking an event that the skilled contemplative and yogi will not have missed it. As a major meditative landmark on the global contemplative and yogic itinerary, it marks the point at which the mind begins to experience a purely subtle realm that is independent of physical processes. In the Catholic case, these include purely spiritual or intellectual apprehensions of the deity apart from all images, forms, and names derived from the activity of the external senses and the lower faculties of the memory and imagination (Poulain 31.46, 49). (This understanding of the intellect as the supreme intuitive faculty of the mind prevailed in the West before Kant. It was once a well-known element of traditional Western philosophy, known as *intellectus* in Latin and *nous* in Greek, but it has been virtually forgotten in contemporary Western philosophy. Yet, ironically and quite naturally, it is making a comeback into contemporary thought through the influence of Indic philosophies, such as Sāṃkhya, where it is known as *buddhi*).

Simplification: The Mind Transcends Itself Factor by Factor

In the *Visuddhimagga*, the process of simplification is expressed as the emergence of a higher *jhāna* from a lower *jhāna* through the sequential suppression of the four chief generating factors of *vitakka, vicāra, pīti*, and *sukha*. In the *Yoga Sūtra*, the process of simplification is expressed as the emergence of the higher levels of *saṃprajñāta-samādhi* through the sequential suppression of the four chief generating factors of *vitarka, vicāra, ānanda*, and *asmitā*. So, in *Des grâces d'oraison*, the process of simplification is expressed as the emergence of the first three stages of mystical union and the two passive nights through the sequential suppression of the chief generating factors of the intellect, understanding, will, imagination, and memory, all of which are suppressed or alienated in ecstatic union. Simplification thus seems to be a general and invariant feature of contemplative and yogic experience.

In the Catholic case, this process of simplification had begun already in the transition from public and vocal prayer to meditative prayer. The preparatory ascetical purification of the mind and will inaugurates a natural falling away of the verbal, conceptual, and physical complexity of the lower stages of prayer (Poulain 2.3). In place of the busyness of religious ceremonies, of recited, antiphonal, and communal prayers, the drama of pilgrimage in the liturgy, and the aid of sacramentals such as sanctified water and prayer beads, the unified and simplified mind begins now to turn inward toward a bright presence that reduces the mind increasingly to silence and draws the meditator away from busyness and verbosity. Here, where the prayer of simplicity edges toward the arid prayer of quiet and the ligature, themselves simplifications of a higher magnitude than previously encountered, the meditator joins company with the yogi who has cultivated *dhāraṇā* to the verge of *dhyāna* and with the *jhāyin* who has cultivated the learning sign to the moment just prior to the dawning of the counterpart sign.

This process of simplification extends also to the cherished doctrines and images of sacred personages in the various traditions, which are volatilized by mystical simplification, and in a process identical to the reduction of particulars to subtler and simpler forms that is one of the chief spiritualizing processes of the Upaniṣads and the *Yoga Sūtra*, the various deities of the world's religions fade away and finally disappear for the most courageous apophatic contemplatives and yogis. Just as the forms that structure *prakṛti* have disappeared by the time the yogi has attained the pure sattvic awareness of *buddhi* (contemplative insight), so all such forms are utterly absent in the indescribable freedom of *puruṣa-khyāti* (immaterial witnessing awareness), just as all such processes are absent in *saññāvedayitanirodha* (cessation of ideation and feeling) in the *Visuddhimagga*. And, perhaps surprising, or even scandalously, to the orthodox thinker, something similar happens in Catholic mystical theology when the so-called "sacred humanity" of Jesus disappears from view,[97] much to the distress and trouble of mystical theologians from the time of Evagrius Ponticus and Dionysius the Areopagite, to the later days of Eckhart and Teresa, and down to our time when the apophatic and implicitly pluralist mystical theology of a figure like Thomas Merton can easily assimilate the apophatic ultimates of Mahāyāna Buddhism alongside a thoroughly pluralized and nonliteral use of theological and biblical language.[98]

Quiescence: The Stilling of the Mind

The final outcome of the processes of convergence, coalescence, and simplification is a stilling, or cessation, of the mind and its processes, a universal feature of contemplative experience that I call "quiescence." As we have seen in the preceding two chapters, this contemplative universal is expressed as the meditative landmarks of unmediated recollection (*asaṃprajñāta-samādhi*) in *patañjala yoga* and as the meditative landmark of the cessation of ideation and feeling (*saññāvedayitanirodha*) in Theravāda Buddhism. In Catholic mystical theology, it is expressed as the suspension of the faculties (*la suspension des puissances*), which is first felt as the passive night of the spirit (or spiritual dereliction) in Catholic mystical theology before maturing into transforming union and the beatific vision (*visio dei*) in the next and last contemplative universal, beatitude, which I will take up in the next section. In the Catholic mystical itinerary since the time of John of the Cross, the so-called dark night of the soul has taken on a central role. Although this evocative phrase has taken on a life of its own outside of the domain of Catholic mystical theology, where it has come to stand for stress, depression, and other difficult passages in life, in mystical theology, this phrase refers to four distinctive moments in the mystical itinerary. The active and passive night of the senses, as we have seen, precede and mark the entrance into the illuminative way, or the mystical proper in the Poulainian itinerary, while the active and passive nights of the spirit precede and mark the entrance into the unitive way. Like the passive night of the senses, the passive night of the spirit is an arid and distressing spiritual experience, yet it marks the beginning of the full transfer of mystical awareness from its customary biological and psychological media to the purity of immediate spiritual abidance in being as it is in itself apart from all mediation, an experience that, not unsurprisingly, may prove to be distressing for the contemplative. While there is no corresponding arid or distressful phase noted in the passage to *asaṃprajñāta-samādhi* in the *Yoga Sūtra* or to *saññāvedayitanirodha* in the *Visuddhimagga*, the latter text, in its sixth stage of the perfection of wisdom ("Purification by Knowledge and Vision of the Way"), describes a series of harrowing events that occur just prior to the dawning of the first stage of deathless, unconstructed *nibbāna*. These include: "Knowledge of Contemplation as Dissolution, Knowledge of Appearance as Terror, Knowledge of Contemplation of Danger" (Vsm 21.1 Ñ). As these expressions suggest, the transition away from awareness mediated by physical, mental, and spiritual processes may be a fraught one for some contemplatives.

Here, at the culmination of the concentrative practices commencing with the cultivation of *recueillement actif*, the contemplative has mastered the art of deafferentation, as described in current neuroscience and as discussed in an earlier chapter. The mystical theologian has learned through a self-enacted mental process supported by meditative and contemplative prayer to decrease neural activity in the posterior superior parietal lobe, thereby causing the onset of a nondual, unitive state of awareness that, as we have seen, Newberg and d'Aquili call "absolute unitary being,"[99] or an "enhanced non-cognitive state."[100] Despite attempts to limit this state to some brain state or process,[101] the distinctively religious claim implicit in contemplative and yogic experience is that awareness itself in its sovereign form will always exceed the brain just as the sun ever stands beyond earth's atmosphere. (This is true only of the pure awareness itself as it happens, although the memory of this experience and reports about it will necessarily rely upon the anatomy and physiology of the brain that records these sorts of experiences).

Beatitude: The Transcending of the Mind

With the transition into transforming union, the Catholic mystic, like the *jhāyin* entering the fourth level of *nibbāna* and the *kevalin* entering the unencumbered awareness of *citi-śakti,* enters the sovereign reality of being through an awareness that is no longer mediated by the physical body and the conditioned mind. As noted in earlier chapters, this is an apparently radical claim in the contemporary academic and scientific establishments, given its pervasive reductionist and materialist ethos.[102] But this is not an incredible claim in the context of traditional religions, given the general assumption that life continues in some form or another after the death of this body and the dissolution of the socially and biologically conditioned mental life associated with that body. But, if it is the case that something essential continues beyond the demise of the body and mind, then the learned ability of the *jhāyin*, yogi, and mystical theologian to experience the depths of being in advance in this life in transforming union by way of a purified awareness that knows intimately its nonphysical and nonmental character is already a participation in *nibbāna*, *puruṣa*, and *visio dei*, or the beatific vision. (It is this radical disconnection of transforming union from the preceding states that, as noted earlier, leads Poulain to follow Teresa in placing transforming union in its own category apart from the prayer of quiet, full union, and ecstatic union, Poulain 3.6).

But, as with the *kevalin* and those who have attained the highest level of *nibbāna* this side of *parinibbāna*, the question arises of whether there is still any need for the mystic who has consummated the spiritual marriage in transforming union to focus on the world revealed by the body and mind. And, given the central incarnational concern of Christianity for the world that, it proclaims, God loves (John 3:16), the saint who has attained to this level will live in the two worlds of pure being and the everyday world where love is a better answer than hate, forgiveness a truer bond than retribution, and mercy a stronger force than wrath. Thomas Keating well summarizes the dual citizenship of the transformed saint: "Transforming union is the goal of the first part of the Christian spiritual journey. Despite its rarity, it should be regarded as the normal Christian life."[103]

Conclusion

After these long and absorbing sojourns along the three contemplative itineraries traced in the last three chapters, it seems evident that each itinerary expresses through its own distinctive set of meditative landmarks the five contemplative universals of the common yogic-mystical itinerary, which is discovered in the deepest patterns of the mind by the yogic contemplative in search of freedom and is engraved in the genetic code of the brain. As the basic grammar of the spiritual life, the five contemplative universals that constitute the common yogic-mystical itinerary are prior to all religious traditions, just as the capacity of human beings for language acquisition precedes any particular language. It is on these general features of mystical experience rather than upon the endlessly fascinating details of this or that mystical tradition that a philosophical and scientific understanding of religious experience can be grounded. While there will always be interest in the cultural and linguistic dimension of the world's many religions, this study supports the nomothetic quest for an understanding of religion that will allow us to say what conditions must prevail and what outcomes can be expected in any context, present or future, where the application of terms like *mystical*, *contemplative*, and *yogic* are applied. In short, I have attempted to present in these pages a justification for a general theory or explanation of the highest mystical and yogic ranges of human spiritual experience in light of the data of religious studies, the findings of science, and the speculations of constructive and comparative philosophy.

In response to the inevitable criticism that my proposed contemplative universals are inadequate generalizations and imaginative constructs, I would argue that they are neither figments of my imagination nor conventional designations without external referents. On this point, but in a pluralist manner, I am in agreement with Reginald Garrigou-Lagrange who claimed that the itinerary of Catholic mystical theology is not "merely a conventional scheme, but a truly vital process founded on the very nature of the spiritual life."[1] In the same spirit, the Upaniṣads proclaim, "I have touched, I have found/The narrow, long and ancient way."[2] It is my hope that this study of the meditative landmarks and contemplative universals of the common yogic-mystical itinerary will help to articulate what is common to religious traditions, thus moving the study of mysticism beyond the agnostic stance of a distanciated religious studies, the particularisms of inclusivist theologies, and the sterility of the constructivist/essentialist debate in the philosophy of mysticism. In so doing, I hope to move toward establishing the reality of religious experience and its power to ground a philosophy of religions capable of providing a foundation for the religious life and, more fundamentally, for a meditatively grounded metaphysics.

Notes

Prologue

1 Chalmers, David J., "Facing Up to the Problem of Consciousness," *Journal of Consciousness Studies* 2, no. 3 (1995): 2002–19.

Introduction

1 Following Bernard McGinn, I will generally use *awareness* rather than *experience*, since the latter term, as McGinn points out, tends to place the focus on "unusual sensations" and "a particular form of feeling or sensible perception," *The Essential Writings of Christian Mysticism* (New York: The Modern Library, 2006), xv–xvi.

2 I define these two types of pluralism in an unpublished presentation, Kenneth Rose, "Can a Religious Pluralist do Comparative Religion or Comparative Theology?" This was presented at the University of Münster, January 19, 2015.

3 A claim pioneered effectively by Gavin D' Costa in "The Impossibility of a Pluralist View of Religions," *Religious Studies* 32 (June 1996): 223–32. A similar stance in the service of an extreme exclusivism influenced by J. H. Bavinck, Hendrik Kraemer, Alvin Plantinga, and Tim Keller is being forcefully extended by Reformed evangelical theologian of religions Daniel Strange, *Their Rock is Not Like Our Rock* (Grand Rapids, MI: Zondervan, 2014), 31–34.

4 As influentially argued by Steven T. Katz in two foundational essays, "Language, Epistemology, and Mysticism," in *Mysticism and Philosophical Analysis*, ed. Steven T. Katz (New York: Oxford University Press, 1978), 22–74 and "The 'Conservative' Character of Mystical Experience," in *Mysticism and Religious Traditions*, ed. Steven T. Katz (Oxford and New York: Oxford University Press, 1983), 3–60.

5 Groundbreaking studies of mystical maps in the study of religion can be found in Jensine Andresen and Robert K. C. Forman, eds., *Cognitive Models and Spiritual Maps: Interdisciplinary Explorations of Religious Experience* (Charlottesville, VA: Imprint Academic, 2000). For pioneering maps, see Roland Fischer, "A Cartography of the Ecstatic and Meditative States," *Science* (November 26, 1971): 897–904, accessed October 16, 2015, doi: 10.1126/science.174.4012.89, and Daniel Goleman, *The Meditative Mind: The Varieties of Meditative Experience* (New York: Jeremy Tarcher/Putnam, 1988).

6 Goleman uses the expression "landmarks" to name characteristic experiences encountered by "experienced meditators" while "traversing the meditative path to the nirvanic state," *The Meditative Mind*, 1–2. More recently, Alan Wallace has employed this term to refer to meditative stages detailed by Kamalaśīla, *The Attention Revolution*, 6. In more recent work, Goleman has summarized current research on attention, or the ability to "lock-in" on some phenomenon, as one of a "handful of essential life abilities" that is sustained by focusing, or what, he

notes, Richard Davidson calls "phase-locking," Daniel Goleman, *Focus: The Hidden Driver of Excellence* (New York: HarperCollins, 2013), Kindle edition, 15–16. Thus, the snapping in feature of *dhyāna* is the result of volitional episodic focusing or concentration (*dhāraṇā*) becoming automatic spontaneous fixed, or stable, focus. This description, as I will show in later chapters, can be repeated identically for the ligature and for the arising of *upacāra-samādhi*. This occurs through long practice as "top-down" processing via the prefrontal cortex (PFC) gives way to "bottom-up" processing as the PFC hands off a mastered task to the basal ganglia, allowing the higher brain to move on to other tasks while leaving routine tasks to the lower brain, Goleman, *Focus*, 25–28.

7 Already in 2000, F. Samuel Brainard was analyzing mystical experience in order "to isolate relevant pancultural similarities in human experience," *Reality and Mystical Experience* (University Park: Pennsylvania State University Press, 2000), 62, a move that was meant to counter the explanatory overreach of the dominant constructivism of that period.

8 The nomothetic-idiographic distinction has been traced back to Hugo Münsterberg by Russell T. Hurlburt and Terry J. Knapp, "Münsterberg in 1898, Not Allport in 1937, Introduced the Terms 'Idiographic' and 'Nomothetic' to American Psychology," *Theory & Psychology* 16 (April 2006): 287–93.

9 For the latter, see Kenneth Rose, "The Singular and the Shared: Making Amends with Eliade after the Dismissal of the Sacred," in *Interreligious Comparisons in Religious Studies and Theology: Comparison Revisited*, ed. Perry Schmidt-Leukel and Andreas Nehring (London: Bloomsbury Academic, forthcoming in 2016).

10 Also referred to as "affective neuroscience," contemplative neuroscience is a new field with prominent researchers including psychologist Richard Davidson, as noted by Teresa Aubele, Stan Wenck, and Susan Reynolds, *Train Your Brain to Get Happy: The Simple Program that Primes Your Gray Cells For Joy, Optimism, and Serenity* (Avon, MA: Adams Media, 2011), 16. See Richard J. Davidson, *The Emotional Life of Your Brain: How Its Unique Patterns Affect the Way You Think, Feel, and Live—and How You Can Change Them*, (New York: Hudson Street Press, 2011), 16; Jonathan David Nash and Andrew Newberg, "Toward A Unifying Taxonomy and Definition for Meditation," *Frontiers in Psychology* 4 (November 2013): 12, accessed August 7, 2015, doi: 10.3389/fpsyg.2013.00806, http://www.ncbi.nlm.nih.gov/pubmed/24312060. For a summary of the background of contemplative neuroscience, Marcia Barinaga, "Buddhism and Neuroscience: Studying the Well-Trained Mind," *Science* (October 3, 2003): 44–46, accessed October 16, 2015, doi: 10.1126/science.302.5642.44. Mainstream neuroscience is likely to be wary of a "contemplative neuroscience," given that contemplative neuroscience is still averse to linking its third-person, functionalist and vestigially behaviorist approach with the study of "human experience," according to James D. Price and James J. Barrell, *Inner Experience and Neuroscience: Merging Both Perspectives* (Cambridge, MA: MIT Press, 2012), 19, 269–70, 279–80.

Chapter 1

1 Francesca Cho and Richard King Squier, "Religion as a Complex and Dynamic System," *Journal of the American Academy of Religion* 81, no. 2 (June 2013): 357, accessed October 16, 2015, doi: 10.1093/jaarel/lft016.

2 Gregory D. Alles, "After the Naming Explosion: Joachim Wach's Unfinished Project," in *Hermeneutics, Politics, and the History of Religions: The Contested Legacies of Joachim Wach and Mircea Eliade*, ed. Christian Wedemeyer and Wendy Doniger (New York: Oxford University Press, 2010), 72.
3 Alles, "After the Naming Explosion," in Wedemeyer and Doniger, *Hermeneutics, Politics, and the History of Religions*, 56–58.
4 Ibid., 72.
5 Ibid.
6 Cho and Squier, "Religion as a Complex and Dynamic System," 386.
7 Alles, "After the Naming Explosion," in Wedemeyer and Doniger, *Hermeneutics, Politics, and the History of Religions*, 64.
8 Clifford Geertz, "Thick Description: Toward an Interpretive Theory of Culture," in *The Interpretation of Cultures*, ed. Clifford Geertz (New York: Basic Books, 1973), 330.
9 Cho and Squier, "Religion as a Complex and Dynamic System," 359.
10 See, for example, Timothy Fitzgerald, *The Ideology of Religious Studies* (New York: Oxford University Press, 2000), 1, 10.
11 Fitzgerald, *The Ideology of Religious Studies*, 10.
12 Roger Schmidt, *Exploring Religion*, 2nd ed. (Belmont, CA: Wadsworth, 1988), xii.
13 Russell T. McCutcheon, *Manufacturing Religion: The Discourse on Sui Generis Religion and the Politics of Nostalgia* (New York: Oxford University Press, 1997), ix–x, 9–11. At least on the theoretical side, this abandonment of the central comparative explanatory activity of religious studies was motivated by comparative typologies that were too abstract and provincial. There is no doubt that any generalizing nomenclature, as Alles shows, "After the Naming Explosion," in Wedemeyer and Doniger, *Hermeneutics, Politics, and the History of Religions*, 73–74, will be ethnocentric, yet this should have spurred the development of more adequate typologies rather than the abandonment of the comparative approach, except as a relic in introductory courses.
14 McCutcheon, *Manufacturing Religion*, 15, 17–18.
15 Mircea Eliade, "Methodological Remarks on the Study of Religious Symbolism," in *The History of Religions: Essays in Methodology*, ed. Mircea Eliade and Joseph Mitsuo Kitagawa (Chicago: University of Chicago Press, 1973), 89–90.
16 Monima Chadha, "On Knowing Universals: The Nyāya Way," *Philosophy East and West* 64, no. 2 (April 2014): 289.
17 Chadha, "On Knowing Universals," 290.
18 Paul C. Hedengren, "Universals as Theoretical Entities" (PhD thesis, University of Toronto, 1983; reformatted, Provo, Utah: Tepran Corporation, 2002), Kindle edition, Introduction.
19 Hedengren, "Universals as Theoretical Entities," Kindle edition, Introduction.
20 To show that the notion of direct intuitive perception of universals is not merely a personal preference of my own, I cite the fact that, according to Chadha, Nava-Nyāya, a school of Hindu logic, holds that human beings "can have non-mediated perceptual acquaintance with universals," a view that Chadha holds is rarely ever met with in Western philosophy, "On Knowing Universals," 287, 289.
21 For a definition of a property, see Theodore Sider, "Introduction," in *Contemporary Debates in Metaphysics*, ed. Theodore Sider, John Hawthorne, and Dean W. Zimmerman (Hoboken: Wiley-Blackwell, 2013), Kindle edition, Introduction.
22 Chadha, "On Knowing Universals," 290.
23 William Kneale and Martha Kneale, *The Development of Logic* (London: Oxford University Press, 1962), 265.

24 Douglas Ehring, "Distinguishing Universals from Particulars," *Analysis* 64, no. 4 (October 2004): 327. The generality that sponsors universals is an ontological reality that, in my view, fundamentally challenges any materialistic cosmology that remains captive to prerelativistic, Newtonian biases because generality is a symptom, or effect, of the immaterial order within which the central and ultimate formal objects—or abstract entities—of religion are situated. Thus, to eliminate religious and contemplative universals would undercut the ground on which the formal object of religion stands.

25 Chadha, "On Knowing Universals," 289. E. J. Lowe notes that, on some accounts, "universals are 'repeatable' and particulars 'non-repeatable' entities," *The Four-Category Ontology: A Metaphysical Foundation for Natural Science* (Oxford and New York: Oxford University Press, 2006), 9.

26 Chris Swoyer, "Abstract Entities," in *Contemporary Debates in Metaphysics*, ed. Theodore Sider, John Hawthorne, and Dean W. Zimmerman (Hoboken: Wiley-Blackwell, 2013), Kindle edition, Chapter 12.

27 Swoyer, "Abstract Entities," in Sider, Hawthorne, and Zimmerman, *Contemporary Debates in Metaphysics*, Kindle edition, Chapter 13.

28 Alles, "After the Naming Explosion," in Wedemeyer and Doniger, *Hermeneutics, Politics, and the History of Religions*, 71–74.

29 Ibid., 66.

30 Alles distinguishes between what he calls "inference-rich" and "inference-poor" concepts, or concepts about which we can infer a good deal of information simply from the stating of the concept, and those about which we can make few or no inferences, Alles, "After the Naming Explosion," in Wedemeyer and Doniger, *Hermeneutics, Politics, and the History of Religions*, 64.

31 Alles, "After the Naming Explosion," in Wedemeyer and Doniger, *Hermeneutics, Politics, and the History of Religions*, 71.

32 Ibid., 69.

33 A view that Alles appears to hold, although he qualifies it by calling it a "somewhat confused claim," Alles, "After the Naming Explosion," in Wedemeyer and Doniger, *Hermeneutics, Politics, and the History of Religions*, 70.

34 Alles, "After the Naming Explosion," in Wedemeyer and Doniger, *Hermeneutics, Politics, and the History of Religions*, 71.

35 Ibid., 70.

36 It is this intensity, or at least a reflection of it, that is key element in the use of the word "religious" when referring to lesser forms of dedication, such as the dedication which leads a devotee of Apple products to camp out for three days to be among the first to own the latest gadget dreamed up in Cupertino, California. Yet, this use of *religious* remains a metaphor, and its widespread use cannot be seriously used to undermine the definition of religion that I propose here.

37 This definition is identical to the one that I proposed in Kenneth Rose, *Pluralism: The Future of Religion* (New York: Bloomsbury, 2013), 12.

38 Jeppe Sinding Jensen, *The Study of Religion in a New Key: Theoretical and Philosophical Soundings in the Comparative and General Study of Religion* (Århus: Aarhus University Press, 2003), 9. Jensen begins his defense of the necessity for a nomothetic study of religion alongside idiographic approaches by employing the distinction between philology and linguistics that was proposed by Louis Hjemslev in 1943. In Hjemslev's view (as restated by Jensen), philology focuses on "specific languages," while linguistics should have "language in general as its true object," Jensen, *The Study of Religion in a New Key*, 174. Indeed, Hjemslev saw linguistics in holistic terms as "sui generis,"

according to Jensen, and, thus, as more than a mere "conglomeration of non-linguistic phenomena," Jensen, *The Study of Religion in a New Key*, 174.

39 As noted by the leading Mircea Eliade scholar, Bryan Rennie, in "The Influence of Eastern Orthodox Christian Theology on Mircea Eliade's Understanding of Religion," in *Hermeneutics, Politics, and the History of Religions: The Contested Legacies of Joachim Wach and Mircea Eliade*, ed. Christian Wedemeyer and Wendy Doniger (New York: Oxford University Press, 2010), 209.

40 Jensen, *The Study of Religion in a New Key*, 9.

41 Ibid., 162–68.

42 Bernard McGinn, "Preface," in McGinn, *The Essential Writings of Christian Mysticism*, xi.

43 McGinn, *The Essential Writings of Christian Mysticism*, xi.

44 William E. Paden, "Elements of a New Comparativism," in *A Magic Still Dwells: Comparative Religion in the Postmodern Age*, ed. Kimberley C. Patton and Benjamin C. Ray (Berkeley, Los Angeles, and London: University of California Press, 2000), 182.

45 Paden, "Elements of a New Comparativism," in Patton and Ray, *A Magic Still Dwells*, 190.

46 Ibid. A pioneering theorist of the new comparativism, Paden, was already arguing in 2001 and earlier that the time has come "to reconsider the uses of a broadened notion of human behaviors underlying and shared by all cultures," William E. Paden, "Universals Revisited: Human Behaviors and Cultural Variables," *Numen* 48, no. 3 (2001): 276–77.

47 Paden, "Universals Revisited," 276–77.

48 Ann Taves, *Religious Experience Reconsidered: A Building-Block Approach to the Study of Religion and Other Special Things* (Princeton and Oxford: Princeton University Press, 2009), xii, 8.

49 Taves, *Religious Experience Reconsidered*, 164.

50 Ibid., 8–9, 10, 12–14, 26–48, 153–64.

51 Ibid., 163–64.

52 Ibid., 163.

53 Ibid., xiv, 118.

54 Daniel Dubuisson, *The Western Construction of Religion: Myths, Knowledge, and Ideology*, trans. William Sayers (Baltimore and London: The Johns Hopkins University Press, 2003; originally published as *L'Occident et la religion. Mythes, science et idéologie*, Bruxelles, Éditions Complexe, 1998), 87.

55 Dubuisson, *The Western Construction of Religion*, 5.

56 Ibid., 4.

57 Ibid., 3–4.

58 Ibid., 8–15, 172.

59 Ibid., 201.

60 Ibid., 199.

61 Ibid., 17, 198–213.

62 Ibid., 196.

63 Ibid., 172–74.

64 Ibid., 87.

65 Sarbacker, *Samādhi*. Sarbacker also synthesizes the perspectives of academics and practitioners and explores the yoga praxis of India and Tibet from philosophical and psychological standpoints.

66 Randall Studstill, *The Unity of Mystical Traditions: The Transformation of Consciousness in Tibetan and German Mysticism* (Leiden and Boston: Brill Academic, 2005), 7–10. This innovative book bucks the constructivist, that is,

localizing, tendency of virtually all current religious studies theorizing about mysticism.

67 Jeffrey J. Kripal, *Authors of the Impossible: The Paranormal and the Sacred* (Chicago and London: The University of Chicago Press, 2010), Kindle edition, 201–02.

68 Gavin Flood, *The Truth Within: A History of Inwardness in Christianity, Hinduism, and Buddhism* (Oxford, UK: Oxford University Press, 2013), 2.

69 Brainard, *Reality and Mystical Experience*, 62, 252, 266. I discuss Brainard's postconstructivist philosophy of mysticism in a review of this book, *Journal of the American Academy of Religion* 71, no. 2 (Summer 2003): 426–28, accessed October 21, 2015, http://www.jstor.org/stable/1466559.

70 Alles relates an anecdote about what appears to be Wach's rather mechanical and unimaginative way of generating the "concrete types" or categories that he devised to bring order to the study of massive amounts of "religious phenomena," "After the Naming Explosion," in Wedemeyer and Doniger, *Hermeneutics, Politics, and the History of Religions*, 51–53.

71 Alles, "After the Naming Explosion," in Wedemeyer and Doniger, *Hermeneutics, Politics, and the History of Religions*, 60–61.

72 Ibid., 60. See also Patton and Ray, who with perhaps some ambivalence summarize the potent and influential postmodern criticism of the comparative enterprise as revealing it, "at worst, as a subjective mélange of culturally biased perceptions that cannot but distort, or at best, as an act of imaginative associative 'play,' " "Introduction," in Patton and Ray, *A Magic Still Dwells*, 2.

Chapter 2

1 Charles Taylor holds that "a widespread response to the world created by Western modernity over the last two centuries" has been a return to religion, or "spiritual life," which "springs from a profound dissatisfaction with a life encased entirely in the immanent order. The sense is that this life is flat, empty, devoid of a higher purpose," *A Secular Age* (Cambridge, MA: Harvard University Press, 2007), 506–07.

2 Wayne Proudfoot, *Religious Experience* (Berkeley: University of California Press, 1985), xi.

3 Friedrich Schleiermacher, *On Religion: Speeches to Its Cultured Despisers*, trans. Richard Crouter (Cambridge: Cambridge University Press, 1988), 102, 104.

4 R. C. Zaehner, *Mysticism: Sacred and Profane* (Oxford: Oxford University Press, 1957), v, ix–xvi, 27–29, 168, 198, 204.

5 Katz, "Language, Epistemology, and Mysticism," in Katz, *Mysticism and Philosophical Analysis*; "The 'Conservative' Character of Mysticism." in *Mysticism and Religious Traditions*.

6 Robert M. Gimello, "Mysticism and Meditation," in *Mysticism and Philosophical Analysis*, ed. Steven T. Katz (New York: Oxford University Press, 1978), 170–99 and "Mysticism and its Contexts," in *Mysticism and Religious Traditions*, ed. Steven T. Katz (New York: Oxford University Press, 1983), 61–88.

7 Proudfoot, *Religious Experience*, 1–40, 228–36, *et* passim.

8 Grace M. Jantzen, "Could There be a Mystical Core of Religion?" *Religious Studies* 26 (1990): 59–71.

9 The English word *mysticism* comes from the Greek *myō* (μύω): to "close, be shut, of the eyes," Henry George Liddell, and Robert Scott, *A Greek-English Lexicon*

(1940), s.v. *myō* (μύω), accessed October 17, 2015, http://www.perseus.tufts.edu/hopper/text?doc=Perseus%3Atext%3A1999.04.0057%3Aentry%3Dmu%2Fw. It can also mean "to conceal," Jerome Gellman, "Mysticism," *Stanford Encyclopedia of Philosophy*, accessed October 17, 2015, http://plato.stanford.edu/entries/mysticism/SEP. In Greek, a *mystēs* ("initiate") is "a person who has been initiated into mysteries, especially religious mysteries," and, consequently, is a "person vowed to keep silence," *The Oxford English Dictionary*, s.v. "mystes, n.," accessed October 17, 2015, http://0-www.oed.com.read.cnu.edu/view/Entry/124646? See also Steven T. Katz, "General Editor's Introduction," in *Comparative Mysticism: An Anthology of Original Sources*, ed. Steven T. Katz (New York: Oxford University Press, 2013), 3.

10 Robert M. Grant with David Tracy, *A Short History of the Interpretation of the Bible*. 2nd ed. (Philadelphia: Fortress Press, 1984), 85. For a detailed account of the exegetical character of early Christian mysticism, see Bernard McGinn, *The Presence of God: A History of Western Christian Mysticism*, Vol. 1, *The Foundations of Mysticism: Origins to the Fifth Century* (New York: Crossroad, 1994), 3–4, 84–130; Philip Sheldrake, *Spirituality: A Very Short Introduction* (Oxford: Oxford University Press, 2012), 46.

11 Jonathan David Nash and Andrew Newberg, "Toward A Unifying Taxonomy and Definition for Meditation," *Frontiers in Psychology* 4 (November 2013): 1–18, accessed August 7, 2015, doi: 10.3389/fpsyg.2013.00806.6.

12 Harvey D. Egan, *An Anthology of Christian Mysticism* (Collegeville, MN: The Liturgical Press, 1996), 4–5.

13 Egan, *An Anthology of Christian Mysticism*, 207–14.

14 As scripted and performed by Pseudo-Dionysius in the five chapters of *The Mystical Theology*, in *Pseudo-Dionysius The Complete Works*, trans. Colm Luibheid (Mahwah, NJ: Paulist Press, 1987), 133–41; in Meister Eckhart's "Poverty Sermon" *Meister Eckhart: Selected Writings*, trans. Oliver Davies (New York: Penguin Books, 1994), Sermon 22 (DW 53), 202–09, and more recently in Thomas Merton's apophatic tour de force, *Contemplative Prayer* (New York: Image Books, 1971; originally published as *The Climate of Monastic Prayer*, Kalamazoo, MI: Cistercian Publications, and Herder and Herder, 1971), 42–45, 75–116.

15 Egan, *An Anthology of Christian Mysticism*, xxi; see also Harvey D. Egan, *Christian Mysticism: The Future of a Tradition* (New York: Pueblo Publishing, 1984), 4.

16 Vladimir Lossky, *The Mystical Theology of the Eastern Church*, trans. anon. (Crestwood, NY: St. Vladimir's Seminary Press, 1976; originally published as *Essai sur la theologie mystique de l'Eglise d'Orient*, Paris: Aubier, 1944), 7.

17 Lossky, *The Mystical Theology of the Eastern Church*, 236. A view more or less affirmed by McGinn, *The Foundations of Mysticism*, xiv.

18 As detailed in André Jean Festugière's classic monograph, *Personal Religion among the Greeks* (Berkeley and Los Angeles: University of California Press, 1954).

19 As in the famous challenge of William Tyndale, who boasted to an opponent, "If God spare my life, ere many years I will cause a boy that driveth the plough shall know more of the Scripture than thou dost," *The Independent Works of William Tyndale*. Vol. 3, *An Answer unto Sir Thomas More's Dialogue*, ed. Anne M. O'Donnell and Jared Wicks (Washington, DC: Catholic University of America Press, 2000), 384.

20 In this brief account of the rise of the contemporary concept of mysticism and the discourse about the world's religions and Orientalism, I generally follow, Tomoko Masuzawa, *The Invention of World Religions: Or, How European Universalism was Preserved in the Language of Pluralism* (Chicago: University of Chicago Press, 2005),

10–13, 107–20, and Richard King, *Orientalism and Religion: Postcolonial Theory, India, and the "Mystic East"* (London and New York: Routledge, 1999), 8–34, 81–95.

21 A somewhat negative, analysis similar to that proposed by King (see preceding footnote) is given by Katz, *Mysticism and Philosophical Analysis*, 1. More positive is Richard Woods, "Introduction," in *Understanding Mysticism*, ed. Richard Woods (New York: Image Books, 1980), 1.

22 Catherine Cornille, *The Im-Possibility of Interreligious Dialogue* (New York: Crossroad, 2008), 4; Catherine Cornille, "The Dynamics of Multiple Belonging," in *Many Mansions? Multiple Religious Belonging and Christian Identity*, ed. Catherine Cornille (Maryknoll, NY: Orbis Books, 2002), 3–4.

23 These phrases are consistent with what Gavin D'Costa unfavorably calls "a pick and mix divine," Gavin D'Costa, "Pluralist Arguments," in *Catholic Engagement with World Religions: A Comprehensive Study*, ed. Karl J. Becker, Ilaria Morali, and Gavin D'Costa (Maryknoll, NY: Orbis Books, 2010), 334. Stephen Prothero has colorfully characterized the religious syncretism evident in the contemporary United States as "the divine-deli-cafeteria religion," quoted in Lisa Miller, "We're All Hindus Now," *Newsweek* (August 24, 2009): 58. Other condescending evaluations include: David Mills, "Spirituality without Spirits," *First Things*, May 28, 2010, accessed August 10, 2015, http://www.firstthings.com/web-exclusives/2010/05/spirituality-without-spirits?utm_source=First+Things+Subscribers&utm_campaign=29364ebaec-Sunday_Spotlight_8_9_2015&utm_medium=email&utm_term=0_28bf775c26-29364ebaec-180570269#print.

24 Linda A. Mercadante breaks new ground by treating SBNRs seriously as bringing about "a sea change in belief," *Belief without Borders: Inside the Minds of the Spiritual but not Religious* (Oxford and New York: Oxford University Press, 2014), 9, 69–71.

25 Charles Taylor defined the "post-secular" era as "a time in which the hegemony of the mainstream master narrative of secularism will be more and more challenged," *A Secular Age*, 534.

26 Referring to the different mystical traditions as "mysticisms" is traceable at least to Katz, "The 'Conservative' Character of Mysticism," in Katz, *Mysticism and Religious Traditions*, 3.

27 Ninian Smart, "Interpretation and Mystical Experience," in Woods, *Understanding Mysticism* (repr. *Religious Studies* 1, no. 1, October, 1975), 91.

28 Katz, "Language, Epistemology, and Mysticism," in Katz, *Mysticism and Philosophical Analysis*, 27, 64; "The 'Conservative' Character of Mystical Experience," in Katz, *Mysticism and Religious Experience*, 4–5. Katz is certainly correct in pointing out that he does not see context as totally determinative of the mystic's context, as is clear from the preceding cited passages. This is a weaker constructivism than the strong constructivism criticized by Sallie B. King, Robert K. C. Forman, and Jensine Andresen, as noted by Torben Hammersholt, "Steven T. Katz's Philosophy of Mysticism Revisited," *Journal of the American Academy of Religion* 81, no. 2 (June 2013): 470.

29 Although raised in as prominent a location as the standard pre-Katzian anglophone philosophical study of mysticism, W. T. Stace's, *Mysticism and Philosophy* (Los Angeles: Jeremy P. Tarcher, 1987, repr. London: Macmillan Press, 1960), 34, this question became central in the wake of the Katzian revolution, as asked, for instance, by Richard Woods in 1980: "Is mystical experience in fact one and the same for all in its essential structure and function, or are there irreducibly plural forms of mystical experience?" "Introduction," in Woods (ed.), *Understanding Mysticism*, 3.

30 The expression *constructivism* is widely used to name the stance introduced by Katz and his collaborators in 1978, yet Katz, as noted by Jason N. Blum, prefers the less familiar term *contextualism*, "The Science of Consciousness and Mystical Experience: An Argument for Radical Empiricism," *Journal of the American Academy of Religion* 82, no. 1 (March 2014): 152. See Steven T. Katz, "Mystical Speech and Mystical Meaning," in *Mysticism and Language*, ed. Steven T. Katz (Oxford and New York: Oxford University Press, 1992), 34n9; Steven T. Katz, "Editor's Introduction," in *Mysticism and Sacred Scripture*, ed. Steven T. Katz (Oxford and New York: Oxford University Press, 2000), 3. Perennialism can be seen as one historical expression of the essentialist approach to mysticism.

31 Bernard McGinn, "Meister Eckhart: An Introduction," in *An Introduction to the Medieval Mystics*, ed. Paul S. Szarmach (Albany: SUNY Press, 1984), 247.

32 This phrase has since the sixteenth century been applied to various, mostly European, religious philosophies, Charles B. Schmitt, "Perennial Philosophy: From Agostino Steuco to Leibniz," *Journal of the History of Ideas* 27, no. 4 (October/December 1966): 515, 532, accessed February 6, 2015, http://www.jstor.org/stable/2708338. It was popularized by Aldous Huxley, *The Perennial Philosophy*, 3rd ed. (New York: Harper and Brothers, 1945), vii, who repurposed it to serve as the name of an approach to mysticism that sees mysticism everywhere as constituted by a small set of basic attributes, an approach associated with Anglophone philosophy of mysticism from William James to Ninian Smart and also with the massively more influential and global "traditionalist school" of mystical studies associated with such names as Ananda Coomaraswamy, René Guenon, Martin Lings, Titus Burckhardt, Fritjof Schuon, Marco Pallis, Seyyed Hossein Nasr, Alain Daniélou, Huston Smith, and Alan Watts, as noted by Alan Watts, *Beyond Theology: The Art of Godmanship*, pbk. ed. (Cleveland and New York: World Publishing, 1966), xi.

33 As an example, James S. Cutsinger notes that the perennialism of Fritjof Schuon involves "a complete disregard for such things as cultural context and historical influence in the exposition of ideas," "Review of *The Essential Writings of Fritjof Schuon*," edited by Seyyed Hossein Nasr, *Journal of the American Academy of Religion* 62, no. 1 (Spring 1989): 209. Cutsinger notes that Schuon's writings are "devoted to describing, defending, and evoking a mode of knowledge or level of insight that is not the effect or result, but the cause by manifestation and condensation, of the empirical, social, physical, and cultural world, *the visible* world, simply taken as given in nearly all our research," ibid., 210, italics in the original.

34 Bernard McGinn, in a masterful history of recent theologies and philosophies of mysticism, characterizes much of anglophone philosophizing on this topic since 1960 as "inbred," "internecine" critical studies of "the inner consistency" of theories of mysticism rather than the actual texts of mysticism, *The Foundations of Mysticism*, 315–24. Wood, "Introduction," in Wood, *Understanding Mysticism*, 3–8, provided, not long after the commencement of the constructivist counterrevolution in anglophone mysticism studies, a balanced evaluation of the what he saw as "a perennial issue" of weighing the relative importance of similarities and differences in evaluating mysticism—or perhaps we should say, mysticisms.

35 Other figures include Robert M. Gimello (mentioned elsewhere in this chapter) and Wayne Proudfoot, who categorically asserted "the impossibility of transcending language in order to discover some aspect of experience which is innocent of conceptual assumptions or grammatical practices," *Religious Experience*, 229. Blum lists other formative figures in the movement, including Hans Penner, Matthew

Bagger, Philip Barnes, and C. J. Arthur, but he sees Katz as the most prominent of the group, "The Science of Consciousness and Mystical Experience," 152, 153. Other major constructivist and "social constructionist" approaches to religious experience have been mounted by Jonathan Z. Smith, Russell T. McCutcheon, Talal Asad, Timothy Fitzgerald, William E. Arnal, and Daniel Dubuisson, according to Benjamin Y. Fong, "On Critics and What's Real: Russell McCutcheon on Religious Experience," *Journal of the American Academy of Religion* 82, no. 4 (December 2014): 1128.

36 Hammersholt surmises that Katz's founding contextualist/constructivist essay, Language, Epistemology, and Mysticism," published in Katz's edited volume *Mysticism and Philosophical Analysis*, is "a strong candidate" for being "the text that has attracted the most scholarly attention within the last thirty years of research on mysticism," "Steven T. Katz's Philosophy of Mysticism Revisited," 467. Robert K. C. Forman earlier made a similar claim, "Introduction: Mysticism, Constructivism, and Forgetting," in Robert K. C. Forman, *The Problem of Pure Consciousness: Mysticism and Philosophy*, pbk. ed. (New York: Oxford University Press, 1997, originally published 1990), 9.

37 Steven T. Katz, "Editor's Introduction," in Katz, *Mysticism and Philosophical Analysis*, 4.

38 Katz, "Language, Epistemology, and Mysticism," in Katz, *Mysticism and Philosophical Analysis*, 65.

39 As Katz notes throughout in his contributions to *Mysticism and Philosophical Analysis*, 2, 25, 28, 29, 30, 31.

40 John Hick, "The Copernican Revolution in Theology," in *God and the Universe of Faiths: Essays in the Philosophy of Religion* (London: Macmillan, 1973), 8, 125–30; see also Kenneth Rose, *Knowing the Real: John Hick on the Cognitivity of Religions and Religious Pluralism* (Peter Lang Publishing, New York, 1996), 66–69.

41 S. Wesley Ariarajah, "Wider Ecumenism: A Threat or a Promise?" *The Ecumenical Review* 50, no. 3 (1998): 321–29, accessed October 17, 2015, doi: 10.1111/j.1758-6623.1998.tb00009.

42 D'Costa, "The Impossibility of a Pluralist View of Religions," 225.

43 Katz claims that, with the exception of Ninian Smart, R. C. Zaehner, and H. P. Owen, no other previous academic student of mysticism recognized the issue as Katz does in this essay, "Language, Epistemology, and Mysticism," in Katz, *Mysticism and Philosophical Analysis*, 68n13. It is clear, however, that Zaehner is much more than a mere predecessor of Katz, but may even be seen as the true originator of constructivism (see *Mysticism: Sacred and Profane*, v, ix–xvi, 27–29, 168, 198, 204, where he expressed a sense of nausea for the mystical core teaching of perennialism), far more than Smart, who, despite clear presentiments of the constructivist approach, would as late as 1975 in the first issue of the prestigious *Religious Studies* assert the phenomenological oneness of mysticism as "everywhere the same," "Interpretation and Mystical Experience," 79–86, 90–91. Smart restates this view cogently, if more tentatively, in the opening essay in Katz's landmark volume, "Understanding Religious Experience," in Katz, *Mysticism and Philosophical Analysis*, 14.

44 Katz, "Language, Epistemology, and Mysticism," in Katz, *Mysticism and Philosophical Analysis*, 26.

45 Ibid. Katz restates this view as late as 2013 in his "General Editor's Introduction," in Katz, *Comparative Mysticism*, 5.

46 Katz, "Language, Epistemology, and Mysticism," in Katz, *Mysticism and Philosophical Analysis*, 26.

47 Katz's views have varied somewhat on whether mystical experience is only partially or totally preformed by context. In his 1978 essay, he qualified the constructivist axiom with the phrase "at least partially," "Language, Epistemology, and Mysticism," in Katz, *Mysticism and Philosophical Analysis*, 26. He repeats this qualification five years later, "The 'Conservative' Character of Mystical Experience," in Katz, *Mysticism and Religious Traditions*, 3. His constructivism was still cautious, as when he spoke of "what may well be the *necessary* [Katz's emphasis] connection between the mystic's way and his goal," "Editor's Introduction," viii. But in a recent essay, Katz is clear and categorical: "Mystical experience(s) reveal a *necessary* [Katz's emphasis] relationship between the prior education of the mystic and their mystical goal, [and] the intentions of the mystic and their actual experiences," Katz, *Comparative Mysticism*, 5. McGinn thinks that Katz's concerns in "Language, Epistemology, and Mysticism," are "almost nominalistic at times," *The Foundations of Mysticism*, 322. This ambiguity animates his argument in Katz, "Language, Epistemology, and Mysticism," in Katz, *Mysticism and Philosophical Analysis*, 26, 40. See also Hammersholt, "Steven T. Katz's Philosophy of Mysticism Revisited," 468. This ambiguity, and Katz's tendency to reject a strong or complete constructivism on one hand while reaffirming it on the other hand, can be seen in the lively interview with Katz conducted by journalist John Horgan, *Rational Mysticism* (Boston and New York: Houghton Mifflin, 2003), 46.

48 Blum summarizes the neo-Kantian—as opposed to merely Kantian—assumptions of constructivism, Blum, "The Science of Consciousness and Mystical Experience," 150–51.

49 Katz, "Language, Epistemology, and Mysticism," in Katz, *Mysticism and Philosophical Analysis*, 25.

50 Illustrative of this dissolution and utterly consistent with strong constructivism is Hans Penner's claim that "'mysticism' is an illusion, unreal, a false category which has distorted an important aspect of religion," "The Mystical Illusion," in *Mysticism and Religious Traditions*, ed. Steven T. Katz (New York: Oxford University Press, 1983), 89.

51 As evidenced in Katz's extensive discussion of the various visionary, doctrinal, and physical phenomena that attend the mysticisms, in "The 'Conservative' Character of Mysticism," in Katz, *Mysticism and Religious Traditions*, 6–43. None of this is to be denied, and all of these phenomena are worthy of study, but this infinitely extendable catalogue only underscores the fact that the archive of mystical evidence also massively witnesses to a centrally important strand of mysticism that Ninian Smart, in the same volume as Katz's catalogue of differences, precisely named "consciousness-purity," and defined it as "the inmost rapture that is imageless and locutionless," "The Purification of Consciousness and the Negative Path," in Katz, *Mysticism and Religious Traditions*, 117, 125, 128n1.

52 For example, Penner's virtuoso-like demonstration that the significance of "Indian mysticism" should be understood as the ascetic complement to caste, which may well be the case from a purely materialist or social-constructionist standpoint, but still leaves the question of the meaning or reality of these mystical traditions *as mystical traditions* and not merely as sociocultural formations unaddressed, "The Mystical Illusion," in Katz, *Mysticism and Religious Traditions*, 104–13.

53 My use of the expression "the mystical" is influenced by Wittgenstein's variously interpreted *das Mystische* at the end of the *Tractatus Logico-Philosophicus*, rev. ed., trans. D. F. Pears and B. F. McGuinness (London and New York: Routledge, 1972; originally published, 1922; a translation of *Logische-Philosophische Abhandlung*, 1922): 6:522.

54 Gimello, "Mysticism in its Contexts," in Katz, *Mysticism and Religious Traditions*, 85.
55 Katz, "Language, Epistemology, and Mysticism," in *Mysticism and Philosophical Analysis*, 36. Stace also understood this difference, as evidenced throughout *Mysticism and Philosophy.*
56 Or, as Stace notes, *Mysticism and Philosophy*, 183, 197, whether they exist, or perhaps subsist, *ante rem* or *in re* (that is, prior to or within a class of related realities) to use the classic distinction between the Platonic and Aristotelian view.
57 As early as 2000 in the long afternoon of the reign of constructivism, F. Samuel Brainard offered the essentialist, nomothetic claim that some aspect of the mysticisms justifies a nonarbitrary use of the term "mystical," since, if this were not the case, mystical experience would be devoid of the "pan-religious scholarly interest" that it clearly possesses, *Reality and Mystical Experience*, 52, 62.
58 Forman distinguishes between what he calls "complete constructivism" and "incomplete constructivism" in "Introduction," in Forman, *The Problem of Pure Consciousness*, 13, a distinction that is rigorously analyzed by Hammersholt, "Steven T. Katz's Philosophy of Mysticism Revisited," 469–74.
59 Sallie B. King, "Two Epistemological Models for the Interpretation of Mysticism," *Journal of the American Academy of Religion* 56, no. 2 (Summer 1988): 257.
60 Blum, "The Science of Consciousness and Mystical Experience," 151.
61 Paul Marshall, *Mystical Encounters with the Natural World: Experiences and Explanations* (Oxford: Oxford University Press, 2005), 190.
62 Stace, *Mysticism and Philosophy*, 95–96. This passage is taken from *The Adornment of the Spiritual Marriage, The Book of the Supreme Truth, The Sparking Stone,*, trans. C. A. Wynschenk (London: J. M. Dent & Sons, 1916), 245 ff.
63 Stace, *Mysticism and Philosophy*, 155.
64 Ibid., 79.
65 Ibid., 94. A view that was cogently and courageously presented by Ninian Smart in what might be seen as the dissenting essay in Katz's *Mysticism and Religious Traditions*, "The Purification of Consciousness and the Negative Path," 117–28. There, Smart names the washing of images from the mind as "consciousness-purification," 117, and reasserts it as "the heart of mysticism," 128n1.
66 Katz, *Comparative Mysticism*, 5.
67 Katz, "Language, Epistemology, and Mysticism," in Katz, *Mysticism and Philosophical Analysis*, 58. He makes a similar claim as recently as 2013: "The forms of consciousness that the mystic brings to experience set structured and limiting parameters on what the experience will be," *Comparative Mysticism*, 5.
68 Huston Smith, "Is there a Perennial Philosophy?" *Journal of the American Academy of Religion* 55, no. 3 (Autumn 1987): 556, accessed February 8, 2015, http://www.jstor.org/stable/1464070.
69 Katz, "Language, Epistemology, and Mysticism," in Katz, *Mysticism and Philosophical Analysis*, 61. Stace reproduces a number of passages similar to this from Ruysbroeck and compares them with a passage from the *Māṇḍūkya Upaniṣad* and concludes that, minus some interpretational doctrines, both traditions express core teachings of what he calls introvertive mysticism. Stace notes, however, that Zaehner, *Mysticism: Sacred and Profane*, 170–74, attempted to explain this similarity away by attributing the mysticism of formlessness and indistinction to a natural state of mysticism that is inferior to the "true, supernatural union with God," which Zaehner sees as much higher than the imageless, indistinct experiences of introvertive mysticism, *Mysticism and Philosophy*, 88–97m 97n44.

70 On Eckhart, see Robert K. C. Forman, "Eckhart, *Gezücken*, and the Ground of the Soul," in Forman, *The Problem of Pure Consciousness*, 30, 32, 38, 101, 103–07.
71 See Rose, *Pluralism*, 125.
72 Stace, *Mysticism and Philosophy*, 86, 110–11, 155. Forman, "Eckhart, *Gezücken*, and the Ground of the Soul," 106, notes that Stace provides forty pages of cross-cultural evidence for what Stace called "introvertive mystical experiences" or states of "pure consciousness," Stace, *Mysticism and Philosophy*, 86, 88–133, or what Forman calls PCEs. Driven more by theory than facts, Katz proactively and surprisingly influentially declared in his paradigm-generating essay that "there is no substantive evidence to suggest that there is any pure consciousness *per se*," Katz, "Language, Epistemology, and Mysticism," 57.
73 Katz, "Language, Epistemology, and Mysticism," 57.
74 See Christopher Chapple's analysis of *samādhi* in the light of the unconditioned consciousness, "The Unseen Seer and the Field: Consciousness in Sāṃkhya and Yoga," in *The Problem of Pure Consciousness: Mysticism and Philosophy*, ed. Robert K. C. Forman (New York: Oxford University Press, 1997), 65–70.
75 Paul Griffiths, "Pure Consciousness and Indian Buddhism," in *The Problem of Pure Consciousness: Mysticism and Philosophy*, ed. Robert K. C. Forman (New York: Oxford University Press, 1997), 78–82–85–92. A similar investigation has been made quite recently by Yaroslav Komarovski, *Tibetan Buddhism and Mystical Experience* (New York: Oxford University Press, 2015), 16, 68–78.
76 Forman, "Introduction," in Forman, *The Problem of Pure Consciousness*, 33, 38–39.
77 Steven Bernhardt, "Is Pure Consciousness Unmediated: A Response to Katz," unpublished essay presented at the American Academy of Religion, November 1985, 12–13, and quoted by Forman, "Eckhart, *Gezücken*, and the Ground of the Soul," in Forman, *The Problem of Pure Consciousness*, 100. A similar article by Steven Bernhardt appears as, "Are Pure Consciousness Events Unmediated," in *The Problem of Pure Consciousness: Mysticism and Philosophy*, ed. Robert K. C. Forman (New York: Oxford University Press, 1997), 220–36.
78 *Kaṭha Upaniṣad*, Patrick Olivelle, trans. *The Upaniṣads* (New York: Oxford University Press, 1996), 4.10.
79 Katz, "Language, Epistemology, and Mysticism," in Katz, *Mysticism and Philosophical Analysis*, 65.
80 Griffiths, "Pure Consciousness and Indian Buddhism," in Forman, *The Problem of Pure Consciousness*, 73, 75.
81 Forman holds that constructivism cannot "plausibly account" for the PCE, "Introduction," in Forman, *The Problem of Pure Consciousness*, 21–25.
82 Although Forman distinguishes between visionary and mystical experience, "Introduction," in Forman, *The Problem of Pure Consciousness*, 7–8, I think that this too narrowly defines mysticism. Rather, I think it more helpful and truer to traditional philosophies of mysticism, to distinguish between visionary mysticisms, which can be seen as cataphatic responses to the mystical reality understood as, in the Advaita Vedānta of Śaṇkara, for instance as *saguṇa brahman*, or having form, and form-transcending mysticisms, which can be seen as apophatic responses to the mystical reality understood as *nirguṇa brahman*. For a short discussion of this distinction, see Eliot Deutsch, *Advaita Vedānta: A Philosophical Reconstruction* (Honolulu: The University Press of Hawai'i, 1969), 12–14.
83 Katz, "Language, Epistemology, and Mysticism," in Katz, *Mysticism and Philosophical Analysis*, 57.

84 Forman, "Introduction," in Forman, *The Problem of Pure Consciousness*, 21.
85 Ibid., 22.
86 Ibid., 24.
87 Ibid., 8.
88 Roland Fischer, "A Cartography of Understanding Mysticism," *Science* (November 26, 1971): 897–904. This essay is reprinted in Woods, *Understanding Mysticism*, 286–305; much of this argument is repeated in Robert K. C. Forman, *Mysticism, Mind, Consciousness* (Albany: State University Press of New York, 1999), 4–7.
89 Forman, "Introduction," in Forman, *The Problem of Pure Consciousness*, 6.
90 Ibid., 7.
91 Ibid., 8.
92 Ibid., 6.
93 Ibid., 7.
94 Smart, "Interpretation and Mystical Experience," 7, quoted in Forman, "Introduction," in Forman, *The Problem of Pure Consciousness*, 7.
95 Stace, *Mysticism and Philosophy*, 111.
96 Fritz Staals endorsed a more essentialist approach when he concludes in a series of essays on the study of mysticism that the "immense variety [of mystical experiences] . . . is consistent with a very small number of basic experiences, or even with one kind of basic experience." Staals goes on to conclude that mystical experiences are "to some extent independent of their interpretations and evaluations," *Exploring Mysticism: A Methodological Essay* (Berkeley: University of California Press, 1975), 189.
97 Zaehner, *Mysticism: Sacred and Profane*, xv.
98 Robert K. C. Forman, "Preface," in *The Innate Capacity: Mysticism, Psychology, and Philosophy*, ed. Robert K. C. Forman (New York and Oxford: Oxford University Press, 1998), viii.
99 Taves, *Religious Experience Reconsidered*, 92–93, 97–98. As William G. Barnard notes in correspondence with Taves, *Religious Experience Reconsidered*, 118, her application of attribution theory to his experiences produces the "prosaic and interesting" result of merely saying that he sought to explain his experience after the fact.
100 Forman, *The Problem of Pure Consciousness*, 13.
101 Taves, *Religious Experience Reconsidered*, 93, 97–98.
102 Ingrid Jordt, *Burma's Mass Lay Movement: Buddhism and the Cultural Construction of Power* (Athens, OH: Ohio University Press, 2007), xi.
103 William James, *The Varieties of Religious Experience: A Study in Human Nature* (New York: Longmans, Green and Co., 1902; repr, New York: Modern Library, n.d.), 371. The potentially endless variety of names and adjectives for what I am calling the mystical in this book indicates that the claim dating back to James that ineffability is a key mark of the mystical is on target. I make this claim in opposition to Proudfoot's notion of the placeholder of the ineffable, which he defines as a "formal operator . . . systematically excluding any differentiating description or predicates that might be proposed," *Religious Experience*, 127 (see also 124–36) because it is the encounter with ineffability that motivates the conception of logical placeholder, I think, and not the reverse, which would be like holding that language is merely an expression of grammar rather than also of contexts external to the grammar of this or that language.
104 Blum, "The Science of Consciousness and Mystical Experience," 168.

105 Ibid., 150.
106 Ibid., 157–59.
107 Ibid., 160–61.
108 Ibid., 160.
109 Ibid., 168.
110 As Fong claims with respect to the findings of cognitive science, "On Critics and What's Real," 1128.
111 Blum, "The Science of Consciousness and Mystical Experience," 168.
112 James, *The Varieties of Religious Experience*, 410.
113 The view of Ralph W. Hood, who defends the common-core thesis over against strong constructivism in the light of the empirical study of religion, or the scientific study of religious experience, which includes neuroscience, and operates for the most part independently of philosophical, theological, and comparative approaches to mysticism, "The Common Core Thesis in the Study of Mysticism," in *Where God and Science Meet: How Brain and Evolutionary Studies Alter Our Understanding of Religion*. Vol. 3, *The Psychology of Religious Experience*, ed. Patrick McNamara (Westport, CT and London: Praeger, 2006), 126–27, 135.

Chapter 3

1 Ross Aden, *Religion Today: A Critical Thinking Approach to Religious Studies* (Lanham, MD: Rowman & Littlefield, 2013), 186. John Hick summarized this conclusion saying, "It seems, then, that the stimulation of the temporal lobe can produce in some people a sense of divine presence," *The New Frontier of Science and Religion: Religious Experience, Neuroscience and the Transcendent* (Basingstoke, Hampshire: Palgrave Macmillan, 2010; reissue of 2006 ed.), 63. For a more popular but balanced account of Persinger's work, see Horgan, *Rational Mysticism*, 91–105. Pehr Granqvist notes that the findings of Persinger's studies, although replicated by Persinger himself multiple times, have failed to be replicated by other researchers, "Religion as a By-Product or Evolved Psychology: The Case of Attachment and Implications for Brain and Religion Research," in *Where God and Science Meet: How Brain and Evolutionary Studies Alter Our Understanding of Religion*. Vol. 2, *The Neurology of Religious Experience*, ed. Patrick McNamara (Westport, CT and London: Praeger, 2006), 125.
2 Aden, *Religion Today*, 186. A view "cautiously" accepted, according to Todd Tremlin, by Ilkka Pyysiäinen, Todd Tremlin, *Minds and Gods: The Cognitive Foundations of Religion* (New York: Oxford University Press, 2006), 125.
3 Aden, *Religion Today*, 186.
4 Or what Aden calls "cultural factors as well as the setting," *Religion Today*, 186.
5 Justin L. Barrett notes that this defense of the naturalness of religious beliefs in god or God from the standpoint of the cognitive science of religion may seem to some theists "like a brutal and effective attack on theism," *Why Would Anyone Believe in God* (Walnut Creek, CA, USA: Altamira Press, 2004), 123.
6 Kripal, *Authors of the Impossible*, 268.
7 Aden, *Religion Today*, 188.
8 Kripal, *Authors of the Impossible*, 268.
9 Victoria Nelson, *The Secret Life of Puppets* (Cambridge, MA: Harvard University Press, 2001), 16; quoted in Kripal, *Authors of the Impossible*, 268.

10 Inaugurated perhaps by F. Max Müller's lectures and writings on "the Science of Religion," beginning with his surmise that "the Science of Religion" might be modeled on "the Science of Language," *Chips from a German Workshop: Essays on The Science of Religion*, Vol. 1 (London: Longmans, Green, 1867), xv. This humanistic approach to developing a science of religion is to be distinguished from an experimental science of religion. As McNamara notes in *The Neuroscience of Religious Experience*, 81, William James was a pioneer of the latter approach, although the meager resources of the neuroscience of his day hampered the development of a robust neuroscience of religion until the 1970s, when the first lines of research that have now branched out into the many disciplines of contemplative neuroscience were first charted. See also Andrew W. Newberg, *Principles of Neurotheology* (Farnham, Surrey, UK: Ashgate, 2010), 11.

11 Instances of this conflation of the two expressions can be seen in Eric J. Sharpe, *Comparative Religion: A History*, 2nd ed. (La Salle, IL, USA: Open Court, 1986), xi–xiii, 22.

12 "Generality is a feature of scientific knowledge," Michael Stausberg, "There is Life in the Old Dog Yet: An Introduction to Contemporary Theories of Religion," in *Contemporary Theories of Religion: A Critical Companion*, ed. Michael Stausberg (London and New York: Routledge, 2009), 1. Here Stausberg draws upon Alan Chalmers, *Science and Its Fabrication* (Minneapolis: University of Minnesota Press, 1990).

13 Ilkka Pyysiäinen, *How Religion Works: Toward a New Cognitive Science of Religion* (Leiden, Boston, Köln: Brill, 2001), vii.

14 Léon P. Turner notes that Edward Slingerland and Joseph Bulbulia have recently begun to call CSR "the evolutionary cognitive science of religion," or ECSR, "Introduction: Pluralism and Complexity in the Evolutionary Cognitive Science of Religion," in *Evolution, Religion, and Cognitive Science*, ed. Fraser Watts and Léon P. Turner (New York and Oxford: Oxford University Press, 2014), 1.

15 Cho and Squier, "Religion as a Complex and Dynamic System," 386. They refer in this context to Stausberg, *Contemporary Theories of Religion*, as "a review of current theories of religion, the majority of which utilize or relate to cognitive science."

16 Steven Engler and Mark Quentin Gardiner, "Religion as Superhuman Agency: On E. Thomas Lawson and Robert N. McCauley, *Rethinking Religion* (1990)," in *Contemporary Theories of Religion: A Critical Companion*, ed. Michal Stausberg (London and New York: Routledge, 2009), 22. Turner, "Introduction," in Watts and Turner, *Evolution, Religion, and Cognitive Science*, 4, points out that "some of the basic premises of CSR were presented by Stewart Guthrie" in his 1980 essay, "A Cognitive Theory of Religion" (*Current Anthropology* 21, no. 2: 181–203), ideas that he later developed in *Faces in the Clouds: A New Theory of Religion* (New York and Oxford: Oxford University Press, 1993).

17 Thomas Lawson and Robert N. McCauley, *Rethinking Religion: Connecting Cognition and Culture* (Cambridge: Cambridge University Press, 1993), 123, quoted in Engler and Gardiner, "Religion as Superhuman Agency," 23.

18 Justin L. Barrett, "Exploring the Natural Foundations of Religion," *Trends in Cognitive Sciences* 4, no. 1 (January 2000): 29.

19 Pascal Boyer, "Evolution of the Modern Mind and the Origins of Culture: Religious Concepts as a Limiting Case," in *Evolution and the Human Mind: Modularity, Language and Meta-Cognition*, ed. Peter Carruthers and Andrew Chamberlain (Cambridge: Cambridge University Press, 2000): 93–112.

20 For example, see Ilkka Pyysiäinen, "Amazing Grace: Religion and the Evolution of the Human Mind," in *Where God and Science Meet: How Brain and Evolutionary Studies Alter Our Understanding of Religion*. Vol. 1, *Evolution, Genes, and the Religious Brain*, ed. Patrick McNamara (Westport, CT and London: Praeger, 2006), 210.

21 Drawing upon the work of anthropologist Stewart Guthrie and E. Thomas Lawson and Robert N. McCauley, J. L. Barrett developed the notion of the HADD in "Exploring the Natural Foundations of Religion," 29–34, and *Why Would Anyone Believe in God?* passim; cited in Engler and Gardiner, "Religion as Superhuman Agency," in Stausberg, *Contemporary Theories*, 23. Although the use of the word *hyperactive* seems more widespread in the literature, Barrett changed this (2004) to *hypersensitive*, which, conveniently, left HADD unchanged, but led to "some terminological confusion in the field," Kelley James Clark and Justin L. Barrett, "Reidian Religious Epistemology and the Cognitive Science of Religion," *Journal of the American Academy of Religion* 79, no. 3 (Summer 2011): 640n.1.

22 Or what, Barrett, in summarizing Pascal Boyer's "conceptual catalog of the supernatural," characterizes as "minor aberrations of natural concepts," in "Exploring the Natural Foundations of Religion," 31.

23 Clark and Barrett, "Reidian Religious Epistemology and the Cognitive Science of Religion," 640. That the ADD is not merely a conceptual construct of ECSR is Todd Tremlin's claim in *Minds and Gods*, 124, based on research by Antonio Damasio and Joseph LeDoux, that the ADD corresponds to a " 'dirty' pathway" in the brain that feeds impulses from the sensory thalamus to the amygdala, which activates a "better safe than sorry" release of adrenaline, increased heartbeat, and a heightening of sensory perception that is sometimes not warranted by actual external events.

24 Lawson and McCauley choose to see the principles governing religious action and cognition as part of humanity's general cognitive capacities rather than as instances of specifically religious cognitive capacities, Lawson and McCauley, *Rethinking Religion*, 79, quoted in Engler and Gardiner, "Religion as Superhuman Agency," 26. Pascal Boyer also holds a similar view, as does Barrett, "Exploring the Natural Foundations of Religion," 29, *Why Would Anyone Believe in God*, 119. See also Turner, "Introduction: Pluralism and Complexity in the Evolutionary Cognitive Science of Religion," in Watts and Turner, *Evolution, Religion, and Cognitive Science*, 3; Stephen Pinker, "The Evolutionary Psychology of Religion," in *Where God and Science Meet: How Brain and Evolutionary Studies Alter Our Understanding of Religion*. Vol. 1, *Evolution, Genes, and the Religious Brain*, ed. Patrick McNamara (Westport, CT and London: Praeger, 2006), 5–8, and Pehr Granqvist, "Religion as a By-Product or Evolved Psychology: The Case of Attachment and Implications for Brain and Religion Research," in *Where God and Science Meet: How Brain and Evolutionary Studies Alter Our Understanding of Religion*. Vol. 2, *The Neurology of Religious Experience*, ed. Patrick McNamara (Westport, CT and London: Praeger, 2006), 105, 138–40.

25 Engler and Gardiner, "Religion as Superhuman Agency," 30; as noted in an earlier footnote, J. L. Barret developed the notion of hyperactive or hypersensitive agency detection in "Exploring the Natural Foundations of Religion," 29–34, and *Why Would Anyone Believe in God*, 31–44, 120.

26 As in the case of Pinker, "The Evolutionary Psychology of Religion," 6–7.

27 Pyysiäinen, *How Religion Works*, 14–23.

28 Ibid., 17.

29 Ibid., 20. In developing this line of argument, Pyysiäinen acknowledges his reliance upon the ideas of Scott Atran, Dan Sperber, and Pascal Boyer, ibid., 19. Elsewhere, Boyer writes, "Religious concepts are constrained by intuitive ontology in two different ways: [1] they include explicit *violations* of intuitive expectations, and [2] they tacitly activate a *background* of non-violated 'default' expectations," "Evolution of the Modern Mind and the Origins of Culture: Religious Concepts as a Limiting Case," in *Evolution and the Human Mind: Modularity, Language and Meta-Cognition*, ed. Peter Carruthers and Andrew Chamberlain (Cambridge: Cambridge University Press, 2000), 100.

30 Pyysiäinen, *How Religion Works*, 21.

31 As developed by figures such as Arthur Deikman, Richard Davidson, Daniel Goleman, Francisco Varela, Jon Kabat-Zinn, and B. Alan Wallace, "Meng Wu Lecture: Richard Davidson, PhD," Stanford University, October 2, 2012, accessed August 17, 2015, https://www.youtube.com/watch?v=AKKg3CDczpA.

32 Herbert Benson, "Foreword: Twenty-fifth Anniversary Update," in *The Relaxation Response*, ed. Herbert Benson with Miriam Z. Klipper (New York: Harper-Collins, 2009; 2nd ed. 2000; 1st ed. 1975), Kindle edition, "Foreword."

33 Benson, "Foreword: Twenty-fifth Anniversary Update," in Benson, *The Relaxation Response*, Kindle edition, "Foreword."

34 Arthur J. Deikman, "Experimental Meditation," *Journal of Nervous Mental Disorders* 136 (April 1963): 329–43.

35 Davidson, "Meng Wu Lecture." Other early articles in what is now known as contemplative neuroscience include, according to Davidson, ibid.: Robert Keith Wallace, "Physiological Effects of Transcendental Meditation," *Science* (March 27, 1970): 1751–54, accessed October 20, 2015, doi: 10.1126/science.167.3926.1751; J. P. Banquet, "Spectral Analysis of the EEG in Meditation," *Journal of Electroencephalography and Clinical Neurophysiology* 35, no. 2 (August 1973): 143–51; Richard J. Davidson, Daniel J. Goleman, and Gary E, Schwartz, "Attentional and Affective Concomitants of Meditation: A Cross-Sectional Study," *Journal of Abnormal Psychology* 85 (1976): 235–38; Richard J. Davidson and Daniel J. Gorman, "The Role of Attention in Meditation and Hypnosis: A Psychobiological Perspective on Transformations of Consciousness," *The International Journal of Clinical and Experimental Hypnosis* 25, no. 4 (October 1977): 291–308; Daniel J. Goleman, "The Buddha on Meditation and States of Consciousness, Part I: The Teachings," *Journal of Transpersonal Psychology* 4, no. 2 (1972): 1–44; "The Buddha on Meditation and States of Consciousness, Part II: A Typology of Meditation Techniques," *Journal of Transpersonal Psychology* 4 (1972): 151–210; Jon Kabat-Zinn, "An Outpatient Program in Behavioral Medicine for Chronic Pain Patients Based on the Practice of Mindfulness Meditation," *General Hospital Psychiatry*, 4 (1982): 33–47, and Francisco J. Varela, "Neurophenomenology: A Methodological Remedy for the Hard Problem," *Journal for Consciousness Studies* 3, no. 4 (1996): 330–49.

36 Davidson, "Meng Wu Lecture."

37 To be noted also is Donald D. Price and James J. Barrell's sensitivity to first-person, experiential, introspective, and phenomenological accounts of conscious experience that has led them over the last four decades to develop a new multidisciplinary approach that blends the natural sciences, especially neuroscience, with what they name "experiential science." They also note the materialistic outlook of current Western science, refute mind-brain identity theories, and look to phenomenologists such as Husserl, Marcel, and Merleau-Ponty to overcome the resistance in

psychology in the twentieth century to "the idea that human meanings underpin psychological responses," *Inner Experience and Neuroscience: Merging Both Perspectives* (Cambridge, MA, London: MIT Press, 2012), 2, 4, 9–14, 22.

38 Dean Hamer, *The God Gene: How Faith is Hardwired into Our Genes* (New York: Anchor), 2005.

39 Hamer, *The God Gene*, 211. The "God Gene" is the VMAT2 gene, whose variations control serotonin and dopamine to produce altered states. Twin studies show that this gene is highly heritable, as measured in the Cloninger Self-Transcendence Scale, ibid., viii, 9–10, 21–35, 72–78.

40 Perla Kaliman, María Jesús Álvarez-López, Marta Cosín-Tomás, Melissa A. Rosenkranz, Antoine Lutz, and Richard J. Davidson, "Rapid Changes in Histone Deacetylases and Inflammatory Gene Expression in Expert Meditators," *Psychoneuroendocrinology* 40 (February 2014): 96–107, accessed October 20, 2015, http://dx.doi.org/10.1016/j.psyneuen.2013.11.004; Belinda Weber, "Meditation Changes Gene Expression, Study Shows," *Medical News Today* (December 12, 2013), accessed October 19, 2014, http://www.medicalnewstoday.com/articles/269910.php.

41 Hamer, *The God Gene*, 8.

42 Patrick McNamara, *The Neuroscience of Religious Experience* (Cambridge: Cambridge University Press, 2009), 137–38.

43 McNamara, *The Neuroscience of Religious Experience*, 127.

44 Ibid.

45 Positive summaries of this research include, Jonathan Haidt, *The Happiness Hypothesis: Finding Modern Truth in Ancient Wisdom* (New York: Basic Books, 2006), 235–37; Horgan, *Rational Mysticism*, 74–75; Hick, *The New Frontier of Religion and Science*, 62, 75; Aubele, Wenck, and Reynolds, *Train Your Brain to Get Happy*, 92, and numerous magazine and newspaper articles.

46 Newberg, *Principles of Neurotheology*, ix.

47 Nash and Newberg, "Toward A Unifying Taxonomy and Definition for Meditation," 8, cite Hans-Otto Karnath, Susanne Ferber, and Marc Himmelbach, "Spatial Awareness is a Function of the Temporal Not the Posterior Parietal Lobe," which suggests that the superior temporal lobe "may play a more important role in body spatial representation," *Nature* 411 (2001): 950–53, accessed October 20, 2015. doi:10.1038/35082075. See also Andrew B. Newberg, "Religious and Spiritual Practices: A Neurochemical Perspective," in *Where God and Science Meet: How Brain and Evolutionary Studies Alter Our Understanding of Religion*. Vol. 2, *The Neurology of Religious Experience*, ed. Patrick McNamara (Westport, CT and London: Praeger, 2006), 22–23, 23.

48 Nash and Newberg, "Toward A Unifying Taxonomy and Definition for Meditation," 8; Andrew Newberg, Eugene d'Aquili, and Vince Rause, *Why God Won't Go Away: Brain Science and the Biology of Belief* 1st trade ed. (New York: Ballantine Books, 2002), 1–10; Eugene d'Aquili, Andrew B. Newberg, *The Mystical Mind: Probing the Biology of Religious Experience* (Minneapolis: Fortress Press, 1999), 110–13; Danny J. J. Wang, Hengyi Rao, Marc Korczykowski, Nancy Wintering, John Pluta, Dharma Singh Khalsa, Andrew B. Newberg, "Cerebral Blood Flow Changes Associated with Different Meditation Practices and Perceived Depth of Meditation," *Psychiatry Research: Neuroimaging* 191 (2011): 60–67, accessed October 20, 2015, doi:10.1016/j.pscychresns.2010.09.011; Andrew Newberg and Mark Robert Waldman, *How God Changes Your Brain: Breakthrough Findings from a Leading Neuroscientist* pbk. ed. (New York: Ballantine Books, 2010), 16–17, 41–63; Patrick McNamara, Raymon

Durso, Ariel Brown, and Erica Harris, "The Chemistry of Religiosity: Evidence from Patients with Parkinson's Disease," in *Where God and Science Meet: How Brain and Evolutionary Studies Alter Our Understanding of Religion*. Vol. 2, *The Neurology of Religious Experience*, ed. Patrick McNamara (Westport, CT and London: Praeger, 2006), 2. These results have not gone unnoticed by theologians and religious-studies scholars, see, for example, Hick, *The New Frontier of Religion and Science*, 62, 75; Taves, *Religious Experience Reconsidered*, 21.

49 Nash and Newberg, "Toward A Unifying Taxonomy and Definition for Meditation," 8; Newberg, "Religious and Spiritual Practices: A Neurobiological Perspective," in McNamara, *Where God and Science Meet*, Vol. 2, 22–23; Newberg, "Religious and Spiritual Practices," 22.

50 Newberg and d'Aquili, *The Mystical Mind*, 13–14, 95, 110–14.

51 Equal, I think, to *asamprajñāta-samādhi* in the *Yoga Sūtra* and *nirodha-samāpatti* in the *Visuddhimagga*. These states are brought about by the cultivation of, what Nash and Newberg call, a "Null Domain" methods, which "purport to create an enhanced empty state that is devoid of phenomenological content—a non-cognitive/non-affective state," Nash and Newberg, "Toward A Unifying Taxonomy and Definition for Meditation," 6–7.

52 Stace, *Mysticism and Philosophy*, 19. In contrast to Stace, who could only argue for the reality of the mystical though comparative literary studies, we can now test the adequacy of this claim through the twin tools of dedicated meditation and neuroscience, thanks to stunning advances in neuroscience in the last forty years and the global rise of two generations of practitioners well trained by traditional teachers in the classic contemplative traditions of Asia. Where Stace wrote as a philosopher sympathetic to and perhaps even sensitized to mysticism, Stace, *Meditation and Philosophy*, 21, but without consistent or profound mystical experiences of his own, the scholar of mysticism is today more likely than a half century ago to be a longtime and well-trained meditator. And, unlike in Stace's day, the student of mysticism can today draw upon the rapidly expanding field of contemplative neuroscience in order to uncover and confirm the universality of various types of mystical and yogic experience, Newberg, d'Aquili, and Rause, *Why God Won't Go Away*, 7, 140–41.

53 Stace, *Mysticism and Philosophy*, 147, 148, 152, 204.

54 Newberg, *Principles of Neurotheology*, 64. Or what, according to Evan Thompson, neuroscientists call the "intrinsic activity" of the brain, which is generated by the brain and not outwardly determined, *Waking, Dreaming, Being: Self and Consciousness in Neuroscience, Meditation, and Philosophy* (New York: Columbia University Press, 2014), Kindle edition, "Prologue: The Dalai Lama's Conjecture."

55 Newberg, *Principles of Neurotheology*, 89.

56 Jensine Andresen and Robert K. C. Forman, "Methodological Pluralism in the Study of Religion: How the Study of Consciousness and Mapping Spiritual Experiences can Reshape Religious Studies Methodology," in Andresen and Forman, *Cognitive Models and Spiritual Maps*, 13.

57 See Newberg and Waldman, *How God Changes Your Brain*, 150–69.

58 Taves, *Religious Experience Reconsidered*, 18–22.

59 Sarbacker, *Samādhi*, 1, 24–25, passim.

60 Summarized by Hick, *The New Frontier of Religion and Science*, 63–65, 75–76, 79, although he interprets this constructivistically.

61 McNamara, *The Neuroscience of Religious Experience*, 127, 129–30.

62 At the juncture of science and religion, pioneering neurotheologian Andrew Newberg suggests that one possible, if "perhaps unlikely," outcome of the discoveries of neurotheology might be a paradigm shift in which "the material world will be found to be secondary to some spiritual or absolute realm," *Principles of Neurotheology*, 59.

63 Hamer clearly places himself in the Jamesian tradition of separating personal spirituality from institutional expressions of religiosity, and clearly indicates that his interest as a researcher is in the latter, Hamer, *The God Gene*, ix–x.

64 To avoid the traditional religious associations associated with words such as *transcendent*, I substitute here the expression *nonordinary*, which is taken from F. Samuel Brainard, *Reality and Mystical Experience*, 49–50 passim.

65 Paul Condon, Gaëlle Desbordes, Willa Miller, and David DeSteno, "Meditation Increases Compassionate Responses to Suffering," *Psychological Science* (August 21, 2013), accessed October 23, 2015, doi:10.1177/0956797613485603; see also David DeSteno, "The Morality of Meditation," *New York Times* (July 5, 2013), accessed October 23, 2015, http://www.nytimes.com/2013/07/07/opinion/sunday/the-morality-of-meditation.html?hpw.

66 Haidt, *The Happiness Hypothesis*, 35–37, 63, 78, 90, 91, 148.

67 Ibid., 235–38. Haidt follows David Sloan Wilson in arguing for this view of religion, *The Happiness Hypothesis*, 233–34.

Chapter 4

1 *Maha-Saccaka Sutta: The Longer Discourse to Saccaka* (Majjhima Nikāya 36), translated from the Pāli by Thanissaro Bhikkhu. *Access to Insight*, accessed May 6, 2014, http://www.accesstoinsight.org/tipitaka/mn/mn.036.than.html. See also Johannes Bronkhorst, *The Two Traditions of Meditation in Ancient India*, 2nd ed. (Delhi: Motilal Banarsidass, 1992, repr. 2000; originally published, Stuttgart: Franz Steiner Verlag, 1986), 22–23.

2 *Maha-Saccaka Sutta*, trans. Thanissaro Bhikkhu, *Access to Insight*.

3 The translation of the terms *vitakka* and *vicāra* is as difficult as their proper conceptual definition. The range of meanings given to these terms runs from seeing them as merely a pair of synonyms for "the normal flow of thought," Roderick S. Bucknell, "Reinterpreting the *Jhānas*," *Journal of the International Association of Buddhist Studies* 16, no. 2 (1993): 397, or "just thought, thinking, only in an emphatic way," *The Pāli Text Society's Pāli-English Dictionary* (London: Pāli Text Society, 1921–25), s.v., *vitakka*, accessed June 14, 2014, http://dsalsrv02.uchicago.edu/cgi-bin/philologic/getobject.pl?c.3:1:1489.pali.1016839; see also Donald Swearer, "Control and Freedom: The Structure of Buddhist Meditation in the Pāli Suttas," *Philosophy East and West* 23, no. 4 (October 1973): 445n49. Somewhat more refined definitions construe *vitakka* as "thinking" and *vicāra* as "pondering," *Poṭṭhapāda Sutta*, in Maurice Walsh, trans., *The Long Discourses of the Buddha: A Translation of the Dīgha Nikāya* (Boston: Wisdom Publications, 1995), 161 (cited in Ayya Khema, *Who is My Self: A Guide to Buddhist Meditation* [Boston: Wisdom Publications, 1997], 41), The most technical definitions see *vitakka* as the effort of fixing the mind in fits and starts on the meditation objects and *vicāra* as a deepening ability to stay focused on the meditation object. This difference is formalized in

Ācariya Anuruddha and Bhikkhu Bodhi, *A Comprehensive Manual of* Abhidhamma: *The* Abhidhammattha Sangaha *of Ācariya Anuruddha*, trans, Mahāthera Nārada, ed. Bhikkhu Bodhi (Seattle: BPS Pariyatti Editions, 2000, first published Kandy, Sri Lanka: Buddhist Publication Society, 1993), 56–57, where it reads concerning *vitakka*: "In the Suttas the word *vitakka* is often used in the sense of thought, but in the Abhidhamma it is used in the precise technical sense to mean the mental factor that mounts or directs the mind to its object," and concerning *vicāra*: "The word *vicāra* usually means examination [in the *suttas*], but here [in the Abhidhamma] it signifies the sustained application of the mind on its object." The *Vimuttimagga* defines *vitakka* in this way: "to perceive, to think, to be composed, to excogitate and to aspire rightly, though without understanding," Arahant Upatissa, *The Path of Freedom (*Vimuttimagga*)*, Arahant Upatissa, trans. N. R. M. Ehara, Soma Thera, and Kheminda Thera (Kandy: Buddhist Publication Society, 1977), 86. My own view on this echoes that of Leigh Brasington, who writes, "it is simply not possible to have one-pointedness [*ekaggatā*] and thinking at the same time, so experiencing *ekaggata* in the same *jhana* as *vitakka* and *vicara* makes no sense," "Five Factors for the First Jhana—Not!" http://www.leighb.com/jhana_4factors.htm, accessed July 8, 2014. I think that "quiet reflection" will also do, as styled by Rolf W. Giebel in his translation of Takasaki Jikido's comments about the meaning of *ch'an/zen/dhyāna/jhāna*, *An Introduction to Buddhism* (Tokyo: The Tōhō Gakkai, 1987), 179.

4 Ayya Khema thinks that "people who have that kind of childhood experience [i.e., Siddhartha's] do enter the jhanas with great ease" later in life, which was true, she thinks, in the case of the older Siddhartha, *Who is My Self*, 48.

5 Bronkhorst concludes, after exhaustive philological analysis of ancient Indian literature, that the earliest form of "authentic Buddhist meditation" in ancient India comprises the Four Dhyānas, the destruction of the intoxicants, or *āsavas*, and the practice of mindfulness, or *smṛti/sati*, *The Two Traditions of Meditation in Ancient India*, 95; see also 22–24, 30, 88, 95, 102, 104, 109, 110, and Johannes Bronkhorst, *Buddhist Teaching in India* (Boston: Wisdom Publications, 2009), 16–17. Tilmann Vetter isolates what he sees as "perhaps the oldest" soteriology in "the most ancient form of Buddhism" as the "use of dhyāna-meditation, which is based on ascetic conduct (P. *sīla*), in aid of the path of discriminating insight (P. *paññā*)," *The Ideas and Meditative Practices of Early Buddhism*, trans. Marianne Oort (Leiden, New York, KØbenhavn, and Köln: E. J. Brill, 1988), xxxv. This view of the teaching of the *suttas*—as opposed to that of the *Visuddhimagga*—is also affirmed by Richard Shankman, *The Experience of Samādhi: An In-depth Exploration of Buddhist Mediation* (Boston and London: Shambhala, 2008), 89, 84. 101.

6 Bodhirājakumāra Sutta (Majjhima Nikāya 85), in Bronkhorst, *The Two Traditions of Meditation in Ancient India*, 17; see also Grzegorz Polak, *Reexamining Jhāna: Towards a Critical Reconstruction of Early Buddhist Soteriology* (Lublin: Wydawnictwo Uniwersytetu Marii Curie-Skłodowskiej, 2011), 184.

7 Just such a synthesis of aspects of the concentrative and wisdom paths is suggested by Michael Barnes, "The Buddhist Way of Deliverance (according to the Pāli Sources)," *Studia* Missionalia 30 (1981): 263, 277. See also, Rupert M. L. Gethin, *The Buddhist Path to Awakening: A Study of the Bodhi-Pakkhiyā Dhammā* (Leiden, New York, and Köln: Brill, 1992), 345. This is also the irenic, synthetic view of Shanta Ratnayaka, *Two Ways of Perfection: Buddhist and Christian* (Colombo: Lake House Investments, 1978), 41–42.

8 As Walpola Rahula observed in an influential introduction to the teachings and practices of Theravāda Buddhism, "There are two forms of meditation. One is the development of mental concentration (*samatha* or *samādhi*), of one-pointedness of mind . . . by various methods . . . leading up to the highest mystic states. . . . This form of meditation existed before the Buddha. Hence it is not purely Buddhist, but is not excluded from the field of Buddhist meditation. However it is not essential for the realization of Nirvāṇa. [The Buddha] discovered the other form of 'meditation' known as vipassanā (Skt. *vipaśyanā* or *vidarśana*), 'Insight' into the nature of things, leading to complete liberation of mind, to the realization of the Ultimate Truth, Nirvāṇa. This is essentially Buddhist 'meditation,' Buddhist mental culture. It is an analytical method based on mindfulness, awareness, vigilance, observation" (Walpola Rahula, *What the Buddha Taught*, 2nd ed. (New York: Grove Press, 1974), 68–69). Bhikkhu Ñāṇamoli makes a similar claim, "Introduction," in Bhadantācariya Buddhaghosa, *The Path of Purification* (*Visuddhimagga*), 1st BPS Pariyatti ed., Bhikkhu Ñāṇamoli trans. (Seattle: BPS Pariyatti Editions, 1999), xliii. In reference to the contemporary *vipassanā* meditation tradition in Burmese Theravāda Buddhism, Polak notes that "it is almost as if jhāna was a forbidden subject to the representatives of this branch of Theravāda Buddhism," *Reexamining Jhāna*, 184.

9 *The Pāli Text Society's Pāli-English Dictionary*, s.v. "*āsava*," accessed May 19, 2014, http://dsalsrv02.uchicago.edu/cgi-bin/philologic/getobject.pl?c.0:1:3098.pali.

10 Bronkhorst, *The Two Traditions of Meditation in Ancient India*, 30. See also Bronkhorst, *Buddhist Teaching in India*, 16–17, and Polak, *Reexamining Jhāna*, 12, 58, where he claims that "contrary to the traditional view, the early Buddhist *jhāna* does not lead to the stopping of the senses." Gethin, in agreement with Bronkhorst and Vetter, and contra Winston King, also holds that "there can be no doubt that for the Nikāyas, the Abhidhamma and the commentaries the *jhānas* represent central, mainstream Buddhism," *The Buddhist Path to Awakening*, 347, 349.

11 *Jhāna* is cognate with the Sanskrit *dhyāna*, and both can be translated as "meditation." But *The Pāli Text Society's Pāli-English Dictionary*, s.v., "Jhāna," clarifies that *jhāna* "never means vaguely meditation," since it is "the technical term" for the four *jhānas*, the whole of which, however, "forms one series of mental states and the stages might have been fixed at other points in the series."

12 Swearer also argues that it is "arguable that concentration of mind [*samādhi*] is a necessary step to the attainment of a higher truth ['an enlightened state of mind'] and the powers accompanying it," "Control and Freedom," 443.

13 In a discussion that can lend support to the renewed emphasis on *jhāna* in this book and in the writings of scholars such as Bronkhorst and Polak, Richard Gombrich traces the evolution of the idea in early Buddhism as far back as the *Suttapiṭaka* that "enlightenment can be attained without meditation [*samatha-bhāvanā*], by a process of intellectual analysis (technically known as *paññā*, insight) alone," *How Buddhism Began: The Conditioned Genesis of the Early Teachings*, 2nd ed. (London and New York: Routledge, 2006, first published 1996), 96, 115. Gombrich judges that "the Theravāda is the only surviving form of Buddhism to accept this idea," ibid., 96, 133. Gombrich's point is that the rejection of *jhāna* in favor of exclusive reliance on *paññā* is not original to the Buddha, but develops, early on admittedly, through monastic debates reflected in the evolving *Suttapiṭaka* and perhaps even through forgery or "a narrative accident," ibid., 106, 110–12, 118, 120–21, 123, 126n21, 127, 131. At 126n21, Gombrich cites Lance Cousins in the seminar on which his book is based as

seeing attainment of the four *jhānas* as "a prerequisite not merely for Enlightenment but even for stream-entry," ibid., 126n21.

14 *The Dhammapada*, trans. Gil Fronsdal (Boston and London: Shambhala, 2006), 96.

15 Polak, *Reexamining Jhāna*, 26. Paul Griffiths has isolated at least five divergent soteriologies in the *Suttapiṭaka* that involve the *jhānas* in varying ways, and he concludes his form-critical analysis of the first four Nikāyas by noting that, contrary to later systematizers, some early Buddhist communities may have regarded the four *jhānas* "as of independent soteriological validity," Paul Griffiths, "Buddhist Jhāna: A Form-Critical Study," *Religion* 13 (1983): 65.

16 This view takes various forms, although its main feature is to prioritize *vipaśyanā/vipassanā*, even where *śamatha/samatha* is preserved as an auxiliary to insight. In some instances the claim is made that because calming practices were common among non-Buddhist ascetics in Buddha's day, they have no essential or ultimate role in genuine Buddhist enlightenment. The following citations are a sampling of the spectrum of views on this topic: *On the Mahāyāna side*: Gimello, "Mysticism and Meditation," in Katz, *Mysticism and Philosophical Analysis*, 187; Polak notes that the Theravāda downplaying of *jhāna* is also a Mahāyāna view, *Reexamining Jhāna*, 24; Thich Nhat Hanh sees the *jhānas* as "wrong concentration" that "hide reality from the practitioner," *Transformation and Healing* (Berkeley: Parallax Press, 1990, repr. 2006), 37, quoted in Polak, *Reexamining Jhāna*, 31; Lati Rinbochay holds that "many non-Buddhists also cultivate these eight absorptions; however, unlike Buddhists, they do not use them to gain other important minds and to progress on the path," "Lati Rinbochay's Oral Presentation of the Concentrations and Formless Absorptions," trans. Jeffrey Hopkins, in *Meditative States in Tibetan Buddhism*, ed. Leah Zahler (Boston: Wisdom Publications, 1997, first pub. 1983), 49; Stuart Ray Sarbacker notes that this Theravāda view is "mirrored by the Mahāyāna view that identifies *śamatha* with yoga," *Samādhi*, 23. *On the Theravāda side*: Polak, *Reexamining Jhāna*, 11; Rahula, as noted above, holds that *samatha* or *samādhi* "is not essential for the realization of Nirvāṇa," *What the Buddha Taught*, 68–69; Henepola Gunaratana sees *samatha-bhāvanā* "as common to both Buddhist and non-Buddhist disciplines," while "insight meditation is held to be the unique discovery of the Buddha and an unparalleled feature of his path," "A Critical Analysis of the Jhānas in Theravada Buddhist Meditation" (PhD thesis, American University, 1980; online version, Buddha Dharma Education Association), 11–12, accessed May 17, 2014, http://www.buddhanet.net/pdf_file/scrnguna.pdf.

17 Vetter, *The Ideas and Meditative Practices of Early Buddhism*.

18 Bronkhorst, *The Two Traditions of Meditation in Ancient India*, 101–02.

19 Polak holds that the *jhāna* formula is repeated often and unchanged in the Pāli Canon because the *jhānas* are "the most important element of the Buddhist doctrine" in the Pāli Canon, *Reexamining Jhāna*, 24–25.

20 Rupert Gethin, *Sayings of the Buddha: A Selection of Suttas from the Pāli Nikāyas* (Oxford and New York: Oxford University Press, 2008), 142. Polak agrees with this view and he cites Tillman Vetter, whom Polak says "rightly points out that it is no longer possible to maintain a view, that the Theravāda theory of meditation is faithful and coherent representation of early Buddhist soteriology," *Reexamining Jhāna*, 30. Sarbacker, following L. S. Cousins and Griffiths, notes that "the paradigm of the Buddha's own awakening experience as alluded to in treatises such as the *Visuddhimagga* does not appear to be at the heart of modern Theravāda practice," *Samādhi*, 23. Thus, as Martin Stuart-Fox points out, over time in the early

Buddhism, "the *Jhāyins* lost" the contest to the intellectualizing Dhammayogas, who were scholastic exegetes, "Jhāna and Buddhist Scholasticism," *Journal of the International Association of Buddhist Studies* 12, no. 2 (1989): 102–03. Yet, it must be said that this does now seem to be changing with the teaching activity of Ayya Khema, Ajahn Brahmavaṃso, Bhante Gunaratana, Pa Auk Sayadaw, Leigh Brasington, Shaila Catherine, Richard Shankman, Christian Feldman, Stephen Snyder, and Tina Rasmussen, and others, and with the increasing interest in recent years in the *jhānas* among Theravāda Buddhist in the West. As Ayya Khema has observed, "the meditative absorptions are part of the path," *Who is My Self*, 39.

21 For example, Ajahn Brahm (Brahmavaṃso), following Ajahn Cha, sees *samatha* and *vipassanā* as two sides of the one hand of Buddhist *bhāvanā* and he further holds that these two practices "cannot be separated," *Mindfulness, Bliss, and Beyond: A Meditator's Handbook* (Boston: Wisdom Publications, 2006), 25. Jeffrey Hopkins, while summarizing the Prāsaṅgika-Mādhyamika view of *śūnyatā*, expresses a similar view in which "special insight" is attained through balancing "stabilizing and analytical meditation," *Meditation on Emptiness* (London: Wisdom Publications, 1983), 558.

22 Bhikkhu Ñāṇamoli summarizes this passage: "According to the Suttas, concentration of jhāna strength is necessary for the manifestation of the path," Buddhaghosa, *The Path of Purification*, 749n21. This was the experience of the Elder Mallaka, who used the *jhāna* pentad to attain the insight that led to Arahantship (Vsm 4.23 Ñ).

23 Bronkhorst, *The Two Traditions of Meditation in Ancient India*, xviii. Paul Griffiths ends his survey of "the radically different kinds of soteriology" represented by *samādhi-bhāvanā* and *vipassanā-bhāvanā* by giving up on the possibility, given our present knowledge, of a "resolution of the whole issue," "Concentration or Insight: The Problematic of Theravāda Buddhist Meditation-Theory," *The Journal of the American Academy of Religion* 49, no. 4 (December 1981): 6, 616, 618.

24 Polak, *Reexamining Jhāna*, 25. Griffiths claims that at least some early Buddhists thought of the four *jhānas* as an independent soteriology, "Buddhist Jhāna," 65.

25 Polak, *Reexamining Jhāna*, 192. Polak carefully analyzes the *jhānas* to show that the Seven Factors of Enlightenment (*bojjhaṅga*) blend with and are completed by the *jhānas* and their factors: "Sati (mindfulness) is present in the last two jhānas, while pīti (rapture) is said to belong to the first two jhānas. Samādhi (concentration) arises for the first time in the second jhāna, and upekkhā (equanimity) appears in the third jhāna and reaches its perfection in the fourth jhāna," *Reexamining Jhāna*, 27.

26 Vetter, *The Ideas and Meditative Practices of Early Buddhism*, xxii, see also xvn9. Earlier L. Schmithausen concluded that "there are already in the Sūtrapiṭaka various, even conflicting view or theories of Liberating Insight (and Enlightenment)," "On Some Aspects of Descriptions or Theories of 'Liberating Insight' and 'Enlightenment' in Early Buddhism," in Klaus Bruhn and Albrecht Wezler, eds., *Studien zum Jainismus und Buddhismus* (Wiesbaden: Franz Steiner Verlag, 1981), 240. Polak provides a catalog of the views of liberative insight in diverse Buddhist soteriologies in the *Suttapiṭaka*, *Reexamining Jhāna*, 191. Griffiths outlines what seem to be at least five soteriologies in early Buddhism, "Buddhist Jhāna," 63–64.

27 Polak, following Vetter and Bronkhorst, rejects the commonplace view that Theravāda Buddhism, unlike Mahāyāna Buddhism, preserves "the meditative teachings of early Buddhism in their pure form," *Reexamining Jhāna*, 11. He thinks that this view can "no longer be maintained," due to "fundamental discrepancies between the early suttas and the later meditative scriptures of Theravāda Buddhism"

and "internal discrepancies" within "the *Suttapiṭaka* itself." *Reexamining Jhāna*, 11. These discrepancies, according to Polak, mostly surround the "status and the role of the meditative state known as 'jhāna,'" Polak, *Reexamining Jhāna*, 11.

28 As displayed in a chart created by Leigh Brasington, the Pāli *suttas*, the Abhidhamma, and the *Visuddhimagga* agree that the first *jhāna* contains *vitakka*, *vicāra*, *pīti*, and *sukha*, "The Traditional Factors of the 8 Jhanas," accessed May 7, 2014, http://www.leighb.com/jhanatrd.htm. Buddhaghosa concedes that *ekaggatā* is not included in the first *jhāna*, as described earlier in the *Vibhaṅga*, yet, because it is included in a later passage in the same work, he asserts that "it is a factor too" (Vsm 4.109 Ñ). See Stuart-Martin, "Jhāna and Buddhist Scholasticism," 87–89.

29 See Rinbochay's "Oral Presentation of the Concentrations and Formless Absorptions," trans. Jeffrey Hopkins, in Lati Rinbochay and Denma Lochö Rinbochay, *Meditative States in Tibetan Buddhism*, 53–83; Alan Wallace provides a chart of the *navākārā cittasthiti*, as well as contemporary renderings of the names of these nine stages in *The Attention Revolution: Unlocking the Power of the Focused Mind* (Boston: Wisdom, 2006), 174–75.

30 Shaila Catherine notes that "when I first wrote *Focused and Fearless [published 2008]*, the term jhāna was not widely used in our insight meditation circles. I think that's changed quite a bit in the last few years," "Jhāna Practice and True Happiness: Talking with Shaila Catherine," *BCBS Insight Journal*, May 14, 2014, accessed May 16, 2014, http://www.bcbsdharma.org/insight-journal/.

31 Among teachers who guide people into the *jhānas* on ten-day retreats, Brasington names Ayya Khema, Bhante Gunaratana, and the Venerable Bhante U Vimalaramsi, "Interpretations of the Jhanas," accessed May 7, 2014, http://www.leighb.com/jhanantp.htm. Brasington also guides people into the *jhānas* on shorter retreats, see Mary Talbot, "A Mind Pure, Concentrated, and Bright: An Interview with Meditation Teacher Leigh Brasington," *Tricycle* 54 (Winter 2004): 69. See also Leigh Brasington, *Right Concentration: A Practical Guide to the Jhānas* (Boston: Shambhala, 2015), Kindle edition, Introduction to Part One, where he says that the *jhānas* "are best learned on a ten-day or longer meditation retreat." Supporting the minimalist camp is Polak's claim that early Buddhist *jhāna* was not like the later, "traditional," or orthodox, Theravāda *jhāna*, since it did not require cessation of external awareness, *Reexamining Jhāna*, 49. From Polak's standpoint, Ajahn Brahmavaṃso's maximalist *jhāna* is not actual *jhāna*—or not the *jhāna* of Buddha and early Buddhists—but an instance of *saññāvedayitanirodha* ("the cessation of ideation and feeling"), which Polak, following Bronkhorst, sees as a later Buddhist incorporation from the indigenous yoga tradition, which early Buddhism rejected, *Reexamining Jhāna*, 183. See also Bronkhorst, *The Two Traditions of Meditation in Ancient India*, 81, 86, 89–90, 99, 102, 108. Steven Collins sees the inclusion of *saññāvedayitanirodha* in "the path to salvation" as a yogic accomplishment that does not cohere well with early Buddhist attempts to see this path as a matter of wisdom or understanding alone, *Nirvana and Other Buddhist Felicities* (Cambridge: Cambridge University Press, 1998), 157. Supporting the minimalist approach would be Richard Gombrich's view that the emergence of *ekodibhāva* in the second *jhāna* "stills all discursive thought," *What the Buddha Thought* (London: Equinox Publishing, 2009), 204. Bucknell argues cogently for what I call the minimalist approach to *jhāna* in "Reinterpreting the *Jhānas*," 403–04. If we take Bucknell's reinterpretation of *jhāna* as a guide, we might say that Ajahn Brahm's first *jhāna* is equivalent to Buddhaghosa's eighth *jhāna*. Stuart-Fox can also be included with the minimalists, since he claims that

"in *jhāna* 1 discursive thought is still present," "Jhāna and Buddhist Scholasticism," 88, a view that he shares with Bucknell, "Reinterpreting the *Jhānas*," 397. Offering the most conclusive evidence for a minimalist view of the first *jhāna* is Gunaratana's Abhidhammic analysis of the "initial attainment" of the first *jhāna* as lasting for "only one great thought-moment" (*javana*), "A Critical Analysis of the Jhānas in Theravada Buddhist Meditation," 152–52 (see also Vsm 4.74, 78 Ñ). Consistent with the *Visuddhimagga*, Bhante Gunaratana, a masterful *jhāna* teacher, points out "the first taste of jhana is usually just a flash, but then you learn to sustain it for longer and longer periods," *Beyond Mindfulness in Plain English: An Introductory Guide to Deeper States of Meditation* (Boston: Wisdom Publications, 2009), 105 (See Vsm 4.78 Ñ). Karen Armstrong's lucid account of Siddhartha's youthful discovery and later rediscovery of the first *jhāna* can be seen as supporting the minimalist view, since she thinks that in the first *jhāna* one is "still able to think and reflect," *Buddha* (New York: Penguin, 2001), 66–72. Also on the minimalist side is the Burmese abbot and meditation master Pa Auk Sayadaw (i.e., the Venerable Acinna or the Venerable Pa-Auk Tawya Sayadaw), a contemporary meditation teacher who holds that meditators can attain *jhāna* "within one or two weeks," if they sit every day two or three times for one or two hours, "Interview with Pa Auk Sayadaw," in Shankman, *The Experience of Samādhi*, 179. Also to be counted as minimalists are his students Stephen Snyder and Tina Rasmussen, who report completing the eight *jhānas* during a two-month retreat in California under Pa Auk Sayadaw's guidance, where he instructed Rasmussen to practice in order to obtain mastery of the first *jhāna* by being able to sit in it unbroken for up to four hours. As preparation for this, they recommend increasing the time that one sits before a retreat begins until one can sit for two hours twice a day. Maximalist as this view appears, it can be counted as minimalist, since it holds that *jhāna* can be attained in shorter sessions, if not mastery, Stephen Snyder and Tina Rasmussen, *Practicing the Jhānas: Traditional Concentration Methods as Presented by the Venerable Pa Auk Sayadaw* (Boston and London: Shambhala, 2009), 4, 45. More on the minimalist side is Ajaan Ṭhānissaro, who thinks that the time it takes to attain *jhāna* and the required context "really varies for the person," "Interview with Ajaan Ṭhānissaro," in Shankman, *The Experience of Samādhi*, 125. As suggested above, Bhante Henepola Gunaratana can also be placed on the minimalist side, since he thinks that "laypeople can attain *jhāna* provided they follow the steps," "Interview with Bhante Gunaratana," in Shankman, *The Experience of Samādhi*, 141. Bhante Gunaratana teaches the practice of the *jhānas* in ten-day retreats at the Bhāvanā Society in West Virginia. The former monk Bhikkhu Visuddhācāra is a student of Sayadaw U Pandita and he teaches a straightforward and practical approach to achieving *jhāna* through intensive *mettā* meditation. Because he sees the *jhāna* that naturally arises through *mettā* meditation lasting as little as five minutes, although it can last for an hour or more for meditators with strong concentration, he can be placed with the *jhāna* minimalists, *Curbing Anger, Spreading Love* (Kandy: Buddhist Publication Society, 1992), 68–69.

32 As a rigorist, Ajahn Brahm sees the first *jhāna* as involving "the complete absence of all five sense activities," *Mindfulness, Bliss, and Beyond*, 158. He claims that "during any jhāna it is impossible to experience the body (e.g., physical pain), hear a sound from outside, or produce any thought—not even a 'good' thought," ibid, 25. Brahm lays down the rule that "[a] jhāna will last a long time. It does not deserve to be called a jhāna if it lasts for only a few minutes. The higher jhānas will last for many hours," ibid. 24. Elsewhere Ajahn Brahm claims that "in jhana—real jhana, not fake

ones—the seen and the heard and sensed all disappear. The external five senses cease," Brahm, "Degrees of Seeing," *Tricycle* 5, no. 1 (Fall 2006): 47. Even more rigorous is Alan Wallace who seems to claim that access concentration (*upacāra-samādhi*) should last four hours and the first *jhāna* should endure for twenty-four hours, *Meditations of a Buddhist Skeptic: A Manifesto for the Mind Sciences and Contemplative Practice*, Kindle edition (New York: Columbia University Press, 2012), Kindle edition, Chapter Nine: "From Agnosticism to Gnosticism"; see also *The Attention Revolution*, 159. Contrary to *jhāna* minimalists, Wallace is skeptical of the claims that the Buddhist first *dhyāna* can be "achieved in a few days or weeks," *Meditations of a Buddhist Skeptic*, Kindle edition, Chapter Nine: "From Agnosticism to Gnosticism." Consistent with this rigorism, he seems to think that in the first *jhāna* there is no awareness of the external world and that the subject-object distinction disappears, ibid., Kindle location, 2793, 2802, 2812, 2831, 2843. Wallace also thinks that it should take about 10,000 hours of practice to come to the stage of *śamatha*, 162. He also seems to think that the attainment of the *paṭibhāga-nimitta* and thus of *upacāra-samādhi*, or *śamatha*, requires "years or months of full-time practice," *The Attention Revolution*, 156–59. The Dalai Lama, on the other hand, seems to take a more middling view when he teaches that "concentrated meditation" can be achieved "within six months" and that the sign of having achieved "calm abiding," or *śamatha* is the ability to stay focused "vividly and continuously" on the meditation object for four hours, *How to Meditate: The Way to a Meaningful* Life, 1st pbk. ed., trans. and ed. Jeffrey Hopkins (New York and London, et al.: Atria Books, 2003), 126–27. The *Visuddhimagga* might seem at first glance to support the maximalists when it says that when *appanā-samādhi* arises it can continue "for a whole night and a whole day" (Vsm 4.33 Ñ). A bit later, Buddhaghosa states that after entering a *jhāna* (which one is not specified), the meditator "remains in the attainment even for a whole day" (Vsm 4.125 Ñ). But this is qualified a few sentences later when Buddhaghosa give advice for one who "wants to remain long in the jhana" (Vsm 4.126 Ñ), which seems to imply that one can stay a shorter period in a jhāna. This is confirmed in the Visuddhimagga, which states that a Bhikkhu whose mind is not fully purified from "states that obstruct concentration . . . soon comes out of that jhāna again." Such a meditator can reach absorption, the attaining of which is equivalent to the first *jhāna*, but cannot make it last. But the Bhikkhu who purifies the mind appropriately can "remain in the attainment for a whole day (Vsm 4.124 Ñ)." The *Visuddhimagga* also defines one form of mastery of *jhāna* as the ability to "remain in jhāna for a moment consisting in exactly a finger-snap or exactly ten finger-snaps" (Vsm 4.134 Ñ). Thus, nothing in the *Visuddhimagga* seems to imply that *upacāra-samādhi*—what to speak of *appanā-samādhi*—should last for four hours to be genuine. The *Visuddhimagga* says, on the one hand, that first *jhāna* absorption can last for "a single conscious moment" (Vsm 4.78 Ñ) or that one can carry "on with a stream of profitable impulsion [*javanas*] for a whole night and for a whole day" (Vsm 433 Ñ). Anuruddha provides the solution to this apparent contradiction by pointing out that *appanā-samādhi*, and thus the first *jhāna*, lasts "for only one javana moment" for beginners, but it can stretch out to days with practice and mastery, Anuruddha and Bodhi, *A Comprehensive Manual of* Abhidhamma, 178.

33 Brasington, "Interpretations of the Jhanas," http://www.leighb.com/jhanantp.htm, accessed May 7, 2014.

34 "Interview with Ajaan Ṭhānissaro," in Shankman, *The Experience of Samādhi*, 128.

35 Brasington, "Interpretations of the Jhanas," http://www.leighb.com/jhanantp.htm, accessed May 7, 2014.

36 Shaila Catherine, a contemporary Insight Meditation and *jhāna* teacher, seems to occupy a middle ground between the minimalists and the maximalists. On the one hand, she holds that "you can maintain an immersion for very long periods of time—jhāna is a deeply steady state," while on the other hand, she says of *jhāna*, "Yes. It's quite accessible. . . . It is something that is very doable for committed lay practitioners. . . . In the earliest discourses, the Buddha encouraged lay people to, 'from time to time,' enjoy the bliss of seclusion, that is, to develop the concentration states of jhāna," Catherine, *Jhāna Practice and True Happiness*. Supporting this latter stance is Bucknell's claim that the first-jhāna factors of *vitakka* and *vicāra* constitute "probably nothing other than the normal process of discursive thought, the familiar but usually unnoticed stream of mental imagery and verbalization, 'Reinterpreting the *Jhānas*,'" 376. This is also the view of Pa Auk Sayadaw's students Stephen Snyder and Tina Rasmussen that "in first jhāna . . . the awareness is so close to normal consciousness that it is quite easy for full absorption to be disrupted," *Practicing the Jhānas*, 73. Also in the middle ground, I would place Christian Feldman, a *jhāna* teacher who thinks that a retreat of at least a month is needed to acquire access concentration and jhānas, "Opening the Gates of Consciousness," *Tricycle* 54 (Winter 2004): 73.

37 Bronkhorst, *The Two Traditions of Meditation in Ancient India*, ix, xvii, 128.

38 Ibid., 53.

39 Ibid., 31–44, 45–53. Polak also notes that: "Not only have we learned that jhāna was not yoga; it was in fact seen in early Buddhism as the direct opposite of Buddhist meditation," *Reexamining Jhāna*, 191

40 Bronkhorst, *Buddhist Teaching in India*, 59. "Bronkhorst speaks of this as the first method" of mainstream meditation in ancient India. In contrast to this, ascetical methods associated with the Jains and preclassical yoga, he describes a second mainstream method, which involves the realization that "the true self does not participate in any activities," a view closer to the wisdom paths of Sāṃkhya, the *jñāna-yoga* of the Bhagavad Gītā, and, later, of Advaita Vedānta. See Bronkhorst, *Two Meditation Traditions in Ancient India*, 54–57.

41 This attainment is also known in Pāli as *saññāvedayitanirodha*, or "the cessation of ideation and feeling," Damien Keown, ed. *A Dictionary of Buddhism* (Oxford: Oxford University Press, 2004), s.v. "saññā-vedayita-nirodha," accessed May 17, 2014, http://www.oxfordreference.com/view/10.1093/acref/9780198605607.001.0001/acref-9780198605607-e-1592?rskey=UFiy6P&result=1. See also Collins, *Nirvana and Other Buddhist Felicities*, 157.

42 Collins, *Nirvana and Other Buddhist Felicities*, 159.

43 This view, which is one of the surprising turnabouts suggested by Bronkhorst and Polak, directly contradicts a standard claim among Theravāda Buddhists that the Buddha is the discoverer of *vipassanā* meditation, while *jhāna* meditation was widely practiced by the other ascetics of Buddha's day. See, for example, Bhante Henepola Gunaratana, "A Critical Analysis of the Jhānas in Theravada Buddhist Meditation," 12, and Rahula, *What the Buddha Taught*, 68–69.

44 Polak, *Reexamining Jhāna*, 25.

45 Brahm, *Mindfulness, Bliss, and Beyond*, 127. See also Brahm, "Degrees of Seeing," 42. See also "Interview with Ajahn Brahmavaṃso," in Shankman, *The Experience of Samādhi*, 166.

46 Brahm, *Mindfulness, Bliss, and Beyond*, 127. See *Gopaka Moggallana Sutta: Moggallana the Guardsman* (Majjhima Nikāya 108), trans. Thanissaro Bhikkhu, accessed May 8, 2014, http://www.accesstoinsight.org/tipitaka/mn/mn.108.than.html. Taking the opposite approach, Robert Gimello subordinates "calming to discernment" and sees Buddhist meditation (as opposed to Buddhist mysticism, which is equivalent to the phenomena of *śamatha*) as ultimately an insight practice of "doctrinal analysis," or the viewing of experiences through the categories of Buddhist teachings. He provides this formula for his *vipaśyanā*-weighted stance: discernment (or *vipaśyanā*) is "a form of meditative analysis" that employs "the concepts and propositions of Buddhist doctrine," "Mysticism and Meditation," in Katz, *Mysticism and Philosophical Analysis*, 185, 187, 188–89. In contrast to Bronkhorst and Polak, Vetter produces a good deal of evidence that indicates that early Buddhists practiced insight without concentration, *The Ideas and Meditative Practices of Early Buddhists*, 35–44. And this seems to be the method employed by Buddha in the *Satipaṭṭhāna Sutta* and other similar *suttas*.

47 These have been conveniently tabulated by Flickstein, *The Meditator's Atlas: A Roadmap of the Inner World* (Boston: Wisdom Publications, 2007; previously published as *Swallowing the River Ganges*), 63.

48 Gimello, "Mysticism and Meditation," in Katz, *Mysticism and Philosophical Analysis*, 181.

49 Goleman, *The Meditative Mind*, 1–38. This book contains a pioneering popularizing introduction in English to the contemplative itinerary of the *Visuddhimagga*, which is then comparatively applied to other contemplative paths. A more comprehensive rendering in the tradition of Bhante Henepola Gunaratana of the *Visuddhimagga* into the form of a practical manual for contemporary meditators is Flickstein's *The Meditator's Atlas* (for the concentration practices, see 27–43). Using the term *dhyana*, William James sketched an early but fluent summary of the *jhānas* in the "Mysticism" chapter of the still widely influential William James, *The Varieties of Religious Experience: A Study in Human Nature* (New York: Longmans, Green; repr, New York: Random House, n. d.), 392–93. His sketch is based on Carl Friedrich Köppen, *Die Religion des Buddha und Ihre Entstehung*, vol. 1 (Schneider: Berlin, 1857), 585–93. A later influential study in German was Friedrich Heiler, *Die buddhistische Versenkung: Eine religionsgeschichtliche Untersuchung*, 2nd ed. (München: E. Reinhardt, 1922; 1st ed., 1918), 14–24. Other influential references to the *jhānas* include Ninian Smart, *Reasons and Faith* (London: Routledge and Kegan Paul, 1958; repr. 2014), 95–105 and Rahula, *What the Buddha Taught*, 48–49.

50 Gunaratana, "A Critical Analysis of the Jhānas in Theravada Buddhist Meditation," 14; *Beyond Mindfulness*, 17.

51 Griffiths concludes that "most modern [before 1981, that is] Theravāda practitioners" only seemed to be interested in insight meditation and that it was difficult as late as 1981 "to find Theravādins able and willing to give instruction in the finer points of *kasiṇa* meditation or to expound on the benefits of *nirodha-samāpatti*," "Concentration or Insight," 617–18.

52 Erik Braun, "Meditation En Masse: How Colonialism Sparked the Global Vipassana Movement," *Tricycle* 23, no. 4 (Spring 2014): 56, 60 and *The Birth of Insight: Meditation, Modern Buddhism, and the Burmese Monk Ledi Sayadaw* (Chicago: University of Chicago Press, 2013), 127–28, 138–41, 161–62. See also Polak, *Reexamining Jhāna*, 16, 78, 174–90 and Jodt, *Burma's Mass Lay Movement*, xii, xvi, 19–55.

53 For the possibility of dry insight, or insight without the *jhānas*, in older, authoritative texts, see *Visuddhimagga*, 1.6, 21.112. See also Collins, *Nirvana and Other Buddhist Felicities*, 160, 160n68.

54 Braun, "Meditation En Masse," 60, Braun, *The Birth of Insight*, 6, 123–24, 145, and Polak, *Reexamining* Jhāna, 177. Polak concludes that "our investigation seems to show that the Theravāda tradition of meditation cannot be seen as an unbroken lineage going back to the Buddha himself," ibid., 180.

55 *Paramattha-mañjūsā*, 9–10, quoted by Ñāṇamoli in Buddhaghosa, *The Path of Purification*, 750n3.

56 Gethin see the *jhānas* as continuing to be of "paramount importance" in the Abhidhamma and the commentaries, and even, to a greater degree than sometimes recognized, in the *Visuddhimagga*, *The Buddhist Path to Awakening*, 350.

57 Polak carefully probes the strengths and weaknesses of the Western critical approach to Buddhism, *Reexamining Jhāna*, 213–24.

58 *Samādhi* in the Buddhist tradition, as indicated in its being part of the name of the last limb of the Noble Eightfold Path, is the name for the whole concentrative path of yogic contemplation. It is synonymous with *samatha* (Skt., *śamatha*), "serenity" or "tranquility," which names one of the major components of Buddhist meditation. See Gunaratana, "A Critical Analysis of the Jhānas in Theravāda Buddhist Meditation," 28.

59 See the discourses in the Asaṅkhata Saṃyutta section of the Saṃyutta Nikāya, for example, *Asaṅkhata Sutta*, 43.12. This *sutta* is referenced by Polak, *Reexamining Jhāna*, 28.

60 As pioneered by Ledi Sayadaw and furthered by Mingun Sayadaw and Mahasi Sayadaw, see Braun, *The Birth of Insight*, 139–41, 161–62.

61 "As we have already noted, *vipassanā* appears rather rarely in the *suttas* and is never described in detail," Polak, *Reexamining Jhāna*, 29.

62 Bronkhorst contrasts the "pleasant experience" of the Buddha's *jhāna* experience with the more difficult and forceful forms of "main stream meditation" in ancient India, *The Two Traditions of Mediation in Ancient India*, 22–24.

63 I follow Bronkhorst's rendition of the account as given in the *Mahāsaccaka Sutta*, *The Two Traditions of Meditation in Ancient India*, 22–23.

64 I am in agreement with Bucknell, who sees Buddhaghosa's account of the stages of meditative practice as "reliable" up until the first *jhāna*, although Bucknell disagrees with Buddhaghosa's doctrinal interpretations of these stages, "Reinterpreting the *Jhānas*," 389.

65 The *Visuddhimagga*, writes Polak, "defines the orthodoxy within Theravāda Buddhism and it has always been held in great esteem. It is also worth noting that the doctrine presented within the Visuddhimagga represents a basis level of Buddhist soteriology, which is accepted by all the schools of Buddhism. From a Mahāyāna and Vajrayāna standpoint, practices contained within Buddhaghosa's work are a safe but slow and strenuous path to liberation. . . . The Visuddhimagga contains the only path to liberation, which is accepted by all the Buddhists, even if by some it is regarded as a lesser level of soteriological road to liberation," Polak, *Reexamining Jhāna*, 32.

66 "Sumangala's Mother," *Therigatha* (*sumaṅgalamātātherīgāthā*), 2.3.23-24, trans. Thanissaro Bhikkhu, *Access to Insight*, accessed May 28, 2014, http://www.accesstoinsight.org/tipitaka/kn/thig/thig.02.03.than.html. The ecstatic dimension of Buddhism is often overlooked, while its intellectual dimension is too often overemphasized. As L. S. Cousins has observed, the importance of *pīti* is often

overlooked in the study of early Buddhism, with the result that early Buddhism "comes to seem a somewhat dry and unemotional form of religion, even perhaps desiccated and intellectual," "Buddhist *Jhāna*: Its Nature and Attainment according to the Pali Sources," *Religion* 3, no. 2 (Autumn 1973): 120, accessed October 24, 2015, doi:10.1016/0048-721X(73)90003-1. Following Cousins on this view of *pīti*, Barnes notes that "so far from being a dry, desiccating, and mainly intellectual discipline, Buddhism sets great store by the experience of largely emotional states," "The Buddhist Way of Deliverance (according to the Pāli Sources)," 259.

67 For the details of this brief historical overview, I follow Bhikkhu Ñāṇamoli's engaging account in his introduction to his translation of the *Visuddhimagga*, *The Path of Purification*, xxiii–xli.

68 Ñāṇamoli, *The Path of Purification*, xxiii–xli.

69 The 14th Dalai Lama refers to it as "this wonderful meditation manual," "Message from His Holiness the Dalai Lama," in Ñāṇamoli, *The Path of Purification*, i. Ram Dass writes of his first encounter with the *Visuddhimagga* in India, "I drank the book like a fine brandy," "Foreword," in Goleman, *The Meditative Mind*, xiv. Edward Conze exclaimed that Buddhaghosa "composed one of the great spiritual classics of mankind. If I had just one book to take with me on a desert island, this [i.e., the *Visuddhimagga*] would be my choice"—although he allows that he might take a volume of Horace along as well! *Buddhist Meditation* (New York: Routledge, 2008; originally published 1956), 25.

70 "It . . . appears that Buddhaghosa did not even supposedly attain the first *jhāna*," Polak, *Reexamining Jhāna*, 188. Surprising as this claim might be about a master of meditative theory, it is not unprecedented that someone might possess encyclopedic theoretical knowledge of Buddhist *bhāvanā* without personal experience of what is being described. Geshe Gedün Lodrö noted at the end of a series of lectures on calm abiding and special insight that he was not giving "an explanation from experience," and he denies having "already attained calm abiding or special insight," a claim that may, however, be meant to preserve modesty about having attained the higher states of adepts, *Calm Abiding and Special Insight: Achieving Spiritual Transformation Through Meditation*, trans. Jeffrey Hopkins, ed. Jeffrey Hopkins, Anne C. Klein, and Leah Zahler (Ithaca, NY, USA: Snow Lion Publications, 1998), 283. The same can also be said of Buddhaghosa and his meditative attainments.

71 Polak, *Reexamining Jhāna*, 188. For a detailed chart of Theravāda Buddhism's thirty-one planes of existence, see Rupert Gethin, *The Foundations of Buddhism* (New York and London: Oxford University Press, 1998), 116–17.

72 Polak, *Reexamining Jhāna*, 188.

73 Ibid.

74 Ñāṇamoli, *The Path of Purification*, xliii.

75 For the Pāli text, I have consulted Buddhaghosa, *Visuddhimagga*, vol. 1 (Yangon, Myanmar: Ministry of Religious Affairs, 2008; Romanized from the Myanmar edition, Aṭṭakathā Series 51, 1970).

76 Buddhaghosa briefly reformulates the fourfold *jhāna* formula in the Pāli Canon to account for the fivefold *jhāna* formula in the Abhidhamma, Vsm 4.198-202 Ñ. In the *Visuddhimagga*, Buddhaghosa generally equates the four *sutta jhānas*, that is, "the jhana tetrad," with the five Abhidhamma *jhānas*, that is, "the jhana pentad," although in the case of Elder Mallaka (Vsm 4.23 Ñ), he speaks of his attaining the *jhāna* pentad rather than the *jhāna* tetrad. I don't think this difference has any soteriological significance.

77 The word *samādhi* seems to be used in a wider sense in Buddhism, where, at least in the Pāli literature, as Henepola Gunaratana points out that it is used "with varying degrees of specificity of meaning. In the narrowest sense, as defined by Buddhaghosa, it denotes the particular mental factor responsible for the concentrating of the mind, namely, one-pointedness. In a wider sense, it can signify the states of unified consciousness that result from the strengthening of concentration, i.e., the meditative attainments of serenity and the stages leading up to them. And in a still wider sense the word *samādhi* can be applied to the method of practice used to produce and cultivate these refined states of concentration, here being equivalent to the development of serenity," "A Critical Analysis of the Jhānas in Theravada Buddhist Meditation," 26. *Samādhi* in the Buddhist sense can thus be taken as a rough synonym for the *saṃyama* of the *Yoga-Sūtras*, unless, of course, we take yoga in the broadest sense as *samādhi*, as the commentator Vyāsa does when he claims that "yoga is *samādhi*" (*yogaḥ samādhiḥ*), Swāmi Harihārananda Āraṇya, *Yoga Philosophy of Patañjali: Containing His Yoga Aphorisms with Commentary of Vyāsa*, trans. P. N. Mukerji (Calcutta: University of Calcutta, 1981), 1.

78 The phrase *parikamma-nimitta* doesn't seem to appear in the *Visuddhimagga*, although *parikamma*, "preliminary work," occurs throughout. Indeed, Buddhaghosa speaks only of "the two signs" (Vsm 5.4 Ñ), which is consistent with the *Vimuttimagga*, 77. Yet the idea of *parikamma-nimitta* is consistent with the teaching of the *Visuddhimagga*, and *parikamma-nimitta* is clearly part of current Theravāda tradition. See Nyanatiloka, *Manual of Buddhist Terms and Doctrines*, 4th ed., ed. Nyanaponika (Kandy, Sri Lanka: Buddhist Publication Society, 1980; first published 1952), s.v. "Nimitta," accessed June 4, 2014, http://www.palikanon.com/english/wtb/n_r/nimitta.htm. The threefold complement of signs is given in the Nārada and Bhikkhu, *A Comprehensive Manual of* Abhidhamma, 331.

79 I take the translation of the first two terms, *vitakka* and *vicāra*, from Bhikkhu Ñāṇamoli (Vsm 4.79) and Bhante Henepola Gunaratana, and I follow Bhante Gunaratana in my translation of *pīti* and *sukha*, Gunaratana, "A Critical Analysis of the Jhānas in Theravada Buddhist Meditation," 80. See also, Collins, *Nirvana and Other Buddhist Felicities*, 304. Since I agree with Stuart-Fox, "Jhāna and Buddhist Scholasticism," 83–85, that *ekaggatā* was a later, Abhidhammic imposition on the Sutta first *jhāna* (nor is it found in the classic *jhāna* description quoted by Buddhaghosa at 4.79 Ñ, 4.69 Myanmar Romanized text), I don't include it here as a fifth *jhānāṅga*). Stuart-Fox subjects the three references to *ekaggatā* in the first *jhāna* in the *Suttapiṭaka* to a persuasive source-critical analysis that sees these references as later interpolations, "Jhāna and Buddhist Scholasticism," 88–90.

80 Bucknell refers to the stereotyped *jhāna* formula as a pericope, "Reinterpreting the *Jhānas*," 377.

81 Buddhaghosa quotes the *jhāna* formula from the *Vibhaṅga*, which is in the Abhidhamma Piṭaka. Although there is much debate over whether the *jhāna* series should include the four immaterial states as the last four *jhānas*, I follow Bucknell and the "many suttas" where the *rūpa* and *arūpa jhānas* are construed "as constituting a single series," "Reinterpreting the *Jhānas*," 377n5.

82 Buddhaghosa quotes from the *Vibhaṅga*, 245.

83 *Catechism of the Catholic Church*, 2000, accessed June 25, 2014, http://www.vatican.va/archive/ccc_css/archive/catechism/p3s1c3a2.htm.

84 Paramattha-mañjūsā, 119, quoted in Visuddhimagga, 4.22 Ñ.

85 Various commentators disagree on whether there are four, eight, or nine *jhānas*. Jikido accepts nine, with *nirodha-samāpatti* as the ninth, *An Introduction to Buddhism*, 181. Collins notes that "there are texts in the *Sutta* collection which place Cessation in a position analogous to that of nirvana, as the ninth and culminating stage of meditative practice," *Nirvana and Other Buddhist Felicities*, 159. The *Visuddhimagga* also accepts the ninefold scheme (Vsm 11.124, 23.18, 23.26 Ñ). It is clear, however, as noted earlier, that the emerging scholarly view of early Buddhism sees the first four *jhānas* as constituting the core of the Buddha's meditative teaching and the addition of the four immaterial states and cessation as the next five *jhānas* is an attempt to blend the traditional, or "mainstream" yogic path and the Buddha's new path of the *jhānas*. Ayya Khema taught a system with nine *jhānas*, with the ninth carrying the name of *abhisaññānirodha*, *Who is My Self*, 95.

86 Bronkhorst, *Buddhist Teaching in India*, 53–54, 54n104, 130.

87 To the standard four *jhāna* factors, one more is usually added. There is much debate over how to name this fifth factor, as well as much debate about whether it is included in the first *jhāna* or not, an innovation that Bucknell lays at Upatissa's and Buddhaghosa's feet, "Reinterpreting the *Jhānas*," 386–87. Jhāna maximalists tend to think that it is, while *jhāna* minimalists think that it is not. For an example of the first view, see "Interview with Ajahn Brahmavaṃso," in Shankman, *The Experience of Samādhi*, 169; for an example of the latter stance, see Bucknell, "Reinterpreting the *Jhānas*," 389, 387–98, 394, 404. Although *ekaggatā* doesn't appear in the *jhāna* formula, it is often named as a fifth Abhidhammic and Commentarial *jhāna* factor, Gunaratana, "A Critical Analysis of the Jhānas in Theravada Buddhist Meditation," 140–41; Brasington, "The Traditional Factors of the 8 *Jhanas*," and it is taken as a synonym for *cetaso ekodibhāva* (Vsm 4.109 Ñ), *cittass' ekaggatā* (Bucknell, "Reinterpreting the *Jhānas*," 397), and *samādhi* (Gunaratana, "A Critical Analysis of the Jhānas in Theravada Buddhist Meditation," 143). And, as we will see, numerous other characteristics are also detailed in the *jhāna* formula, with the most important being *upekkhā* and *sati*, although these are not included in either the fourfold or fivefold listing of *jhāna* factors. Gunaratana points out that "these elements are not themselves *jhāna* factors," ibid., 206.

88 At this point, according to the standard *jhāna* formula, *cetaso ekodibhāva*, or "oneness of mind," makes its entrance as a *jhāna* factor. The appearance of *cetaso ekodibhāva* is consistent with the fact that *pīti* and *sukha* arise from *samādhi*, or concentration, in the second *jhāna* rather than from separation (*viveka*), as in the first *jhāna*. Arising alongside *cetaso ekodibhāva* is *ajjhatta sampasādana*, which makes its sole appearance in this *jhāna*, and which Bucknell translates as "inner tranquility," "Reinterpreting the *Jhānas*," 378, and Ñāṇamoli as "internal confidence" (Vsm 4.139 Ñ).

89 Reflecting the inconsistency of the *sutta jhāna* formula (see Bucknell, "Reinterpreting the *Jhānas*," 382–83), and to the distraction of later systematizers, *cetaso ekodibhāva* is replaced in the third *jhāna* by *upekhaka* or *upekkhā* ("equanimous") and *ajjhatta sampasādana* is left unmentioned (Vsm 4.153 Ñ). Appearing now for the first time are "mindful" (*sata* or *sati*), the condition of being "fully aware" (*sampajāna* or *sampajañña*), and feeling "bliss" (*sukha*) with one's "body" (*sukañ ca kāyena paṭisaṃvedeti*, Vsm 4.153 Ñ; Pāli text from Bucknell, "Reinterpreting the *Jhānas*," 377n7). The doubling of the terms here reflects the adjectival forms of the terms as given, in the first instances, in the Pāli text and, in the second, the noun forms as given by Gunaratana, "A Critical Analysis of the Jhānas in Theravada Buddhist Meditation," 173, Bucknell, "Reinterpreting the *Jhānas*," 380–81, and Johannes Bronkhorst, *Buddhist Teaching in India*, 16–17.

90 As in the third *jhāna*, "mindfulness" (*sati*) remains in the fourth *jhāna*, but it, along with *upekkhā*, is now said to be *pārisuddhi*, which *The Pali Text Society's Pali-English Dictionary* translates as "clean," "clear," "pure," and "perfect," s.v. *pārisuddhi*, accessed October 24, 2015, http://dsalsrv02.uchicago.edu/cgi-bin/philologic/getobject.pl?c.2:1:2214.pali.1016701, and which Ñāṇamoli translates as "purity" (Vsm 4.183 Ñ). The fourth *jhāna* also has unique elements. Along with the characteristic fourth *jhāna* feature of abandoning happiness (*sukha*), pain (dukkha), which is first mentioned here, is also abandoned; two other characteristics unique to this *jhāna*, *somanassa* and *domanassa* or "mental pleasure" and "mental pain" (Bucknell, "Reinterpreting the *Jhānas*," 399), are said not only to be to be absent from this *jhāna*, but to have previously, at an unstated point, disappeared.

91 Gombrich, *How Buddhism Began*, 112.

92 As noted in a comment in *Paramattha-mañjūsā* 122, quoted in Vsm 763n8 Ñ.

93 For specific details concerning the red silk-cotton tree, see "Bombax ceiba," accessed July 3, 2014, http://en.wikipedia.org/wiki/Bombax_ceiba, and "Bombax ceiba, red silk cotton tree," accessed October 24, 2015, http://plants.usda.gov/core/profile?symbol=BOCE2.

94 Anuruddha and Bodhi, *A Comprehensive Manual of* Abhidhamma, 54.

95 "Change-of-lineage" (*gotrabhū*) refers to both to the attainment of *appanā-samādhi*, which notes a transition from the realm of the senses and desires to the subtle realms, and to the attainment of the first of the four levels of *saintliness*, Anuruddha and Bodhi, *A Comprehensive Manual of* Abhidhamma, 168.

96 Bodhi's translation, *A Comprehensive Manual of* Abhidhamma, 389. Ñāṇamoli prefers "cognitive series," Vsm 4n13 Ñ.

97 Anuruddha and Bodhi, *A Comprehensive Manual of* Abhidhamma, 122–24.

98 Ibid.

99 Ibid., 158, 389.

100 Ibid., 124.

101 Shaila Catherine, *Wisdom Wide and Deep: A Practical Handbook for Mastering Jhāna and Vipassanā* (Boston: Wisdom Publications, 2011), 268, 498.

102 Buddhaghosa, *Visuddhimagga*, vol. 1, Myanmar edition, 4.69.

103 Anuruddha and Bodhi, *A Comprehensive Manual of* Abhidhamma, 372n8.

104 Ibid, 167–68.

105 Whether one experiences four or five *javanas* until absorption is a function of whether one has "keen" or "average" faculties, Anuruddha and Bodhi, *A Comprehensive Manual of* Abhidhamma, 168.

106 Bodhi points out that *appanā-samādhi*, and thus the first *jhāna*, lasts "for only one javana moment" for beginners, but which can stretch out to days with practice and mastery, Anuruddha and Bodhi, *A Comprehensive Manual of* Abhidhamma, 178, a point implied also by Gunaratana, *A Critical Analysis of the Jhānas in Theravada Buddhist Meditation*," 22.

107 Gunaratana, "A Critical Analysis of the Jhānas in Theravada Buddhist Meditation," 205–06, 226.

108 Collins, *Nirvana and Other Buddhist Felicities*, 157.

109 Ibid., 160.

110 *The Pāli Text Society's Pāli-English Dictionary* s.v. "*parinibbāna*," accessed October 24, 2015, http://dsalsrv02.uchicago.edu/cgi-bin/philologic/getobject.pl?c.2:1:1955.pali.895303.

111 As recounted by Collins, *Nirvana and Other Buddhist Felicities*, 159–60.

112 Collins, *Nirvana and Other Buddhist Felicities*, 160; see also Vsm 23.51 Ñ).

113 Collins sees each of these as possibilities in some texts of early Buddhism, *Nirvana and Other Buddhist Felicities*, 160. *The Pāli Text Society's Pāli-English Dictionary*, on the contrary, is far less ambivalent about equating *nibbāna* with *nirodha*: "In many cases [it] is synonymous with nibbāna & parinibbāna; it may be said to be even a stronger expression as far as the *active* destruction of the causes of life is concerned," s.v. "*Nirodha*," accessed October 24, 2015, http://dsalsrv02.uchicago.edu/cgi-bin/philologic/getobject.pl?c.2:1:503.pali.217381.

114 Newberg and d'Aquili, *The Mystical Mind*, 13–14, 95, 110–14.

115 Equal, I think, to *asamprajñāta-samādhi* in the *Yoga Sūtra* and *nirodha-samāpatti* in the *Visuddhimagga*. These states are brought about by the cultivation of a "Null Domain" method, according to Nash and Newberg, "Toward A Unifying Taxonomy and Definition for Meditation," 6–7.

116 Collins characterizes it as "a conditioned phenomenon, even though it is an 'experience' with 'nirvana as its object.'" Collins cites here the Buddha reference to "the signless concentration of mind," which Collins equates with *nibbāna*, as "conditioned and volitionally produced," and, "as a consequence," "subject to cessation," *Nirvana and Other Buddhist Felicities*, 160; *The Shorter Discourse on Voidness* (*Cūḷasuññata Sutta*), in *The Middle Length Discourses of the Buddha: A Translation of the Majjhima Nikāya*, trans. Bhikkhu Ñāṇamoli and Bhikkhu Bodhi, 3rd ed. (Boston: Wisdom Publications & Barre Center for Buddhist Studies, 2005), 121.9, 969.

117 For the distinction between and the synonymy of these terms in early Buddhism, see Collins, *Nirvana and Other Buddhist Felicities*, 147–51.

118 This is consistent with *The Pāli Text Society's Pāli-English Dictionary*, which cites a litany of poetic description of *nibbāna*: "the harbour of refuge, the cool cave, the island amidst the floods, the place of bliss, emancipation, liberation, safety, the supreme, the transcendental, the uncreated, the tranquil, the home of ease, the calm, the end of suffering, the medicine for all evil, the unshaken, the ambrosia, the immaterial, the imperishable, the abiding, the further shore, the unending, the bliss of effort, the supreme joy, the ineffable, the detachment, the holy city, and many others," s.v. "*Nibbāna*," accessed October 24, 2015, http://dsalsrv02.uchicago.edu/cgi-bin/philologic/getobject.pl?c.2:1:324.pali.116987.

Chapter 5

1 David Gordon White, *The Yoga Sutra of Patanjali: A Biography* (Princeton and Oxford: Princeton University Press, 2014), Kindle edition, xv. This shift appears to have begun with the iconoclastic and original scholarship of N. E. Sjoman, whose paradigm-shifting *The Yoga Tradition of the Mysore Palace* (Delhi: Abhinav Publications, 1996) seems to have opened the way for iconoclastic works by White and Mark Singleton, which will figure prominently in these pages. See 35–38.

2 David Gordon White, *Sinister Yogis*, pbk. ed. (Chicago: University of Chicago Press, 2011), xiv, 33, 44, 60–73, 78. White, following Louis Renou and Boris Oguibénine, notes that "the most common rigvedic meaning of the verb **yuj* in its middle conjugation (*yuje*, etc.) was 'to yoke one's self to a chariot' and, by extension, 'to prepare for battle,'" ibid., 63.

3 White, *Sinister Yogis*, 63.

4 Valerie J. Roebuck writes, "*Upāsanā* is often used as a way of moving from grosser to subtler concepts of truth," in *The Upaniṣads*, trans. Valerie J. Roebuck (London, New York, etc.: Penguin Books, 2003), xxxiii. An example can be found in the *Bṛhadāraṇyaka Upaniṣad* (2.2), where the *brāhmaṇa* sage Bālāki Gārgya finds himself to be no match for King Ajātaśatru. In offering subtler definitions that played off of the more concrete definitions of Bālāki Gārgya, Ajātaśatru demonstrates that mystical insight is a gradual perceiving of a subtle, abstract spiritual order as reflected through a grosser, physical vesture. On "subtilization," or *pratiprasava*, in the *Yoga Sūtra*, see Christopher Key Chapple, *Yoga and the Luminous: Patañjali's Spiritual Path to Freedom* (Albany: State University of New York Press, 2008), 104–08.

5 White, *Sinister Yogis*, 37; David Gordon White, "Introduction: Yoga, Brief History of an Idea," in *Yoga in Practice*, ed. David Gordon White (Princeton and New York: Princeton University Press, 2012), 11.

6 *Ṛg Veda* 5.81.1: "Seers of the vast illumined seer yogically [*yuñjante*] control their minds and their intelligence," trans. Mikel Burley, *Haṭha Yoga: Its Context, Theory and Practice* (Delhi: Motilal Banarsidass, 2000), 25.

7 *Kaṭha Upaniṣad* 2.12, 6.11; *Śvetāśvatara Upaniṣad* 1.3, 2.1-5, 8-15, *Maitrī Upaniṣad* 6.18-29. Clear evidence of yogic meditation is present in the *Kaṭha Upaniṣad*, where, according to Burley, *Haṭha-Yoga*, 33, "Yama defines yoga as 'the steady holding' [*dhāraṇā*] of the senses (*KU* 6.11), i.e., fixing the mind's attention upon a single point." Willard L. Johnston notes that, as clearly indicated in *Śvetāśvatara Upaniṣad* 1.3 (*te dhyānyogānugatāḥ*), the "Upaniṣadic speculators practiced yoga (the śramaṇa system of self-discipline) and meditation," Willard Johnson, *Poetry and Speculation of the Ṛg Veda* (Berkeley: University of California Press, 1980), 123.

8 Dominik Wujastyk argues that "the yoga tract in the *Compendium* [i.e., the *Carakasaṃhitā*] is older than Patañjali's yoga system," "The Path to Liberation through Yogic Mindfulness in Early Āyurveda," in White, *Yoga in Practice*, 33.

9 A part of the great epic that, according to White, "contains the greatest concentration of narrative accounts of yoga practice," *Sinister Yogis*, 43.

10 White, *Sinister Yogis*, 38–41.

11 Ibid.

12 Ibid., 29.

13 Ibid., 38. White's emphasis.

14 Andrew J. Nicholson, "Review of *Sinister Yogis*," by David Gordon White, *Journal of the American Oriental Society* 130, no. 2 (April to June 2010): 277.

15 James Mallinson, "The Yogīs' Latest Trick," *Journal of the Royal Asiatic Society* 24, no. 1 (July 2014): 2.

16 White, *Sinister Yogis*, 47.

17 White, *The Yoga Sutra of Patanjali*, 110, 116–42.

18 White, *Sinister Yogis*, 45.

19 Ibid., 45.

20 Ibid., 45–46; see 263n30, where White cites Elizabeth De Michelis's discussion of Vivekananda's identification of *rāja-yoga* and *pātañjala yoga*. See Swāmi Vivekānanda, *Rāja Yoga: Or Conquering the Internal Nature* (London, New York, and Bombay: Longmans, Green, and Co., 1896), ix–x.

21 White, *The Yoga Sutra of Patanjali*, 124.

22 Mallinson agrees with White's attempt to undo Swami Vivekananda's "identification of *rājayoga* with Patañjali's *aṣṭāṅgayoga*," "The Yogīs' Latest Trick," 7.

23 White, *Sinister Yogis*, 45–47. See also Mallinson, "The Yogīs' Latest Trick," 7, and Mark Singleton, *Yoga Body: The Origins of Modern Posture Practice* (New York and London: Oxford University Press, 2010), 27–29.

24 White, *The Yoga Sutra of Patanjali*, 113–14. See Svātmārāma, *Hatha Yoga Pradipika: An English Translation*, trans. Brian Dana Akers (Woodstock, NY: YogaVidya, 2002), 84–85, which lists fifteen synonyms for *rāja-yoga* including *samādhi*, *advaita*, and *jīvanmukti.*

25 *The Gheranda Samhita: An English Translation*, trans. James Mallinson (Woodstock, NY: YogaVidya, 2004), loc. 145–152n1.

26 Mallinson points out that *haṭha yoga* has been practiced in either *mumukṣu* or *bubhukṣu* varieties, that is a type oriented toward liberation and another oriented toward the attainment of *siddhis*, or extraordinary powers, Mallinson, "The Yogīs' Latest Trick," 4. Burley sees *haṭha yoga* as the culmination of *rāja-yoga* rather than as "a set of mental techniques which must be appended to haṭha-yoga," Burley, *Haṭha-Yoga*, 242. Gerald James Larson translates *haṭha yoga* as "Exertion Yoga," "Pātañjala Yoga in Practice," in White, *Yoga in Practice*, 73.

27 White, *The Yoga Sutra of Patanjali*, 115.

28 White, *Sinister Yogis*, 47; Dermot Killingley, "Manufacturing Yogis: Swami Vivekananda as a Yoga Teacher," in *Gurus of Modern Yoga*, ed. Mark Singleton and Ellen Goldberg (New York and Oxford: Oxford University Press, 2014), 29.

29 Elizabeth De Michelis, *A History of Modern Yoga: Patañjali and Western Esotericism* (London and New York: Continuum, 2004), 178.

30 In the *Dattātreyayogaśāstra*, according to Mallinson, "The Yogīs' Latest Trick," 7, 13. See a short summary of the history of *haṭha yoga* in Singleton, *Yoga Body*, 27–29. Singleton also seeks to drive a wedge between traditional *haṭha yoga* and "transnational 'hatha' yoga" (27), yet even he has to admit that this can only be pushed so far, although he seems to think that the innovations of current *haṭha yoga* are a consequence of "India's encounter with modernity" (33).

31 James Mallinson, "*Haṭhayoga's* Philosophy: A Fortuitous Union of Non-Dualities," *Journal of Indian Philosophy* 42, no. 1 (March 2014): 226, accessed October 25, 2015, 10.1007/s10781-013-9217-0. White also notes that the meaning of the expression *haṭha yoga* "has remained relatively stable" since the eleventh century, *The Yoga Sutra of Patanjali*, 113.

32 Burley, *Haṭha-Yoga*, 39.

33 White, *Sinister Yogis*, 42; James Mallinson, "Yogis in Mughal India," in *Yoga: The Art of Transformation*, ed. Debra Diamond (Washington, DC: Freer Gallery and Arthur M. Sackler Gallery, Smithsonian Institute, 2013), 69–70, 81n8.

34 *Kaṭha Upaniṣad* 2.12, 6.11; *Śvetāśvatara Upaniṣad* 2.1-5, 8-15, *Maitrī Upaniṣad* 6.18-29.

35 *Maitrī Upaniṣad* 6.18. The omission of *āsana* in this list of six limbs leads White to conclude that *āsana* is a later addition to an emerging meditative and philosophical yoga tradition, which is discontinuous with the yogic ascent of Vedic chariot warriors, the seated *jhāna* practice of the Buddha, and the seated ascetic often identified with Śiva in the Mohenjo-Daro clay seal no. 420, White, *Sinister Yogis*, 49–56.

36 *Bhagavad Gītā* 6.10-32.

37 Mallinson, "The Yogīs' Latest Trick," 2, 5–7.

38 White, "Introduction," in White, *Yoga in Practice*, 15.

39 A similar project of debunking the authenticity of contemporary yoga can be found in Singleton, *Yoga Body*, 3–7, 15–16, 21–22, 33 passim. One of the pioneers of this

attitude of "fundamental skepticism" toward contemporary yoga is Joseph S. Alter, whose diffuse, historicistic, and deconstructive dismantling of yoga, particularly in its modern, "transnational" expressions was undertaken in *Yoga in Modern India: The Body Between Science and Philosophy* (Princeton: Princeton University Press, 2004), xii, xix, 10, 14–18. Another pioneer of this approach is Elizabeth De Michelis, who is aware, however, that overly Orientalizing studies of contemporary yoga can veer into becoming "ultimately self-defeating forms of radical deconstructivism," *A History of Modern Yoga*, 9.

40 White, *Sinister Yogis*, xii, 42–45, where he identifies meditative practice not with yoga as such but with the Buddhist *jhāna*-practice. See also, White, *The Yoga Sutra of Patanjali*, 16, 113.

41 White, *The Yoga Sutra of Patanjali*, xvi, 6, 40–52, 148–71, 203. Mallinson's reconstruction of this history in "The Yogīs' Latest Trick" and "Yogis in Mughal India" is more balanced.

42 In the millennium before the rise of the tantric and *bhakti* movements, which reshaped the whole of Indian life in the second half of the first millennium, orthodox Vedic and popular religion in medieval India was influenced by the *śramaṇic* traditions of Buddhism and Jainism, which are closer in spirit to the *Yoga Sūtra* than they are to Vedānta and Brāhmaṇism, with their focus on *varṇa* duties, ritualism, and, later, highly developed expressions of henotheism, which can be thought of as focusing on a supreme divinity that reveals itself in multiple supreme expressions. Gavin Flood envisions at the beginning of this period that "a common heritage of meditation and mental discipline [was] practiced by renouncers with varying affiliations to non-orthodox (Veda-rejecting) and orthodox (Veda-accepting) traditions," *An Introduction to Hinduism* (Cambridge: Cambridge University Press, 1996), 82. The gradual eclipse of the *Yoga Sūtra* in the last millennium thus makes sense in an India where a resurgent Brāhmaṇism (or "Hinduism") expressed itself forcefully in the rise and organizational power of Advaita Vedānta and widely influential devotional movements, see White, *The Yoga Sutra of Patanjali*, 16, 44. Out of step with these developments is the minimalist theism of the *Yoga Sūtra*, which seems like a poorly integrated graft in the *Yoga Sūtra* and lacks the normative monotheistic attributes of the deities of the great devotional movements. Also, the Buddhist-influenced themes in the *Yoga Sūtra* would have made the text less attractive in an India where Buddhism had been vanquished and had virtually disappeared from India below the Himalayas. For example, the claim that "everything is indeed suffering for the wise" (YS 2.15), terminology such as *nirodha*, *samādhi*, *samāpatti*, *saṃskāra*, *duḥkha*, and *dharmamegha-samādhi* (YS 4.29), and doctrinal complexes such as the first two constituents of *samprajñāta-samādhi*, that is, *vitarka* and *vicāra* (YS 1.17), which figure in the first two *jhānas*, the *brahmavihāras* (YS 1.33), and the concept of an eightfold path (YS 2.29) suggest Buddhist influence. See, among others, Polak, *Reexamining Jhāna*, 189–90; Barbara Stoler Miller, *Yoga: Discipline of Freedom*, pbk. ed. (New York: Bantam, 1998, originally published, Berkeley: University of California Press, 1996), 114n22; Edwin F. Bryant, *The Yoga Sūtras of Patañjali* (New York: North Point Press, 2009), 128; Sarbacker, *Samādhi*, 21, and Knut A. Jacobsen, "The Wisdom of Kapila's Cave; Sāṃkhya-Yoga as Practice," in *Studying Hinduism in Practice*, ed. Hillary P. Rodrigues (London and New York: Routledge, 2011), 113. Also significant in the decline of the influence of the *Yoga Sūtra* is the relatively sudden and subcontinentally influential rise of tantrism—what White calls "a wave of

genius"—that swept over India beginning in the sixth century, *The Alchemical Body: Siddha Traditions in Medieval India* (Chicago and London: University of Chicago Press, 1997), which, with its world-affirming accent, is far more in line with a return to Hindu *dharma* and ritualism and the rise of devotional movements that give new life to the personal self as a devotee of the divine. By contrast, the spirituality of the *Yoga Sūtra*, which, apart from the third *pāda*, cultivates, like the radical world-renouncing mood of early Buddhism and monastic Jainism, a supreme indifference to everything seen and unseen except for *puruṣa* (YS 1.16).

43 White, *The Yoga Sutra of Patanjali*, xv. This dismissive academic view seems to be at odds with another academic trend of the last forty years, noted by White as well, in which yoga scholarship, apparently supporting the view that White wants to dismantle, has "become a growth industry in the American and European academies," *The Yoga Sutra of Patanjali*, 8. White offers a similarly dismissive and reductive characterization of contemporary global yoga—the yoga of "hipsters" and "flat-tummied yoga babes"—in "Introduction," in White, *Yoga in Practice*, 1.

44 White, *The Yoga Sutra of Patanjali*, xv; White, "Introduction," in White, *Yoga in Practice*, 1–3, 18–22, 24, 27.

45 White's exoticizing of yogis and yoga "opens White to accusations of an Orientalist bias," according to Mallinson, "The Yogīs' Latest Trick," 13.

46 A similar point is made by William K. Mahony, *The Artful Universe: An Introduction to the Vedic Religious Imagination* (Albany: State University of New York Press, 1998), 233–34, who early pushed back against the indiscriminate use of the conceit of Orientalism against westerners interested in India. He notes that this move has been called "reverse Eurocentrism" by Wilhelm Halbfass, *Tradition and Reflection: Explorations in Indian Thought* (Albany: State University of New York Press, 1991), 12 (quoted in Mahony, ibid.).

47 Quoted in Diana L. Eck, *India: A Sacred Geography* (New York: Harmony Books, 2012), Kindle edition, Chapter Two, "What is India." Eck notes here that "resistance to ideas of India's unity is embedded in colonial thought and often in postcolonial thought as well," ibid.

48 An apparent softening of his earlier, more stridently dismissive claims about contemporary yoga appears in a later essay, where White allows that "the complex of transformative practices that we know as yoga today is itself the product of some four thousand years of transformation," "Yoga in Transformation," in Diamond, *Yoga*. 35, 40. His views in this essay are decidedly more temperate than in his earlier *Sinister Yogis* (2009) and the later *The Yoga Sutra of Patanjali* (2014). See also the more moderate, polyvocalic view of yoga in White, "Introduction," in White, *Yoga in Practice*, 2. One does sense that White may be of two minds on these matters, which is perhaps why Mallinson "sometimes suspects that White himself is aware that his argument is one-sided," "The Yogīs' Latest Trick," 8.

49 *Ṛg Veda* 5.81.1: "Seers of the vast illumined seer yogically [*yuñjante*] control their minds and their intelligence," Burley, *Haṭha Yoga*, 25.

50 White, *Sinister Yogis*, 62.

51 Mallinson, "The Yogīs' Latest Trick," 4.

52 Ibid., 5n17, 6.

53 White, "Introduction," in White, *Yoga in Practice*, 13.

54 Mallinson, "The Yogīs' Latest Trick," 4.

55 White, "Introduction," in White, *Yoga in Practice*, 3–4.

56 A characterization to be discussed at length later in this section.

57 White, "Introduction," in White, *Yoga in Practice*, 26.
58 Ibid., 4, 8.
59 In his review of *Sinister Yogis*, Andrew J. Nicholson writes that, "although Patañjali's widely repeated definition of yoga at YS 1.2 features the idea of disjunction (or *nirodha*, cessation), his widely overlooked third section dealing with supernormal powers (*vibhūtis*) portrays numinous engagement with other beings in the world as part of the yogic path," Review of *Sinister Yogis* by David Gordon White, 278. Mallinson also notes that the *Yoga Sūtra* enumerates the *siddhis* that yoga produces, "The Yogīs' Latest Trick," 3.
60 Mallinson, "The Yogīs' Latest Trick," 11. This point has been acknowledged implicitly by White, *The Yoga Sutra of Patanjali*, 110–11.
61 Mallinson, "Yogis in Mughal India," in Diamond, *Yoga*, 76.
62 Sjoman, *The Yoga Tradition of the Mysore Palace*, 35. Sjoman also claims that there is a "total absence of connection between the traditional sources and modern traditions," 39.
63 Singleton, *Yoga Body*, 33, where he allows that it is going too far to delink "modern postural yoga" from traditional Indian *āsana* traditions, which is a version of Sjoman's hypothesis. Yet, elsewhere, he either categorically or nearly categorically negates this relationship, 3, 5, 21, 23, 27, 29–33.
64 White, "Introduction," in White, *Yoga in Practice*, 21.
65 Gerald James Larson, "Introduction to the Philosophy of Yoga," in *Encyclopedia of Indian Philosophies*, Vol. 12, *Yoga India's Philosophy of Meditation*, ed. Gerald James Larson and Ram Shankar Bhattacharya (Delhi: Motilal Banarsidass, 2008), 148.
66 Autumn Jacobsen accepts but moderates Sjoman's view by noting that eighteen of the one hundred and twenty-two *āsanas* in Mummadi Krishnaraja Wodeyar's nineteenth-century *Śrītattvanidhi* are, in fact, found in the *haṭha yoga* textual tradition, "Contemporary Yoga Movements," in Larson and Bhattacharya, Encyclopedia of Indian Philosophies, Vol. 12, 149.
67 "Modern" is favored by Alter, *Yoga in Modern India*, xiii, passim, and De Michelis, *A History of Modern Yoga*, 1, passim, while "Modern Postural Yoga" appears to have been coined by De Michelis, *A History of Modern Yoga*, 4, and was adopted by Singleton, *Yoga Body*, 3, passim. The essentialized typology of "Modern Yoga," which has become a standard conceptual item in contemporary academic studies of yoga, originated with De Michelis, *A History of Modern Yoga*, 187–94; see also Elizabeth De Michelis, "Modern Yoga: History and Forms," in *Yoga in the Modern World: Contemporary Perspectives*, ed. Mark Singleton and Jean Byrne (London and New York: Routledge, 2008), 19–22. "Transnational" seems to have been deployed first by Sarah Strauss (see Alter, *Yoga in Modern India*, xix), and is deployed frequently by Singleton, Yoga Body, 3, passim. "Anglophone" is a favored term for Singleton, Yoga Body, 4, passim, as in "transnational anglophone yoga," 9.
68 Jacobsen, "Contemporary Yoga Movements," in Larson and Bhattacharya, *Encyclopedia of Indian Philosophies*, Vol. 12, 150; Sjoman, *The Yoga Tradition of the Mysore Palace*, 55.
69 Singleton, *Yoga Body*, 178–84, 198–206.
70 Sjoman, *The Yoga Tradition of the Mysore Palace*, 39.
71 Ibid., 49.
72 Ibid. As Sjoman indicates, this evidence includes the twelfth- or thirteenth-century *Mallapurāṇa*, which includes eighteen *āsanas*, including the *śīrṣāsana*, and references to *āsanas* in twelfth-century Jaina and Vīraśaiva texts, 56–57. See also

60–61, where Sjoman appears to trace āsana back to Patañjali via Prince Wodeyar's Śrītattvanidhi.

73 White notes that evidence for seated, meditative *āsanas* goes back to the sixth chapter of the *Bhagavad Gītā*, perhaps to the *Yoga Sūtra* itself, to the *Yoga-Bhāṣya*, Vyāsa's fifth-century commentary on the *Yoga Sūtra* (2.46), and to iconographic representations of and textual references to Lakulīṣa in the fourth century forward and to fifth century and later portrayals of him with a *yoga-paṭṭa*, or yoga-band, wrapped around his knees. This evidence leads White "to place the earliest incontrovertible references to the yoga of postures in . . . middle of the first millennium of the common era," *Sinister Yogis*, 79. Singleton also acknowledges that "a small number of seated postures" can be found in "early Tantric works," *Yoga Body*, 27. Indeed, in contradiction to the claim that there is no connection between traditional *haṭha yoga* and modern yoga, Singleton also admits that the *Haṭhapradīpikā* "outlines fifteen āsanas," some with "curative properties," and that the *Gheraṇḍa Saṃhitā* describes thirty-two *āsanas*, ibid., 29. Singleton also acknowledges murals and other illustrations in India predating the "postural yoga revivals of the twentieth century," ibid., 32–33. Dominik Wujastyk, "The Earliest Accounts of *Āsana* in the Yoga Literature," unpublished presentation, slides 19–29, accessed April 5, 2015, https://www.academia.edu/11798611/The_Earliest_Accounts_of_%C4%80sana_in_the_Yoga_Literature, notes that the *āsanas* named by Vyāsa in his commentary were also commented upon and described by Śaṅkara in the *Vivaraṇa*, his commentary on the *Yoga Sūtra*. Bryant provides a detailed synthesis of the *āsanas* mentioned by Vyāsa and commented upon by other classical commentators, Bryant, *The Yoga Sūtras of Patañjali*, 285–87. James Mallinson notes that "most of the varieties of yoga practiced around the world today derive from *haṭha yoga*," "The Original *Goraṣaśataka*," in White, *Yoga in Practice*, 257. Mallinson also notes that the first texts to teach the practices of *haṭha yoga* "appeared soon after the beginning of the second millennium," ibid, and that "the more complex *āsanas*" associated with *hatḥa yoga*, beginning with the *Haṭhapradīpikā* in the fifteenth century, were first described in the *Vasiṣṭhasaṃhitā*, a thirteenth-century text that accommodated "Tantric Kuṇḍalinī yoga within an orthodox Vedic soteriology," ibid, 258. Olle Qvarnström and Jason Birch note that the even earlier *Vivekamārtaṇḍa* (eleventh to twelfth century) points "to the possibility of innumerable *āsanas*," "Jain Yoga of the Terāpanthī Tradition," in White, *Yoga in Practice*, 368. The question of the number of pre-twentieth-century *āsanas* needs more research in their view, since a significant amount of manuscript material remains unexamined in Indian libraries about *āsana*.

74 Sjoman, *The Yoga Tradition of the Mysore Palace*, 39, 40. Georg Feuerstein notes that this mid-fourteenth-century text describes sixteen *āsanas*, *The Deeper Dimension of Yoga: Theory and Practice* (Boston and London: Shambhala, 2003), 232. Burley gives the number as fifteen, *Haṭha-Yoga*, 198.

75 Jacobsen, "Contemporary Yoga Movements," in Larson and Bhattacharya, *Encyclopedia of Indian Philosophies*, Vol. 12, 149.

76 Miller, *Yoga*, 56.

77 Ibid., 57. Burley also notes this as an aspect of *āsana*, *Haṭha-Yoga*, 198.

78 Sjoman, *The Yoga Tradition of the Mysore Palace*, 45.

79 Ibid., 46.

80 Ibid., 61.

81 Ibid., 39. Feuerstein notes that *Gorakṣa-Paddhati* (1.9) holds that of the 8,400,000 varieties of *āsana* taught by Śiva, only eighty-four are useful, *The Deeper Dimension*

of Yoga, 232. Feuerstein, ibid., also notes that the seventeenth-century *Gheraṇḍa-Saṃhitā* describes thirty-two *āsanas*.

82 *Yoga-Bhāṣya*, 2.46. See Burley, *Haṭha-Yoga*, 62; Feuerstein, *The Deeper Dimension of Yoga*, 231–32.

83 Thomas McEvilley, "An Archaeology of Yoga," *Anthropology and Aesthetics* 1, no. 1 (Spring, 1981): 44–49, accessed: April 27, 2016, http://www.jstor.org/stable/20166655.

84 Bryant, *The Yoga Sūtras of Patañjali*, xxvii.

85 Miller, *Yoga*, 8. On the basis of seals found in Mohenjo-daro, Stanley Wolpert speaks of Śiva as a "yogic fertility deity." *A New History of India*, 6th ed. (New York: Oxford University Press, 2000), 18.

86 Ramdas Lamb, "Rāja Yoga, Asceticism, and the Rāmānanda Saṃpradāy," in *Theory and Practice of Yoga: Essays in Honor of Gerald James Larson*, ed. Knut A. Jacobsen (Leiden: Brill, 2005), 317.

87 David Frawley, "Foreword," in Burley, *Haṭha-Yoga*, x.

88 Chapple, *Yoga and the Luminous*, 2.

89 Jean Varenne, *Yoga and the Hindu Tradition*, trans. Derek Coltman (Chicago and London: University of Chicago Press, 1976; originally published as *Le yoga et la tradition hindoue*, Paris: Cultures, Arts, Loisirs, 1973), 1.

90 As noted in 1964 by Herbert P. Sullivan, "A Re-Examination of the Religion of the Indus Civilization," *History of Religions* 4, no. 1 (Summer 1964): 115.

91 David R. Kinsley seems inclined to see the seals as representing bulls, *Hinduism: A Cultural Perspective*, 2nd ed. (Upper Saddle River, NJ, USA: Prentice-Hall, 1993), 11. This view was suggested by Sullivan, who speculated that what Sir John Marshall thought was the three heads of Śiva, or proto-Śiva, could also be "the head of a Brahmani bull" or "the short-horned bull," "A Re-Examination of the Religion of the Indus Civilization," 120.

92 This is the stance of Singleton in his review of the current status of the academic discussion of this matter, *Yoga Body*, 25.

93 White, *Sinister Yogis*, 82.

94 Ibid., 81.

95 Andrea R. Jain, "Who Is to Say Modern Yoga Practitioners Have It All Wrong? On Hindu Origins and Yogaphobia," *Journal of the American Academy of Religion* 82, no. 2 (June 2014): 428, 429–30, 431, 441, 443, 448–49, 456, 458. See also, Andrea R. Jain, *Selling Yoga: From Counterculture to Pop Culture* (New York: Oxford University Press, 2015), 131.

96 De Michelis, *A History of Modern Yoga*, 9, 42, 53, 55.

97 With respect to De Michelis's broad use of the expression *New Age* throughout *A History of Modern Yoga*, it should be pointed out that in the historical context of Swami Vivekananda, the expression *New Thought* was current, while *New Age*, as in New Age spirituality, which draws upon New Thought spirituality, only emerged decades later in the late 1960s. See Catherine L. Albanese, *America: Religions and Religion*, 5th ed. (Boston: Cengage, 2012), 195–99, 238–40, 269–70.

98 De Michelis, *A History of Modern Yoga*, 110–26.

99 Ibid.

100 See Ibid., 11–13, 35–40, 91–92, 110–26, 173–74.

101 De Michelis, *A History of Modern Yoga*, 110–14, 150–55, 174, 179.

102 Jeffery D. Long points out that it "seems to have become *de rigueur* in scholarly writing on Swami Vivekananda over the course of the last few years (beginning with the work of Paul Hacker) to question the integrity, motives, and character of this pivotal figure

in the history of both Modern Yoga and Modern Hinduism," "The Transformation of Yoga and Hinduism: Negotiating Authenticity, Innovation, and Identity in a Global Context," *Religious Studies Review* 40, no. 3 (September 2014): 131.

103 De Michelis, *A History of Modern Yoga*, 37.

104 See Kenneth Rose, *Pluralism: The Future of Religion* (New York: Bloomsbury, 2013), 73–87. William H. Harrison, *In Praise of Mixed Religion: The Syncretism Solution in a Multifaith World* (Montreal and Kingston: McGill-Queen's University Press, 2014), 17–19; Perry Schmidt-Leukel, *Transformation by Integration: How Inter-Faith Encounter Changes Christianity* (London: SCM Press, 2009), 67–88; Jain, "Who Is to Say Modern Yoga Practitioners Have It All Wrong," 455, 459.

105 Singleton, *Yoga Body*, 6.

106 Mark Singleton and Jean Byrne, "Introduction," in Singleton and Byrne, *Yoga in the Modern World: Contemporary Perspectives*, 6.

107 Singleton, *Yoga Body*, 15; see also 17.

108 Singleton and Byrne, "Introduction," in Singleton and Byrne, *Yoga in the Modern World: Contemporary Perspectives*, 4–5; 2: Ellen Goldberg and Mark Singleton, "Introduction," in Singleton and Goldberg, *Gurus of Modern Yoga*, 2; Mark Singleton, "Globalized Modern Yoga," in *Yoga: The Art of Transformation*, ed. Debra Diamond (Washington, DC: The Freer Gallery of Art and the Arthur M. Sackler Gallery, 2013), 95.

109 For example, De Michelis writes that "the misidentification between Vivekananda's *rājayoga* and *The Yoga Sūtras of Patañjali* . . . betrays a cognitive confusion which causes a typically esoteric variety of yoga (further occultized by Vivekananda and his followers) to be understood not only in terms of mainstream yoga, but as the most important and universally applicable form of yoga," *A History of Modern Yoga*, 179; see also 110–14. But Dermot Killingley notes that Swami Vivekananda "repudiated" Blavatsky's "esotericism," particularly with respect to the restriction of the role of the adept to Blavatsky and her Tibetan Mahatmas, "Manufacturing Yogis," in Singleton and Goldberg, *Gurus of Modern Yoga*," 25.

110 Vivekānanda, *Rāja Yoga*, 12.

111 Ibid., 44, 47.

112 Ibid., 47.

113 For example, *Praśna Upaniṣad* 3.3. See also *Maitri Upaniṣad*. Burley points out that the *Maitri Upaniṣad* among the major Upaniṣads is "the one that contains the most explicit description of a methodology akin to that presented in the later haṭha manuals." He also points out that it "emphasizes *prāṇāyāma* as the foremost means of bringing the mind to a point of stillness" (MU 6.19), Burley, *Haṭha-Yoga*, 37.

114 Vivekānanda, *Rāja Yoga*, 100–01, 104 (1.2).

115 Vivekānanda, *Rāja Yoga*, 1–7, 9–10, 34–37, 81, 102–03 (1.1), 132–33 (1.34). See Sam Harris, *Waking Up: A Guide to Spirituality Without Religion* (New York: Simon & Schuster, 2014), 29–49. Carol A. Horton claims that, "considered in light of contemporary neuroscience, some of Vivekananda's claims regarding the veracity of 'yogic science' hold up remarkably well today," *Yoga Ph.D.: Integrating the Life of the Mind and the Wisdom of the Body* (Chicago: Kleio Books, 2012), Kindle edition, Chapter 3, "In Praise of Modern Yoga," and she cites a passage from *Rāja Yoga* where Swamiji clearly anticipates the recent, revolutionary discovery of the brain's neuroplasticity, ibid.

116 Alter, *Yoga in Modern India*, 6. Even White agrees that Vivekananda's commentary, if only formally, followed the traditional method, *The Yoga Sutra of Patanjali*, 125.

117 A stance that challenges the sweeping, overly suspicious, extended ad hominem critique leveled at Swami Vivekananda's *Rāja-Yoga* by De Michelis, 179.

118 Vivekānanda, *Rāja Yoga*, 124, 125 (1.27). Killingley, "Manufacturing Yogis," in Singleton and Goldberg, *Gurus of Modern Yoga*, 30.
119 Vivekānanda, *Rāja Yoga*, 121 (1.24)
120 Ibid., 131, 132 (1.34).
121 Ibid., (YS 1.34).
122 White, *Sinister Yogis*, 45–46. White seems to be dependent here upon the historical judgment of De Michelis, who states that it was Blavatsky who first made a distinction between "'an inferior' *haṭhayoga* and 'superior' *rājayoga*," *A History Of Modern Yoga*, 178. De Michelis doesn't seem to claim here that Swami Vivekananda took this distinction or the expression "classical yoga" from Blavatsky, as White implies. And, even on the evidence that White provides in this context, the subordination of *haṭhayoga* to *rājayoga* occurs as early as in the *Haṭhapradīpikā*, White, *Sinister Yogis*, 47.
123 Vivekānanda, *Rāja Yoga*, 13–14, 30–32, 115 (1.17), 130–32 (1.34), 140 (1.45), 149 (2.6), 164–66 (2.19).
124 De Michelis, *A History of Modern Yoga*, 174, 157.
125 Ibid., 30–62.
126 Ibid., 48, 52, 60, 2 (1.34).
127 Ibid., 48, 51, 53–55, 58–59, 185 (2.49).
128 Sir John George Woodroffe (a.k.a. Arthur Avalon), *The Serpent Power: Being the Sat-Cakra-Nirupana and Paduka-Pañcaka* (London: Luzac, 1919).
129 Vivekānanda, *Rāja Yoga*, 43.
130 Killingley, "Manufacturing Yogis," in Singleton and Goldberg, *Gurus of Modern Yoga*, 33.
131 Swāmi Vivekānanda, "Paper on Hinduism," in *Complete Works of Swami Vivekananda*, accessed September 24, 2014, http://www.ramakrishnavivekananda.info/vivekananda/volume_1/addresses_at_the_parliament/v1_c1_paper_on_hinduism.htm.
132 Horton refers to Swami Vivekananda's "spectacular success in the U.S." and gives a sampling of the widespread positive and even rapturous response of the mainstream media of that day to the Swami's discourses and public appearances at the Parliament and afterwards in his travels across the United States, *Yoga Ph.D.*, Kindle edition, Chapter 3, "In Praise of Modern Yoga."
133 Vivekānanda, *Rāja Yoga*, 10.
134 Singleton, *Yoga Body*, 4, 44, where, as often in his account, Singleton acknowledges, against his thesis, that "elements [of *haṭha* yoga] are not entirely absent" from Swami Vivekananda's teaching, *Yoga Body*, 45, 49, 70–75, 78, 80.
135 Vivekānanda, *Rāja Yoga*, 28–29.
136 Ibid., 19; Singleton *Yoga Body*, 71.
137 Killingley, "Manufacturing Yogis," in Singleton and Goldberg, *Gurus of Modern Yoga*, 29. See also Singleton, *Yoga Body*, 72–74.
138 Long, "The Transformation of Yoga and Hinduism," 127.
139 Singleton, *Yoga Body*, 115–16.
140 Ibid., 116–22.
141 Ibid., 174–210.
142 Harrison, *In Praise of Mixed Religion*, 17–19; Schmidt-Leukel, *Transformation by Integration*, 67–88; Jain, "Who Is to Say Modern Yoga Practitioners Have It All Wrong," 455, 459.
143 Singleton, *Yoga Body*, 36–44.

144 White, *The Yoga Sutra of Patanjali*, 64, 73–74, 92–102.
145 As described by Singleton, *Yoga Body*, 55–70.
146 Singleton, *Yoga Body*, 33.
147 Chapple, *Yoga and the Luminous*, 249–59. A view shared by Jain, "Who Is to Say Modern Yoga Practitioners Have It All Wrong," 455, 459.
148 Chapple, *Yoga and the Luminous*, 249.
149 Singleton, *Yoga Body*, 33.
150 Varenne, *Yoga and the Hindu Tradition*, 82–83.
151 Ibid.
152 Ibid.
153 Ibid., 83.
154 Miller, *Yoga*, 1.
155 Stephen Phillips, *Yoga, Karma, and Rebirth: A Brief History and Philosophy* (New York: Columbia University Press, 2009), vi–vii, 2, 5–6, 41.
156 Phillips, Yoga, Karma, and Rebirth, 6.
157 Horton, *Yoga Ph.D.*, Kindle edition, Chapter 1, "The Professor and the Yogini."
158 Yoga-Sūtra 2.30. See Chapple, *Yoga and the Luminous*, 105.
159 Bryant, *The Yoga Sūtras of Patañjali*, 140.
160 Ibid.
161 See, for example, Horton's positive view of Swami Vivekananda as an Indian reformer who creatively brought together important aspects of Indian and Western cultures of his day, *Yoga Ph.D.*, Kindle edition, Chapter 7, "Yoga, Modernity, and the Body."
162 Bryant, *The Yoga Sūtras of Patañjali*, 140.
163 White, *The Yoga Sutra of Patanjali*, 146.
164 Ian Whicher, *The Integrity of the Yoga Darśana: A Reconsideration of Classical Yoga* (Albany: State University of New York Press, 1998), 38–39, 42.
165 White, *The Yoga Sutra of Patanjali*, 17, 44, 148–71; *Sinister Yogis*, 202.
166 As noted by Bryant, *The Yoga Sūtras of Patañjali*, 87. That theistic meditation in the *Yoga Sūtra* is optional is indicated by the use of the particle *vā* in YS 1.23 (*īśvara praṇidhānādvā*). Nalini Kanta Brahma notes that the idea of God—better to write *īśvara*, I think—is "very unimportant" in *pātañjala-yoga* and is but "one of many methods of attaining concentration," Philosophy of Hindu Sādhanā (Delhi: Book Faith India, 1999; repr. London: Kegan Paul, Trench, Trubner, 1932 ed.), 126.
167 Whicher, *The Integrity of the Yoga Darśana*, 308.
168 As noted elsewhere in the pages, *dhyāna* is generally translated as "meditation," which can be confusing or vague, given the history of this word as referring to deep reflection in Western traditions and its use in the last century in Western contexts as a general term to refer to the whole range of the two distinctive sets of concentrative and insight practices in Hinduism, Buddhism, and other contemplative traditions. Although I will retain "meditation" because it has become the standard translation of *dhyāna*, I will also supplement it with other translations such as "concentrative stability," "focused meditation," and "locked-in meditation" (the latter expression has been influenced by Richard Davidson's research on attention and focus as involving a state of "phase-locking," which Daniel Goleman explains as activating "key circuitry in the prefrontal cortex [that] gets into a synchronized state with the object of that beam of awareness," *Focus: The Hidden Driver of Excellence*, 15).
169 Jeanine Miller, *The Vedas: Harmony, Meditation and Fulfilment* (London: Rider, 1974), 45; quoted in Burley, *Haṭha-Yoga*, 24.

170 "Everything is indeed hardship for those who sift *puruṣa* from *prakṛti*" (*duḥkham eva sarvaṃ vivekinaḥ*, YS 2.15). This obvious reference to Buddhism's first noble truth does not merely show the influence of Buddhism on Patañjali, it also shows a qualification of this universal claim when it limits this insight to the wise, to those, that is, who are able to extract *prakṛti* from *puruṣa*. As a teacher, it has long been my experience that many people do not intuitively and immediately agree that their lives are characterized by *duḥkha*. This Pātañjalian modification answers to this apparent disconfirmation of the Buddha's claim.

171 Chapple suggests that there are more than twenty training methods in the *Yoga Sūtra*, of which ten are to be found in the first *pāda*, *Yoga and the Luminous*, 103–04.

172 Chapple notes that the cultivation of *abhyāsa* and *vairāgya* is the first of more than twenty training methods in the *Yoga Sūtra*, *Yoga and the Luminous*,103.

173 An enumeration that agrees with Chapple's count, *Yoga and the Luminous*, 104.

174 Georg Feuerstein, *The Philosophy of Classical Yoga* (Rochester, VT: Inner Traditions, 1996), 28.

175 Whicher, *The Integrity of the Yoga Darśana*, 145, passim.

176 Although Chapple, *Yoga and the Luminous*, 104–08, sees "subtilization" (*pratiprasava*) as the central concern of the *Yoga Sūtra*, I have derived my primary understanding of the process of subtilization through which the manifest is reduced to the unmanifest from the teaching of the Upaniṣadic figure Raikva, which is known as the *saṃvarga vidyā* and is recounted in *Chāndogya Upaniṣad* 4.1-3.

177 It is also so characterized by Swami Vivekānanda, *Rāja-Yoga*, 168. See also Miller, *Yoga*, 45. In support of this view, Patañjali seems to imply that *īśvara-praṇidhāna* leads only to *samprajñāta-samādhi*. See Bryant's translation of YS 1.23, where "this previously mentioned state" seems to refer to this degree of *samādhi*, *The Yoga Sūtras of Patañjali*, 81.

178 The interpretation of the commentator Vyāsa, Āraṇya, *Yoga Philosophy of Patañjali*,114.

179 As recommended by the commentator Vijñāna Bhikṣu and others, according to Bryant, *The Yoga Sūtras of Patañjali*, 170–71.

180 *Monier-Williams Online Dictionary*, 1899, s.v. "*vivic*," accessed October 27, 2015, http://www.sanskrit-lexicon.uni-koeln.de/scans/MWScan/2014/web/webtc/indexcaller.php/; *Wilson Sanskrit-English Dictionary*, s.v. "*viveka*," accessed March 17, 2015, http://www.sanskrit-lexicon.uni-koeln.de/scans/WILScan/2014/web/webtc2/index.php; William Dwight Whitney, *The Roots, Verb-Forms, and Primary Derivatives of the Sanskrit Language* (Delhi: Motilal Banarsidass, 1994; original ed. 1885), s.v. "vic."

181 Vyāsa refers to the *aṣṭāṅgāni* as *sādhanas*, *Yoga-Bhāṣya*, 3.1, Āraṇya, *Yoga Philosophy of Patañjali*, 248.

182 An integrative view of the end state of yoga as articulated by I. K. Taimni in his commentary on YS 2.19, *The Science of Yoga*, 4th ed. (Wheaton, IL, Madras, and London: The Theosophical Publishing House, 1975), 185; see also Whicher, The Integrity of the Yoga Darśana, 307–08.

183 The five *yamas* taken together are called *mahāvrata*, or "the Great Vow," in YS 2.31 (and it is also translated this way by Āraṇya and also I. K. Taimni). These are identical with the Five Great Vows in Jainism. *Yama*, according to Monier-Williams, is "any great moral rule or duty" (as opp. to *niyama*, "a minor observance"). *Monier-Williams Online Dictionary*, 1899, s.v. *yama*, accessed October 27, 2015, http://www.sanskrit-lexicon.uni-koeln.de/sc ans/MWScan/2014/web/webtc/indexcaller.php.

Thus, according to Monier-Williams, a *niyama* is a "penance" that is a "lesser vow or minor observance dependent on external conditions and not so obligatory as *yama*," *Monier-Williams Online Dictionary*, 1899, s.v. "niyama," accessed October 27, 2015, http://www.sanskrit-lexicon.uni-koeln.de/scans/MWScan/2014/web/webtc/indexcaller.php.

184 See Bryant, *The Yoga Sūtras of Patañjali*, 252.

185 *Monier-Williams Online Dictionary*, 1899, s.v. "*śauca*," accessed October 27, 2015, http://www.sanskrit-lexicon.uni-koeln.de/scans/MWScan/2014/web/webtc/indexcaller.php.

186 Bryant, *The Yoga Sūtras of Patañjali*, 295.

187 A point suggested with respect to meditation by Bryant, *The Yoga Sūtras of Patañjali*, 284, who follows Śaṅkara and Vijñāna Bhikṣu on this matter.

188 Chapple, *Yoga and the Luminous*, 76.

189 A classic illustration suggested by the commentator Vyāsa, Āraṇya, *Yoga Philosophy of Patañjali*, 245.

190 Bryant, *The Yoga Sūtras of Patañjali*, 301.

191 Ibid.

192 Ibid.

193 This term seems to appear in the *Yoga Sūtra* only in the name of the third *pāda*, that is, *vibhūti-pāda*.

194 A term also used in this context by Miller, *Yoga*, 75.

195 For these terms as translations of *antinomian*, see Georg Feuerstein, *Tantra: The Path of Ecstasy* (Boston: Shambhala, 1998), 8.

196 See the exquisite depiction by Swami Vivekananda of mothering *prakṛti*, whose gentle ministrations are no longer needed by *puruṣa* at this point, *Rāja-Yoga*, 267, also quoted in Swami Prabhavananda and Christopher Isherwood, *How to Know God: The Yoga Aphorisms of Patanjali*, pbk. ed. (Hollywood, CA: Vedanta Press, 1983; orig. pub., 1953), 221–22.

197 See Feuerstein, *The Philosophy of Classical Yoga*, 52–53, where he links *citi-śakti* (YS 4.34) to *dṛśeḥ kaivalya* (2.25) and *dṛśi-mātra* (2.20).

198 See *Monier-Williams Online Sanskrit-English Dictionary*, 1899, s.v. "*saṃyama*," accessed October 27, 2015, http://www.sanskrit-lexicon.uni-koeln.de/scans/MWScan/2014/web/webtc/indexcaller.php.

199 Vyāsa, *Yoga-Bhāṣya*, 3.1, Āraṇya, *Yoga Philosophy of Patañjali*, 249.

200 Vyāsa, *Yoga-Bhāṣya*, 1.1, Āraṇya, *Yoga Philosophy of Patañjali*, 1.

201 Āraṇya, *Yoga Philosophy of Patañjali*, 251.

202 Current scholarly consensus seems to hold that the *Yoga Sūtra* of Patañjali and the *Yoga-Bhāṣya* of Vyāsa are a unified composition datable to the beginning of the fifth century, Wujastyk, "The Earliest Accounts of *Āsana* in the Yoga Literature," slide 3. See Larson, "Pātañjala Yoga in Practice," in White, *Yoga in Practice*, 74, who allows that this might possible.

203 Larson, "Pātañjala Yoga in Practice," in White, *Yoga in Practice*, 73; Vyāsa, *Yoga-Bhāṣya*, 1.1, Āraṇya, *Yoga Philosophy of Patañjali*, 6–7.

204 *Samāpatti* is an important term in Theravāda Buddhism, where the *Visuddhimagga* postulates a ninefold scheme of *jhānas*, culminating in *nirodha-samāpatti* (Vsm 11.124, 23.18, 23.26 Ñ), as discussed by Mircea Eliade, *Yoga, Immortality, and Freedom*, trans. and ed. Willard R. Trask (Princeton, NJ: Princeton University Press, 2009; English translation originally published 1958; a translation of *Le Yoga: Liberté et immortalité*, Paris: Librairie Payot, 1954), 169–77. See also *The Pāli Text Society's*

Pāli-English Dictionary, s.v. "*samāpatti*," accessed April 7, 2015, http://dsalsrv02.uchicago.edu/cgi-bin/philologic/getobject.pl?c.3:1:3411.pali.1829823; Miller, *Yoga*, 112n8. These considerations suggest to me that the deployment of *samāpatti* in the *Visuddhimagga* is far more consistent than its deployment in the *Yoga Sūtra*. See also Stuart Ray Sarbacker, *Samādhi: The Numinous and the Cessative in Indo-Tibetan Yoga* (Albany: State University Press of New York Press, 2005), 86.

205 Whicher, *The Integrity of the Yoga Darśana*, 375n242.

206 Larson, "Pātañjala Yoga in Practice," in White, *Yoga in Practice*, 84; Āraṇya offers a similar, if not quite identical, distinction, *Yoga Philosophy of Patañjali*, 89.

207 Feuerstein, *The Philosophy of Classical Yoga*, 88.

208 A gap that leads Sarbacker to question the status of the *Yoga Sūtra* as a "unitary text," *Samādhi*, 91–92.

209 This also seems to be the solution offered by Vyāsa, *Yoga-Bhāṣya*, 1.46, Āraṇya, *Yoga Philosophy of Patañjali*, 103.

210 Bryant, *The Yoga Sūtras of Patañjali*, 68, 153–54, 157.

211 Larson, "Pātañjala Yoga in Practice," in White, *Yoga in Practice*, 84; Bryant, The *Yoga Sūtras of Patañjali*, 84–86.

212 Feuerstein, *The Philosophy of Classical Yoga*, 90.

213 Larson, "Pātañjala Yoga in Practice," in White, *Yoga in Practice*, 84; Bryant, *The Yoga Sūtras of Patañjali*, 62. Bryant, following the taxonomy of Vācaspati Miśra, allows that there might be nine (or ten, if he includes *dharmamegha-samādhi*) degrees of *samādhi*, ibid., 156. Taimni offers an elaborate illustration of the taxonomy of Vācaspati Miśra, albeit without naming the classical commentator, *The Science of Yoga*, 179–85. Gaspar M. Koelman assumes the model of eight *samāpattis* proposed by Vācaspati Miśra in the *Tattvavaiśāradi* comment on YS 1.46, although he notes that this schema is not accepted by all commentators, *Pātañjala Yoga: From Related Ego to Absolute Self* (Poona: Papal Athenaeum, 1970), 198, 212, 223–24.

214 Wujastyk, "The Earliest Accounts of *Āsana* in the Yoga Literature," slide 29.

215 Neither of the last two *samprajñāta-samādhis* listed in YS.1.17 has a *samāpatti* as a counterpart in the *Yoga Sūtra*, although Bryant implies that they are included in the subtle levels of *prakṛti* that the yogi accesses beyond the level of *nirvicāra-samāpatti*, *The Yoga Sūtras of Patañjali*, 154–55. See also Feuerstein, *The Philosophy of Classical Yoga*, 90–92.

216 Bryant, *The Yoga Sūtras of Patañjali*, 153; Whicher, *The Integrity of the Yoga Darśana*, 255; Feuerstein, *The Philosophy of Classical Yoga*, 89; Feuerstein, *Yoga*, 197.

217 As indexed in John Grimes, *A Concise Dictionary of Indian Philosophy: Sanskrit Terms Defined in English*, new and rev. ed. (Albany: State University of New York Press, 1996), s.v. "*nirvikalpa-pratyakṣa*," 209–10; see also Bryant, *The Yoga Sūtras of Patañjali*, 148.

218 Larson, "Pātañjala Yoga in Practice," in White, *Yoga in Practice*, 85; Brahma, *Philosophy of Hindu Sādhanā*, 132–32.

219 Concisely discussed by Sarbacker, *Samādhi*, 91–92.

220 See Bryant, *The Yoga Sūtras of Patañjali*, 157, 166–68, Whicher, *The Integrity of the Yoga Darśana*, 201, Āraṇya, *Yoga Philosophy of Patañjali*, 103, and Brahma, *Philosophy of Hindu Sādhanā*, 132. Taimni disagrees that they are synonyms. In his taxonomy, he alternates various stages of *saṃprajñāta-samādhi* with *asaṃprajñāta-samādhi* as instances of *sabīja-samādhi*, which are mediated forms of *samādhi* preceding the unmediated *samādhi* just prior to *dharmamegha-samādhi*, which he

names *nirbīja-samādhi*, *The Science of Yoga*, 32–41. See also Mircea Eliade, *Yoga, Immortality, and Freedom*, 83.

221 Since, as Whicher notes, *The Integrity of the Yoga Darśana*, 201, there can be no misidentification of any manifestation of *prakṛti* in *nirbīja-samādhi*, which he equates with *asaṃprajñāta-samadhi.*

222 In the view of Vijñāna Bhikṣu, according to Feuerstein, *The Philosophy of Classical Yoga*, 91.

223 This common approach is seen widely in secondary literature, See, for example, Flood, *An Introduction to Hinduism*, 96, and it is found in Vyāsa's commentary, *Yoga-Bhāṣya*, 1.43, in Āraṇya, *Yoga Philosophy of Patañjali*, 93–94; see also Bryant, *The Yoga Sūtras of Patañjali*, 157. I agree with Bryant's enumeration of the *samādhis*, except for my taking *dharmamegha-samādhi* as a distinctive stage of *asaṃprajñāta-samādhi.*

224 Feuerstein, *The Philosophy of Classical Yoga*, 92.

225 Whicher, *The Integrity of the Yoga Darśana*, 209; see also, Sarbacker, *Samādhi*, 92.

226 Feuerstein cogently analyzes and offers a chart of Vācaspati Miśra's eight *samāpattis*, *The Philosophy of Classical Yoga*, 90–91.

227 Bryant, *The Yoga Sūtras of Patañjali*, 452, YS 4.29-30.

228 Research on the relationship between the Buddhist series and the Pātañjalian series is summarized and evaluated by Sarbacker, *Samādhi*, 93.

229 Bryant, *The Yoga Sūtras of Patañjali*, 158.

230 Ibid., 62–63.

231 *Prasava*, *sava*, and √ *su* or *sū* call to mind the "pressing out" of the juice of the Soma plant, which was central to the spirituality of the *Ṛg-Veda*, see *Monier-Williams Online Dictionary*, 1899, s.v. "*prasava*," accessed October 27, 2015, http://www.sanskrit-lexicon.uni-koeln.de/scans/MWScan/2014/web/webtc/indexcaller.php, "*sava*," accessed October 27, 2015, http://www.sanskrit-lexicon.uni-koeln.de/scans/MWScan/2014/web/webtc/indexcaller.php, and "*su*," accessed October 27, 2015, http://www.sanskrit-lexicon.uni-koeln.de/scans/MWScan/2014/web/webtc/indexcaller.php.

232 I diverge here from the various translations for the cognate Pāli words, *vitakka* and *vicāra*, that I used in the last chapter when discussing Theravāda Buddhism, which is due to the shifting of the meaning of these terms in the Sāṅkhya-inflected *Yoga Sūtra*. For a detailed discussion of the shifts in meaning of these terms among different Buddhist schools and the yoga *darśana*, see Sarbacker, *Samādhi*, 75–109, particularly, 91–92.

233 Swami Satchidananda, *The Yoga Sutras of Patanjali* (Yogaville, VA: Integral Yoga Publications, 1990), 36.

234 See Whicher, *The Integrity of the Yoga Darśana*, 221, 249.

235 Vyāsa, *Yoga-Bhāṣya*, 2.19, Āraṇya, *Yoga Philosophy of Patañjali*, 169. In commenting on YS 2.19, Taimni neatly charts this and the subsequent three correlations between the phases of the *guṇas* and the factors of *saṃprajñāta-samādhi*, *The Science of Yoga*, 174–85. Feuerstein rejects Taimni's correlations and suggests his own. Similarly, Whicher provides his own version of correlations, which are also divergent from Taimni's crisp summation, 207–08, 218–22–23, 229–30, 241, although Whicher notes that the commentators are divided on this matter of interpretation, ibid., 241. I have followed the latter two contemporary commentators for the most part, though, since these attempts at correlation are traceable to the early commentaries, not to Patañjali, I have felt free to articulate my own understanding of the stages of *liṅga*

and *aliṅga*, which is influenced by Taimni's approach. See Mikel Burley, *Classical Sāṃkhya and Yoga: An Indian Metaphysics of Experience* (London and New York: Routledge, 2007), 53–54.

236 As listed in Gerald J. Larson, *Classical Sāṃkhya*, 2nd ed. (Delhi: Motilal Banarsidass, 1979), 236.

237 Vyāsa, *Yoga-Bhāṣya*, 2.19 in Āraṇya, *Yoga Philosophy of Patañjali*, 169; Whicher, *The Integrity of the Yoga Darśana*, 207.

238 Also known as *sāmānya* in contrast to *viśeṣa* in the Nyāya and Vaiśeṣika schools of philosophy, Bryant, *The Yoga Sūtras of Patañjali*, 159–60.

239 See Surendranath Dasgupta, *A History of Indian Philosophy*, Vol. 1 (Delhi: Motilal, Banarsidass, 1988; repr. 1975 ed.; orig. pub., London: Cambridge University Press, 1922), 251.

240 Vyāsa, *Yoga-Bhāṣya*, 2.19, Āraṇya, *Yoga Philosophy of Patañjali*, 170; Feuerstein, *The Philosophy of Classical Yoga*, 45.

241 Āraṇya, *Yoga Philosophy of Patañjali*, 171; *The Yoga Sūtras of Patañjali*, 218.

242 Bryant, *The Yoga Sūtras of Patañjali*, 218; Sarvepalli Radhakrishnan, *Indian Philosophy*, Vol. 2, 2nd ed. (Delhi: Blackie & Son, 1985; repr., orig., pub. Oxford: Oxford University Press, 1923), 267.

243 Larson, Classical Sāṃkhya, 190.

244 Larson, "Pātañjala Yoga in Practice," in White, *Yoga in Practice*, 87.

245 Bryant, *The Yoga Sūtras of Patañjali*, lvi.

246 Larson, "Pātañjala Yoga in Practice," in White, *Yoga in Practice*, 86–88.

247 Bryant, *The Yoga Sūtras of Patañjali*, 62.

248 Taimni also uses the example of a rose as a meditation object, but he doesn't develop it beyond *savitarka-samādhi* in this context, *The Science of Yoga*, 106.

249 Bryant, *The Yoga Sūtras of Patañjali*, 273–78; Feuerstein, *The Philosophy of Classical Yoga*, 1–14.

250 Bryant holds that YS 1.17 "initiates the esoteric teachings of yoga," *The Yoga Sūtras of Patañjali*.

251 Feuerstein notes that the *Yoga Sūtra* (YS 1.50, 3.9-10) speaks of two kinds of *saṃskāras*, one kind which produces ordinary consciousness and another kind that initiates the overcoming of the ordinary, karma-implicated thought processes, *The Philosophy of Classical Yoga*, 68. A similar point is made by Whicher, *The Integrity of the Yoga Darśana*, 259.

252 Taimni sees these as emanating from *puruṣa*, *The Science of Yoga*, 111–12.

253 Thus Feuerstein sees *vitarka* and *vicāra* as instances not of ordinary discursive reasoning, which can be included in the three kinds *pramāṇa-vṛttis*: *pratyakṣa*, *anumāna*, and *āgama* (YS 1.6, 7), but rather as expression of *prajña*, or "wisdom." Bryant accordingly refers to the activity of *vitarka* and *vicāra* in *saṃprajñāta-samādhi* as "wisdom *saṃskāras*," Bryant, *The Yoga Sūtras of Patañjali*, 162.

254 As implied by the word *saṅkīrṇa* in YS 1.42. This lowest degree of *samādhi* is neither fully one-pointed (*ekāgratā*) nor devoid of various mental contents, as noted by Vyāsa in his commentary on YS 1.42 and as noted and explained by Whicher, *The Integrity of the Yoga Darśana*, 224–25.

255 Although this discussion of the development in *saṃprajñāta-samādhi* of the meditation object of the chosen deity is grounded in the author's own theological and contemplative practice over the decades, it parallels in striking ways the similar account offered by Bryant, *The Yoga Sūtras of Patañjali*, 152–53. These similarities point clearly to a natural apophatic mystical process that strips and purifies theistic

conceptions of external, contingent elements in the movement of contemplation to the heights of mystical union, a topic that we will take up in greater detail in the next chapter.

256 Taimni, The Science of Yoga, 110.

257 Katz, "Language, Epistemology, and Mysticism," in Katz, *Mysticism and Philosophical Analysis*, 57. Author's italics.

258 As suggested by Bryant, *The Yoga Sūtras of Patañjali*, 148.

259 Vyāsa, *Yoga-Bhāṣya*, 1.43, in Āraṇya, *Yoga Philosophy of Patañjali*, 93.

260 Āraṇya, *Yoga Philosophy of Patañjali*, 100.

261 Vyāsa, *Yoga-Bhāṣya*, 1.43, in Āraṇya, *Yoga Philosophy of Patañjali*, 94–95. This is discussed as well by Bryant, *The Yoga Sūtras of Patañjali*, 146, 147, and by Whicher, *The Integrity of the Yoga Darśana*, 226–29.

262 Whicher, *The Integrity of the Yoga Darśana*, 228.

263 Bryant, *The Yoga Sūtras of Patañjali*, 150–51; Radhakrishnan, *Indian Philosophy*, v. 2, 271; Feuerstein, *The Philosophy or Classical Yoga*, 45.

264 Feuerstein raises the issue of whether Patañjali made us of the notion of *tanmātras, The Philosophy of Classical Yoga*, 46. I use Larson's terminology here for the *tanmātras, Classical Sāṃkhya*, 236.

265 I use Larson's terminology here for the *mahābhūtas, Classical Sāṃkhya*, 236.

266 For a discussion of the derivation of the Latin *universalis* from the Aristotelian corpus, see Riin Sirkel, "The Problem of *Katholou* (Universals) in Aristotle" (2010). Ph.D. Dissertation, University of Western Ontario, *Electronic Thesis and Dissertation Repository*, Paper 62 (December 2010): 1n1, accessed October 12, 2015, http://ir.lib.uwo.ca/cgi/viewcontent.cgi?article=1099&context=etd.

267 Plotinus, *Ennead, Volume I: Porphyry on the Life of Plotinus. Ennead I*, trans. D. H. Armstrong (Cambridge, MA: Harvard University Press, 1969), 260 (1.6.25).

268 Larson notes that the *Sāṃkhya-Kārikā* is opaque on the question of how the *mahābhūtas* emerge from the *tanmātras*, although various theories have been proposed, *Classical Sāṃkhya*, 188. As noted by Larson, ibid., Dasgupta offers a detailed exposition of how the *tanmātras* emerge from the *mahābhūtas, A History of Indian Philosophy*, vol. 1, 251–56, none of which, as Feuerstein notes, *The Philosophy of Classical Yoga*, 44, resolves the "obscurity" surrounding the nature of the *tanmātras.*

269 Feuerstein distinguishes between the "deep" and "surface structure" of *prakṛti, The Philosophy of Classical Yoga*, 29.

270 Vyāsa, *Yoga-Bhāṣya*, 1.44, in Āraṇya, *Yoga Philosophy of Patañjali*, 98.

271 See Feuerstein's discussion of this point, *The Philosophy of Classical Yoga*, 45.

272 *Meister Eckhart: Selected Writings*, trans. Oliver Davies (New York: Penguin Books, 1994), Sermon 22 (DW 52, W87), 205. Oliver Davies, *The God Within: The Mystical Tradition of Northern Europe*, rev. ed. (Hyde Park, NY: New City Press, 2006), 45–46.

273 Paul Tillich, *The Courage to Be*, 2nd ed. (New Haven, CT: Yale University Press, 2000) 15, 187.

274 Gordon D. Kaufman, *God the Problem* (Cambridge, MA: Harvard University Press, 1972), 86.

275 Taimni, *The Science of Yoga*, 113.

276 I follow Mikel Burley and his paradigm-shifting idealist and "abolitionist" view of the Sāṃkhya and Yoga *darśanas* in seeing *prakṛti* as providing "the matter of experience" rather than seeing *prakṛti* as an external extramental, objective reality, *Classical Sāṃkhya and Yoga*, ix–xi, 1, 5–7, 10–13, 56, 69–90, 156–58, passim.

Burley stresses the psychological rather than the cosmological significance of the *tattvas*, which follows from his near Kantian turn of seeing them as transcendental categories, or conditions of experience, rather than physical and subtle realities existing external to consciousness.

277 *Chāndogya Upaniṣad*, 6.10.

278 Stace, *Mysticism and Philosophy*, 112–13.

279 Bryant, *The Yoga Sūtras of Patañjali*, 152.

280 Taimni, The Science of Yoga, 113.

281 Jan van Ruysbroeck, *The Adornment of the Spiritual Marriage*, quoted by Katz, in "Language, Epistemology, and Mysticism," in Katz, *Mysticism and Philosophical Analysis*, 61.

282 Sarbacker, *Samādhi*, 91–92.

283 Whicher, *The Integrity of the Yoga Darśana*, 238.

284 Whicher makes a similar point, *The Integrity of the Yoga Darśana*, 238.

285 Bryant, *The Yoga Sūtras of Patañjali*, 64–65.

286 Ibid., 65.

287 Āraṇya, *Yoga Philosophy of Patañjali*, 44.

288 Bryant, *The Yoga Sūtras of Patañjali*, 165.

289 I follow Whicher here in taking *liṅga-mātra*, and thus *buddhi* (*mahat*) as the stage into which the mind coalesces in *asmitā-samādhi*, *The Integrity of the Yoga Darśana*, 241. Taimni correlates *asmitā-samādhi* with *aliṅga*, *The Science of Yoga*, 122–23.

290 See Feuerstein, *The Philosophy of Classical Yoga*, 93–95.

291 See Bryant, *The Yoga Sūtras of Patañjali*, 157.

292 See Feuerstein, *The Philosophy of Classical Yoga*, 92.

293 Vyāsa, *Yoga-Bhāṣya*, 1.18, in Āraṇya, *Yoga Philosophy of Patañjali*, 45.

294 Āraṇya, *Yoga Philosophy of Patañjali*, 111.

295 Vyāsa, *Yoga-Bhāṣya*, 1.18, in Āraṇya, *Yoga Philosophy of Patañjali*, 46, see also 111.

296 Bryant uses the figure of a thorn rather than a stick in this context, *The Yoga Sūtras of Patañjali*, 162; see also Koelman, *Pātañjala Yoga*, 218–24.

297 Vyāsa, *Yoga-Bhāṣya*, 1.18, in Āraṇya, *Yoga Philosophy of Patañjali*, 45,

298 See Bryant, *The Yoga Sūtras of Patañjali*, 164.

299 Vyāsa, *Yoga-Bhāṣya*, 1.51, in Āraṇya, *Yoga Philosophy of Patañjali*, 111; see also YS 1.16.

300 Where it is the tenth *bhūmi*, or stage, in the *Bodhisattva's* itinerary, as charted in the *Daśabhūmikasūtra*, see Bryant, *The Yoga Sūtras of Patañjali*, 452, Miller, *Yoga*, 82n.22, and Klaus Klostermaier, "*Dharmamegha samādhi*: Comments on *Yogasūtra* IV, 29," *Philosophy East and West* 36, no. 3 (July 1986): 254–62, accessed April 4, 2015, http://www.jstor.org/stable/1398774. Klostermaier traces this originally Buddhist expression back to the *Milindapañha*, ibid., 258. Klostermaier traces only one use of the term in classical Hindu texts in the *Pañcadaśī*, ibid., 254.

301 I translate *dharma* here as "beatitude," which is justified by the equation of *brahmānanda*, or the "bliss of Brahman" realization with *dharma* by Swāmī Vijñānāśrama, as noted and explained by Klostermaier, "*Dharmamegha samādhi*," 254.

302 Klostermaier, "*Dharmamegha samādhi*," 260.

303 Bryant, *The Yoga Sūtras of Patañjali*, 452, YS 4.29-30.

304 Bryant makes a similar point, *The Yoga Sūtras of Patañjali*, 311.

305 Feuerstein doubts that Patañjali taught a *jīvanmukta* doctrine, which he attributes to Vedānta, Feuerstein, *Yoga*, 198.

306 Vyāsa, *Yoga-Bhāṣya*, 4.30, in Āraṇya, *Yoga Philosophy of Patañjali*, 398.
307 Vivekānanda, *Rāja-Yoga*, 221.
308 These three are the traditional triad of *ādhyātmika*, *ādhibhautika*, and *ādhidaivika*. See *Sāṃkhyakārikā* of Īśvarakṛṣṇa, 1, in Larson, *Classical Sāṃkhya*, 255; see also ibid., 155–56.
309 Newberg and d'Aquili, *The Mystical Mind*, 13–14, 95, 110–14.
310 Equal, I think, to *asamprajñāta-samādhi* in the *Yoga Sūtra* and *nirodha-samāpatti* in the *Visuddhimagga*. These states are brought about by the cultivation of a "Null Domain" method, according to Nash and Newberg, "Toward A Unifying Taxonomy and Definition for Meditation," 6–7.
311 Excluding Chapple and Whicher, as noted by Burley, *Classical Sāṃkhya and Yoga*, 138–41.
312 See the often-cited pericope in the *Sāṃkhyakārikā* of Īśvarakṛṣṇa, 49–53, in Larson, *Classical Sāṃkhya*, 274.
313 Whicher, *The Integrity of the Yoga Darśana*, 277–80, 114, 380n112 (the latter for Chapple's influence on his position). See also Burley, *Classical Sāṃkhya and Yoga*, 140.
314 A conclusion reasserted by Burley, *Classical Sāṃkhya and Yoga*, 141, and upheld also by such scholars, notes Whicher, as Eliade, Koelman, Feuerstein, and Larson, which makes for a formidable consensus, *The Integrity of the Yoga Darśana*, 380n110.
315 *Sāṃkhyakārikā* of Īśvarakṛṣṇa, 67, in Larson, *Classical Sāṃkhya*, 275. See K. P. Bahadur, *The Wisdom of Saankhya* (New Delhi: Sterling Publishers, 1978), 142–44; see also Burley, *Classical Sāṃkhya and Yoga*, 140.
316 See Feuerstein, *The Philosophy of Classical Yoga*, 53, 54, 55.
317 A stance obviously associated with Buddhism, although it was and remains a widespread conviction in Indian spiritualities, Bryant, *The Yoga Sūtras of Patañjali*, 204.
318 Bryant, *The Yoga Sūtras of Patañjali*, 393–94.
319 Ibid., 396.
320 Johannes Bronkhorst, *Buddhist Teaching In India* (Boston: Wisdom Publications, 2009), 53.

Chapter 6

1 Wendy Wright's comprehensive, irenic, and highly readable contemporary Catholic manual, *The Essential Spirituality Handbook*, stands as a successor to the old manualists as well as to numerous newer trends in Catholic spirituality, yet, as far as I can see by looking over her lists of sources cited and recommendations for further reading, none of the names of the earlier manualists is mentioned.
2 William Johnston, *Mystical Theology: The Science of Love* (Maryknoll, NY: Orbis, 1998), 2.
3 Augustin-François Poulain, *The Graces of Interior Prayer: A Treatise on Mystical Theology*, trans. Leonora L. Yorke Smith (London: Kegan Paul, Trench, Trubner & Co, 1928); fourth impression, originally published 1910; fifth impression, 1950; translation of *Des grâces d'oraison: traité de théologie mystique*, 10th ed. (Paris: Gabriel Beauchesne, 1922; 1st ed., 1901). Given that Smith's translation was published well before the public-domain cutoff year of 1923 in 1910 and given that the fourth impression of Poulain's text (1923) is an exact reproduction of earlier impressions, this impression is in the public domain, as is the French edition that I use herein, which was published in 1922.

4 J. V. Bainvel, "Introduction to the Tenth Edition," in Poulain, *The Graces of Interior Prayer*, fifth impression, lxvii.
5 Michael Murphy, a cofounder of the Esalen Institute, views Poulain's treatise on mystical theology as "perhaps the most thorough account of Catholic contemplative experience produced in the twentieth century," *The Future of the Body*, 523; See also Edward F. Kelly and Ian Whicher, who refer to Poulain as "a major commentator," "Patañjali's *Yoga Sūtras* and the *Siddhis*," in *Beyond Physicalism: Toward Reconciliation of Science and Spirituality*, ed. Edward F. Kelly, Adam Crabtree, and Paul Marshall (Lanham, MD: Rowman & Littlefield, 2015), 324.
6 Pike, *Mystic Union*, xi, 42–44, 51, 56, 58, 81, 166–70; William P. Alston, *Perceiving God: The Epistemology of Religious Experience* (Ithaca and London: Cornell University Press, 1991), 52–53. Both philosophers take seriously Poulain's descriptive approach to mystical experience, especially his claim that the mystic experiences God with five senses in various states of mystical union.
7 See the "Approbation of His Holiness Pope Pius X," ix, and a reviewer in the British Spiritualist journal *Light*, who called Poulain's book "a mine of gold" as "a record of spiritualistic happenings," in Poulain, *The Graces of Interior Prayer*, back matter. It was also favorably reviewed by HJS in *The Occult Review*, ibid., back matter.
8 According to the title page of the eleventh edition, which was published in Paris in 1931 by Gabriel Beauchesne.
9 Bainvel, "Introduction à la dixième édition," in Poulain, *Des grâces d'oraison*, xii.
10 Bainvel, "Introduction," in Poulain, *The Graces of Interior Prayer*, fifth impression, xxxvi, lxvii.
11 Which was noted and lamented by Catholic mystical theologian Émile Lamballe, *Mystical Contemplation: Or The Principle of Mystical Theology*, trans. W. H. Mitchell (New York: Benziger Brothers, 1913; originally published as *La contemplation, ou principes de théologie mystique* [Paris: Pierre Tequi, 1912]), v–vi.
12 Michael Murphy, *The Future of the Body: Explorations into the Future Evolution of Nature* (Los Angeles: Tarcher, 1992), 465–67, 478–526, 630–33.
13 A feature of Poulain's book that has been noted by Pike, *Mystic Union*, 167 and by Poulain himself, Poulain, 30.4b.
14 Bainvel, "Introduction," in Poulain, *The Graces of Interior Prayer*, fifth impression, xxxvi, and "Introduction à la dixième édition," in Poulain, *Des grâces d'oraison*, xii.
15 Bainvel, "Introduction," in Poulain, *The Graces of Interior Prayer*, fifth impression, xxxv–xxxvii.
16 Poulain, *The Graces of Interior Prayer*, xiii.
17 An unnamed reviewer of *The Graces of Interior Prayer* in a journal simply referred to here as *Light*, in Poulain, *The Graces of Interior Prayer*, back matter.
18 Daniel Considine, "Preface to the English Translation," in Poulain, *The Graces of Interior Prayer*, xi–xii.
19 Bainvel, "Introduction," in Poulain, *The Graces of Interior Prayer*, fifth impression, lxvi.
20 His somewhat awkward attempts to sustain his claim that mystical states are purely supernatural graces passively received without any effort on the part of the contemplative often runs up against his more naturalistic view of mystical states as continuous with the process of simplification that moves from the verboseness of meditation, or discursive prayer, to the mood of simple awareness of the meditation subject in the prayer of simplicity (Poulain 2.11, E12).

21 Considine referred to it as "an example of modern scientific methods applied to . . . mysticism," "Preface to the English Translation," in Poulain, *The Graces of Interior Prayer*, xi.

22 Poulain writes "*à la loupe*," which is a handheld magnifying glass used by jewelers, *dictionary.com*, s.v. "loupe," accessed April 30, 2015, http://dictionary.reference.com/browse/loupe?s=t.

23 Bainvel, "Introduction à la dixième édition," in Poulain, *Des grâces d'oraison*, xi.

24 The manual, which runs to over 800 pages in the French editions and to over 600 in the English translation includes, besides a detailed description of twelve characteristics of mystical union, the four stages of mystical union, and the two nights of the soul, long sections on ancillary mystical phenomena such as revelation, visions, the physical and psychological effects of mystical states, and a discussion of numerous theoretical issues concerning mysticism, all in an informed and conservational style that suggests mastery of the science of mystical theology as well as of its practice and realization.

25 It is used by Kelly and Whicher as an authoritative source for mystical phenomena paralleling in many instances the *siddhis* cataloged in the *Yoga Sūtra*, "Patañjali's *Yoga Sūtras* and the *Siddhis*," in Kelly, Crabtree, and Marshall, *Beyond Physicalism*, 326–27, 336. The authors refer to Poulain's discussions of the ligature, which they see as providing documentation in the Catholic tradition for the often similar *siddhis* described in the *Yoga Sūtra*, but for which documentation is less available, ibid. 323–27, 336.

26 McGinn, *The Foundations of Mysticism*, 171. Among Catholic and Orthodox Christians, mysticism has an older, more precise technical name: *mystical theology* (*theologia mystica*). Mystical theology is distinguished from dogmatic theology, which is concerned with presenting revealed truth, and ascetical theology, which is concerned with the disciplines that lead through the ordinary ways of prayer toward contemplation. Mystical theology takes direct experience of God as its field of study. Maturinus Corderius, a sixteenth-century mystical theologian characterized mystical theology as naming "a sort of holy and secret awareness of God and things divine" (*mystica theologia . . . designat quandam sacram et arcanam de Deo divinisque rebus notitiam*), quoted in William Ralph Inge, *Christian Mysticism: Considered in Eight Lectures Delivered before the University of Oxford* (London: Methuen, 1899), 335.

27 Noted also, among others theologians, by Mark McIntosh, *Mystical Theology: The Integrity of Spirituality and Theology* (Malden, MA: Wiley-Blackwell, 1998), 7–8, 19.

28 See, for example, Wright, *The Essential Spirituality Handbook*, 133.

29 Paul Lejeune, *Manuel de théologie mystique* (Paris: Librairie Ch. Poussielgue, 1897), 14–15; Bainvel, "Introduction to the Tenth Edition," in Poulain, *The Graces of Interior Prayer*, fifth impression, xi. See Thomas Keating, *Open Mind, Open Heart: The Contemplative Dimension of the Gospel* (New York: Continuum, 2002, orig. pub., Warwick, NY: Amity House, 1986), 23–24, whose concise statement of Quietism's "ingenious" teaching not only shows it to be virtually identical to the act of faith made by evangelicals when they accept Jesus as their savior, but, ironically, as virtually identical to the kind of dry faith espoused stoutly by Ruth Burrows, *Interior Castle Explored: St Teresa's Teaching on the Life of Deep Union with God* (Mahwah, NJ: HiddenSpring, 2007; orig. pub., London: Sheed and Ward, 1981), 37, and more tentatively by Keating, *Open Mind, Open Heart*, 23–24. See Poulain 15.43.

30 Poulain sees both Quietism and Protestantism as similarly pessimistic about human action due to the sin of Adam (Poulain 27.5; 489).

31 A phrase still used to refer what are now thought to be rare and inessential counterparts to contemplative prayer, which in its essence is distinct from subjective experiences. See, for example, Keating, *Open Mind, Open Heart*, 10–11.

32 Réginald Garrigou-Lagrange rejects the equation of the infused mystical graces encountered in mystical contemplation with extraordinary graces and sees them instead as the ordinary outworking of actual, habitual, or sanctifying grace, *The Three Ages of the Interior Life: Prelude of Eternal Life*, trans. M. Timothea Doyle (London: Catholic Way Publishing, 2013; orig. pub. St. Louis: Herder, 1948; a translation of *Les trois âges de la vie intérieure: prélude de celle du ciel*, Paris: Aubin, 1938), Kindle edition, part 1, Chapter 1. (This is a view that Bainvel sees as imprecise, "Introduction," in Poulain, *The Graces of Interior Prayer*, fifth impression, xxiii). In this, Garrigou-Lagrange clearly tried to find a way through the currently dominant view of the mystical graces as inessential and nonmystical and the earlier, pervasive view, associated with such great figures as Teresa and John of the Cross and many of the manualists, including Lejeune, *Manuel de théologie mystique*, 94, and Poulain, 4.6 passim, that they are infused complements to the sanctifying grace necessary for Christian perfection. The views of Poulain on this topic are briefly discussed in Edward Yarnold, "The Theology of Christian Spirituality," in *The Study of Spirituality*, ed. Cheslyn P. M. Jones, Geoffrey Wainwright, and Edward Yarnold (New York and Oxford: Oxford University Press, 1986),15, and, in Poulain's larger context, in Lejeune, *An Introduction to the Mystical Life*, 2nd ed., trans. Basil Levett (London: R & T Washbourne, 1915; a translation of *Introduction à la vie mystique*, Paris: Lethielleux, 1911), 7–32.

33 Thus Wright claims that these experiences—what traditionally were called "the mystical graces" are "not mystical," but are, rather, "secondary phenomena occasioned by the purgative process." The mystical, on the contrary, is, in her view, "the union of wills, the cleaving of lives, and the aligning of hearts," *The Essential Spirituality Handbook* (Liguori, MS: Liguori Publications, 2009), 135.

34 Thomas Keating, *Invitation to Love: The Way of Christian Contemplation* (New York: Continuum, 1992), 93.

35 Keating, *Open Mind, Open Heart*, 11; Johnston's view of the mystical experiences of the laity and married people in the active life is far more positive, *Mystical Theology*, 8.

36 Burrows, *Interior Castle Explored*, 121.

37 Réginald Garrigou-Lagrange, *The Three Conversions in the Spiritual Life*, trans. unknown (Rockford, IL, USA, 2002; a translation of *Les trois conversions et les trois voies*, Juvisy-Seine-Et-Oise: Les Éditions du Cerf, 1933, 140), 81.

38 What was traditionally called "actual grace" in Catholic theology, J. Pohle, "Actual Grace," *The Catholic Encyclopedia* (New York: Robert Appleton Company, 1909). Online edition accessed June 6, 2015, http://www.newadvent.org/cathen/06689x.htm. As far back as the *Kaṭha Upaniṣad*, 2.20, the idea of grace was acknowledged as a causal factor in the process of attaining *mokṣa* in the Vedānta traditions of Hinduism.

39 See also Poulain, *The Graces of Interior Prayer*, xv.

40 As evidenced, for example, in the manuals of Louis Bouyer and Adolphe Tanquerey, who devote much less space to the unfolding of the strictly contemplative and mystical dimension of Catholic spirituality than to ascetical matters. Bouyer devotes only the last two of twelve chapters of *Introduction to Spirituality*, pbk. ed., trans. Mary Perkins Ryan (Collegeville, MN: Liturgical Press, 1961); a translation of *Introduction à la vie spirituelle: précis de théologie ascétique et mystique*, Paris:

Desclée, 1960, to mystical theology in the strict sense, while Tanquerey devotes only about a seventh of over 700 pages in English to mystical theology in his *Précis de théologie ascétique et mystique, Catholique du net* Internet ed. of the 14th ed., 2003; originally published, 1924, accessed June 10, 2015, https://eti.martin.free.fr/la-mystique/TANQUEREY.doc, trans. Herman Branderis, *The Spiritual Life: A Treatise on Ascetical and Mystical Theology*, 2nd rev. ed. Tournai: Desclée, 1932 (reprinted and updated after 1954; orig. pub. in two volumes, Paris, Tournai, Rome, New York: Desclée, 1923–24). In contrast, the *Visuddhimagga* devotes more than two-thirds of its length to the unfolding of its maps of yogic progress.

41 My version of the chart, which is presented here, is a synthetic adaptation of the traditional itinerary of the *via triplex*, which is informed by and modifies in various ways the itinerary and its terminology as expounded by Poulain 1.1, 1.11-14, 2.1, 3.5-9, 15.1-20, 15.42, 29.3-7; John of the Cross, *The Dark Night* in *The Collected Works of St. John of the Cross*, trans. Kieran Kavanaugh and Otilio Rodriguez (Washington, DC: ICS Publications, 1979), 297–98 (1.1.1); Keating, *Invitation to Love*, 90–94, Thomas Keating, *Intimacy with God: An Introduction to Centering Prayer* (New York: Crossroad, 1994), 40; Thomas Merton, *The Inner Experience*, ed. William H. Shannon (San Francisco: HarperSanFrancisco, 2003), 57–79, *Contemplative Prayer*, 29–33, 42–45,67–71, 75–11; William G. Most, *Our Father's Plan: God's Arrangements and Our Response* (Manassas, VA: Trinity Communications, 1988), online edition accessed October 31, 2015, http://www.catholicculture.org/culture/library/most/getwork.cfm?worknum=232, Chapter 21, "Mental Prayer," Chapter 22, "Mystical Rose," and Chapter 23, "Spouse of the Holy Spirit"; Tanquerey, *The Spiritual Life*, 297–304, passim (§618–634 passim); Evelyn Underhill, *Mysticism: A Study in the Nature and Development of Man's Spiritual Consciousness*, 4th ed. (New York: Dutton, 1912; first ed. 1911), 204–07, 357–54; Mary Margaret Funk, "Lectio Divina," in *The Gethsemani Encounter: A Dialogue on the Spiritual Life by Christian and Buddhist Monastics*, ed. Donald W. Mitchell and James Wiseman (New York: Continuum, 2003, orig. pub. 1997), 64; Jordan Aumann, *Spiritual Theology* (New York: Continuum, 2006 repr. London: Sheed & Ward, 1980), 316–57; McGinn, *The Essential Writings of Christian Mysticism*, 150–51; Garrigou-Lagrange, *The Three Ages of the Interior Life*, Kindle edition, part 4, Chapter 51.

42 For a current example, see Wright, *The Essential Spirituality Handbook*, 128.

43 Evan Thompson reports on studies by Antoine Lutz and Richard Davidson that demonstrate increases and decreases in the amplitude of gamma brain waves corresponding to changes of degrees of clarity in the meditative awareness of advanced meditators, *Waking, Dreaming, Being*, Kindle edition, 76.

44 The rudiments of the classic Christian *via mystica*, which has antecedents in the pedagogy of the Greeks, are traceable as far back as Clement of Alexandria, Origen, and Dionysius the Areopagite. Dionysius traced a path of ascent with three clearly defined stages (*via triplex*) of experiential union with God that came to be known as *purgatio, illuminatio*, and *unio* (or *katharsis, phōtismos*, and *henōsis* or *teleiōsis*). See Inge, *Christian Mysticism*, 354–55, who concisely and illuminatingly relates the Christian three ways of the mystical life to the Greek Mysteries; McGinn, *The Foundations of Mysticism*, 105, 117, 158; Auguste Saudreau, *The Degrees of the Spiritual Life: A Method of Directing Souls according to their Progress in Virtue*, vol. 1., trans. Bede Camm (New York, Cincinnati, and Chicago: Benziger Brothers, 1907), vii–ix, and Andrew Louth, *The Origins of the Christian Mystical Tradition; From Plato to Denys* (Oxford: Oxford University Press, 1981), 163.

45 Tanqueray, *The Spiritual Life*, 171–72 (§340). See also Thomas Aquinas, *Summa Theologiae*, II.II, Q. 183, art. 4; *The Oxford Dictionary of the Christian Church*, 2nd ed., ed. F. L. Cross and E. A Livingstone (New York: Oxford University Press, 1974), s.v., "Ascetical theology."

46 Based on Maximus the Confessor see Urban T. Holmes, *A History of Christian Spirituality: An Analytical Introduction* (Harrisburg, PA: Morehouse Publishing, 2002), 50; Thomas Aquinas, *Summa Theologiae*, II.II, Q. 183; Tanqueray, *The Spiritual Life*, 297–98 (§619).

47 Garrigou-Lagrange, *The Three Ages of the Interior Life*, Kindle edition, part 1, Chapter 18, section C.

48 I will generally use the term *mind* instead of *soul* except in quotations, while expounding the teachings of Catholic mystical theology since *mind*, in the broad sense of referring collectively to the cognitive, affective, and conative faculties can serve as a translation of the Latin *anima*, the Greek *psychē*, the Sanskrit *antaḥkaraṇa*, and the Sanskrit and Pāli *citta*.

49 This list of eight sins, or vices (*logismoi*), goes back to Evagrius Ponticus (McGinn, *The Essential Writings of Christian Mysticism*, 55), and it differs markedly from the traditional list of seven sins listed by Thomas Aquinas, *Summa Theologiae*, I.II, Q. 84. See also Dennis Okholm, *Dangerous Passions, Deadly Sins: Learning from the Psychology of Ancient Monks* (Grand Rapids, MI: Brazos Press, 2014), 2–6.

50 A point cogently expressed by Wright, *The Essential Spirituality Handbook*, 118.

51 As cogently explained, for example, by Stephen Batchelor, "Foreword," in *Waking, Dreaming, and Sleeping: Self and Consciousness in Neuroscience, Meditation, and Philosophy*, ed. Evan Thompson (New York: Columbia University Press, 2014), xi.

52 As classically expressed in Joseph Simler, *Catechism of Mental Prayer*, 3rd ed. (Rockford, IL: TAN Books, 1984; orig. pub. Dayton: Brothers of Mary, 1911; 1st ed., 1888).

53 Guigo II, *The Ladder of Monks* (*Scala claustralium: epistola de vita contemplativa*), trans. L. Dysinger (Paris, 1970), accessed June 9, 2015, http://www.ldysinger.com/@texts2/1180_guigo-2/02_lad_sel-lec.htm. This translation is based on *Guigo II: The Ladder of Monks and Twelve Meditations*, trans. Edmund Colledge and James Walsh (New York: Image, 1978), 81–89.

54 Keating, *Intimacy with God*, 47.

55 Teresa of Ávila, *The Way of Perfection*, trans. E. Allison Peers (New York: Image, 2004; reissue of 1964 ed.), 177.

56 Keating, *Intimacy with God*, 47.

57 John of the Cross, *Ascent of Mount Carmel*, trans. E. Allison Peers (Garden City, NY: Image Books, 1958), 103 (1.1.1).

58 Garrigou-Lagrange, *The Three Conversions in the Spiritual Life*, 31–47. Garrigou-Lagrange sees the passive night of the senses as the "threshold" of the illuminative way, *The Three Ages of the Interior Life*, Kindle edition, part 2, Chapter 24.

59 "*C'est un état d'âme complexe*," Tanquerey, *Précis de théologie ascétique et mystique*, 453 (§1421), *The Spiritual Life*, 668.

60 Tanquerey, *Précis de théologie ascétique et mystique*, 453 (§1420), *The Spiritual Life*, 667. Poulain makes a similar distinction, although he appears to keep the night of the senses in the borderland between the prayer of simplicity and the prayer of quiet (Poulain 15.3; 31.37). Yet, at another point, he calls both nights "two kinds [*sortes*] of contemplation" (Poulain 31.38, E575, F609; 31.43), which, given the precise equation in this tradition of contemplation with the mystical graces, would place the night of the senses, at least in its passive phase, in the illuminative way.

61 Thomas Merton, *Contemplative Prayer*, 77.
62 Tanquerey, Précis de théologie ascétique et mystique, 453 (§1421).
63 Garrigou-Lagrange, *The Three Ages of the Interior Life*, Kindle edition, part 3, Chapter 4.
64 Tanquerey, *The Spiritual Life*, 651 (§1388), *Précis de théologie ascétique et mystique*, 422. Author's italics.
65 Lamballe, *Mystical Contemplation*, 44.
66 Poulain was aware that applying the name *God* and the doctrinal matter, including the whole catechism of the Catholic Church to the unitive experiences of the Catholic mystics seems arbitrary to sympathetic students of mysticism who hold no special brief for Catholicism or Christianity, as in his quotation of Gustav Belot, who, in a 1905 conference of the *Société française de philosophie* in Paris, questioned the legitimacy of Catholic mystics in calling by the name of *God* "this confused, vague, and inexpressible reality" (*cette réalité confuse, indéterminée, inexprimable*) of mystical experience, when the source of this experience is interpreted differently by Buddhists, "Pantheists," and followers of other deities and conceptions of the divine (quoted in Poulain, 31.49, E583, F618, a view that I see as an expression of the apophatic mystical pluralism that I argued for in my last book, *Pluralism: The Future of Religion*, and which underlies and justified the comparative approach that I am pursuing in this book). For the proceedings of the Paris conference, see Henri Delacroix, *Le développement des états mystiques chez sainte Thérèse, Bulletin de la Société française de philosophie* 6 (1906): 1–42. For critical analysis of the proceedings at this conference, see Louise Nelstrop and Bradley B Onishi, *Mysticism in the French Tradition: Eruptions from France* (Farnham, Surrey, UK and Burlington, VY, USA: Ashgate Publishing, 2015), 18–21.
67 Merton, *Contemplative Prayer*, 21. Poulain uses neither of these two traditional names for this kind of prayer in this context.
68 Keating, *Invitation to Love*, 91.
69 Réginald Garrigou-Lagrange, *Reality: A Thomistic Synthesis*, trans., Patrick Cummins (South Bend, IN, USA: Ex Fontibus, 2012; repr., St. Louis: Herder, 1950; orig. French ed., Paris: Desclée de Brouwer, 1946), 195.
70 Poulain acknowledges this intellectual power, but only as a "supernatural" intellectual vision granted by God (Poulain 20.13).
71 Garrigou-Lagrange offers a traditional analysis of the powers of the mind, *The Three Ages of the Interior Life*, Kindle edition, part 1, Chapter 3, section 1.
72 Elmer O'Brien, *The Essential Plotinus* (Indianapolis: Hackett, 1964), 29–30.
73 Garrigou-Lagrange, *The Three Ages of the Interior Life*, Kindle edition, part 4, Chapter 51. Poulain disagrees with this view, yet he traces it to Teresa and Francis de Sales (Poulain 9.18-23, 33-37).
74 Garrigou-Lagrange, *The Three Ages of the Interior Life*, Kindle edition part 4, Chapter 51.
75 Ibid.
76 Ibid.
77 Poulain comes close to a nondual perspective when he claims that God grants a divine knowledge in which all is blended into one (*tout est fondu*), yet he maintains the formal distinction of the divine and human natures, which his theology requires (Poulain 18.25n*/1, E250, F 261) and, consistently, rejects the views of "Monists" (*monistes*, Poulain 18.30, E252, F263).

78 I have removed the hyphens in the technical theological term *aseity*, which were introduced by the translator (i.e., *a-se-ity*) because they are unnecessary and were not used by Poulain, who writes *l'aséité*.
79 Poulain is dubious about this point, which he quotes, not, it seems, with complete disagreement from other mystical theologians.
80 Garrigou-Lagrange, *The Three Ages of the Interior Life*, Kindle edition part 4, Chapter 51.
81 Ibid., Chapter 1.
82 Poulain here provides a number of extracts from the writings of John of the Cross.
83 Keating, *Invitation to Love*, 95.
84 Ibid., 98. See also Merton, *Contemplative Prayer*, 98.
85 Keating, *Invitation to Love*, 99. See also Merton, *Contemplative Prayer*, 76–78.
86 Topics treated by Teresa of Ávila in the Sixth Mansions in *The Interior Castle*, trans. E. Allison Peers (New York: Image Books, 1961), 169–78.
87 Keating, *Invitation to Love*, 102.
88 Garrigou-Lagrange, *The Three Ages of the Interior Life*, Kindle edition part 3, Chapter 4.
89 John of the Cross, *Ascent of Mount Carmel*, 103 (1.1.3).
90 As noted by Tanquerey, *Précis de théologie ascétique et mystique*, 434 (§1363).
91 Vyāsa, *Yoga-Bhāṣya*, 2.54, cited in Bryant, *The Yoga Sūtras of Patañjali*, 297.
92 Tanquerey, *Précis de théologie ascétique et mystique*, 434 (§1363).
93 Vyāsa, *Yoga-Bhāṣya*, 1.1, Āraṇya, *Yoga Philosophy of Patañjali*, 1.
94 Garrigou-Lagrange, *The Three Ages of the Interior Life*, Kindle edition, part 1, Chapter 25.
95 Ibid.
96 See, for example, Āraṇya, *Yoga Philosophy of Patañjali*, 251.
97 A persistent danger for Catholic mystics, and to which Burrows refers, *Guidelines for Mystical Prayer*, 12. See Tanquerey, *Précis de Théologie Ascétique et Mystique*, 474 (§1486.4), *The Spiritual Life*, 698; Poulain, 14.41; Thomas Keating, *The Better Part: Stages of Contemplative Living* (New York and London: Continuum, 2000), 102, and Keating, *Intimacy with God*, 36–37.While these writers anxiously try to preserve imagery of Jesus into the highest contemplative states, one of the earliest and most influential theorists of mystical theology, Evagrius Ponticus (fl. 344–99), argued that the highest form of contemplation moves beyond ideas and images, including "the humanity of the Savior," as noted by Louis Boyer, *Introduction to Spirituality*, 77–78. This issue is addressed without clarifying "the place of the humanity of Christ in the higher stages of the mystical life" by John Eudes Bamberger, "Introduction," in *The* Praktikos *and Chapters on Prayer*, ed. Evagrius Ponticus, trans. John Eudes Bamberger (Kalamazoo, MI: Cistercian Publications, 1981), xciii–xciv, xcivnn291, 292.
98 As implicit in later writings such as *Contemplative Prayer* and as explicit in works such as Thomas Merton, *Asian Journal of Thomas Merton*, ed. Naomi Burton, Patrick Hart, and James Laughlin (New York: New Directions Press, 1973).
99 Newberg and d'Aquili, *The Mystical Mind*, 13–14, 95, 110–14.
100 Equal, I think, to *asamprajñāta-samādhi* in the *Yoga Sūtra* and *nirodha-samāpatti* in the *Visuddhimagga*. These states are brought about by the cultivation of a "Null Domain" method, according to Jonathan D. Nash and Andrew Newberg, "Toward A Unifying Taxonomy and Definition for Meditation," *Frontiers in Psychology* 4 (November 2013): 6–7, accessed October 20, 2015, doi: 10.3389/fpsyg.2013.00806.

101 Thompson, *Waking, Dreaming, Being: Self and Consciousness in Neuroscience, Meditation, and Philosophy*, Kindle edition, "Prologue: The Dalai Lama's Conjecture."

102 Although this dogmatic stance has been challenged on many fronts, most recently and effectively by Edward F. Kelley, "Introduction: Science and Spirituality at a Crossroads," in Kelly, Crabtree, and Marshall, *Beyond Physicalism*, xii–xxiv, its authority is so strong that Evan Thompson feels the need to find a middle ground between the view that pure awareness is either dependent on the brain or not, *Waking, Dreaming, Being: Self and Consciousness in Neuroscience, Meditation, and Philosophy*, Kindle edition, "Prologue: The Dalai Lama's Conjecture."

103 Keating, *Invitation to Love*, 103.

Conclusion

1 Garrigou-Lagrange, *The Three Conversions in the Spiritual Life*, 79–80.

2 *Bṛhadāraṇyaka Upaniṣad* 4.4.8, Roebuck translation.

Bibliography

Azari, Nina P. "Neuroimaging Studies of Religious Experience: A Critical Review." In *Where God and Science Meet: How Brain and Evolutionary Studies Alter Our Understanding of Religion*. Vol. 2, *The Neurology of Religious Experience*, edited by Patrick McNamara, 33–54. Westport, CT and London: Praeger, 2006.

Aden, Ross. *Religion Today: A Critical Thinking Approach to Religious Studies*. Lanham, MD: Rowman & Littlefield, 2013.

Akers, Brian Dana, trans. *Hatha Yoga Pradipika: An English Translation*. Woodstock, NY: YogaVidya, 2002.

Albanese, Catherine L. *America: Religions and Religion*. 5th ed. Boston: Cengage, 2012.

Alles, Gregory D. "After the Naming Explosion: Joachim Wach's Unfinished Project." In *Hermeneutics, Politics, and the History of Religions: The Contested Legacies of Joachim Wach and Mircea Eliade*, edited by Christian Wedemeyer and Wendy Doniger, 51–78. New York: Oxford University Press, 2010.

Alston, William P. *Perceiving God: The Epistemology of Religious Experience*. Ithaca and London: Cornell University Press, 1991.

Alter, Joseph S. *Yoga in Modern India: The Body Between Science and Philosophy.* Princeton: Princeton University Press, 2004.

Andresen, Jensine and Robert K. C. Forman, eds. *Cognitive Models and Spiritual Maps: Interdisciplinary Explorations of Religious Experience*. Charlottesville, VA: Imprint Academic, 2000.

Andresen, Jensine and Robert K. C. Forman, "Methodological Pluralism in the Study of Religion: How the Study of Consciousness and Mapping Spiritual Experiences Can Reshape Religious Studies Methodology." In *Cognitive Models and Spiritual Maps: Interdisciplinary Explorations of Religious Experience*, edited by Jensine Andresen and Robert K. C. Forman, 7–14. Charlottesville, VA: Imprint Academic, 2000.

Anonymous. *Light*. No place. No date. In Augustin-François Poulain. *The Graces of Interior Prayer: A Treatise on Mystical Theology,* back matter. Fourth impression. Translated by Leonora L. Yorke Smith. London: Kegan Paul, Trench, Trubner and Co., 1928. Original publication, 1910. A translation of *Des grâces d'oraison: traité de théologie mystique*. 10th ed. Paris: Gabriel Beauchesne, 1922. 1st ed., 1901.

Anuruddha, Ācariya. *A Comprehensive Manual of Abhidhamma*: *The* Abhidhammattha Sangaha *of Ācariya Anuruddha*. Translated by Mahāthera Nārada and Bhikkhu Bodhi. Edited by Bhikkhu Bodhi. Seattle: BPS Pariyatti Editions, 2000. First published Kandy, Sri Lanka: Buddhist Publication Society, 1993.

Āraṇya, Swāmi Harihārananda. *Yoga Philosophy of Patañjali: Containing His Yoga Aphorisms with Commentary of Vyāsa*. Translated by P. N. Mukerji. Calcutta: University of Calcutta, 1981.

Ariarajah, S. Wesley. "Wider Ecumenism: A Threat or a Promise?" *The Ecumenical Review* 50, no. 3 (1998): 321–29. Accessed October 17, 2015. doi: 10.1111/j.1758-6623.1998.tb00009.

Armstrong, Karen. *Buddha*. New York: Penguin, 2001.

Aubele, Teresa, Stan Wenck, and Susan Reynolds, *Train Your Brain to Get Happy: The Simple Program that Primes Your Gray Cells For Joy, Optimism, and Serenity*. Avon, MA: Adams Media, 2011.

Aumann, Jordan. *Spiritual Theology*. New York: Continuum, 2006. Reprint, London: Sheed & Ward, 1980.

Bahadur, Krishna Prakash. *The Wisdom of Saankhya*. New Delhi: Sterling Publishers, 1978.

Bainvel, Jean-Vincent. "Introduction à la dixième édition." In *Des grâces d'oraison: traité de théologie mystique*, edited by Augustin-François Poulain, 10th ed. xxxi–cxii. Paris: Gabriel Beauchesne, 1922. 1st ed. Paris, 1901.

Bainvel, Jean-Vincent. "Introduction to the Tenth Edition." In *The Graces of Interior Prayer: A Treatise on Mystical Theology*, edited by Augustin-François Poulain, 10th ed. 5th impression. Translated by Leonora L. Yorke Smith. London: Kegan Paul, Trench, Trubner & Co, 1950. A translation of *Des grâces d'oraison: traité de théologie mystique* 10th ed. Paris: Gabriel Beauchesne, 1922. 1st ed. 1901.

Bamberger, John Eudes. "Introduction." In *The Praktikos and Chapters on Prayer*, edited by Evagrius Ponticus, translated by John Eudes Bamberger, xxii–xciv. Kalamazoo, MI: Cistercian Publications, 1981.

Banquet, J. P. "Spectral Analysis of the EEG in Meditation." *Journal of Electroencephalography and Clinical Neurophysiology* 35, no. 2 (August 1973): 143–51.

Barinaga, Marcia. "Buddhism and Neuroscience: Studying the Well-Trained Mind." *Science*, October 3, 2003, 44–46. Accessed October 16, 2015. doi: 10.1126/science.302.5642.44.

Barnes, Michael. "The Buddhist Way of Deliverance (according to the Pāli Sources)." *Studia Missionalia* 30 (1981): 233–77.

Barret, Justin L. "Exploring the Natural Foundations of Religion." *Trends in Cognitive Science* 4, no. 1 (2000): 29–34.

Barrett, Justin L. *Why Would Anyone Believe in God*. Walnut Creek: Altamira Press, 2004.

Barth, Karl. *The Epistle to the Romans*. 6th ed. Paperback, edited and translated by Edwyn C. Hoskyns. London: Oxford University Press, 1968. Original edition, 1933. This is a translation of *Der Römerbrief*. 6th ed. Zürich, 1928.

Batchelor, Stephen. "Foreword." In *Waking, Dreaming, and Sleeping: Self and Consciousness in Neuroscience, Meditation, and Philosophy*, edited by Evan Thompson, xi–x. New York: Columbia University Press, 2014.

Benson, Herbert. "Foreword: Twenty-fifth Anniversary Update." In *The Relaxation Response*, edited by Herbert Benson with Miriam Z. Klipper, 2nd ed, Kindle ed. "Foreword." New York: Harper-Collins, 2009. 1st ed. 1975.

Bernhardt, Steven. "Is Pure Consciousness Unmediated: A Response to Katz." Unpublished essay presented at the American Academy of Religion, November 1985.

Bernhardt, Steven. "Are Pure Consciousness Events Unmediated." In *The Problem of Pure Consciousness: Mysticism and Philosophy*, edited by Robert K. C. Forman, 220–36. Paperback ed. New York: Oxford University Press, 1997. Original publication, 1990.

Bhikkhu, Thanissaro. "Sumangala's Mother." *Access to Insight*. Accessed May 28, 2014. http://www.accesstoinsight.org/tipitaka/kn/thig/thig.02.03.than.html. A translation of *sumaṅgalamātātherīgāthā*.

Blum, Jason N. "The Science of Consciousness and Mystical Experience: An Argument for Radical Empiricism." *Journal of the American Academy of Religion* 82, no. 1 (March 2014): 150–73.

Bouyer, Louis. *Introduction à la vie spirituelle: précis de théologie ascétique et mystique*. Paris: Desclée, 1960.

Bouyer, Louis. *Introduction to Spirituality.* Translated by Mary Perkins Ryan. Paperback ed. Collegeville, MN: Liturgical Press, 1961. A translation of *Introduction à la vie spirituelle: précis de théologie ascétique et mystique.* Paris: Desclée, 1960.

Boyer, Pascal. "Evolution of the Modern Mind and the Origins of Culture: Religious Concepts as a Limiting Case." In *Evolution and the Human Mind: Modularity, Language and Meta-Cognition*, edited by Peter Carruthers and Andrew Chamberlain, 93–112. Cambridge: Cambridge University Press, 2000.

Brahm (Brahmavaṃso), Ajahn. *Mindfulness, Bliss, and Beyond: A Meditator's Handbook.* Boston: Wisdom Publications, 2006.

Brahm (Brahmavaṃso), Ajahn. "Degrees of Seeing." *Tricycle* 5, no. 1 (Fall 2006): 42–47.

Brahm (Brahmavaṃso), Ajahn. "Interview with Ajahn Brahmavaṃso." In *The Experience of Samādhi: An In-depth Exploration of Buddhist Meditation*, edited by Richard Shankman, 166–73. Boston and London: Shambhala, 2008.

Brahma, Nalini Kanta. *Philosophy of Hindu Sādhanā.* Delhi: Book Faith India, 1999. Reprint, London: Kegan Paul, Trench, Trubner, 1932.

Brainard, F. Samuel. *Reality and Mystical Experience.* University Park: Pennsylvania State University Press, 2000.

Brasington, Leigh. "Five Factors for the First Jhana—Not!" Accessed July 8, 2014. http://www.leighb.com/jhana_4factors.htm.

Brasington, Leigh. "Interpretations of the Jhanas." Accessed May 7, 2014. http://www.leighb.com/jhanantp.htm.

Brasington, Leigh. "The Traditional Factors of the 8 Jhanas." Accessed May 7, 2014, http://www.leighb.com/jhanatrd.htm.

Brasington, Leigh. *Right Concentration: A Practical Guide to the Jhānas.* Boston: Shambhala, 2015.

Braun, Erik. *The Birth of Insight: Meditation, Modern Buddhism, and the Burmese Monk Ledi Sayadaw.* Chicago: University of Chicago Press, 2013.

Braun, Erik. "Meditation En Masse: How Colonialism Sparked the Global Vipassana Movement." *Tricycle* 23, no. 4 (Spring 2014): 56–62, 105.

Bronkhorst, Johannes. *The Two Traditions of Meditation in Ancient India.* 2nd ed. Delhi: Motilal Banarsidass, 1992. Original publication, Stuttgart: Franz Steiner Verlag, 1986.

Bronkhorst, Johannes. *Buddhist Teaching In India.* Boston: Wisdom Publications, 2009.

Bryant, Edwin F. *The Yoga Sūtras of Patañjali.* New York: North Point Press, 2009.

Bucknell, Roderick S. "Reinterpreting the *Jhānas*." *Journal of the International Association of Buddhist Studies* 16, no. 2 (1993): 375–409.

Buddhaghosa, Bhadantācariya. *Visuddhimagga.* Volume 1, *Paṭhamo Bhāgo.* Yangon, Myanmar: Ministry of Religious Affairs, 2008; Pāli text Romanized from the Myanmar ed. Aṭṭakathā Series 51, 1970.

Buddhaghosa, Bhadantācariya. *The Path of Purification* (*Visuddhimagga*). 1st BPS Pariyatti ed. Translated by Bhikkhu Ñāṇamoli. Seattle: BPS Pariyatti Editions, 1999.

Burley, Mikel. *Haṭha Yoga: Its Context, Theory and Practice.* Delhi: Motilal Banarsidass, 2000.

Burley, Mikel. *Classical Sāṃkhya and Yoga: An Indian Metaphysics of Experience.* London and New York: Routledge, 2007.

Burrows, Ruth. *Guidelines for Mystical Prayer.* London: Burns & Oates, 1976.

Burrows, Ruth. *Interior Castle Explored: St Teresa's Teaching on the Life of Deep Union with God.* Mahwah, NJ: HiddenSpring, 2007. Original publication, London: Sheed and Ward, 1981.

Catherine, Shaila. "*Wisdom Wide and Deep: A Practical Handbook for Mastering Jhāna and Vipassanā*. Boston: Wisdom Publications, 2011.

Catherine, Shaila. "Jhāna Practice and True Happiness: Talking with Shaila Catherine." *BCBS Insight Journal*. May 14, 2014. Accessed May 16, 2014. http://www.bcbsdharma.org/insight-journal/.

Catholic Church. *Catechism of the Catholic Church*. Accessed June 25, 2014. http://www.vatican.va/archive/ccc_css/archive/catechism/p3s1c3a2.htm.

Chadha, Monima. "On Knowing Universals: The Nyāya Way." *Philosophy East and West* 64, no. 2 (April 2014): 287–302.

Chalmers, Alan. *Science and Its Fabrication*. Minneapolis: University of Minnesota Press, 1990.

Chalmers, David J. "Facing Up to the Problem of Consciousness." *Journal of Consciousness Studies* 2, no. 3 (1995): 200–19.

Chapple, Christopher Key. "The Unseen Seer and the Field: Consciousness in Sāṃkhya and Yoga." In *The Problem of Pure Consciousness: Mysticism and Philosophy*, edited by Robert K. C. Forman, 53–70. Paperback ed. New York: Oxford University Press, 1997. Original publication, 1990.

Chapple, Christopher Key. *Yoga and the Luminous: Patañjali's Spiritual Path to Freedom*. Albany: State University of New York Press, 2008.

Cho, Francesca and Richard King Squier. "Religion as a Complex and Dynamic System." *Journal of the American Academy of Religion* 81, no. 2 (June 2013): 357. Accessed October 16, 2015. doi: 10.1093/jaarel/lft016.

Clark, Kelley James and Justin L. Barrett, "Reidian Religious Epistemology and the Cognitive Science of Religion." *Journal of the American Academy of Religion* 79, no. 3 (Summer 2011): 639–75.

Collins, Steven. *Nirvana and Other Buddhist Felicities*. Cambridge: Cambridge University Press, 1998.

Condon, Paul, Gaëlle Desbordes, Willa Miller, and David DeSteno. "Meditation Increases Compassionate Responses to Suffering." *Psychological Science* (August 21, 2013). Accessed October 23, 2015. doi:10.1177/0956797613485603.

Considine, Daniel. "Preface to the English Translation." In *The Graces of Interior Prayer: A Treatise on Mystical Theology*. Fourth impression, edited by Augustin-François Poulain and translated by Leonora L. Yorke Smith. London: Kegan Paul, Trench, Trubner and Co., 1928. Original publication, 1910. A translation of *Des grâces d'oraison: traité de théologie mystique*. 10th ed. Paris: Gabriel Beauchesne, 1922. 1st ed., 1901.

Conze, Edward. *Buddhist Meditation*. New York: Routledge, 2008. Original publication, 1956.

Cornille, Catherine. "The Dynamics of Multiple Belonging." In *Many Mansions? Multiple Religious Belonging and Christian Identity*, edited by Catherine Cornille, 1–6. Maryknoll, NY: Orbis Books, 2002.

Costa, Gavin D. "The Impossibility of a Pluralist View of Religions." *Religious Studies* 32 (June 1996): 223–32.

Costa, Gavin D. "Pluralist Arguments." In *Catholic Engagement with World Religions: A Comprehensive Study*, edited by Karl J. Becker, Ilaria Morali, and Gavin D'Costa, 329–44. Maryknoll, NY: Orbis Books, 2010.

Cousins, L. S. "Buddhist *Jhāna*: Its Nature and Attainment according to the Pali Sources." *Religion* 3, no. 2 (Autumn 1973): 115–31. Accessed October 24, 2015. doi:10.1016/0048-721X(7390003-1.

Cutsinger, James S. Review of *The Essential Writings of Fritjof Schuon*, edited by Seyyed Hossein Nasr. *Journal of the American Academy of Religion* 62, no. 1 (Spring 1989): 209–13.

d'Aquili, Eugene and Andrew B. Newberg. *The Mystical Mind: Probing the Biology of Religious Experience*. Minneapolis: Fortress Press, 1999.

Dasgupta, Surendranath. *A History of Indian Philosophy*. Vol. 1, *Philosophy of Buddhist, Jaina and Six Systems of Indian Thought*. Delhi: Motilal, Banarsidass, 1988. Reprint, 1975 ed. Original publication, London: Cambridge University Press, 1922.

Dass, Ram. "Foreword." In *The Meditative Mind: The Varieties of Meditative Experience*, edited by Daniel J. Goleman, ix–xvi. New York: Tarcher/Putnam, 1988.

Davidson, Richard J. *The Emotional Life of Your Brain: How Its Unique Patterns Affect the Way You Think, Feel, and Live—and How You Can Change Them*. New York: Hudson Street Press, 2011.

Davidson, Richard J. "Meng Wu Lecture: Richard Davidson, PhD." A Lecture Presented at Stanford University, Palo Alto, CA, October 2, 2012. Accessed August 17, 2015. https://www.youtube.com/watch?v=AKKg3CDczpA.

Davidson, Richard J. and Daniel J. Goleman. "The Role of Attention in Meditation and Hypnosis: A Psychobiological Perspective on Transformations of Consciousness." *The International Journal of Clinical and Experimental Hypnosis* 25, no. 4 (October 1977): 291–308. Accessed November 14, 2015. doi: 10.1080/00207147708415986.

Davidson, Richard J., Daniel J. Goleman, and Gary E, Schwartz. "Attentional and Affective Concomitants of Meditation: A Cross-Sectional Study." *Journal of Abnormal Psychology* 85 (1976): 235–38. Accessed November 14, 2015. doi/10.1037/0021-843X.85.2.235.

Davies, Oliver. *The God Within: The Mystical Tradition of Northern Europe*. Rev. ed. Hyde Park, NY: New City Press, 2006.

De Michelis, Elizabeth. *A History of Modern Yoga: Patañjali and Western Esotericism*. London and New York: Continuum, 2004.

De Michelis, Elizabeth. "Modern Yoga: History and Forms." In *Yoga in the Modern World: Contemporary Perspectives*, edited by Mark Singleton and Jean Byrne, 1–35. London and New York: Routledge, 2008.

Deikman, Arthur J. "Experimental Meditation." *Journal of Nervous Mental Disorders* 136 (April 1963): 329–43.

Delacroix, Henri. "Le développement des états mystiques chez sainte Thérèse." *Bulletin de la Société française de philosophie* 6 (1906): 1–42.

DeSteno, David. "The Morality of Meditation." *New York Times*, July 5, 2013. Accessed October 23, 2015. http://www.nytimes.com/2013/07/07/opinion/sunday/the-morality-of-meditation.html?hpw.

Deutsch, Eliot. *Advaita Vedānta: A Philosophical Reconstruction*. Honolulu: The University Press of Hawai'i, 1969.

Dionysius the Areopagite. "The Mystical Theology." In *Pseudo-Dionysius The Complete Works*. Translated by Colm Luibheid, 133–41. Mahwah, NJ: Paulist Press, 1987.

Dubuisson, Daniel. *The Western Construction of Religion: Myths, Knowledge, and Ideology*. Translated by William Sayers. Baltimore and London: The Johns Hopkins University Press, 2003. A translation of *L'Occident et la religion. Mythes, science et idéologie*. Bruxelles: Éditions Complexe, 1998.

Eck, Diana L. *India: A Sacred Geography*. Kindle ed. New York: Harmony Books, 2012.

Eckhart, Meister. *Meister Eckhart: Selected Writings*. Translated by Oliver Davies. New York: Penguin Books, 1994.

Egan, Harvey D. *Christian Mysticism: The Future of a Tradition*. New York: Pueblo Publishing, 1984.

Egan, Harvey D. *An Anthology of Christian Mysticism*. Collegeville, MN: The Liturgical Press, 1996.

Ehring, Douglas. "Distinguishing Universals from Particulars." *Analysis* 64, no. 4 (October 2004): 326–32.

Eifring, Halvor. "Meditation in Judaism, Christianity, and Islam: Technical Aspects of Devotional Practices." In *Meditation in Judaism, Christianity, and Islam*, edited by Halvor Eifring, 3–13. London and New York: Bloomsbury, 2013.

Eliade, Mircea. *Yoga, Immortality, and Freedom*. Edited and Translated by Willard R. Trask. Princeton, NJ: Princeton University Press, 2009. English translation originally published 1958. Translation of *Le Yoga: Liberté et immortalité*. Paris: Librairie Payot, 1954.

Eliade, Mircea. "Methodological Remarks on the Study of Religious Symbolism." In *The History of Religions: Essays in Methodology*, edited by Mircea Eliade and Joseph Mitsuo Kitagawa, 89–90. Chicago: University of Chicago Press, 1973.

Engler, Steven and Mark Quentin Gardiner. "Religion as Superhuman Agency: On E. Thomas Lawson and Robert N. McCauley, *Rethinking Religion*. 1990." In *Contemporary Theories of Religion: A Critical Companion*, edited by Michal Stausberg, 22–38. London and New York: Routledge, 2009.

Feldman, Christian. "Opening the Gates of Consciousness." *Tricycle* 54 (Winter 2004): 73.

Festugière, André Jean. *Personal Religion among the Greeks*. Berkeley and Los Angeles: University of California Press, 1954.

Feuerstein, Georg. *The Philosophy of Classical Yoga*. Rochester, VT: Inner Traditions, 1996.

Feuerstein, Georg. *Tantra: The Path of Ecstasy*. Boston: Shambhala, 1998.

Fischer, Roland. "A Cartography of the Ecstatic and Meditative States." *Science* (November 26, 1971). Accessed October 16, 2015. doi: 10.1126/science.174.4012.89. Reprint, *Understanding Mysticism*, edited by Richard Woods, 286–305. New York: Image Books, 1980.

Fitzgerald, Timothy. *The Ideology of Religious Studies*. New York: Oxford University Press, 2000.

Flickstein, *The Meditator's Atlas: A Roadmap of the Inner World*. Boston: Wisdom Publications, 2007. Previous title, *Swallowing the River Ganges*, 2001.

Fong, Benjamin Y. "On Critics and What's Real: Russell McCutcheon on Religious Experience." *Journal of the American Academy of Religion* 82, no. 4 (December 2014): 1127–48.

Forman, Robert K. C. "Eckhart, *Gezücken*, and the Ground of the Soul." In *The Problem of Pure Consciousness: Mysticism and Philosophy*, edited by Robert K. C. Forman, 98–120. Paperback ed. New York: Oxford University Press, 1997. Original publication, 1990.

Forman, Robert K. C. "Introduction: Mysticism, Constructivism, and Forgetting." In *The Problem of Pure Consciousness: Mysticism and Philosophy*, edited by Robert K. C. Forman, 3–49. Paperback ed. New York: Oxford University Press, 1997. Original publication 1990.

Forman, Robert K. C., ed. *The Problem of Pure Consciousness: Mysticism and Philosophy*. Paperback ed. New York: Oxford University Press, 1997. Original publication, 1990.

Forman, Robert K. C. "Preface." In *The Innate Capacity: Mysticism, Psychology, and Philosophy*, edited by Robert K. C. Forman, vii–ix. New York and Oxford: Oxford University Press, 1998.

Forman, Robert K. C. *Mysticism, Mind, Consciousness*. Albany: State University Press of New York, 1999.

Fronsdal, Gil, trans. *The Dhammapada*. Boston and London: Shambhala, 2006.

Funk, Mary Margaret. "Lectio Divina." In *The Gethsemani Encounter: A Dialogue on the Spiritual Life by Christian and Buddhist Monastics*, edited by Donald W. Mitchell and James Wiseman, 60–67. New York: Continuum, 2003. Original publication, 1997.

Garrigou-Lagrange, Réginald. *The Three Conversions in the Spiritual Life*. Unknown translator. Rockford, IL, USA, 2002. A translation of *Les trois conversions et les trois voies*. Juvisy-Seine-Et-Oise: Les Éditions du Cerf, 1933.

Garrigou-Lagrange, Réginald. *The Three Ages of the Interior Life: Prelude of Eternal Life*. Kindle ed. Translated by M. Timothea Doyle. London: Catholic Way Publishing, 2013. Original publication, St. Louis: Herder, 1948. A translation of *Les trois âges de la vie intérieure: prélude de celle du ciel*. Paris: Aubin, 1938.

Garrigou-Lagrange, Réginald. *Reality: A Thomistic Synthesis*. Translated by Patrick Cummins. South Bend, IN, USA: Ex Fontibus Co., 2012. Reprint, St. Louis: Herder, 1950. A translation of *La synthèse thomiste*. Paris: Desclée de Brouwer, 1946.

Gavin, Flood. *An Introduction to Hinduism*. Cambridge: Cambridge University Press, 1996.

Gavin, Flood. *The Truth Within: A History of Inwardness in Christianity, Hinduism, and Buddhism*. Oxford, UK: Oxford University Press, 2013.

Geertz, Clifford. "Thick Description: Toward an Interpretive Theory of Culture." In *The Interpretation of Cultures: Selected Essays by Clifford Geertz*, edited by Clifford Geertz, 3–30. New York: Basic Books, 1973.

Gellman, Jerome. "Mysticism." *Stanford Encyclopedia of Philosophy*. Accessed October 17, 2015. http://plato.stanford.edu/entries/mysticism/SEP.

Gethin, Rupert M. L. *The Buddhist Path to Awakening: A Study of the Bodhi-Pakkhiyā Dhammā*. Leiden, New York, Köln: Brill, 1992.

Gethin, Rupert M. L. *Sayings of the Buddha: A Selection of Suttas from the Pāli Nikāyas*. Oxford and New York: Oxford University Press, 2008.

Gimello, Robert M. "Mysticism and Meditation." In *Mysticism and Philosophical Analysis*, edited by Steven T. Katz, 170–99. New York: Oxford University Press, 1978.

Gimello, Robert M. "Mysticism in its Contexts." In *Mysticism and Religious Traditions*, edited by Steven T. Katz, 61–88. New York: Oxford University Press, 1983.

Goldberg, Ellen and Mark Singleton, "Introduction." In *Gurus of Modern Yoga*, edited by Mark Singleton and Ellen Goldberg, 1–14. New York: Oxford University Press, 2014.

Goleman, Daniel J. "The Buddha on Meditation and States of Consciousness, Part I: The Teachings." *Journal of Transpersonal Psychology* 4, no. 2 (1972): 1–44.

Goleman, Daniel J. "The Buddha on Meditation and States of Consciousness, Part II: A Typology of Meditation Techniques." *Journal of Transpersonal Psychology* 4 (1972): 151–210.

Goleman, Daniel J. *The Meditative Mind: The Varieties of Meditative Experience*. New York: Tarcher/Putnam, 1988. Republication of *The Varieties of Meditative Experience*. New York: Irvington Publishers, 1977.

Goleman, Daniel J. *Focus: The Hidden Driver of Excellence*. Kindle ed. New York: HarperCollins, 2013.

Gombrich, Richard. *How Buddhism Began: The Conditioned Genesis of the Early Teachings*. 2nd ed. London and New York: Routledge, 2006. Original publication, 1996.

Gopaka Moggallana Sutta: Moggallana the Guardsman (Majjhima Nikāya 108). Translated by Thanissaro Bhikkhu. *Access to Insight*. Accessed May 8, 2014. http://www.accesstoinsight.org/tipitaka/mn/mn.108.than.html.

Graham, Ward. "Theology and Postmodernism: Is It All Over?" *Journal of the American Academy of Religion* 80, no. 2 (June 2012): 467–68.

Granqvist, Pehr. "Religion as a By-Product or Evolved Psychology: The Case of Attachment and Implications for Brain and Religion Research." In *Where God and Science Meet: How Brain and Evolutionary Studies Alter Our Understanding of Religion*.

Vol. 2, *The Neurology of Religious Experience*, edited by Patrick McNamara, 105–50. Westport, CT and London: Praeger, 2006.

Grant, Robert M. and David Tracy, *A Short History of the Interpretation of the Bible*. 2nd ed. Philadelphia: Fortress Press, 1984.

Griffiths, Paul. "Concentration or Insight: The Problematic of Theravāda Buddhist Meditation-Theory." *The Journal of the American Academy of Religion* 49, no. 4 (December 1981): 605–24.

Griffiths, Paul. "Buddhist Jhāna: A Form-Critical Study." *Religion* 13 (1983): 55–68.

Griffiths, Paul. "Pure Consciousness and Indian Buddhism." In *The Problem of Pure Consciousness: Mysticism and Philosophy*, edited by Robert K. C. Forman, 71–97. Paperback ed. New York: Oxford University Press, 1997. Original publication, 1990.

Grimes, John. *A Concise Dictionary of Indian Philosophy: Sanskrit Terms Defined in English*. Rev ed. Albany: State University of New York Press, 1996.

Guigo II. *The Ladder of Monks (Scala claustralium: epistola de vita contemplativa)*. Translated by L. Dysinger. Paris, 1970. Accessed June 9, 2015. http://www.ldysinger.com/@texts2/1180_guigo-2/02_lad_sel-lec.htm.

Guigo II. *Guigo II: The Ladder of Monks and Twelve Meditations*. Translated by Edmund Colledge and James Walsh. New York: Image, 1978.

Gunaratana, Henepola. "A Critical Analysis of the Jhānas in Theravada Buddhist Meditation." Online ed. PhD diss., American University, 1980. Buddha Dharma Education Association. Accessed May 17, 2014. http://www.buddhanet.net/pdf_file/scrnguna.pdf.

Gunaratana, Bhante. *Beyond Mindfulness in Plain English: An Introductory Guide to Deeper States of Meditation*. Boston: Wisdom Publications, 2009.

Gunaratana, Henepola. "Interview with Bhante Gunaratana." In *The Experience of Samādhi: An In-depth Exploration of Buddhist Meditation*, edited by Richard Shankman, 136–45. Boston and London: Shambhala, 2008.

Guthrie, Stewart. "A Cognitive Theory of Religion." *Current Anthropology* 21, no. 2 (April 1980): 181–203. Accessed November 14, 2015. http://www.jstor.org/stable/2741711.

Guthrie, Stewart. *Faces in the Clouds: A New Theory of Religion*. New York: Oxford University Press, 1993.

Haidt, Jonathan. *The Happiness Hypothesis: Finding Modern Truth in Ancient Wisdom*. New York: Basic Books, 2006.

Halbfass, Wilhelm. *Tradition and Reflection: Explorations in Indian Thought*. Albany: State University of New York Press, 1991.

Hamer, Dean. *The God Gene: How Faith is Hardwired into Our Genes*. New York: Anchor, 2005.

Hammersholt, Torben. "Steven T. Katz's Philosophy of Mysticism Revisited." *Journal of the American Academy of Religion* 81, no. 2 (June 2013): 467–90.

Hanh, Thich Nhat. *Transformation and Healing*. Berkeley: Parallax Press, 1990, Reprint, 2006.

Harris, Sam. *Waking Up: A Guide to Spirituality Without Religion*. New York: Simon & Schuster, 2014.

Harrison, William H. *In Praise of Mixed Religion: The Syncretism Solution in a Multifaith World*. Montreal and Kingston: McGill-Queen's University Press, 2014.

Hedengren, Paul C. "Universals as Theoretical Entities." PhD diss., University of Toronto, 1983. Reformatted, Provo, Utah: Tepran Corporation, 2002.

Heiler, Friedrich. *Die buddhistische Versenkung: Eine religionsgeschichtliche Untersuchung*. 2nd ed. München: E. Reinhardt, 1922.

Hick, John. *God and the Universe of Faiths: Essays in the Philosophy of Religion*. London: Macmillan, 1973.

Hick, John. *The New Frontier of Science and Religion: Religious Experience, Neuroscience and the Transcendent*. Basingstoke, UK: Palgrave Macmillan, 2010. Reprint, 2006.

HJS. "The Occult Review." In *The Graces of Interior Prayer: A Treatise on Mystical Theology*. Fourth impression. Edited by Augustin-François Poulain. Translated by Leonora L. Yorke Smith, back matter. London: Kegan Paul, Trench, Trubner and Co., 1928. Original publication, 1910. A translation of *Des grâces d'oraison: traité de théologie mystique*. 10th ed. Paris: Gabriel Beauchesne, 1922. 1st ed., 1901.

Hogue, Michael S. "After the Secular: Toward a Pragmatic Public Theology." *Journal of the American Academy of Religion* 78, no. 2 (June 2010): 346–74. Accessed February 17, 2015. doi:10.1093/jaarel/lfp081.

Holmes, Urban T. *A History of Christian Spirituality: An Analytical Introduction*. Harrisburg, PA: Morehouse Publishing, 2002.

Hood, Ralph W. "The Common Core Thesis in the Study of Mysticism." In *Where God and Science Meet: How Brain and Evolutionary Studies Alter Our Understanding of Religion*. Vol. 3, *The Psychology of Religious Experience*, edited by Patrick McNamara, 119–38. Westport, CT and London: Praeger, 2006.

Hopkins, Jeffrey. *Meditation on Emptiness*. London: Wisdom Publications, 1983.

Horgan, John. *Rational Mysticism*. Boston and New York: Houghton Mifflin, 2003.

Horton, Carol A. *Yoga Ph.D.: Integrating the Life of the Mind and the Wisdom of the Body*. Kindle ed. Chicago: Kleio Books, 2012.

Hurlburt, Russell T. and Terry J. Knapp. "Münsterberg in 1898, Not Allport in 1937, Introduced the Terms 'Idiographic' and 'Nomothetic' to American Psychology." *Theory & Psychology* 16 (April 2006): 287–93.

Huxley, Aldous. *The Perennial Philosophy*. 3rd ed. New York: Harper and Brothers, 1945.

Inge, William Ralph. *Christian Mysticism: Considered in Eight Lectures Delivered before the University of Oxford*. London: Methuen, 1899.

Jacobsen, Autumn. "Contemporary Yoga Movements." In *Encyclopedia of Indian Philosophies*. Vol. 12, *Yoga India's Philosophy of Meditation*, edited by Gerald James Larson and Ram Shankar Bhattacharya, 148–59. Delhi: Motilal Banarsidass, 2008.

Jacobsen, Knut A. "The Wisdom of Kapila's Cave: Sāṃkhya-Yoga as Practice." In *Studying Hinduism in Practice*, edited by Hillary P. Rodrigues, 104–17. London and New York: Routledge, 2011.

Jain, Andrea R. "Who Is to Say Modern Yoga Practitioners Have It All Wrong? On Hindu Origins and Yogaphobia." *Journal of the American Academy of Religion* 82, no. 2 (June 2014): 427–71.

Jain, Andrea R. *Selling Yoga: From Counterculture to Pop Culture*. New York: Oxford University Press, 2015.

James, William. *The Varieties of Religious Experience: A Study in Human Nature*. New York: Longmans, Green and Co., 1902, Reprint, New York: Modern Library, n.d.

Jantzen, Grace M. "Could There be a Mystical Core of Religion?" *Religious Studies* 26 (1990): 59–71.

Jensen, Jeppe Sinding. *The Study of Religion in a New Key: Theoretical and Philosophical Soundings in the Comparative and General Study of Religion*. Århus: Aarhus University Press, 2003.

Jikido, Takasaki. *An Introduction to Buddhism*. Tokyo: The Tōhō Gakkai, 1987.

Jodt, Ingrid. *Burma's Mass Lay Movement: Buddhism and the Cultural Construction of Power*. Athens: Ohio University Press, 2007.

John of the Cross, *Ascent of Mount Carmel*. Translated by E. Allison Peers. Garden City, NY: Image Books, 1958.

John of the Cross. *The Dark Night*. In *The Collected Works of St. John of the Cross*. Translated by Kieran Kavanaugh and Otilio Rodriguez, 293–389. Washington, DC: ICS Publications, 1979.

Johnson, Willard. *Poetry and Speculation of the Ṛg Veda*. Berkeley: University of California Press, 1980.

Johnston, William. *Mystical Theology: The Science of Love*. Maryknoll, NY: Orbis, 1998.

Kabat-Zinn, Jon. "An Outpatient Program in Behavioral Medicine for Chronic Pain Patients Based on the Practice of Mindfulness Meditation." *General Hospital Psychiatry* 4 (1982): 33–47.

Kaliman, Perla, María Jesús Álvarez-López, Marta Cosín-Tomás, Melissa A. Rosenkranz, Antoine Lutz, and Richard J. Davidson. "Rapid Changes in Histone Deacetylases and Inflammatory Gene Expression in Expert Meditators." *Psychoneuroendocrinology* 40 (February 2014): 96–107. Accessed October 20, 2015. doi.org/10.1016/j.psyneuen.2013.11.004.

Karnath, Hans-Otto, Susanne Ferber, and Marc Himmelbach. "Spatial Awareness is a Function of the Temporal Not the Posterior Parietal Lobe." *Nature* 411 (2001): 950–53. Accessed October 20, 2015. doi:10.1038/35082075.

Katz, Steven T. "Language, Epistemology, and Mysticism." In *Mysticism and Philosophical Analysis*, edited by Steven T. Katz, 22–74. New York: Oxford University Press, 1978.

Katz, Steven T., ed. *Mysticism and Philosophical Analysis*. New York: Oxford University Press, 1978.

Katz, Steven T., ed. *Mysticism and Religious Traditions*. Oxford and New York: Oxford University Press, 1983.

Katz, Steven T. "The 'Conservative' Character of Mystical Experience." In *Mysticism and Religious Traditions*, edited by Steven T. Katz, 3–60. New York: Oxford University Press, 1983.

Katz, Steven T., ed. *Mysticism and Language*. New York: Oxford University Press, 1992.

Katz, Steven T. "Mystical Speech and Mystical Meaning." In *Mysticism and Language*, edited by Steven T. Katz, 3–41. New York: Oxford University Press, 1992.

Katz, Steven T., ed. *Mysticism and Sacred Scripture*. New York: Oxford University Press, 2000.

Katz, Steven T. "Editor's Introduction." In *Mysticism and Sacred Scripture*, edited by Steven T. Katz, 3–6. New York: Oxford University Press, 2000.

Katz, Steven T., ed. *Comparative Mysticism: An Anthology of Original Sources*. New York: Oxford University Press, 2013.

Katz, Steven T. "General Editor's Introduction." In *Comparative Mysticism: An Anthology of Original Sources*, edited by Steven T. Katz, 3–22. New York: Oxford University Press, 2013.

Kaufman, Gordon D. *God the Problem*. Cambridge, MA: Harvard University Press, 1972.

Keating, Thomas. *Invitation to Love: The Way of Christian Contemplation*. New York: Continuum, 1992.

Keating, Thomas. *Intimacy with God: An Introduction to Centering Prayer*. New York, Crossroad, 1994.

Keating, Thomas. *The Better Part: Stages of Contemplative Living*. New York and London: Continuum, 2000.

Keating, Thomas. *Open Mind, Open Heart: The Contemplative Dimension of the Gospel*. Continuum: New York, 2002. Originally published, Warwick, NY: Amity House, 1986.

Kelley, Edward F. "Introduction: Science and Spirituality at a Crossroads." In *Beyond Physicalism: Toward Reconciliation of Science and Spirituality*, edited by Edward F. Kelly, Adam Crabtree, and Paul Marshall, xii–xxiv. Lanham, MD: Rowman and Littlefield, 2015.

Kelley, Edward F. and Ian Whicher. "Patañjali's *Yoga Sūtras* and the *Siddhis*." In *Beyond Physicalism: Toward Reconciliation of Science and Spirituality*, edited by Edward F. Kelly, Adam Crabtree, and Paul Marshall, 315–48. Lanham, MD: Rowman and Littlefield, 2015.

Khema, Ayya. *Who is My Self: A Guide to Buddhist Meditation*. Boston: Wisdom Publications, 1997.

Killingley, Dermot. "Manufacturing Yogis: Swami Vivekananda as a Yoga Teacher." In *Gurus of Modern Yoga*, edited by Mark Singleton and Ellen Goldberg, 17–37. New York and Oxford: Oxford University Press, 2014.

King, Richard. *Orientalism and Religion: Postcolonial Theory, India, and the "Mystic East."* London and New York: Routledge, 1999.

King, Sallie B. "Two Epistemological Models for the Interpretation of Mysticism." *Journal of the American Academy of Religion* 56, no. 2 (Summer 1988): 257–79.

Kinsley, David R. *Hinduism: A Cultural Perspective*. 2nd ed. Upper Saddle River, NJ, USA: Prentice-Hall, 1993.

Klostermaier, Klaus. "*Dharmamegha samādhi*: Comments on *Yogasūtra* IV, 29." *Philosophy East and West* 36, no. 3 (July 1986): 253–62. Accessed April 4, 2015. http://www.jstor.org/stable/1398774.

Kneale, William and Martha Kneale. *The Development of Logic*. London: Oxford University Press, 1962.

Koelman, Gaspar M. *Pātañjala Yoga: From Related Ego to Absolute Self.* Poona: Papal Athenaeum, 1970.

Komarovski, Yaroslav. *Tibetan Buddhism and Mystical Experience*. New York: Oxford University Press, 2015.

Köppen, Carl Friedrich. *Die Religion des Buddha und Ihre Entstehung*. Vol. 1, *Die Religion des Buddha und ihre Enstehung*. Schneider: Berlin, 1857.

Kripal, Jeffrey J. *Authors of the Impossible: The Paranormal and the Sacred*. Kindle ed. Chicago and London: The University of Chicago Press, 2010.

Lamb, Ramdas. "Rāja Yoga, Asceticism, and the Rāmānanda Saṃpradāy." In *Theory and Practice of Yoga: Essays in Honor of Gerald James Larson*, edited by Knut A. Jacobsen, 317–31. Leiden: Brill, 2005.

Lamballe, Émile. *Mystical Contemplation: Or The Principle of Mystical Theology.* Translated by W. H. Mitchell. New York: Benziger Brothers, 1913. A translation of *La contemplation, ou principes de théologie mystique*. Paris: Pierre Tequi, 1912.

Larson, Gerald James. *Classical Sāṃkhya*. 2nd ed. Delhi: Motilal Banarsidass, 1979.

Larson, Gerald James. "Introduction to the Philosophy of Yoga." In *Encyclopedia of Indian Philosophies*. Vol. 12, *Yoga India's Philosophy of Meditation*, edited by Gerald James Larson and Ram Shankar Bhattacharya, 21–148. Delhi: Motilal Banarsidass, 2008.

Larson, Gerald James. "Patañjala Yoga in Practice." In *Yoga in Practice*, edited by David Gordon White, 76–96. Princeton and New York: Princeton University Press, 2012.

Lawson, E. Thomas and Robert N. McCauley. *Rethinking Religion: Connecting Cognition and Culture*. Cambridge: Cambridge University Press, 1993.

Lejeune, Paul. *Manuel de théologie mystique*. Paris: Librairie Ch. Poussielgue, 1897.

Lejeune, Paul. *An Introduction to the Mystical Life*. 2nd ed. Translated by Basil Levett. London: R & T Washbourne, 1915. A translation of *Introduction à la vie mystique*. Paris: Lethielleux, 1911.

Lodrö, Geshe Gedün. *Calm Abiding and Special Insight: Achieving Spiritual Transformation Through Meditation.* Edited by Jeffrey Hopkins, Anne C. Klein, and Leah Zahler. Translation Jeffrey Hopkins. Ithaca, NY, USA: Snow Lion Publications, 1998.

Long, Jeffery D. "The Transformation of Yoga and Hinduism: Negotiating Authenticity, Innovation, and Identity in a Global Context." *Religious Studies Review* 40, no. 3 (September 2014): 125–32.

Lossky, Vladimir. *The Mystical Theology of the Eastern Church.* Anonymous translator. Crestwood, NY: St. Vladimir's Seminary Press, 1976. Originally published as *Essai sur la theologie mystique de l'Eglise d'Orient.* Paris: Aubier, 1944.

Louth, Andrew. *The Origins of the Christian Mystical Tradition: From Plato to Denys.* Oxford: Oxford University Press, 1981.

Lovelace, Richard F. "Evangelical Spirituality: A Church Historian's Perspective." *Journal of the Evangelical Theological Society* 3, no. 1 (March 1988): 25–35.

Lowe, E. J. *The Four-Category Ontology: A Metaphysical Foundation for Natural Science.* Oxford and New York: Oxford University Press, 2006.

Maha-Saccaka Sutta: The Longer Discourse to Saccaka (Majjhima Nikāya 36). Translated by Thanissaro Bhikkhu. *Access to Insight.* Accessed May 6, 2014. http://www.accesstoinsight.org/tipitaka/mn/mn.036.than.html.

Mahony, William K. *The Artful Universe: An Introduction to the Vedic Religious Imagination.* Albany: State University of New York Press, 1998.

Mallinson, James, trans. *The Gheranda Samhita: An English Translation.* Woodstock, NY: YogaVidya, 2004.

Mallinson, James. "Yogis in Mughal India." In *Yoga: The Art of Transformation*, edited by Debra Diamond, 69–83. Washington, DC: Freer Gallery and Arthur M. Sackler Gallery, Smithsonian Institute, 2013.

Mallinson, James. "*Haṭhayoga's* Philosophy: A Fortuitous Union of Non-Dualities." *Journal of Indian Philosophy* 42, no. 1 (March 2014): 225–47. Accessed October 25, 2015. doi.10.1007/s10781-013-9217-0.

Mallinson, James. "The Yogīs' Latest Trick." *Journal of the Royal Asiatic Society* 24, no. 1 (July 2014): 1–16.

Marshall, Paul. *Mystical Encounters with the Natural World: Experiences and Explanations.* Oxford: Oxford University Press, 2005.

Masuzawa, Tomoko. *The Invention of World Religions: Or, How European Universalism was Preserved in the Language of Pluralism.* Chicago: University of Chicago Press, 2005.

Maurice Walsh, trans. *The Long Discourses of the Buddha: A Translation of the Dīgha Nikāya.* Boston: Wisdom Publications, 1995.

McCutcheon, Russell T. *Manufacturing Religion: The Discourse on Sui Generis Religion and the Politics of Nostalgia.* New York: Oxford University Press, 1997.

McEvilley, Thomas. "An Archaeology of Yoga." *Anthropology and Aesthetics* 1, no. 1 (Spring, 1981): 44–77. Accessed April 27, 2016. http://www.jstor.org/stable/20166655.

McGinn, Bernard. "Meister Eckhart: An Introduction." In *An Introduction to the Medieval Mystics*, edited by Paul S. Szarmach, 237–57. Albany: SUNY Press, 1984.

McGinn, Bernard. *The Presence of God: A History of Western Christian Mysticism.* Vol. 1, *The Foundations of Mysticism: Origins to the Fifth Century.* New York: Crossroad, 1994.

McGinn, Bernard, ed. *The Essential Writings of Christian Mysticism.* New York: The Modern Library, 2006.

McGinn, Bernard. "Preface." In *The Essential Writings of Christian Mysticism*, edited by Bernard McGinn, xi–xii. New York: The Modern Library, 2006.

McIntosh, Mark. *Mystical Theology: The Integrity of Spirituality and Theology.* Malden, MA: Wiley-Blackwell, 1998.

McNamara, Patrick, Raymon Durso, Ariel Brown, and Erica Harris, "The Chemistry of Religiosity: Evidence from Patients with Parkinson's Disease." In *Where God and Science Meet: How Brain and Evolutionary Studies Alter Our Understanding of Religion*. Vol. 2, *The Neurology of Religious Experience*, edited by Patrick McNamara, 1–14. Westport, CT and London: Praeger, 2006.

McNamara, Patrick, ed. *Where God and Science Meet: How Brain and Evolutionary Studies Alter Our Understanding of Religion*. Vol. 1, *Evolution, Genes, and the Religious Brain*. Westport, CT and London: Praeger, 2006.

McNamara, Patrick, ed. *Where God and Science Meet: How Brain and Evolutionary Studies Alter Our Understanding of Religion*. Vol. 2, *The Neurology of Religious Experience*. Westport, CT and London: Praeger, 2006.

McNamara, Patrick, ed. *Where God and Science Meet: How Brain and Evolutionary Studies Alter Our Understanding of Religion*. Vol. 3, *The Psychology of Religious Experience*. Westport, CT and London: Praeger, 2006.

McNamara, Patrick. *The Neuroscience of Religious Experience*. Cambridge: Cambridge University Press, 2009.

Mercadante, Linda A. *Belief without Borders: Inside the Minds of the Spiritual but not Religious*. Oxford and New York: Oxford University Press, 2014.

Merton, Thomas. *Contemplative Prayer*. New York: Image Books, 1971. Originally published as *The Climate of Monastic Prayer*. Kalamazoo, MI: Cistercian Publications, and Herder and Herder, 1971.

Merton, Thomas. *Asian Journal of Thomas Merton*. Edited by Naomi Burton, Patrick Hart, and James Laughlin. New York: New Directions Press, 1973.

Merton, Thomas. *The Inner Experience*. Edited by William H. Shannon. San Francisco: HarperSanFrancisco, 2003.

Miller, Barbara Stoler. *Yoga: Discipline of Freedom*. Paperback ed. New York: Bantam, 1998. Originally published, Berkeley: University of California Press, 1996.

Miller, Jeanine. *The Vedas: Harmony, Meditation and Fulfilment*. London: Rider, 1974.

Miller, Lisa. "We're All Hindus Now." *Newsweek*, August 24, 2009.

Mills, David. "Spirituality without Spirits." *First Things*, May 28, 2010. Accessed August 10, 2015, http://www.firstthings.com/web-exclusives/2010/05/spirituality-without-spirits?utm_source=First+Things+Subscribers&utm_campaign=29364ebaec-Sunday_Spotlight_8_9_2015&utm_medium=email&utm_term=0_28bf775c26-29364ebaec-180570269#print.

Most, William G. *Our Father's Plan: God's Arrangements and Our Response*. Online ed. Manassas, VA: Trinity Communications, 1988. Accessed October 31, 2015. http://www.catholicculture.org/culture/library/most/getwork.cfm?worknum=232.

Müller, F. Max. *Chips from a German Workshop: Essays on The Science of Religion*. Vol. 1, *Essays on the Science of Religion*. London: Longmans, Green, 1867.

Murphy, Michael. *The Future of the Body: Explorations into the Future Evolution of Nature*. Los Angeles: Tarcher, 1992.

Ñāṇamoli, Bhikkhu. "Introduction." In *The Path of Purification* (*Visuddhimagga*). 1st BPS Pariyatti edn. Edited by Bhadantācariya Buddhaghosa and Translated by Bhikkhu Ñāṇamoli. Seattle: BPS Pariyatti Editions, 1999.

Nash, Jonathan David and Andrew Newberg. "Toward A Unifying Taxonomy and Definition for Meditation." *Frontiers in Psychology* 4 (November 2013): 1–18. Accessed August 7, 2015. doi: 10.3389/fpsyg.2013.00806.

Nelson, Victoria. *The Secret Life of Puppets*. Cambridge, MA: Harvard University Press, 2001.

Nelstrop, Louise and Bradley B. Onishi, *Mysticism in the French Tradition: Eruptions from France.* Farnham, Surrey, UK and Burlington, VT, USA: Ashgate Publishing, 2015.

Newberg, Andrew B., Eugene G. d'Aquili, and Vince Rause. *Why God Won't Go Away: Brain Science and the Biology of Belief.* 1st trade ed. New York: Ballantine, 2002.

Newberg, Andrew B. "Religious and Spiritual Practices: A Neurochemical Perspective." In *Where God and Science Meet: How Brain and Evolutionary Studies Alter Our Understanding of Religion.* Vol. 2, *The Neurology of Religious Experience*, edited by Patrick McNamara, 15–31. Westport, CT and London: Praeger, 2006.

Newberg, Andrew B. *Principles of Neurotheology.* Farnham, Surrey, UK: Ashgate, 2010.

Newberg, Andrew B. and Mark Robert Waldman. *How God Changes Your Brain: Breakthrough Findings from a Leading Neuroscientist.* Paperback ed. New York, Ballantine Books, 2010.

Nicholson, Andrew J. "Review of *Sinister Yogis.*" *Journal of the American Oriental Society* 130, no. 2 (April to June 2010): 277–79.

Nyanatiloka. *Manual of Buddhist Terms and Doctrines.* 4th ed. Edited by Nyanaponika. Kandy, Sri Lanka: Buddhist Publication Society, 1980. First published 1952. Accessed June 4, 2014. http://www.palikanon.com/english/wtb/n_r/nimitta.htm.

O'Brien, Elmer. *The Essential Plotinus.* Indianapolis: Hackett, 1964.

Okholm, Dennis. *Dangerous Passions, Deadly Sins: Learning from the Psychology of Ancient Monks.* Grand Rapids, MI: Brazos Press, 2014.

Olivelle, Patrick, trans. *The Upaniṣads.* New York: Oxford University Press, 1996.

Paden, William E. "Elements of a New Comparativism." In *A Magic Still Dwells: Comparative Religion in the Postmodern Age*, edited by Kimberley C. Patton and Benjamin C. Ray, 182–92. Berkeley, Los Angeles, and London: University of California Press, 2000.

Paden, William E. "Universals Revisited: Human Behaviors and Cultural Variables." *Numen* 48, no. 3 (2001): 276–77.

Penner, Hans. "The Mystical Illusion." In *Mysticism and Religious Traditions*, edited by Steven T. Katz, 89–116. New York: Oxford University Press, 1983.

Phillips, Stephen. *Yoga, Karma, and Rebirth: A Brief History and Philosophy.* New York: Columbia University Press, 2009.

Pinker, Stephen. "The Evolutionary Psychology of Religion." In *Where God and Science Meet: How Brain and Evolutionary Studies Alter Our Understanding of Religion.* Vol. 1, *Evolution, Genes, and the Religious Brain*, edited by Patrick McNamara, 1–9. Westport, CT and London: Praeger, 2006.

Pius X. "Approbation of His Holiness Pope Pius X." In *The Graces of Interior Prayer: A Treatise on Mystical Theology.* Fourth impression, edited by Augustin-François Poulain and translated by Leonora L. Yorke Smith, back matter. London: Kegan Paul, Trench, Trubner and Co., 1928. Original publication, 1910. A translation of *Des grâces d'oraison: traité de théologie mystique.* 10th ed. Paris: Gabriel Beauchesne, 1922. 1st ed., 1901.

Plotinus, *Plotinus, Volume* 1. Translated by D. H. Armstrong. Cambridge, MA: Harvard University Press, 1969.

Pohle, J. "Actual Grace." *The Catholic Encyclopedia.* Online ed. New York: Robert Appleton Company, 1909. Accessed June 6, 2015. http://www.newadvent.org/cathen/06689x.htm.

Polak, Grzegorz. *Reexamining Jhāna: Towards a Critical Reconstruction of Early Buddhist Soteriology.* Lublin: Wydawnictwo Uniwersytetu Marii Curie-Skłodowskiej, 2011.

Poulain, Augustin-François. *Des grâces d'oraison: traité de théologie mystique.* 10th ed. Paris: Gabriel Beauchesne, 1922. 1st ed., 1901.

Poulain, Augustin-François. *The Graces of Interior Prayer: A Treatise on Mystical Theology*. Fourth impression. Translated by Leonora L. Yorke Smith. London: Kegan Paul, Trench, Trubner and Co., 1928. Original publication, 1910. A translation of *Des grâces d'oraison: traité de théologie mystique*. 10th ed. Paris: Gabriel Beauchesne, 1922. 1st ed., 1901.

Prabhavananda, Swami and Christopher Isherwood. *How to Know God: The Yoga Aphorisms of Patanjali*. Paperback ed. Hollywood, CA: Vedanta Press, 1983. Originally published, 1953.

Price, James D. and James J. Barrell. *Inner Experience and Neuroscience: Merging Both Perspectives* (Cambridge, MA: MIT Press, 2012).

Proudfoot, Wayne. *Religious Experience*. Berkeley: University of California Press, 1985.

Pyysiäinen, Ilkka. *How Religion Works: Toward a New Cognitive Science of Religion*. Leiden, Boston, Köln: Brill, 2001.

Pyysiäinen, Ilkka. "Amazing Grace: Religion and the Evolution of the Human Mind." In *Where God and Science Meet: How Brain and Evolutionary Studies Alter Our Understanding of Religion*. Vol. 1, *Evolution, Genes, and the Religious Brain*, edited by Patrick McNamara, 209–25. Westport, CT and London: Praeger, 2006.

Qvarnström, Olle and Jason Birch. "Jain Yoga of the Terāpanthī Tradition." In *Yoga in Practice*, edited by David Gordon White, 365–82. Princeton and New York: Princeton University Press, 2012.

Radhakrishnan, Sarvepalli. *Indian Philosophy*, Vol. 2. 2nd ed. Delhi: Blackie & Son, 1985; Reprint, Oxford: Oxford University Press, 1929.

Rahula, Walpola. *What the Buddha Taught*. 2nd ed. New York: Grove Press, 1974.

Ratnayaka, Shanta. *Two Ways of Perfection: Buddhist and Christian*. Colombo: Lake House Investments, 1978.

Rennie, Bryan. "The Influence of Eastern Orthodox Christian Theology on Mircea Eliade's Understanding of Religion." In *Hermeneutics, Politics, and the History of Religions: The Contested Legacies of Joachim Wach and Mircea Eliade*, edited Christian Wedemeyer and Wendy Doniger, 197–214. New York: Oxford University Press, 2010.

Rinbochay, Lati. "Lati Rinbochay's Oral Presentation of the Concentrations and Formless Absorptions." Translated by Jeffrey Hopkins. In *Meditative States in Tibetan Buddhism*, edited by Leah Zahler, 21–25. Boston: Wisdom Publications, 1997, first pub. 1983.

Roebuck, Valerie J., trans. *The Upaniṣads*. Penguin Books, 2003.

Rose, Kenneth. *Knowing the Real: John Hick on the Cognitivity of Religions and Religious Pluralism*. New York: Peter Lang Publishing, 1996.

Rose, Kenneth. "Review of Brainard." *Reality and Mystical Experience, Journal of the American Academy of Religion* 71, no. 2 (Summer 2003): 426–28. Accessed October 21, 2015. http://www.jstor.org/stable/1466559.

Rose, Kenneth. *Pluralism: The Future of Religion*. New York: Bloomsbury, 2013.

Rose, Kenneth. "Can a Religious Pluralist do Comparative Religion or Comparative Theology?" Unpublished presentation, University of Münster, January 19, 2015.

Rose, Kenneth. "The Singular and the Shared: Making Amends with Eliade after the Dismissal of the Sacred." In *Interreligious Comparisons in Religious Studies and Theology: Comparison Revisited*. edited by Perry Schmidt-Leukel and Andreas Nehring, 110–29. London: Bloomsbury Academic, forthcoming in 2016.

Sarbacker, Stuart Ray. *Samādhi: The Numinous and the Cessative in Indo-Tibetan Yoga*. Albany: State University Press of New York Press, 2005.

Satchidananda, Swami. *The Yoga Sutras of Patanjali*. Yogaville, VA: Integral Yoga Publications, 1990.

Saudreau, Auguste. *The Degrees of the Spiritual Life: A Method of Directing Souls according to their Progress in Virtue*. Vol. 1. Translated by Bede Camm. New York, Cincinnati, and Chicago: Benziger Brothers, 1907.

Sayadaw, Pa Auk (The Venerable Acinna or the Venerable Pa-Auk Tawya Sayadaw). "Interview with Pa Auk Sayadaw." In *The Experience of Samādhi: An In-depth Exploration of Buddhist Meditation*, edited by Richard Shankman, 174–81. Boston and London: Shambhala, 2008.

Schleiermacher, Friedrich. *On Religion: Speeches to Its Cultured Despisers*. Translated by Richard Crouter. Cambridge: Cambridge University Press, 1988.

Schmidt, Roger. *Exploring Religion*, 2nd ed. Belmont, CA: Wadsworth, 1988.

Schmidt-Leukel, Perry. *Transformation by Integration: How Inter-Faith Encounter Changes Christianity*. London: SCM Press, 2009.

Schmithausen, L. "On Some Aspects of Descriptions or Theories of 'Liberating Insight' and 'Enlightenment' in Early Buddhism." In *Studien zum Jainismus und Buddhismus*, Edited by Klaus Bruhn and Albrecht Wezler, 199–250, 240. Wiesbaden: Franz Steiner Verlag, 1981.

Schmitt, Charles B. "Perennial Philosophy: From Agostino Steuco to Leibniz." *Journal of the History of Ideas* 27, no. 4 (October/December 1966): 505–32. Accessed February 6, 2015. http://www.jstor.org/stable/2708338.

Shankman, Richard. *The Experience of Samādhi: An In-depth Exploration of Buddhist Meditation*. Boston and London: Shambhala, 2008.

Sharpe, Eric J. *Comparative Religion: A History*. 2nd ed. La Salle, IL: Open Court, 1986.

Sheldrake, Philip. *Spirituality: A Very Short Introduction*. Oxford: Oxford University Press, 2012.

Sider, Theodore. "Introduction." In *Contemporary Debates in Metaphysics*, Kindle ed. edited by Theodore Sider, John Hawthorne, and Dean W. Zimmerman. Malden: Wiley-Blackwell, 2013.

Simler, Joseph. *Catechism of Mental Prayer*. 3rd ed. Rockford, IL: TAN Books, 1984. Originally published, Dayton: Brothers of Mary, 1911.

Singleton, Mark. *Yoga Body: The Origins of Modern Posture Practice*. New York: Oxford University Press, 2010.

Singleton, Mark. "Globalized Modern Yoga." In *Yoga: The Art of Transformation*, edited by Debra Diamond, 95–102. Washington, DC: Freer Gallery and Arthur M. Sackler Gallery, Smithsonian Institute, 2013.

Singleton, Mark and Jean Byrne, "Introduction." In *Yoga in the Modern World: Contemporary Perspectives*, edited by Mark Singleton and Jean Byrne, 1–14. London and New York: Routledge, 2008.

Singleton, Mark and Jean Byrne, eds. *Yoga in the Modern World: Contemporary Perspectives*. London and New York: Routledge, 2008.

Singleton, Mark and Ellen Goldberg. *Gurus of Modern Yoga*. New York: Oxford University Press, 2014.

Sirkel, Riin. "The Problem of *Katholou*. Universals in Aristotle." PhD., diss. University of Western Ontario, 2010. *Electronic Thesis and Dissertation Repository* (Paper 62), December 2010. Accessed October 12, 2015. http://ir.lib.uwo.ca/cgi/viewcontent.cgi?article=1099&context=etd.

Sjoman, N. E. *The Yoga Tradition of the Mysore Palace*. Delhi: Abhinav Publications, 1996.

Smart, Ninian. *Reasons and Faith*. Routledge & Kegan Paul, 1958, Reprint, 2014.

Smart, Ninian. "The Purification of Consciousness and the Negative Path." In *Mysticism and Religious Traditions*, edited by Steven T. Katz, 117–28. New York: Oxford University Press, 1983.

Smith, Huston. "Is there a Perennial Philosophy?" *Journal of the American Academy of Religion* 55, no. 3 (Autumn 1987): 556–66. Accessed February 8, 2015. http://www.jstor.org/stable/1464070.

Snyder, Stephen and Tina Rasmussen. *Practicing the Jhānas: Traditional Concentration Methods as Presented by the Venerable Pa Auk Sayadaw*. Boston and London: Shambhala, 2009.

Staals, Fritz. *Exploring Mysticism: A Methodological Essay*. Berkeley: University of California Press, 1975.

Stace, W. T. *Mysticism and Philosophy*. Los Angeles: Jeremy P. Tarcher, 1987. Reprint, London: Macmillan Press, 1960.

Stausberg, Michael, ed. *Contemporary Theories of Religion: A Critical Companion*. London and New York: Routledge, 2009.

Stausberg, Michael. "There is Life in the Old Dog Yet: An Introduction to Contemporary Theories of Religion." In *Contemporary Theories of Religion: A Critical Companion*, edited by Michael Stausberg, 1–21. London and New York: Routledge, 2009.

Strange, Daniel. *Their Rock is Not Like Our Rock*. Grand Rapids, MI: Zondervan, 2014.

Stuart-Fox, Martin. "Jhāna and Buddhist Scholasticism." *Journal of the International Association of Buddhist Studies* 12, no. 2 (1989): 79–102, 102–03.

Studstill, Randall. *The Unity of Mystical Traditions: The Transformation of Consciousness in Tibetan and German Mysticism*, Leiden and Boston: Brill Academic, 2005.

Sullivan, Herbert P. "A Re-Examination of the Religion of the Indus Civilization." *History of Religions* 4, no. 1 (Summer 1964): 115–25.

Surendranath, Dasgupta. *A History of Indian Philosophy*. Volume 1. Delhi: Motilal, Banarsidass, 1988, Reprint, 1975. Originally published, London: Cambridge University Press, 1922.

Swearer, Donald. "Control and Freedom: The Structure of Buddhist Meditation in the Pāli Suttas." *Philosophy East and West* 23, no. 4 (October 1973): 435–55.

Swoyer, Chris. "Abstract Entities." In *Contemporary Debates in Metaphysics*, Chapter 12. Kindle. ed. Edited by Theodore Sider, John Hawthorne, and Dean W. Zimmerman. Malden: Wiley-Blackwell, 2013.

Taimni, I. K. *The Science of Yoga*. 4th ed. Wheaton, IL: The Theosophical Publishing House, 1975.

Talbot, Mary. "A Mind Pure, Concentrated, and Bright: An Interview with Meditation Teacher Leigh Brasington." *Tricycle* 54 (Winter 2004): 66–71.

Tanquerey, Adolphe. *Précis de théologie ascétique et mystique*. 14th ed. Internet ed. *Catholique du net*, 2003. Original published, 1924. Accessed June 10, 2015. https://eti.martin.free.fr/la-mystique/TANQUEREY.doc.

Tanquerey, Adolphe. *The Spiritual Life: A Treatise on Ascetical and Mystical Theology*. 2nd rev. ed. Translated by Herman Branderis. Tournai: Desclée, 1932. Reprinted and updated after 1954. Originally published in two volumes, Paris, Tournai, Rome, New York: Desclée, 1923–24.

Taves, Ann. *Religious Experience Reconsidered: A Building-Block Approach to the Study of Religion and Other Special Things*. Princeton and Oxford: Princeton University Press, 2009.

Taylor, Charles. *A Secular Age*. Cambridge, MA: Harvard University Press, 2007.

Teresa of Ávila. *The Interior Castle*. Translated by E. Allison Peers. New York: Image Books, 1961.

Teresa of Ávila, *The Way of Perfection*. Translated by E. Allison Peers. New York: Image, 2004, Reissue, 1964.

Ṭhānissaro, Ajaan. "Interview with Ajaan Ṭhānissaro." In *The Experience of Samādhi: An In-depth Exploration of Buddhist Meditation,* edited by Richard Shankman, 117–29. Boston and London: Shambhala, 2008.

The Dalai Lama. "Message from His Holiness the Dalai Lama." In Buddhaghosa, Bhadantācariya. *The Path of Purification* (*Visuddhimagga*), preceding page i. 1st BPS Pariyatti ed. Translated by Bhikkhu Ñāṇamoli. Seattle: BPS Pariyatti Editions, 1999.

The Dalai Lama. *How to Practice: The Way to a Meaningful* Life. 1st pbk. ed. Translated and Edited by Jeffrey Hopkins. New York: Atria Books, 2003.

The Shorter Discourse on Voidness. Cūḷasuññata Sutta. In *The Middle Length Discourses of the Buddha: A Translation of the Majjhima Nikāya,* 3rd ed. Translated by Bhikkhu Ñāṇamoli and Bhikkhu Bodhi, 965–70. Boston: Wisdom Publications and Barre Center for Buddhist Studies, 2005.

Thompson, Evan. *Waking, Dreaming, Being: Self and Consciousness in Neuroscience, Meditation, and Philosophy.* Kindle ed. New York: Columbia University Press, 2014.

Tillich, Paul. *The Courage to Be.* 2nd ed. New Haven, CT: Yale University Press, 2000.

Tremlin, Todd. *Minds and Gods: The Cognitive Foundations of Religion.* New York: Oxford University Press, 2006.

Turner, Léon P. "Introduction: Pluralism and Complexity in the Evolutionary Cognitive Science of Religion." In *Evolution, Religion, and Cognitive Science,* edited by Fraser Watts and Léon P. Turner, 1–20. New York: Oxford University Press, 2014.

Tyndale, William. *The Independent Works of William Tyndale.* Vol. 3, *An Answer unto Sir Thomas More's Dialogue.* Edited by Anne M. O'Donnell and Jared Wicks. Washington, DC: Catholic University of America Press, 2000.

Underhill, Evelyn. *Mysticism: A Study in the Nature and Development of Man's Spiritual Consciousness.* 4th ed. New York: Dutton, 1912.

Upatissa, Arahant. *The Path of Freedom* (*Vimuttimagga*). Translated by N. R. M. Ehara, Soma Thera, and Kheminda Thera. Kandy: Buddhist Publication Society, 1977.

Varela, Francisco J. "Neurophenomenology: A Methodological Remedy for the Hard Problem." *Journal for Consciousness Studies* 3, no. 4 (1996): 330–49.

Varenne, Jean. *Yoga and the Hindu Tradition.* Translated by Derek Coltman. Chicago and London: University of Chicago Press, 1976. A translation of *Le yoga et la tradition hindoue.* Paris: Cultures, Arts, Loisirs, 1973.

Vetter, Tilmann. *The Ideas and Meditative Practices of Early Buddhism.* Translated by Marianne Oort. Leiden, New York, KØbenhavn, and Köln: E. J. Brill, 1988.

Visuddhācāra, Bhikkhu. *Curbing Anger, Spreading Love.* Kandy: Buddhist Publication Society, 1992.

Vivekānanda, Swāmi. "Paper on Hinduism." In *Complete Works of Swami Vivekananda.* Accessed September 24, 2014. http://www.ramakrishnavivekananda.info/vivekananda/volume_1/addresses_at_the_parliament/v1_c1_paper_on_hinduism.htm.

Vivekānanda, Swāmi. *Rāja Yoga: Or Conquering the Internal Nature.* London, New York and Bombay: Longmans, Green, and Co., 1896.

Wallace, Alan. *The Attention Revolution: Unlocking the Power of the Focused Mind.* Boston: Wisdom, 2006.

Wallace, Alan. *Meditations of a Buddhist Skeptic: A Manifesto for the Mind Sciences and Contemplative Practice.* Kindle ed. New York: Columbia University Press, 2012.

Wallace, Robert Keith. "Physiological Effects of Transcendental Meditation." *Science,* March 27, 1970. Accessed October 20, 2015. doi: 10.1126/science.167.3926.1751.

Wang, Danny J. J., Hengyi Rao, Marc Korczykowski, Nancy Wintering, John Pluta, Dharma Singh Khalsa, and Andrew B. Newberg. "Cerebral Blood Flow Changes

Associated with Different Meditation Practices and Perceived Depth of Meditation." *Psychiatry Research: Neuroimaging* 191 (2011): 60–67. Accessed October 20, 2015. doi:10.1016/j.pscychresns.2010.09.011.

Watts, Alan. *Beyond Theology: The Art of Godmanship.* Paperback ed. Cleveland and New York: World Publishing, 1966.

Weber, Belinda. "Meditation Changes Gene Expression, Study Shows." *Medical News Today,* December 12, 2013. Accessed October 19, 2014. http://www.medicalnewstoday.com/articles/269910.php.

Wedemeyer, Christian and Wendy Doniger, *Hermeneutics, Politics, and the History of Religions: The Contested Legacies of Joachim Wach and Mircea Eliade.* New York: Offord University Press, 2010.

Whicher, Ian. *The Integrity of the Yoga Darśana: A Reconsideration of Classical Yoga.* Albany: State University of New York Press, 1998.

White, David Gordon. *The Alchemical Body: Siddha Traditions in Medieval India.* Chicago and London: University of Chicago Press, 1997.

White, David Gordon. *Sinister Yogis.* Paperback ed. Chicago and London: The University of Chicago Press, 2009.

White, David Gordon. "Introduction: Yoga, Brief History of an Idea." In *Yoga in Practice,* edited by David Gordon White, 1–23. Princeton and New York: Princeton University Press, 2012.

White, David Gordon. "Yoga in Transformation." In *Yoga: The Art of Transformation,* edited by Debra Diamond, 35–45. Washington, DC: Freer Gallery and Arthur M. Sackler Gallery, Smithsonian Institute, 2013.

White, David Gordon. *The* Yoga Sutra of Patanjali: *A Biography.* Kindle ed. Princeton and Oxford: Princeton University Press, 2014.

Whitney, William Dwight. *The Roots, Verb-Forms, and Primary Derivatives of the Sanskrit Language.* Delhi: Motilal Banarsidass, 1994. Original ed. 1885.

Wittgenstein, Ludwig. *Tractatus Logico-Philosophicus.* Translated by D. F. Pears and B. F. McGuinness. Revised ed. London and New York: Routledge, 1972. Originally published, 1922. A translation of *Logische-Philosophische Abhandlung,* 1922.

Wolpert, Stanley. *A New History of India.* 6th ed. New York: Oxford University Press, 2000.

Woodroffe, John George, Sir (a.k.a. Arthur Avalon). *The Serpent Power: Being the Sat-Cakra-Nirupana and Paduka-Pañcaka.* London, Luzac, 1919.

Woods, Richard, ed. *Understanding Mysticism.* New York: Image Books, 1980.

Woods, Richard. "Introduction." In *Understanding Mysticism,* edited by Richard Woods, 1–15. New York: Image Books, 1980.

Wright, Wendy. *The Essential Spirituality Handbook.* Liguori, MS: Liguori Publications, 2009.

Wujastyk, Dominik. "The Earliest Accounts of *Āsana* in the Yoga Literature." Unpublished presentation posted online. Accessed April 5. 2015. https://www.academia.edu/11798611/The_Earliest_Accounts_of_%C4%80sana_in_the_Yoga_Literature.

Wujastyk, Dominik. "The Path to Liberation through Yogic Mindfulness in Early Āyurveda." In *Yoga in Practice,* edited by David Gordon White, 31–42. Princeton and New York: Princeton University Press, 2012.

Yarnold, Edward. "The Theology of Christian Spirituality." In *The Study of Spirituality,* edited by Cheslyn P. M. Jones, Geoffrey Wainwright, and Edward Yarnold, 9–17. New York and Oxford: Oxford University Press, 1986.

Zaehner, R. C. *Mysticism: Sacred and Profane.* Oxford: Oxford University Press, 1957.

Index

Note: Page locators followed by 'n' indicate notes section.

CPSIA information can be obtained
at www.ICGtesting.com
Printed in the USA
LVHW031549201218
601089LV00009B/120/P

9 781350 065260